国际财务报告准则

财务报告概念框架

（汉英对照）

中国会计准则委员会　组织翻译

中国财经出版传媒集团
中国财政经济出版社

图书在版编目（CIP）数据

财务报告概念框架：汉英对照/中国会计准则委员会组织翻译．
—北京：中国财政经济出版社，2019.6
书名原文：Conceptual Framework For Financial Reporting
ISBN 978－7－5095－9081－2

Ⅰ.①财… Ⅱ.①中… Ⅲ.①会计报表－概念－汉、英 Ⅳ.①F231.5

中国版本图书馆 CIP 数据核字（2019）第 125010 号

责任编辑：宋学军　吴檬檬　　　　　　　责任校对：黄亚青

中国财政经济出版社 出版

URL：http://www.cfeac.com
E－mail：cfeac@cfemg.cn

（版权所有　翻印必究）

社址：北京市海淀区阜成路甲 28 号　邮政编码：100142
营销中心电话：010－88191522
天猫网店：中国财政经济出版社旗舰店
网址：https://zgczjjcbs.tmall.com
三河市宏图印务有限公司印刷　各地新华书店经销
787×1092 毫米　16 开　21 印张　434 000 字
2019 年 7 月第 1 版　2019 年 7 月河北第 1 次印刷
定价：80.00 元
ISBN 978－7－5095－9081－2
（图书出现印装问题，本社负责调换）
本社质量投诉电话：010－88190744
打击盗版举报热线：010－88191661　QQ：2242791300

Conceptual Framework for Financial Reporting is issued by the International Accounting Standards Board (Board).

Disclaimer: To the extent permitted by applicable law, the Board and the IFRS Foundation (Foundation) expressly disclaim all liability howsoever arising from this publication or any translation thereof whether in contract, tort or otherwise to any person in respect of any claims or losses of any nature including direct, indirect, incidental or consequential loss, punitive damages, penalties or costs.

Information contained in this publication does not constitute advice and should not be substituted for the services of an appropriately qualified professional.

ISBN for complete publication: 978 – 7 – 5095 – 9081 – 2

Copyright © 2018 IFRS Foundation

All rights reserved. Reproduction and use rights are strictly limited. Please contact the Foundation for further details at licences@ifrs.org.

Copies of IASB ® publications may be obtained from the Foundation's Publications Department. Please address publication and copyright matters to publications@ifrs.org or visit our web shop at https://shop.ifrs.org.

The Foundation has trade marks registered around the world (Marks) including 'IAS ® ', 'IASB ® ', the IASB ® logo, 'IFRIC ® ' 'IFRS ® ', the IFRS ® logo, 'IFRS for SMEs ® ', the IFRS for SMEs ® logo, the 'Hexagon Device', 'International Accounting Standards ® ', 'International Financial Reporting Standards ® ', 'NIIF ® ' and 'SIC ® '. Further details of the Foundation's Marks are available from the Foundation on request.

The Foundation is a not – for – profit corporation under the General Corporation Law of the State of Delaware, USA and operates in England and Wales as an overseas company (Company number FC023235) with its principal office at 30 Cannon Street, London, EC4M 6XH.

《财务报告概念框架》由国际会计准则理事会("理事会")发布。

免责声明：在适用法律允许的范围内，国际会计准则理事会和国际财务报告准则基金会（"基金会"）对所有因本出版物或任何与之相关的翻译所引致的涉及任何人士的责任（无论是因合同、侵权或其他方式导致的任何性质的索赔或损失，包括直接、间接、附带或结果性损失、惩罚性赔偿、处罚或费用）概不负责。

本出版物中所含内容并不构成任何建议，且不应以此取代任何适当合资格专业人士的服务。

本书的 ISBN：978-7-5095-9081-2

Copyright © 2018 IFRS Foundation

版权所有。本出版物的复制及使用权受到严格限制。如需了解进一步详情，请联系国际财务报告准则基金会（licences@ifrs.org）。

您可以从国际财务报告准则基金会的出版部门获取国际会计准则理事会（IASB®）的出版物。有关出版物和版权事宜，请发送电子邮件至 publications@ifrs.org 或访问我们的电子商城 http://shop.ifrs.org。

国际财务报告准则基金会在全球拥有多个注册商标（"商标"），包括"IAS®"，"IASB®"，"IFRIC®"，"IFRS®"，国际财务报告准则 IFRS® 标识，中小主体国际财务报告准则 IFRS for SMEs® 标识，"Hexagon Device"，"International Accounting Standards®"，"International Financial Reporting Standards®"，"NIIF®"和"SIC®"。可以向国际财务报告准则基金会申请提供有关国际财务报告准则基金会商标的进一步详情。

国际财务报告准则基金会是按照美国特拉华州《普通公司法》成立的非营利性公司，总部设在英格兰与威尔士并在该地以海外分公司运营（公司号码：FC023235），办公地址：30 Cannon Street, London, EC4M 6XH。

国际财务报告准则中文翻译审核专家组

组长： 高一斌　财政部会计司司长、会计准则委员会主任，国际财务报告准则咨询委员会委员

组员： 张为国　清华大学、上海财经大学教授，博士生导师
　　　　黄世忠　厦门国家会计学院院长，教授，博士生导师
　　　　支晓强　中国人民大学商学院教授，博士生导师
　　　　毛新述　北京工商大学商学院教授，博士生导师
　　　　杨　征　新华人寿保险股份有限公司副总裁，国际财务报告准则解释委员会委员
　　　　杨金忠　上海证券交易所国际发展部副总经理
　　　　孙　玫　安永华明会计师事务所合伙人
　　　　张青波　毕马威华振会计师事务所合伙人
　　　　邱连强　致同会计师事务所合伙人
　　　　郑先弘　立信会计师事务所合伙人
　　　　陈　瑜　财政部会计司准则二处处长，国际会计准则理事会会计准则咨询论坛委员
　　　　徐华新　会计准则委员会研究处副处长，研究员

出版说明

2018年，国际会计准则理事会完成了其概念框架修订项目，发布了修订后的《财务报告概念框架》，将于2020年1月1日起生效，允许提前采用，但对国际会计准则理事会和国际财务报告准则解释委员会自发布之日起生效。《财务报告概念框架》取代了国际会计准则理事会2010年发布的《编报财务报表的框架》，是其制定国际财务报告准则的概念基础，且有助于报表编制者理解和应用国际财务报告准则。

我国2006年发布的企业会计准则体系实现了与国际财务报告准则的趋同。2010年，财政部发布了《中国企业会计准则与国际财务报告准则持续趋同路线图》。为借鉴国际财务报告准则完善我国企业会计准则体系，实现中国会计准则与国际财务报告准则的持续趋同，会计准则委员会组织人员对《财务报告概念框架》进行了翻译。经国际财务报告准则基金会认可的中文翻译审核专家组审核，该《财务报告概念框架》中文版是国际财务报告准则基金会认可的国际财务报告准则官方译本，为国际财务报告准则基金会的正式出版物。

在翻译审校过程中，财政部会计司陈瑜、朱琳、黄赟和邱颖等同志对本书译稿进行了校译；财政部会计司巡视员应唯同志和财政部会计司司长、会计准则委员会主任高一斌同志对全部译稿进行了审阅。值此《财务报告概念框架》汉英对照版出版之际，特别感谢安永华明会计师事务所（特殊普通合伙）、厦门大学会计发展研究中心、国际财务报告准则中文翻译审核专家组以及中国财经出版传媒集团的有关同志为本书的翻译出版工作所付出的辛勤劳动！

会计准则委员会
2019年4月

总　目　录

财务报告概念框架 …………………………………………………………… 1
《财务报告概念框架》结论基础 …………………………………………… 71

Conceptual Framework for Financial Reporting ……………………………… 159
Basis for Conclusions on the Conceptual Framework for Financial Reporting ……… 235

财务报告概念框架

目 录

	起始段落
《概念框架》的现状和目的 ……………………………………………	**SP1.1**
第 1 章——通用目的财务报告的目标	
引言 ………………………………………………………………………	**1.1**
通用目的财务报告的目标、有用性以及局限性 ……………………	**1.2**
关于报告主体经济资源、对主体的求偿权以及经济资源与求偿权变动的信息	
……………………………………………………………………………	**1.12**
经济资源与求偿权 ………………………………………………	1.13
经济资源与求偿权的变动 ………………………………………	1.15
权责发生制会计所反映的财务业绩 ……………………………	1.17
过去现金流量所反映的财务业绩 ………………………………	1.20
非因财务业绩导致的经济资源与求偿权的变动 ………………	1.21
关于主体经济资源使用的信息 ……………………………………	1.22
第 2 章——有用财务信息的质量特征	
引言 ………………………………………………………………………	**2.1**
有用财务信息的质量特征 …………………………………………	**2.4**
基本质量特征 ……………………………………………………	**2.5**
提升性质量特征 …………………………………………………	**2.23**
有用财务报告的成本限制 …………………………………………	**2.39**
第 3 章——财务报表和报告主体	
财务报表 …………………………………………………………………	**3.1**
财务报表的目标和范围 …………………………………………	3.2
报告期间 …………………………………………………………	3.4
财务报表中采用的角度 …………………………………………	3.8
持续经营假设 ……………………………………………………	3.9
报告主体 …………………………………………………………………	**3.10**
合并与非合并财务报表 …………………………………………	3.15
第 4 章——财务报表要素	
引言 ………………………………………………………………………	**4.1**

资产的定义	**4.3**
权利	4.6
产生经济利益的潜力	4.14
控制	4.19
负债的定义	**4.26**
义务	4.28
经济资源的转移	4.36
由于过去事项而形成的现时义务	4.42
资产和负债	**4.48**
核算单元	4.48
待执行合同	4.56
合同权利和合同义务的实质	4.59
权益的定义	**4.63**
收益和费用的定义	**4.68**

第5章——确认和终止确认

确认流程	**5.1**
确认标准	**5.6**
相关性	5.12
如实反映	5.18
终止确认	**5.26**

第6章——计量

引言	**6.1**
计量基础	**6.4**
历史成本	6.4
现行价值	6.10
特定计量基础提供的信息	**6.23**
历史成本	6.24
现行价值	6.32
选择计量基础时考虑的因素	**6.43**
相关性	6.49
如实反映	6.58
提升性质量特征和成本限制	6.63
初始计量的特殊因素	6.77
一种以上计量基础	6.83
权益的计量	**6.87**
基于现金流量的计量技术	**6.91**

第7章——列示和披露
  列示和披露作为沟通工具……………………………………………… 7.1
  列示和披露的目标和原则……………………………………………… 7.4
  分类……………………………………………………………………… 7.7
    资产和负债的分类……………………………………………… 7.9
    权益的分类……………………………………………………… 7.12
    收益和费用的分类……………………………………………… 7.14
  汇总……………………………………………………………………… 7.20

第8章——资本和资本保全概念
  资本概念………………………………………………………………… 8.1
  资本保全概念和利润的确定…………………………………………… 8.3
  资本保全调整…………………………………………………………… 8.10

附录——术语表

《财务报告概念框架》由理事会于2018年3月批准发布

《概念框架》的现状和目的

SP1.1 《财务报告概念框架》(以下简称"《概念框架》")阐述了通用目的财务报告的目标和概念。《概念框架》有助于:

(1) 协助国际会计准则理事会(以下简称"理事会")基于一致的概念制定国际财务报告准则(以下简称"准则");

(2) 协助编制者在某一特定交易或事项无适用准则、或者某项准则允许会计政策选择时制定一致的会计政策;以及

(3) 协助各方理解和解读准则。

SP1.2 《概念框架》并非准则。其中的任何内容均不可凌驾于准则或准则中的规定之上。

SP1.3 为了达成通用目的财务报告的目标,理事会有时会提出偏离《概念框架》内容的具体要求。若发生此种情况,理事会将在相应准则的结论基础部分解释该偏离情况。

SP1.4 理事会将基于《概念框架》的工作经验,随时对其进行修订。对《概念框架》的修订,不会自动导致准则的改变。理事会对准则作出的任何修订决定,均须通过应循程序,将修订项目添加至理事会议程,并制定针对该准则的相应修订内容。

SP1.5 《概念框架》有助于国际财务报告准则基金会和隶属于基金会的理事会达成其设定的使命。该使命是制定出为全球金融市场带来透明度、公众受托责任和效率的准则。理事会通过促进全球经济中的信任、增长和长期金融稳定等工作,来服务于公众利益。《概念框架》为准则提供基础,以便:

(1) 通过提高财务信息的国际可比性和质量来提高透明度,有助于投资者和其他市场参与者作出明智的经济决策。

(2) 通过减少资本提供方与受托方之间的信息不对称来强化受托责任。基于《概念框架》制定的准则所提供的信息,有助于明确管理层职责。作为全球可比信息的来源,这些准则对全球的监管机构都至关重要。

(3) 通过协助投资者识别全球机遇与风险来提高经济效率,从而优化资本配置。对于企业,基于《概念框架》制定的准则产生单一、可信的会计语言,使用该语言能降低资本成本以及国际报告成本。

国际财务报告准则

财务报告
概念框架

起始段落

第 1 章——通用目的财务报告的目标

引言	**1.1**
通用目的财务报告的目标、有用性以及局限性	**1.2**
关于报告主体经济资源、对主体的求偿权以及经济资源与求偿权变动的信息	**1.12**
经济资源与求偿权	1.13
经济资源与求偿权的变动	1.15
权责发生制会计所反映的财务业绩	1.17
过去现金流量所反映的财务业绩	1.20
非因财务业绩导致的经济资源与求偿权的变动	1.21
关于主体经济资源使用的信息	**1.22**

引言

1.1 通用目的财务报告的目标构成了《概念框架》的基础。《概念框架》的其他方面——有用财务信息的质量特征和成本限制、报告主体概念、财务报表要素、确认和终止确认、计量、列示和披露等——都是由目标逻辑推演而来的。

通用目的财务报告的目标、有用性以及局限性

1.2 通用目的财务报告的目标①是提供关于报告主体的、有助于现有和潜在投资者、贷款人和其他债权人作出有关向主体②提供资源的决策的财务信息。这些决策包括：

（1）买入、卖出或持有权益和债务工具；

（2）提供或清偿贷款及其他形式的信贷；或者

（3）对管理层影响主体经济资源使用的行动行使表决权或施加影响。

1.3 第1.2段中所述的决策取决于现有和潜在投资者、贷款人和其他债权人的预期回报，如股利、本金和利息的支付或市场价格增长。投资者、贷款人及其他债权人对回报的预期，取决于他们对主体未来净现金流入（前景）的金额、时间分布和不确定性的评估，以及对管理层对主体经济资源受托责任履行情况的评估。现有和潜在投资者、贷款人和其他债权人需要信息来帮助其进行上述评估。

1.4 在进行第1.3段所述的评估前，现有和潜在投资者、贷款人和其他债权人需要关于以下方面的信息：

（1）主体的经济资源、对主体的求偿权以及经济资源与求偿权变动的信息（参见第1.12段至第1.21段）；以及

（2）主体管理层和治理层③履行其使用主体经济资源之职责的效率和效果程度（参见第1.22段至第1.23段）。

1.5 很多现有和潜在投资者、贷款人及其他债权人无法要求报告主体直接向其提供信息，因而必须依赖通用目的财务报告来获取其所需的诸多财务信息。因此，他们是通用目的财务报告的主要使用者。④

1.6 但是，通用目的财务报告不会且无法为现有和潜在的投资者、贷款人及其

---

① 除非特别说明，整个《概念框架》中，"财务报告"均指通用目的财务报告。
② 除非特别说明，整个《概念框架》中，"主体"均指报告主体。
③ 除非特别说明，整个《概念框架》中，"管理层"均指主体的管理层和治理层。
④ 整个《概念框架》中，"主要使用者"和"使用者"均指依赖通用目的财务报告来获取所需信息的现有和潜在投资者、贷款人及其他债权人。

他债权人提供其所需的全部信息。这些使用者需要考虑从其他渠道获取相关信息，例如宏观经济状况和预期、政治事件和政治气候、行业和公司前景。

1.7 通用目的财务报告并非意在反映一个报告主体的价值；而是提供有关信息以协助现有和潜在的投资者、贷款人及其他债权人估计报告主体的价值。

1.8 财务报告主要使用者个体之间的信息需求和关注事项各不相同，甚至可能相互抵触。理事会在制定财务报告准则时，力求所提供的信息集能满足尽可能多的主要使用者的需求。然而，专注于通用信息的需求，并不妨碍报告主体为主要使用者中的一些特定群体提供对其最有用的补充信息。

1.9 报告主体的管理层同样关注主体的财务信息。但是，管理层不需要依赖通用目的财务报告，因为他们可以从主体内部获取财务信息。

1.10 其他群体（例如，监管机构以及除投资者、贷款人及其他债权人以外的公众人士）也可能认为通用目的财务报告是有用的。但是，此类报告并非主要为这些群体而编制。

1.11 在很大程度上，财务报告是基于估计、判断和模型，而非精确描述。《概念框架》构建了用以指导估计、判断和模型的概念。这些概念是理事会以及财务报告编制者力求达到的目标。和大多数目标一样，《概念框架》关于理想财务报告的愿景也不大可能完全实现，至少在短期内是如此，因为，用以分析交易和其他事项的新方法，需要时间来理解、接受和应用。尽管如此，为使财务报告能够通过不断改进提高其有用性，确立一个努力的目标，确有必要。

关于报告主体经济资源、对主体的求偿权以及经济资源与求偿权变动的信息

1.12 通用目的财务报告提供关于报告主体财务状况的信息，也就是关于主体的经济资源和对报告主体的求偿权的信息。财务报告同时提供关于改变报告主体经济资源和求偿权的交易及其他事项影响的信息。这两类信息均为作出是否向主体提供资源的有关决策提供有用的输入值。

经济资源与求偿权

1.13 有关报告主体经济资源和求偿权的性质和金额的信息，有助于使用者识别报告主体的财务优势和劣势。这些信息可帮助使用者评估报告主体的流动性和偿债能力、额外的融资需求，以及成功获得该融资的可能性，也可帮助使用者评估管理层对主体经济资源受托责任的履行情况。关于现有求偿权的优先顺序和支付需求的信息，有助于使用者预测未来现金流量在对报告主体有求偿权的各方之间如何分配。

1.14 不同类型的经济资源会对使用者评估报告主体的未来现金流量前景有不同的影响。有些未来现金流量直接从现有的经济资源中产生，如应收账款。其他现金流

量则从综合使用不同的资源生产并向客户销售商品或提供服务中产生。尽管这些现金流量不能归之于某单项经济资源（或求偿权），但是，财务报告的使用者需要了解报告主体经营活动中可使用的资源的性质和金额。

经济资源与求偿权的变动

1.15 报告主体的经济资源和求偿权的变动，源自报告主体的财务业绩（参见第1.17段至第1.20段）以及其他事项和交易（如发行债务或权益工具）（参见第1.21段）。为了恰当评估报告主体未来净现金流入前景和管理层对主体经济资源受托责任的履行情况，使用者需要能够识别这两类变动。

1.16 关于报告主体财务业绩的信息，能帮助使用者理解报告主体通过使用其经济资源获得的回报。关于报告主体回报的信息，能帮助使用者评估管理层对主体经济资源受托责任的履行情况。关于主体回报的波动程度和组成部分的信息也十分重要，尤其在评估主体未来现金流量的不确定性时。关于报告主体过去财务业绩和管理层履行其受托责任情况的信息，通常有助于预测主体经济资源的未来回报。

权责发生制会计所反映的财务业绩

1.17 权责发生制会计是描述交易及其他事项和情况在其发生实际影响的期间对报告主体的经济资源和求偿权的影响，即使由此产生的现金收入或支付在不同的期间内发生。这样反映信息是很重要的，因为与只提供当期现金收付的信息相比，关于报告主体在某一期间内经济资源和求偿权及其变动的信息，能够为评估主体过去和未来的业绩，提供更好的依据。

1.18 关于报告主体某一期间内由经济资源和求偿权变动所反映的财务业绩（不包括直接从投资者和债权人获得的额外资源，参见第1.21段）的信息，有助于评估主体过去及未来产生净现金流入的能力。这些信息反映了报告主体增加其可用经济资源的程度，进而反映该主体通过其经营（而非直接从投资者和债权人获得额外资源）产生净现金流入的能力。关于报告主体某一期间内财务业绩的信息，能帮助使用者评估管理层对主体经济资源受托责任的履行情况。

1.19 关于报告主体某一期间内财务业绩的信息，亦能反映市场价格或利率变动等事项对主体的经济资源和求偿权增加或减少的影响程度，进而影响主体产生净现金流入的能力。

过去现金流量所反映的财务业绩

1.20 关于报告主体某一期间内现金流量的信息，有助于使用者评估主体产生未来净现金流入的能力，还有助于评估管理层对主体经济资源受托责任的履行情况。这些信息反映报告主体如何获取及消耗现金，包括关于主体借款和还款信息、现金股利和其他对投资者的现金分配、以及可能影响主体流动性及偿债能力的其他因素的信息。关于现金流量的信息有助于使用者理解报告主体的经营情况，评价其筹资及投资活动，评估其流动性及偿债能力，以及解释关于财务业绩的其他信息。

非因财务业绩导致的经济资源与求偿权的变动

1.21 报告主体的经济资源和求偿权也可能由于财务业绩之外的其他原因（例如发行债务或权益工具）而发生变动。关于这类变动的信息对于使用者来说是必要的，能够使其完整理解报告主体经济资源及求偿权变动的原因，以及这些变动对未来财务业绩的影响。

关于主体经济资源使用的信息

1.22 关于主体管理层履行其使用主体经济资源职责的效率和效果程度的信息，有助于使用者评估管理层对这些资源履行受托责任的情况。这些信息还可用于预测管理层在未来期间对主体经济资源使用的效率和效果程度。因此，它能用于评估主体未来净现金流入的前景。

1.23 管理层使用主体经济资源职责的例子包括：保护主体资源免受价格和技术变动等经济因素的不利影响，确保主体遵守适用的法律、法规以及合同条款。

起始段落

第 2 章——有用财务信息的质量特征

引言 ··	**2.1**
有用财务信息的质量特征 ··	**2.4**
基本质量特征 ···	**2.5**
相关性 ···	**2.6**
重要性 ···	**2.11**
如实反映 ···	**2.12**
基本质量特征的应用 ···	**2.20**
提升性质量特征 ···	**2.23**
可比性 ···	**2.24**
可验证性 ···	**2.30**
及时性 ···	**2.33**
可理解性 ···	**2.34**
提升性质量特征的应用 ··	**2.37**
有用财务报告的成本限制 ··	**2.39**

引言

2.1 本章所讨论的有用财务信息的质量特征，阐述了当现有和潜在投资者、贷款人及其他债权人根据主体财务报告中的信息（财务信息）作出关于报告主体的决策时，可能对其最为有用的信息类型。

2.2 财务报告提供的信息是关于报告主体的经济资源、对报告主体的求偿权、以及改变这些经济资源及求偿权的交易和其他事项及其状况的影响信息（《概念框架》将此类信息称为关于经济现象的信息）。有些财务报告同时提供关于管理层对报告主体的预期和战略进行解释的材料以及其他类型的前瞻性信息。

2.3 有用财务信息的质量特征①适用于财务报表中的财务信息以及通过其他方式提供的财务信息。由于成本对报告主体提供有用财务信息的能力构成普遍限制，因此成本限制也适用于上述财务信息。然而，对不同种类的信息而言，在应用质量特征和成本限制中的考虑可能各不相同。例如，将质量特征和成本限制应用于前瞻性信息，可能不同于将其应用于现有经济资源和求偿权及此类资源和求偿权变动的信息。

有用财务信息的质量特征

2.4 有用的财务信息必须具有相关性并且如实反映其意在反映的内容。如果财务信息具有可比性、可验证性、及时性和可理解性，则财务信息的有用性将得到提升。

基本质量特征

2.5 财务信息的基本质量特征是相关性和如实反映。

相关性

2.6 具有相关性的财务信息能够对使用者的决策产生影响。即便某些使用者选择不利用这些信息，或者已从其他渠道获悉这些信息，这些信息仍可能影响决策。

2.7 如果财务信息具有预测价值、证实价值或两者兼有，则能够对决策产生影响。

2.8 如果财务信息能够被使用者在其预测未来结果的过程中作为输入值，则该财务信息具有预测价值。财务信息本身不一定是预测或预报才具有预测价值。具有预

---

① 整个《概念框架》中，"质量特征"和"成本限制"指有用财务信息的质量特征及其受到的成本限制。

测价值的财务信息由使用者在作出自己预测时所使用。

2.9 如果财务信息提供关于之前评估的反馈（证实或更改），则该财务信息具有证实价值。

2.10 财务信息的预测价值和证实价值是相互关联的。具有预测价值的财务信息通常具有证实价值。例如，本年度的收入信息，可用来作为预测未来年度收入的基础，也可用来与过去年度预测的本年度收入进行对比。这些对比的结果可帮助使用者修正及改善其之前用以作出预测的流程。

重要性

2.11 通用目的财务报告提供了关于特定报告主体的财务信息，如果省略或误报某信息会影响通用目的财务报告（参见第 1.5 段）的主要使用者基于这些报告所作出的决策，则该信息就具有重要性。换言之，重要性是基于个别主体财务报告信息所涉及项目的性质或金额大小或两者兼有而确定的，体现出对特定主体的相关性。因此，理事会不能为重要性制定一个统一的量化标准或预先决定在特定情况下什么是重要的。

如实反映

2.12 财务报告以文字和数字反映经济现象。有用的财务信息不仅必须反映相关现象，而且必须如实反映其意在反映的现象的实质。很多情况下，经济现象的实质和它的法律形式相同。若不相同，仅提供关于法律形式的信息无法如实反映经济现象（参见第 4.59 段至第 4.62 段）。

2.13 要达到完美地如实反映，描述应具备三个特征：完整、中立和无误。当然，完美无法企及。理事会的目标是尽可能最大限度地提升这些质量。

2.14 完整描述包含使用者理解所描述现象所必需的全部信息，包括所有必要的说明和解释。例如，对一组资产的完整描述至少应包括关于这组资产性质的描述、所有资产的量化描述、以及对量化描述所反映内容（例如，历史成本或公允价值）的说明。对于某些项目而言，完整描述可能也需要解释关于此项目质量和性质的重要事实、可能影响此项目质量和性质的因素和情形、以及确定其量化描述所采用的过程。

2.15 中立描述是指以不带偏见的方式选择或列报财务信息。中立描述不具有倾向性、未权衡轻重、未片面强调、未故意弱化或用其他方式操纵，以提高使用者乐于或不乐于接受财务信息的可能性。中立的信息并不是指没有目的或对行为没有影响的信息。相反，根据其定义，相关的财务信息能够影响使用者的决策。

2.16 审慎性的运用有助于保持中立性。审慎性是指在不确定性条件下进行判断时运用谨慎。审慎性的运用，是指不高估资产或收益，不低估负债或费用[①]。同样地，运用审慎性也不允许低估资产或收益，或者高估负债或费用。这类错报会导致未

---

① 资产、负债、收益和费用的定义见表 4.1。它们是财务报表要素。

来期间高估或低估收益或费用。

2.17 审慎性的运用并不意味着需要保持不对称性,例如,确认资产或收益的支持证据所需要的说服力系统性地高于确认负债或费用的证据所需要的说服力。该不对称性并非有用财务信息的质量特征。但是,如果出于选择如实反映其意在反映的最相关信息的目的,则特定准则可能包括具有不对称性的相关规定。

2.18 如实反映并不意味着在所有方面都精确。无误是指对现象的描述不存在错误或遗漏,以及用于生成所报告信息的流程在选择和应用的过程中没有发生差错。在这样的情况下,无误不是指在所有方面都完全精确。例如,对不可观察的价格或价值的估计值无法判定其是否精确。然而,如果该金额被清晰准确地描述为估计值、并已说明估计流程的性质和局限性、且选择和应用适当的估计流程时没有发生差错,则该估计值就是如实反映的。

2.19 如果财务报告中的货币金额不可直接观察,而是必须进行估计,则计量不确定性相应产生。在编制财务信息时必然要使用合理估计。如果能够对估计进行清晰准确的描述与解释,则使用合理估计并不会有损信息的有用性,即使是高程度的计量不确定性,也不一定会有碍此估计提供有用信息(参见第 2.22 段)。

基本质量特征的应用

2.20 有用信息必须既具有相关性又能如实反映其意在反映的内容。无论是如实反映不相关的现象,还是未如实反映相关现象,都不能帮助使用者作出好的决策。

2.21 通常,应用基本质量特征最为高效且有效的流程如下(会受本示例中并未考虑的提升性质量特征和成本限制的影响)。首先,识别能够为报告主体财务信息的使用者提供有用信息的经济现象。其次,识别关于此现象最为相关的信息类型。再次,确定此信息是否可获取,以及是否能够如实反映经济现象。如果满足以上条件,则符合基本质量特征的流程已完成。如果不能满足以上条件,则应针对次相关的信息类型重复上述流程。

2.22 某些情况下,可能需要在各基本质量特征间加以权衡,以实现财务报告的目标,即提供关于经济现象的有用信息。例如,关于某经济现象的最具有相关性的信息可能是高度不确定的估计。某些情况下,进行估计时涉及的计量不确定性的程度高,以至于对该估计是否充分地如实反映该现象存有疑问。在某些此类情况下,最有用的信息可能是高度不确定的估计,附以对此估计的描述以及对影响此估计的不确定性作出的解释。在其他一些此类情况下,如果该信息不能充分地如实反映该现象,则最有用的信息可能包括相关性稍低但计量不确定性也更低的另一类型估计。在有限情况下,或许不存在可提供有用信息的估计。在这些有限情况下,可能有必要提供不依赖估计的信息。

提升性质量特征

2.23 有用的信息必须相关,且如实反映其意在反映的信息,可比性、可验证性、及时性和可理解性是能够提升信息有用性的质量特征。当描述某一现象的两种方式所提供的相关性和如实反映程度相同时，提升性质量特征也可有助于确定应使用哪种方式。

可比性

2.24 使用者的决策涉及在各个可选方案之间进行选择，例如，出售或持有某项投资，或者对哪一个报告主体进行投资。因此，如果有关某报告主体的信息能够与其他报告主体的类似信息进行比较、以及能够与同一报告主体其他期间或时点的信息进行比较，则该信息将更加有用。

2.25 可比性是能够让使用者识别和理解各项目之间的相似性和差异的质量特征。与其他质量特征不同的是，可比性不是仅与某个单一项目相关。至少需要两个项目才能进行比较。

2.26 一致性尽管与可比性有关，但却不同于可比性。一致性是指同一报告主体在不同报告期间、或者不同的主体在同一报告期间针对相同的项目使用相同的处理方法。可比性是目标；一致性有助于实现这一目标。

2.27 可比性不是整齐划一。为了使信息可比，相同的事项必须看起来相同，而不同的事项必须看起来不同。让不同的事项看起来相同，并不会比让相同的事项看起来不同对可比性提升更多。

2.28 一定程度的可比性有可能通过符合基本质量特征来实现。对相关经济现象的如实反映，与另一报告主体对类似相关经济现象的如实反映，自然应当具有一定程度的可比性。

2.29 尽管某一经济现象可通过多种方式实现如实反映，但允许对同一经济现象采用不同的会计方法将削弱可比性。

可验证性

2.30 可验证性帮助使用者确信有关信息如实反映了其意在反映的经济现象。可验证性意味着具有必备知识的不同独立观察者能够就某一特定描述是否如实反映达成共识，尽管其意见不一定完全一致。量化信息无需是单点估计才是可验证的。可能金额的区间及其相关概率也是可验证的。

2.31 验证可以是直接的，也可以是间接的。直接验证是指通过直接观察来验证某一金额或其他陈述，例如通过现金盘点。间接验证是指检查模型的输入值、公式或其他技术，并采用相同的方法重新计算输出结果。例如，通过检查输入值（数量和成本）并运用相同的成本流转假设（例如，使用先进先出法）重新计算期末存货来验证存货的账面价值。

2.32 某些说明及前瞻性财务信息可能要直至未来的某一期间才能被验证。为协助使用者决定其是否希望使用该信息，通常有必要披露基础假设、信息汇编的方法以及支持该信息的其他因素和情况。

及时性

2.33 及时性意味着为决策者及时提供能够影响其决策的信息。通常而言,信息越陈旧就越缺乏有用性。然而,某些信息在报告期间结束后一段相当长的时间内仍具有及时性,例如,有些使用者可能需要识别和评估趋势。

可理解性

2.34 清晰和简明地对信息进行分类、界定其特征和列报,使信息具有可理解性。

2.35 某些现象具备固有的复杂性并且无法使其易于理解。从财务报告中剔除关于这些现象的信息可能使财务报告中的信息更容易理解。然而,这样的报告会因不完整而可能产生误导。

2.36 财务报告是为具有合理的业务和经济活动知识以及认真审阅和分析财务报表的使用者而编制的。有时,即使是掌握足够信息的和勤勉的使用者也需要寻求顾问的帮助来理解关于复杂经济现象的信息。

提升性质量特征的应用

2.37 应尽可能最大限度地应用提升性质量特征。然而,如果信息并不相关或无法如实反映其意在反映的现象,则提升性质量特征无论是单独还是作为一个整体都不能使信息有用。

2.38 提升性质量特征的应用是一个持续反复的过程且并不依照既定的顺序进行。有时,可能需要削弱某个提升性质量特征以最大程度地符合另一个质量特征。例如,以未来适用的方式应用某项新准则造成的信息可比性的暂时降低,对于在更长时期内提高相关性或如实反映而言可能是值得的。适当的披露可以部分弥补不可比的情况。

有用财务报告的成本限制

2.39 成本对财务报告可提供的信息具有普遍限制。报告财务信息必然耗费成本,重要的是报告此类信息所产生的效益能够证明相关成本是合理的。有几类成本和效益值得考虑。

2.40 财务信息的提供者为收集、处理、验证和发布财务信息的诸多努力所花费的成本,最终由使用者以降低回报的形式承担。财务信息的使用者在分析和解释所提供的信息时,也会产生成本;如果所需的信息未被提供,则使用者为了从其他来源获得信息或作出估计,将发生额外的成本。

2.41 报告相关和如实反映的财务信息,能够帮助使用者更有信心地作出决策。

这使得资本市场的运作更加高效，并使经济整体的资本成本更低。单个投资者、贷款人或其他债权人也可以通过作出更有依据的决策而获益。然而，通用目的财务报告无法提供每一个使用者都认为相关的全部信息。

2.42 考虑到成本限制，理事会评估报告特定信息带来的效益是否有可能证明提供和使用该信息的成本是合理的。在制定准则过程中考虑成本限制时，理事会向财务信息的提供者、使用者、审计师、学者及其他方征询关于该准则的效益和成本的预期性质和数量的信息。在大多数情况下，评估是基于定量和定性信息综合作出的。

2.43 由于固有的主观性，不同的个体对报告特定项目财务信息的成本和效益的评估结果各不相同。因此，理事会致力于考虑一般情况下财务报告的成本和效益，而非仅考虑与个别报告主体相关的成本和效益。这并不意味着对成本和效益的评估能表明针对所有主体应用相同的报告要求总是合理的。由于主体规模不同、融资方式不同（公募或私募）、不同使用者的需求不同或其他原因，区别处理可能是恰当的。

起始段落

第 3 章——财务报表和报告主体

财务报表 ⋯⋯⋯⋯⋯⋯⋯⋯⋯⋯⋯⋯⋯⋯⋯⋯⋯⋯⋯⋯⋯⋯⋯⋯⋯⋯⋯⋯⋯⋯⋯⋯⋯⋯	**3.1**
财务报表的目标和范围 ⋯⋯⋯⋯⋯⋯⋯⋯⋯⋯⋯⋯⋯⋯⋯⋯⋯⋯⋯⋯⋯⋯⋯⋯⋯⋯	3.2
报告期间 ⋯⋯⋯⋯⋯⋯⋯⋯⋯⋯⋯⋯⋯⋯⋯⋯⋯⋯⋯⋯⋯⋯⋯⋯⋯⋯⋯⋯⋯⋯⋯⋯⋯	3.4
财务报表中采用的角度 ⋯⋯⋯⋯⋯⋯⋯⋯⋯⋯⋯⋯⋯⋯⋯⋯⋯⋯⋯⋯⋯⋯⋯⋯⋯⋯	3.8
持续经营假设 ⋯⋯⋯⋯⋯⋯⋯⋯⋯⋯⋯⋯⋯⋯⋯⋯⋯⋯⋯⋯⋯⋯⋯⋯⋯⋯⋯⋯⋯⋯⋯	3.9
报告主体 ⋯⋯⋯⋯⋯⋯⋯⋯⋯⋯⋯⋯⋯⋯⋯⋯⋯⋯⋯⋯⋯⋯⋯⋯⋯⋯⋯⋯⋯⋯⋯⋯⋯⋯	**3.10**
合并与非合并财务报表 ⋯⋯⋯⋯⋯⋯⋯⋯⋯⋯⋯⋯⋯⋯⋯⋯⋯⋯⋯⋯⋯⋯⋯⋯⋯⋯	3.15

财务报表

3.1 第1章和第2章讨论通用目的财务报告所提供的信息,第3章至第8章讨论通用目的财务报表——通用目的财务报告的特定形式——所提供的信息。财务报表①提供了关于报告主体经济资源、对主体的求偿权以及资源与求偿权变动的信息,它们符合财务报表要素的定义(参见表4.1)。

财务报表的目标和范围

3.2 财务报表的目标是向财务报表的使用者提供关于主体资产、负债、权益、收益和费用②的有用的财务信息,帮助其评估报告主体未来净现金流入的前景及管理层对主体经济资源受托责任的履行情况(参见第1.3段)。

3.3 有用财务信息通过以下方式提供:
(1)在财务状况表中确认资产、负债和权益;
(2)在财务业绩表③中确认收益和费用;以及
(3)在其他报表和附注中列示和披露以下有关信息:
①已确认的资产、负债、权益、收益和费用(参见第5.1段),包括关于这些项目的性质和这些已确认资产和负债引起的风险的信息;
②未确认的资产和负债(参见第5.6段),包括有关这些资产和负债的性质及其引起的风险的信息;
③现金流量;
④权益持有者的投入以及对其分配;以及
⑤对已列示或已披露金额进行估计时所使用的方法、假设和判断,以及这些方法、假设和判断的变化。

报告期间

3.4 财务报表针对特定的时间段(报告期间)进行编制,并提供关于以下方面的信息:
(1)报告期末或报告期间存在的资产和负债(包括未确认的资产和负债)以及权益;以及
(2)报告期间的收益和费用。

3.5 为帮助财务报表使用者识别并评估变化和趋势,财务报表还至少提供之前

---

① 整个《概念框架》中,"财务报表"均指通用目的财务报表。
② 资产、负债、权益、收益和费用的定义见表4.1。它们均为财务报表要素。
③ 《概念框架》未特别指出财务业绩表包含一张报表还是两张报表。

一个报告期间的比较信息。

3.6 如果可能发生的未来交易和其他可能的未来事项的信息（前瞻性信息）满足以下条件，则该信息将被纳入财务报表：

（1）与主体在报告期末或报告期间存在的资产或负债（包括未确认的资产或负债）或权益相关，或与报告期间的收益或费用相关；并且

（2）对财务报表使用者有用。

例如，如果一项资产或负债通过估计未来现金流量进行计量，则关于这些预计未来现金流量的信息可能有助于财务报表使用者理解报告中的计量数据。财务报表通常不会提供其他类型的前瞻性信息，例如，关于管理层预期和报告主体战略的解释性材料。

3.7 如果提供报告期结束后发生的交易和其他事项的相关信息，对于实现财务报表的目标是必要的，则财务报表应包括此类信息（参见第 3.2 段）。

财务报表中采用的角度

3.8 财务报表从报告主体整体的角度提供关于交易和其他事项的相关信息，而非从主体现有或潜在投资者、贷款人或其他债权人的特定群体的角度出发。

持续经营假设

3.9 财务报表的编制通常是基于报告主体持续经营，并在可预见的将来会继续经营的假设。因此，假定主体既没有意图也不需要进入清算程序或终止交易。如果存在这种意图或需要，则财务报表可能要按照不同的基础编制。如果是这样，则财务报表应当披露所采用的基础。

报告主体

3.10 报告主体是被要求或主动选择编制财务报表的主体。报告主体可以是单个主体或主体的一部分，也可以由一个以上主体构成。一个报告主体并不必然是一个法律主体。

3.11 有时一个主体（母公司）拥有对另一个主体（子公司）的控制。如果报告主体由母公司及其子公司构成，则报告主体的财务报表称为"合并财务报表"（参见第 3.15 段至第 3.16 段）。如果报告主体仅为母公司，则报告主体的财务报表称为"非合并财务报表"（参见第 3.17 段至第 3.18 段）。

3.12 如果报告主体由两个或两个以上主体构成，且这些主体不都是母子公司关系，则报告主体的财务报表称为"汇总财务报表"。

3.13 如果报告主体具有以下特征，则确定报告主体的边界是困难的：

(1) 不是法律主体；并且

(2) 不是仅由具有母子公司关系的法律主体构成。

3.14 此类情况下，报告主体的边界主要由报告主体财务报表主要使用者的信息需求来确定。这些使用者需要能如实反映其意在反映、且具有相关性的信息。如实反映有如下要求：

(1) 报告主体边界内不包含随意划分的一组经济活动或不完整的一组经济活动；

(2) 将这些经济活动纳入报告主体边界内会带来中立的信息；以及

(3) 就报告主体边界的确定方式以及报告主体的构成提供描述信息。

合并与非合并财务报表

3.15 合并财务报表提供关于母公司及其子公司作为一个报告主体的资产、负债、权益、收益和费用的信息。这些信息对母公司现有和潜在投资者、贷款人和其他债权人评估母公司未来净现金流入前景是有用的，原因是母公司的净现金流入包含子公司对母公司的分配，而这些分配又依赖于子公司的净现金流入。

3.16 合并财务报表不用于提供任一特定子公司资产、负债、权益、收益和费用的单独信息。上述信息由子公司自身的财务报表提供。

3.17 非合并财务报表意在提供关于母公司资产、负债、权益、收益和费用的信息，而非子公司的上述信息。此类信息对母公司现有和潜在投资者、贷款人和其他债权人而言是有用的，因为：

(1) 针对母公司的求偿权通常不会赋予权利人针对子公司的求偿权；以及

(2) 在某些国家或地区，可合法分配至母公司权益持有者的金额依赖于母公司的可分配盈余。

另一种提供关于母公司资产、负债、权益、收益和费用的部分或全部信息的方法，是将其披露在合并财务报表的附注中。

3.18 非合并财务报表中提供的信息通常不足以满足母公司现有和潜在投资者、贷款人和其他债权人的信息需求。因此，当必须提供合并财务报表时，非合并财务报表无法代替合并财务报表。尽管如此，母公司可能会被要求或选择在合并财务报表之外，编报非合并财务报表。

国际财务报告准则

财务报告
概念框架

起始段落

第 4 章——财务报表要素

引言	4.1
资产的定义	**4.3**
权利	4.6
产生经济利益的潜力	4.14
控制	4.19
负债的定义	**4.26**
义务	4.28
经济资源的转移	4.36
由于过去事项而形成的现时义务	4.42
资产和负债	**4.48**
核算单元	4.48
待执行合同	4.56
合同权利和合同义务的实质	4.59
权益的定义	**4.63**
收益和费用的定义	**4.68**

引言

4.1《概念框架》中定义的财务报表要素为:
(1) 与报告主体财务状况相关的资产、负债和权益;以及
(2) 与报告主体财务业绩相关的收益和费用。

4.2 上述要素与第1章中所讨论的经济资源、求偿权和经济资源与求偿权的变动有关,其定义见表4.1。

表 4.1　　　　　　　　　财务报表要素

第1章讨论的项目	要素	定义或描述
经济资源	资产	主体由于过去的事项而控制的现时经济资源。 经济资源指具备产生经济利益潜力的权利。
求偿权	负债	主体由于过去的事项而承担的转移经济资源的现时义务。
	权益	主体资产扣除所有负债后的剩余利益。
反映财务业绩的经济资源与求偿权的变动	收益	引起权益增加的资产增加或负债减少,但不包括权益持有者的投入。
	费用	引起权益减少的资产减少或负债增加,但不包括对权益持有者的分配。
经济资源与求偿权的其他变动	—	权益持有者的投入或对其分配。
	—	未导致权益增加或减少的资产或负债交换。

资产的定义

4.3 资产是主体由于过去的事项而控制的现时经济资源。
4.4 经济资源指具备产生经济利益潜力的权利。
4.5 本部分讨论了上述定义的三个方面:
(1) 权利(参见第4.6段至第4.13段);

(2) 产生经济利益的潜力（参见第 4.14 段至第 4.18 段）；以及
(3) 控制（参见第 4.19 段至第 4.25 段）。

权利

4.6　具备产生经济利益潜力的权利，形式多样，包括：
(1) 与另一方的义务相关的权利（参见第 4.39 段），例如：
①收取现金的权利。
②收取商品或服务的权利。
③在有利条件下与另一方交换经济资源的权利。例如，此类权利包括以当前有利的条款购买经济资源的远期合同，或购买经济资源的期权。
④如果未来某一特定不确定事项发生，从另一方转移经济资源的义务中获益的权利（参见第 4.37 段）。
(2) 不与另一方的义务相关的权利，例如：
①对不动产、厂场和设备或存货等实物对象的权利。例如，此类权利包括对某实物标的的使用权，或从租入对象的剩余价值中获益的权利。
②使用知识产权的权利。

4.7　许多权利是根据合同、法规或类似方式确立的。例如，主体可通过拥有或租赁实物对象、拥有债务工具或权益工具，或拥有已注册专利的方式获得权利。然而，主体也可通过其他方式获得权利，例如：
(1) 通过取得或创建不公开的专有技术（参见第 4.22 段）而获得权利；或者
(2) 通过另一方的义务而获得权利，该义务是由于另一方没有违反其惯例、政策或声明的实际能力（参见第 4.31 段）而产生。

4.8　某些商品或服务——例如员工服务——在收到之时即被消耗。主体在消耗此类商品或服务产生的经济利益之时才取得相应权利。

4.9　并非主体的所有权利均为该主体的资产——权利在成为主体的资产前必须满足两个条件：具备为该主体产生经济利益的潜力且该经济利益超出所有其他方可从中获得的经济利益（参见第 4.14 段至第 4.18 段）；以及，由该主体控制（参见第 4.19 段至第 4.25 段）。例如，各方无需重大成本均可获得的权利，如道路公共使用权等使用公共财产的权利，或属于公开的专有技术，这些通常不属于持有该权利的主体的资产。

4.10　主体不可拥有从自身获得经济利益的权利。因此：
(1) 主体发行并回购而持有的债务工具或权益工具，如库存股，不属于该主体的经济资源；以及
(2) 若报告主体包含一个以上法律主体，由其中一个法律主体发行、并由其中的另一个法律主体持有的债务工具或权益工具，不属于该报告主体的经济资源。

4.11　原则上，主体的每项权利均为单独资产。但是，从会计角度出发，相关的多项权利通常被当作单一核算单元（即单一资产）（参见第 4.48 段至第 4.55 段）。

例如，一项实物对象的法定所有权可能产生多项权利，包括：

（1）使用该对象的权利；

（2）出售依附于该对象相关权利的权利；

（3）抵押与该对象相关权利的权利；以及

（4）（1）至（3）中未列出的其他权利。

4.12 多数情况下，因实物对象法定所有权而产生的一系列权利被作为单一资产进行会计处理。从概念上讲，经济资源指该系列权利，而非该实物对象。尽管如此，将该系列权利描述为实物对象，通常能够以最简洁、可理解的方式如实反映这些权利。

4.13 在某些情况下，一项权利存在与否，具有不确定性。例如，一个主体可能就该主体是否拥有从另一主体收取经济资源的权利而与另一主体产生争议。在不确定性消除（如通过法庭裁决）之前，主体是否拥有权利是不确定的，相应地，一项资产是否存在具有不确定性。（对于存在具有不确定性的资产，第5.14段讨论了其确认问题。）

产生经济利益的潜力

4.14 经济资源指具备产生经济利益潜力的权利。"存在潜力"意味着权利所产生经济利益并不需要是确定的，或是很可能的。只要权利已经存在，且至少在一种情况下能够为主体产生高于所有其他方可能从中获得的经济利益即可。

4.15 即使产生经济利益的可能性低，一项权利能够满足经济资源的定义，就可以是一项资产。但低可能性会影响对该资产应提供哪些信息和如何提供此类信息的判断，包括是否确认该资产（参见第5.15段至第5.17段）以及如何计量。

4.16 通过使主体有权或可以从事以下一项或各项事情，一项经济资源能够为该主体产生经济利益：

（1）收取合同约定的现金流量或其他经济资源；

（2）在有利条件下与另一方交换经济资源；

（3）通过以下方式产生现金流入或避免现金流出，例如：

①单独利用该经济资源或将其与其他经济资源相结合，用以生产商品或提供服务；

②利用该经济资源提高其他经济资源的价值；或者

③将该经济资源出租给另一方；

（4）出售该经济资源以收取现金或其他经济资源；或者

（5）转移该经济资源以清偿负债。

4.17 尽管经济资源的价值来源于其能产生未来经济利益的现时潜力，但经济资源是指包含该潜力的现时权利，而非该权利可能产生的未来经济利益。例如，购入期权的价值来源于通过在未来某日行使该期权而产生经济利益的潜力。但是，经济资源是指现时权利，即在未来某日行使期权的权利。经济资源并不是指行使期权后持有者可收取的未来经济利益。

4.18 虽然发生支出和获得资产之间存在紧密联系，但二者不必然同时发生。因此，当主体发生支出时，可能证明主体已经在寻找未来经济利益，但并不能够提供主体已经获得资产的确凿证据。同样地，未发生相关支出，并不能妨碍一个项目满足资产的定义。例如，资产可包括政府免费授予主体的权利或另一方赠与主体的权利。

控制

4.19 控制将主体与某一经济资源联系起来。评估是否存在控制有助于主体识别其所核算的经济资源。例如，主体可控制某项房产中一定比例的份额，而无须控制源于房产所有权的各项权利。在此情况下，主体的资产为由其控制的房产份额，而非不由主体控制的源于房产所有权的权利。

4.20 如果主体拥有主导经济资源的使用并且获得该资源可能产生的经济利益的现时能力，则主体控制该经济资源。控制包括阻止其他方主导该经济资源使用的现时能力和获得该经济资源可能产生的经济利益的现时能力。换言之，如果有一方控制某一经济资源，则任何其他方均不具备对该资源的控制。

4.21 如果主体拥有在其活动中调配某一经济资源的权利或允许另一方在该方活动中调配该资源的权利，则主体具有主导该经济资源使用的现时能力。

4.22 主体对某一经济资源的控制通常来自其行使法定权利的能力。如果主体以其他方式确保其自身而非其他方拥有现时能力，能主导该经济资源的使用和获得该经济资源可能产生的经济利益，则主体同样可获得对该资源的控制。例如，如果主体拥有一项不公开的专有技术，且拥有保守专有技术秘密的现时能力，即使该专有技术不受注册专利的保护，主体仍可控制该专有技术的使用权。

4.23 一个主体控制了某一经济资源，则该经济资源产生的经济利益须直接或间接流入该主体，而非其他方。这并不意味着该主体能确保该经济资源在所有情况下都可以产生经济利益，而是表示如果该资源产生经济利益，该主体是可直接或间接获取该经济利益的那一方。

4.24 如果主体受经济资源产生的经济利益金额重大波动的影响，可能表明主体控制该资源，但这仅是整体评估控制是否存在时所考虑的因素之一。

4.25 有时一方（主要责任人）委托另一方（代理人）作为其代表并为其利益行事。例如，主要责任人可聘用代理人安排由主要责任人控制的商品的销售。如果代理人仅负责保管由主要责任人控制的经济资源，该经济资源不属于代理人的资产。此外，如果代理人有义务将由主要责任人控制的经济资源转移至第三方，由于被转移的是主要责任人的经济资源，而非代理人的，因此该义务不属于代理人的负债。

负债的定义

4.26 负债是主体由于过去的事项而承担的转移经济资源的现时义务。

4.27 负债的存在须满足以下三个条件：
（1）主体承担义务（参见第 4.28 段至第 4.35 段）；
（2）该义务将导致经济资源的转移（参见第 4.36 段至第 4.41 段）；以及
（3）该义务是由于过去事项而形成的现时义务（参见第 4.42 段至第 4.47 段）。

义务

4.28 负债的第一个标准是主体承担了义务。

4.29 义务是指主体无实际能力避免的职责或责任。义务总是对应着另一方（或多方）。另一方（或多方）可以是个人或另一主体、一群人或一组其他主体，或全社会。无须识别该义务对应的另一方（或多方）的身份。

4.30 如果一方有转移经济资源的义务，则另一方（或多方）就有收取该经济资源的权利。要求一方确认负债并按照特定金额计量负债，不意味着另一方（或多方）必须确认资产或按照相同金额计量资产。例如，准则可能针对一方的负债和另一方（或多方）的资产提出了不同的确认标准或计量要求，前提是这些不同的标准或要求是为了选择能够如实反映其实质的最具相关性的信息。

4.31 义务主要是通过合同、法规或类似方式确立的而且其所对应的另一方（或多方）具有法律执行力。还有一些义务是由主体的惯例、已发布政策或特定声明产生的，前提是主体没有违反上述惯例、政策或声明的实际能力。此类情况下产生的义务有时被称为"推定义务"。

4.32 某些情况下，主体转移经济资源的职责或责任取决于主体未来可能采取的特定措施。此类措施包括经营特定业务或在具体未来时日在特定的市场开展经营活动，或行使合同范围内的特定选择权。此类情况下，如果主体没有避免采取上述措施的实际能力，则将承担义务。

4.33 如果依据持续经营假设编制主体财务报表是适当的，则由此可以推导出另一结论，即除了清算或终止运营外，主体没有实际能力去避免转移一项资源。

4.34 评估主体是否有避免转移经济资源的实际能力的因素，可能取决于主体职责或责任的性质。例如，某些情况下，如果主体为避免转移所能采取的任何措施，会带来比转移本身更为重大不利的经济后果，则主体没有避免转移的实际能力。但是，无论是该主体具有转移意图，还是发生转移的可能性高，均不足以作为充分理由，得出主体没有避免转移的实际能力的结论。

4.35 某些情况下，是否存在义务并不确定。例如，另一方就主体被指证的不当行为寻求补偿时，不当行为是否已发生、该行为是否由主体作出或相关法律如何适用等等，都可能是不确定的。在义务存在与否的不确定性消除（如通过法庭裁决）之前，对于主体是否对寻求补偿的一方承担义务以及因义务产生的负债存在与否，均存在不确定性。（对于存在具有不确定性的负债，第 5.14 段讨论了其确认问题。）

经济资源的转移

4.36 负债的第二个标准是主体所承担的义务是转移一项经济资源。

4.37 为满足此条件，该义务必须具有要求主体将经济资源转移至另一方（或多方）的潜力。"存在潜力"意味着要求主体转移经济资源并不需要是确定的，或是很可能的，例如，主体可能仅在特定的不确定未来事项发生时才会被要求转移经济资源。只要义务已经存在，且至少在一种情况下能够要求主体转移经济资源即可。

4.38 即使转移经济资源的可能性低，一项义务仍能满足负债的定义。但低可能性会影响有关针对该负债提供哪些信息和如何提供此类信息的决定，包括是否确认该负债（参见第5.15段至第5.17段）以及如何计量。

4.39 转移经济资源的义务包括以下例子：

（1）支付现金的义务。

（2）交付商品或提供服务的义务。

（3）在不利条件下与另一方交换经济资源的义务。例如，此类义务包括以当前不利条款销售经济资源的远期合同，或使另一方有权从主体购买经济资源的期权。

（4）当特定的不确定的未来事项发生时，转移经济资源的义务。

（5）发行一项要求主体必须转移一项经济资源的金融工具的义务。

4.40 除了履行义务将经济资源转移至有权接收该资源的一方外，主体有时会决定采取其他措施，例如：

（1）通过协商免除义务；

（2）将义务转移至第三方；或者

（3）通过达成新的交易，将转移经济资源的义务替换为其他义务。

4.41 在第4.40段所述的情况中，在义务被清偿、转移或替换之前，主体负有转移经济资源的义务。

由于过去事项而形成的现时义务

4.42 负债的第三个标准为该义务是由于过去事项而形成的现时义务。

4.43 由于过去事项而形成的现时义务仅在同时发生如下情况时存在：

（1）主体已获得经济利益或已采取行动；并且

（2）主体因此将要或可能必须转移本不必转移的经济资源。

4.44 主体所获得的经济利益可能包括诸如商品或服务。所采取的行动包括诸如经营特定业务或在特定市场开展经营活动。如果主体是在一段时间内获得经济利益或采取行动，则由此产生的现时义务也将随时间累积。

4.45 如果出台了新的法规，则由主体获得适用新法规的经济利益或采取了适用新法规的相关行动，主体的现时义务仅在其将要或可能必须转移本不必转移的经济资源时出现。法规出台本身不足以使主体承担现时义务。类似地，由于主体适用第

4.31 段的惯例、已发布政策或特定声明而获得经济利益或采取了相关行动，此类惯例、政策或声明仅在主体将要或可能必须转移本不必转移的经济资源时会引起现时义务。

4.46 即使经济资源的转移只能在未来某个时间点执行，现时义务仍然存在。例如，即使一项合同仅要求主体在未来某日进行付款，主体当前即承担支付现金的合同负债。类似地，即使交易对手仅能在未来某日要求主体执行工作，主体当前即承担执行此工作的合同义务。

4.47 如果主体尚不满足第4.43段的条件，即主体尚未获得经济利益或采取行动使其将要或可能必须转移本不必转移的经济资源，则主体不承担转移经济资源的现时义务。例如，如果主体与员工签订合同，通过支付薪酬的方式换取员工的服务，则主体仅在获取员工服务后才承担支付薪酬的现时义务。在此之前合同为待执行合同，即主体具有向员工支付未来薪酬以换取未来服务的一组权利和义务（参见第4.56段至第4.58段）。

资产和负债

核算单元

4.48 核算单元是指适用确认标准和计量概念的一项权利或一组权利、一项义务或一组义务，或者一组权利和义务。

4.49 在考虑确认标准和计量概念如何应用于资产或负债以及相关收益和费用时，会为该资产或负债选择一个核算单元。在某些情况下，可能会为确认选择一个核算单元，为计量选择另一核算单元。例如，合同有时可单独确认，但须作为合同组合的一部分进行计量。对于列示和披露，资产、负债、收益和费用可能需要汇总或拆分成为数个组成部分。

4.50 如果主体转移部分资产或部分负债，核算单元可能会随之改变，使得已转移部分和保留部分成为不同的核算单元（参见第5.26段至第5.33段）。

4.51 选择核算单元意在提供有用信息，这意味着：

（1）所提供的关于资产或负债以及相关收益和费用的信息必须具有相关性。在以下情况下，将一组权利和义务作为单一核算单元进行处理所提供的信息，可能会比将每项权利或义务分别作为单独的核算单元进行处理更相关，例如：

①权利和义务不可能或不太可能是单独交易的对象；

②权利和义务不可能或不太可能以不同的模式到期；

③权利和义务具有相似的经济特征和风险，因此很可能对主体未来预期净现金流入或净现金流出具有相似的影响；或

④在主体为产生现金流量而开展的业务活动中，权利和义务被一并使用，并参照

其相互依存的未来现金流量的估计对其进行计量。

（2）所提供的关于资产或负债以及相关收益和费用的信息，必须如实反映产生上述信息的交易或其他事项的实质。因此，可能有必要将产生于不同来源的权利或义务作为单一核算单元进行处理，或将产生于同一来源的权利或义务分开处理（参见第4.62段）。同样地，为如实反映不相关的权利和义务，可能有必要将其分开确认和计量。

4.52 正如成本会限制其他财务报告决策一样，成本也会限制核算单元的选择。因此，在选择核算单元时，重要的是考虑通过选择核算单元为财务报表使用者提供的信息所带来的效益，是否很可能证明提供和使用该信息的成本是合理的。一般而言，与资产、负债、收益和费用的确认和计量相关的成本，会随着核算单元的缩小而增加。因此，通常而言，只有在分开处理后得到的信息更加有用，且效益大于成本的情况下，产生于同一来源的权利或义务才会被分开处理。

4.53 有时，权利和义务产生于同一来源。例如，一些合同会同时确立各方的权利和义务。这些权利和义务如果是相互依存，不能拆分的，则组成了单一不可拆分的资产或负债，因此构成了单一核算单元。例如，待执行合同就属于这种情况（参见第4.57段）。相反，如果权利和义务是可区分的，则有时宜将权利和义务分组，最终识别一项或多项单独的资产和负债。在其他情况下，将可区分的权利和义务组合为同一核算单元，作为单一资产或单一负债进行处理可能更合适。

4.54 将一组权利和义务作为单一核算单元处理，不同于抵销资产和负债（参见第7.10段）。

4.55 核算单元可能包括：

（1）单项权利或单项义务；

（2）产生于同一来源（如一项合同）的所有权利、所有义务，或所有权利和义务；

（3）这些权利和/或义务的子集。例如，一项资产（不动产、厂场和设备）的部分权利在使用寿命和消耗模式上不同于该项资产的其他权利；

（4）由类似项目组合产生的一组权利和/或义务；

（5）由不同项目组合产生的一组权利和/或义务，例如，将在同一交易中处置的资产和负债组合；以及

（6）一个项目组合中的一个风险敞口。如果一个项目组合面临某一共同风险，会计处理时可能会关注组合中该种风险的总体敞口。

待执行合同

4.56 待执行合同是双方同等程度地未履行的合同或合同的一部分，即，双方均未履行任何义务，或双方均履行了部分义务且履约程度相当。

4.57 待执行合同确立了交换经济资源的一组权利和义务。这些权利和义务相互依存，不可分割。因此，这组权利和义务构成了单一资产或负债。如果交易条款当前

是有利的，则主体拥有资产；如果交易条款当前是不利的，则主体承担负债。是否将该资产或负债纳入财务报表既取决于针对该资产或负债所选的确认标准（参见第5章），也取决于所选的计量基础（参见第6章），包括测试合同是否为亏损合同（如适用）。

4.58 只要合同中的任何一方履行了合同义务，合同便不再属于待执行合同。如果报告主体首先履行了合同义务，其履约行为会促使其交换经济资源的权利和义务转变为接收经济资源的权利，该权利是一项资产。如果另一方首先履行了合同义务，则其履约行为会促使报告主体交换经济资源的权利和义务转变为转移经济资源的义务，该义务是一项负债。

合同权利和合同义务的实质

4.59 合同条款确立了主体作为合同一方的权利和义务。为如实反映这些权利和义务，财务报表须报告其实质（参见第2.12段）。在某些情况下，合同的法律形式明确了权利和义务的实质；而在其他情况下，则需要分析合同或一组或一系列合同的条款以甄别权利和义务的实质。

4.60 主体应考虑合同中的所有条款——无论是明示还是隐含条款，除非其不具有实质内容。隐含条款可能包括法律规定的义务，如签订向客户销售商品的合同的主体需承担法定质保义务。

4.61 无实质内容的条款可忽略。如某条款对合同的经济意义没有可辨认的影响，则认为该条款无实质内容。无实质内容的条款可能包括：
（1）对双方均无约束力的条款；或
（2）持有者在任何情况下都不具备实际能力行使的权利（包括期权）。

4.62 一组或一系列合同可能实现或被设计用于实现某一总体商业目的。为报告此类合同的实质，可能需要将该组或该系列合同产生的权利和义务作为单一核算单元进行处理。例如，如果一项合同中的权利或义务仅仅是宣布与同一交易对手同时签订的另一合同中的所有权利和义务无效，则合并效果即为两项合同最终未确立权利或义务。相反，如果某一合同确立了可能本需由两项或两项以上单一合同确立的两组或两组以上权利或义务，就可能需要单独对每一组权利或义务进行会计处理，如同这组权利和义务产生于单独的合同一样，从而实现如实反映权利与义务（参见第4.48段至第4.55段）。

权益的定义

4.63 权益是主体资产扣除所有负债后的剩余利益。

4.64 权益求偿权是对主体资产扣除所有负债后的剩余利益的求偿权。换言之，权益求偿权是对主体提出的、不符合负债定义的求偿权。此类求偿权可能通过合同、法规或类似方式确立，不符合负债定义的权益求偿权包括：

（1）主体发行的各类股份；以及

（2）主体发行另一权益求偿权的某些义务。

4.65 不同类别的权益求偿权（如普通股和优先股）可能会赋予其持有者不同的权利，例如，收取主体部分或所有以下权益的权利：

（1）股利，前提是主体决定向符合条件的持有者支付股利；

（2）在清算时全额或在其他时间部分清偿权益求偿权的所得；或

（3）其他权益求偿权。

4.66 有时，法律、法规或其他要求会影响权益的特定组成部分，如股本或留存收益。例如，某些规定仅允许主体在拥有该规定允许分配的足够累积盈余的情况下，才能向权益求偿权持有者分配。

4.67 业务活动也经常由独资企业、合伙企业、信托或各类政府事业单位等主体开展。这些主体的法律和监管框架通常与适用于公司类主体的框架不同。例如，对此类主体向权益求偿权持有者分配的限制可能很少。但是，《概念框架》第4.63段中的权益定义适用于所有报告主体。

收益和费用的定义

4.68 收益是指引起权益增加的资产增加或负债减少，但不包括权益求偿权持有者的投入。

4.69 费用是指引起权益减少的资产减少或负债增加，但不包括对权益求偿权持有者的分配。

4.70 根据上述收益和费用的定义，权益求偿权持有者的投入不属于收益，而对权益求偿权持有者的分配不属于费用。

4.71 收益和费用是与主体财务业绩相关的财务报表要素。财务报表使用者既需要了解主体的财务状况相关信息，也需要了解财务业绩相关信息。因此，尽管收益和费用是根据资产和负债的变动来定义的，但收益和费用的信息与资产和负债的信息同样重要。

4.72 不同的交易和其他事项会产生具有不同特征的收益和费用。对具有不同特征的收益和费用分别提供信息有助于财务报表使用者了解主体的财务业绩（参见第7.14段至第7.19段）。

第 5 章——确认和终止确认

起始段落

确认流程	5.1
确认标准	5.6
相关性	5.12
存在的不确定性	5.14
经济利益流入或流出的可能性低	5.15
如实反映	5.18
计量的不确定性	5.19
其他因素	5.24
终止确认	5.26

确认流程

5.1 确认指将符合资产、负债、权益、收益和费用定义的财务报表要素项目纳入财务状况表或财务业绩表的过程。确认涉及以文字和金额表述一个项目（单独或与其他项目汇总在一起）并将该金额纳入财务状况表或财务业绩表的一项或多项合计中。资产、负债或权益在财务状况表中确认的金额被称为其"账面价值"。

5.2 财务状况表和财务业绩表以结构化汇总的方式描述主体确认的资产、负债、权益、收益和费用，意在使财务信息具有可比性和可理解性。这些汇总结构的一项重要特征是将报表中确认的金额包括在合计（以及小计，如适用的话）之中，这些合计或小计与报表中确认的项目相关联。

5.3 确认将财务报表要素与财务状况表和财务业绩表联系起来（参见图5.1）：

（1）在报告期初和期末的财务状况表中，资产总额减负债总额等于权益总额；以及

（2）报告期间确认的权益变动包括：

①财务业绩表中确认的收益减费用；加上

②权益求偿权持有者的投入，减去对权益求偿权持有者的分配。

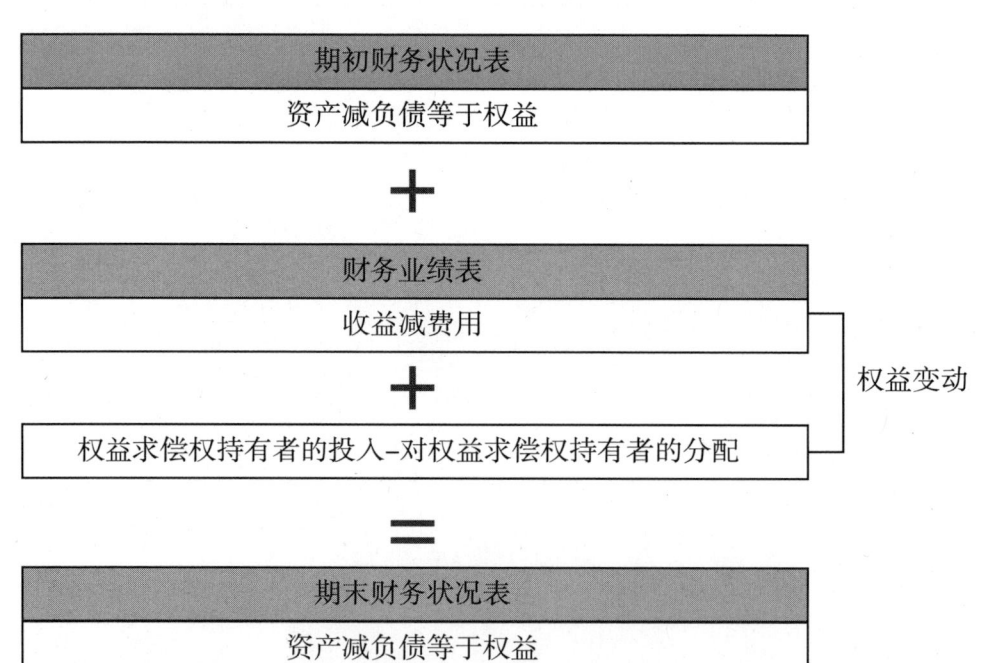

图5.1 确认将财务报表各要素联系起来的方式

5.4 由于确认某一项目（或其账面价值变动）需要确认或终止确认一项或多项其他项目（或一项或多项其他项目的账面价值变动），因此报表之间是相互联系的。例如：

（1）收益在以下情况发生时确认：

①资产初始确认时，或资产的账面价值增加时；或者

②负债终止确认时，或负债的账面价值减少时。

（2）费用在以下情况发生时确认：

①负债初始确认时，或负债的账面价值增加时；或者

②资产终止确认时，或资产的账面价值减少时。

5.5 由交易或其他事项引起的资产或负债的初始确认，可能导致同时确认收益和相关费用。例如，现金销售商品会导致确认收益（确认一项资产——现金）和费用（终止确认另一资产——售出的商品）。同时确认收益和相关费用有时被视为成本与收益的配比。确认资产和负债的变动时，对《概念框架》中这些概念的应用，会导致这种配比。但是，成本与收益配比不是《概念框架》的目标。《概念框架》不允许在财务状况表中确认不符合资产、负债或权益定义的项目。

确认标准

5.6 只有符合资产、负债或权益定义的项目才能在财务状况表中予以确认。同样，只有符合收益或费用定义的项目才能在财务业绩表中予以确认。但是，并非所有符合这些要素定义的项目均可予以确认。

5.7 未确认符合某一要素定义的项目会导致财务状况表和财务业绩表不够完整，并可能使财务报表遗漏有用信息。另一方面，在某些情况下，确认符合某一要素定义的项目将不会提供有用的信息。只有在确认了资产或负债以及由此产生的收益、费用或权益变动，能为财务报表使用者提供有用的信息时，该项资产或负债才予以确认。也就是说，这些信息必须是：

（1）关于资产或负债以及由此产生的收益、费用或权益变动的具有相关性的信息（参见第5.12段至第5.17段）；以及

（2）对资产或负债以及由此产生的收益、费用或权益变动的如实反映（参见第5.18段至第5.25段）。

5.8 正如成本会限制其他财务报告决策一样，成本也会限制确认决策。确认资产或负债是有成本的。财务报表编制者在计量资产或负债时会产生成本。财务报表使用者在分析和解读所提供的信息时也会产生成本。如果通过确认向财务报表使用者提供的信息所带来的效益，有可能证明提供和使用该信息的成本是合理的，则确认资产或负债。在某些情况下，确认的成本可能超过其效益。

5.9 准确界定在何种情况下资产或负债的确认将为财务报表使用者提供有用信

息，且成本不会超过其效益，是不可能的。信息对使用者是否有用，取决于项目以及具体的事实和情况。因此，在决定是否确认某一项目时需要运用判断，所以不同准则之间或在同一准则内的确认要求可能不同。

5.10 在作出关于确认的决策时，一项重要考虑是：如果不确认该项资产或负债而需要提供的信息。例如，如果在支出发生时未确认任何资产，一项费用则被确认。在某些情况下，按期间确认费用会提供有用信息，例如有助于财务报表使用者了解趋势。

5.11 如果符合资产或负债定义的项目未予以确认，主体可能需要在附注中披露该项目的信息。重要的是，主体需要考虑如何有效地使这些信息明辨可见，以弥补其未出现在财务状况表以及财务业绩表（如适用）所提供的结构化汇总中的不足。

相关性

5.12 资产、负债、权益、收益和费用的信息对财务报表使用者来说是相关的。但是，确认特定资产或负债以及由此产生的收益、费用或权益变动可能并不总能够提供具有相关性的信息。例如：

（1）资产或负债是否存在尚不确定（参见第5.14段）；或者

（2）存在资产或负债，但经济利益流入或流出的可能性低（参见第5.15段至第5.17段）。

5.13 即使发生第5.12段所述的一种或两种情况，也不会自动得出结论认为通过确认提供的信息缺乏相关性。此外，第5.12段所述以外的因素也可能影响结论。确认是否提供具有相关性的信息的结论取决于多种因素共同作用，而非任何单一因素。

存在的不确定性

5.14 第4.13段和第4.35段讨论了资产或负债是否存在具有不确定性的情况。某些情况下，如果同时伴随着经济利益流入或流出的可能性低和可能结果极为宽泛的情况，不确定性可能意味着确认一项资产或负债——且以单一金额计量——无法提供具有相关性的信息。无论资产或负债是否被确认，主体均须在财务报表中披露与资产或负债相关的不确定性的解释信息。

经济利益流入或流出的可能性低

5.15 即使经济利益流入或流出的可能性低，资产或负债仍可能存在（参见第4.15段和第4.38段）。

5.16 如果经济利益流入或流出的可能性低，则有关资产或负债的最具相关性的信息包括可能流入或流出的量级、可能的时间分布以及影响其发生可能性的因素。此类信息通常披露于财务报表附注中。

5.17 即使经济利益流入或流出的可能性低，对资产或负债的确认仍可提供除第5.16段所描述的信息之外的相关信息。所提供信息是否具有相关性取决于多种因素，例如：

（1）如果主体按照市场条款进行交换交易时取得了资产或承担了负债，其成本通常反映了经济利益流入或流出的可能性。因此，此类成本可能是具有相关性的信息，且通常易于获取。此外，不确认资产或负债会导致在交易时确认费用或收益，而这可能不是对该交易的如实反映［参见第5.25（1）段］。

（2）如果资产和负债由非交换交易事项引起，则对资产或负债的确认通常会引起对收益或费用的确认。如果资产或负债引起经济利益流入或流出的可能性低，则财务报表使用者可能不认为资产和收益的确认或负债和费用的确认能提供具有相关性的信息。

如实反映

5.18 如果对特定资产或负债的确认不仅能提供具有相关性的信息，还可如实反映该资产或负债以及由此产生的收益、费用或权益变动，则确认该资产或负债是恰当的。能否如实反映，受与资产或负债相关的计量不确定性程度或其他因素的影响。

计量的不确定性

5.19 一项资产或负债如需确认，必须进行计量。许多情况下，此类计量必须进行估计，由此受计量不确定性的影响。如第2.19段所述，编制财务信息需要使用合理估计时，如果能够对估计进行清晰准确的描述与解释，则使用合理估计并不会有损财务信息的有用性。即使是高程度的计量不确定性，也不必然防碍用此估计提供有用的信息。

5.20 某些情况下，资产或负债计量的估计过程中涉及的不确定性程度很高，因此很难确定该估计是否可充分地如实反映该项资产或负债以及由此产生的收益、费用或权益变动。例如，如果资产或负债计量的唯一估计方式是使用基于现金流量的计量技术，且存在以下一种或多种情况，则计量不确定性的程度很高：

（1）可能结果的范围极为宽泛，且每种结果的可能性极难估计。

（2）计量极易受到对不同结果的可能性估计的微小变动影响。例如，如果发生未来现金流入或流出的可能性极低，但一旦发生，这些现金流入或流出的量级将极大。

（3）资产或负债的计量过程中须进行难度极大或极为主观的现金流量分配，该现金流量不仅仅与被计量的资产或负债相关。

5.21 第5.20段所述的部分情况中，最有用的信息可能是依赖高度不确定估计的计量，并附以对此估计的描述和对影响此估计不确定性的解释。如果该计量是与资产或负债最相关的计量，则更是如此。其他情况中，如果上述信息无法充分地如实反映资产或负债以及由此产生的收益、费用或权益变动，则最有用的信息可能是相关性稍低但计量不确定性也低的其他计量方式（附以必要的描述与解释）。

5.22 在有限情况下，受计量高度不确定性影响，所有可用（或可获取的）的资产或负债的相关计量都无法提供关于该资产或负债（以及由此产生的收益、费用或权益变动）的有用信息，即使该计量附有对所使用的相关估计的描述和对影响此估计的不确定性的解释。在这类有限情况下，资产或负债不应被确认。

5.23 无论资产或负债是否被确认，对资产或负债的如实反映均须包括解释性信息，说明与资产或负债存在性或计量相关的不确定性，或与最终由资产或负债引起的经济利益流入或流出的金额或时间分布（即资产或负债的结果）的不确定性（参见第6.60段至第6.62段）。

其他因素

5.24 已确认资产、负债、权益、收益或费用的如实反映不仅包含对这些项目的确认，还包含对这些项目的计量，以及对相关信息的列示和披露（参见第6章至第7章）。

5.25 因此，评估对资产或负债的确认是否能够如实反映该资产或负债时，主体不仅有必要考虑财务状况表中对该资产或负债的描述和计量，还有必要考虑：

（1）由此产生的收益、费用和权益变动的描述。例如，如果主体通过支付对价取得一项资产，不确认该资产会导致费用确认，进而减少主体的利润与权益。比如某些情况下，如果主体未立即消耗该资产，上述结果会提供一个误导性信息，表明主体财务状况发生恶化。

（2）相关资产和负债是否被确认。如果未被确认，则可能造成确认的不一致性（会计错配），这会导致不能提供一个可理解或如实反映的信息，以反映引起资产或负债的交易或其他事项的总体影响，即使附注中提供了解释信息。

（3）资产或负债和由此产生的收益、费用或权益变动的信息的列示和披露。完整的描述需提供财务报表使用者用于了解所表述经济现象的所有必要信息，包括所有必要的描述与解释。因此，相关信息的列示和披露可使已确认金额成为如实反映资产、负债、权益、收益或费用的一部分。

终止确认

5.26 终止确认是指从主体的财务状况表中移除全部或部分已确认的资产或负债。主体通常在相关项目不再满足资产或负债定义时，进行终止确认：

（1）对于资产，终止确认通常发生在主体丧失对全部或部分已确认资产的控制时；以及

（2）对于负债，终止确认通常发生在主体对全部或部分已确认负债不再承担现时义务时。

5.27 终止确认的会计要求意在如实反映：

（1）在导致终止确认的交易或其他事项之后保留的资产和负债（包括作为交易或其他事项的一部分被收购、发生或创建的任何资产或负债）；以及

（2）由该交易或其他事项引起的主体资产和负债的变动。

5.28　第5.27段所述的目标通常由以下方式完成：

（1）终止确认已过期或已被消耗、已收取、已履行或已转移的资产或负债，并确认由此产生的收益或费用。在本章余下部分中，"已转移部分"均指所有此类资产和负债；

（2）继续确认保留的资产和负债，此类保留的资产和负债（如有）称为"保留部分"，并与已转移部分区分开来，单独作为核算单元。因此，不会因对已转移部分的终止确认而对保留部分确认收益或费用，除非终止确认会改变适用于保留部分的计量要求；以及

（3）应用如下一个或多个程序，前提是该程序是实现第5.27段所述的一个或两个目标的必要程序：

①在财务状况表中单独列报任何保留部分；
②在财务业绩表中单独列报由已转移部分终止确认引起的收益和费用；或者
③提供解释信息。

5.29　某些情况下，主体表面上已转移资产或负债，但此类资产或负债可能仍为主体的资产或负债。例如：

（1）如果主体表面上转移了资产，但仍受该资产所形成的经济利益重大波动的影响，这有时说明主体仍控制该资产（参见第4.24段）；或者

（2）如果主体已将资产转移至另一方，另一方是以主体代理人身份持有该资产，则转出方仍控制该资产（参见第4.25段）。

5.30　第5.29段所描述的情况中，因主体无法实现第5.27段所述的任一情形，终止确认该资产或负债，并不恰当。

5.31　当主体不再拥有已转移部分时，终止确认已转移部分可如实反映这一事实。但某些情况下，终止确认可能无法如实反映交易或其他事项对主体资产或负债的影响程度，甚至在执行第5.28（3）段所述的一项或多项程序后仍无法如实反映。此时对已转移部分的终止确认可能意味着主体财务状况的变化程度大于实际情况。例如，这可能在如下情况下发生：

（1）主体已转移资产，且在同一时间达成的另一项交易又赋予主体重新收购该资产的现时权利或现时义务。此类现时权利或现时义务可能源于远期合同、签出的看跌期权或买入的看涨期权。

（2）主体不再控制已转移部分，但受该部分产生的经济利益重大有利或不利波动的影响。

5.32　对于终止确认不足以实现第5.27段所述目标，甚至在执行第5.28（3）段所述的一项或多项程序后仍无法实现的，有时可通过继续确认已转移部分来实现目标。这种情况会产生如下结果：

（1）对由于交易或其他事项产生的、保留部分和已转移部分均未确认收益或费用；

（2）资产（或负债）转移时所收取（或支付）的对价被作为已收取（或已发放）的贷款；以及

（3）需在财务状况表中单独列报已转移部分或提供解释信息，以描述主体不再拥有任何由已转移部分产生的权利或义务的事实。同样地，主体还有必要在转移后提供与由已转移部分引起的收益或费用的信息。

5.33 有一种情况，由于合同的修改造成主体现有权利或义务被削弱或消除，会引起终止确认的问题。确定如何对合同修改进行会计处理时，有必要考虑哪个核算单元为财务报表使用者提供了关于合同修改后被保留资产和负债，以及合同修改如何造成主体资产和负债变动的最有用信息：

（1）如果合同的修改仅消除了现有权利或义务，则在确定是否终止确认这些权利或义务时，需考虑第5.26段至第5.32段的讨论；

（2）如果合同的修改仅增加了新的权利或义务，则有必要确定是将新增的权利或义务作为单独的资产或负债，还是与现有权利或义务一起作为同一核算单元的一部分（参见第4.48段至第4.55段）；以及

（3）如果合同的修改既消除了现有权利或义务，同时增加了新的权利或义务，则有必要考虑这些修改引起的单独影响和综合影响。在某些这种情况下，合同修改实质上是以新资产或负债替换了旧资产或负债。在此种修改情况下，主体可能需对原资产或负债进行终止确认，同时确认新增资产或负债。

第 6 章——计量

起始段落

引言	**6.1**
计量基础	**6.4**
历史成本	**6.4**
现行价值	**6.10**
公允价值	**6.12**
使用价值和履约价值	**6.17**
现行成本	**6.21**
特定计量基础提供的信息	**6.23**
历史成本	**6.24**
现行价值	**6.32**
公允价值	**6.32**
使用价值和履约价值	**6.37**
现行成本	**6.40**
选择计量基础时考虑的因素	**6.43**
相关性	**6.49**
资产或负债的特征	**6.50**
未来现金流量的产生	**6.54**
如实反映	**6.58**
提升性质量特征和成本限制	**6.63**
历史成本	**6.69**
现行价值	**6.72**
初始计量的特殊因素	**6.77**
一种以上计量基础	**6.83**
权益的计量	**6.87**
基于现金流量的计量技术	**6.91**

引言

6.1 财务报表中确认的要素以货币形式量化,这要求选择计量基础。计量基础是指被计量项目的一项已识别特征,例如历史成本、公允价值或履约价值等。对资产或负债应用计量基础也就是为该资产或负债以及相关收益和费用创建一个计量。

6.2 出于对有用财务信息的质量特征和成本限制的考虑,针对不同资产、负债、收益和费用,选择的计量基础可能不同。

6.3 一项准则可能需要描述如何实施该准则中所选的计量基础。该描述包括:

(1) 详细说明对采用特定计量基础的计量方法进行估计时可以或必须使用的技术;

(2) 详细说明可能与首选计量基础提供类似信息的简化计量方法;或者

(3) 解释如何修改计量基础,例如,从负债的履约价值中剔除主体未能履行其负债的可能性的影响(自身信用风险)。

计量基础

历史成本

6.4 历史成本计量,利用形成资产、负债及相关收益和费用的交易或其他事项的价格获取的相关信息(至少部分相关信息),提供关于这些要素的货币信息。与现行价值不同,历史成本不反映价值变动,但与资产减值或负债致损相关的变动除外[参见第6.7(3)段和第6.8(2)段]。

6.5 取得或创建资产时,该资产的历史成本即为取得或创建此资产时所产生成本的价值,包括为取得或创建资产所支付的对价加上交易成本。产生或承担负债时,负债的历史成本为产生或承担负债所收取的对价减去交易成本。

6.6 当主体取得或创建资产、产生或承担负债时,如果主体未按市场条件进行交易(参见第6.80段),则可能无法识别成本,或该成本无法提供关于资产或负债的相关信息。在某些这种情况下,会在初始确认时将资产或负债的现行价值作为认定成本,并将该认定成本作为以历史成本后续计量的起点。

6.7 资产的历史成本随时间更新,以描述如下事项(如适用的话):

(1) 构成资产的部分或全部经济资源的消耗(折旧或摊销);

(2) 处置部分或全部资产所收取的付款;

(3) 造成资产部分或全部历史成本不再可收回的事项的影响(减值);以及

(4) 反映资产融资组成部分的应计利息。

6.8 负债的历史成本随时间更新,以描述如下事项(如适用的话):

(1)履行部分或全部负债,例如通过清偿部分或全部负债或履行商品交付义务等方式;

(2)某些事项的影响,会使履行负债转移经济资源的义务价值有所增加,直至该负债成为致损负债。当一项负债的历史成本不足以描述履行此负债的义务,该负债为致损负债;以及

(3)反映负债融资组成部分的应计利息。

6.9 对金融资产和金融负债应用历史成本计量基础的一种方式是对其以摊余成本计量。金融资产或金融负债的摊余成本反映了对未来现金流量的估计,并按照初始确认时确定的折现率进行折现。对于可变利率工具,需要更新折现率以反映可变利率的变动。金融资产或金融负债的摊余成本随时间更新,以对应计利息、金融资产减值和收取付款等后续变动进行描述。

现行价值

6.10 现行价值计量,利用能够反映计量日具体情况的更新信息,提供关于资产、负债与相关收益和费用的货币信息。因现行价值计量利用的是更新信息,所以资产和负债的现行价值可反映自前一计量日起,对此类现行价值中反映的现金流量和其他因素估计的变动情况(参见第 6.14 段至第 6.15 段和第 6.20 段)。与历史成本不同,资产或负债的现行价值并非来自(甚至并非部分来自)形成资产或负债的交易或其他事项的价格。

6.11 现行价值计量基础包括:

(1)公允价值(参见第 6.12 段至第 6.16 段);

(2)资产的使用价值和负债的履约价值(参见第 6.17 段至第 6.20 段);以及

(3)现行成本(参见第 6.21 段至第 6.22 段)。

公允价值

6.12 公允价值是指市场参与者之间在计量日进行的有序交易中,出售一项资产所能收到或转移一项负债所需支付的价格。

6.13 公允价值可反映主体可进入的市场中所有参与方的预期。资产或负债在计量时应采用市场参与者给资产或负债定价时使用的同一假设,即市场参与者以获得最大经济利益为目标的假设。

6.14 在某些情况下,公允价值可通过观察活跃市场中的价格直接确定。在其他情况下,公允价值是通过计量技术间接确定的,例如使用基于现金流量的计量技术(参见第 6.91 段至第 6.95 段),以反映出如下因素:

(1)对未来现金流量的估计。

(2)由现金流量固有的不确定性引起的,被计量资产或负债的未来现金流量的估计金额或时间分布的可能波动。

（3）货币的时间价值。

（4）承担现金流量固有不确定性的价格（风险溢价或风险折扣）。承担该不确定性的价格受不确定性程度的影响。这也反映了如下事实，即投资者在通常情况下对具有不确定现金流量的资产所支付的要少于具有确定现金流量的资产因承担具有不确定现金流量的负债所要求的要多于具有确定现金流量的负债。

（5）其他因素，例如清算，前提是市场参与者已将这些因素纳入考虑。

6.15 第6.14（2）段和第6.14（4）段所提及因素包括对手方未能履行其债务的可能性（信用风险）或主体未能履行其债务的可能性（自身信用风险）。

6.16 因公允价值并非来自（甚至并非部分来自）产生资产或负债的交易或其他事项的价格，因此公允价值不会因取得资产时发生的交易成本而上升，也不会因发生或承担负债时发生的交易成本而下降。此外，公允价值不反映最终处置资产时或转移或清偿负债时将要产生的交易成本。

使用价值和履约价值

6.17 使用价值是指主体预期从使用资产及其最终处置中取得的现金流量或其他经济利益的现值。履约价值是指主体预期其履行负债时有义务转移的现金或其他经济资源的现值。此处现金或其他经济资源的金额不仅包含将转移至负债对手方的金额，还包含主体预期有义务转移至其他方以协助主体履行其负债的金额。

6.18 因使用价值和履约价值均以未来现金流量为基础，因此其不包含取得资产或承担负债时产生的交易成本。然而，使用价值和履约价值包含主体预期在最终资产处置或履行负债时产生的交易成本的现值。

6.19 使用价值和履约价值反映的是特定主体的假设，而非市场参与者的假设。实务中，有时市场参与者与主体本身所用的假设之间差异甚微。

6.20 使用价值和履约价值无法直接观察，而是通过基于现金流量的计量技术进行确定（参见第6.91段至第6.95段）。使用价值和履约价值所反映的因素与第6.14段公允价值所反映的因素相同，但不同的是，使用价值和履约价值是从特定主体的角度而非市场参与者的角度进行描述。

现行成本

6.21 资产的现行成本是指在计量日取得一项同等资产的成本，它包括应在计量日支付的对价加上可能发生的交易成本。负债的现行成本是指在计量日形成一项同等负债所收到的对价减去计量日可能产生的交易成本。现行成本与历史成本类似，是一种进入价值：反映主体在市场中取得资产或承担负债的价格。因此，现行成本与公允价值、使用价值和履约价值不同，后三者均为脱手价值。然而，与历史成本不同的是，现行成本所反映的是计量日的具体状况。

6.22 某些情况下，现行成本无法通过观察活跃市场价格直接确定，而必须通过其他方式间接确定。例如，如果仅能获得新资产的价格，则已使用资产的现行成本可能需要通过调整新资产的现行价格来估计，以反映主体所持有资产的现行使用年限和状况。

特定计量基础提供的信息

6.23　选择计量基础时，重要的是考虑所选计量基础在财务状况表和财务业绩表中所产生的信息的性质。表6.1对该信息进行了汇总，第6.24段至第6.42段进行了额外讨论。

历史成本

6.24　由于历史成本使用的信息（或至少部分信息）来自于生成资产或负债的交易或其他事项的价格，因此，按照历史成本计量资产或负债所提供的信息，对财务报表使用者可能具有相关性。

6.25　通常，如果主体在基于市场条件的近期交易中取得一项资产，则主体预期该资产会提供充足的经济利益，确保主体至少可收回成本。同样地，如果所产生或承担的负债是由基于市场条件的近期交易导致，则主体预期履行负债所需转移经济资源的义务的价值通常不大于所收取对价减去交易成本的价值。因此，在这种情况下，按照历史成本对资产或负债进行计量，可提供关于资产或负债以及生成该资产或负债的交易价格的具有相关性的信息。

6.26　由于为了反映资产消耗及其减值会减少其历史成本，因此，预期从按历史成本计量的资产中收回的金额至少等于其账面价值。类似地，负债的历史成本会在其成为致损负债时相应增加，因此，履行负债所需转移经济资源的义务的价值不大于负债的账面价值。

6.27　如果对金融资产之外的资产按照历史成本进行计量，消耗或出售资产或部分资产所产生的费用是以已消耗或已出售的资产或部分资产的历史成本计量的。

6.28　资产出售对价被确认为收益的同时，应确认相应的费用。收益与费用之间的差额为出售产生的毛利。将资产消耗产生的费用与相关收益进行比较，可以提供关于毛利的信息。

6.29　类似地，如果为取得对价产生或承担了非金融负债，且按照历史成本计量，则履行全部或部分负债会产生收益，该收益按照已履行部分所收取对价的价值进行计量。履行负债产生的收益与费用之间的差额，为履行负债产生的毛利。

6.30　关于已出售或已消耗资产的成本（包括立即消耗的商品和服务，参见第4.8段）和已收取对价的信息具有预测价值。该信息可作为一项输入值，用来预测未来销售商品（包括主体当前未持有的商品）和提供服务所产生的未来毛利，从而评估主体未来净现金流入的前景。为评估主体未来现金流量的前景，财务报表使用者经常会关注多个期间内产生未来毛利的前景，而不仅仅是已持有商品产生毛利的前景。

按照历史成本计量的收益和费用信息也具有证实价值,因为它会为财务报表使用者之前对现金流量或毛利的预测提供反馈。已出售或已消耗资产成本的相关信息,还有助于评估主体管理层履行其使用主体经济资源的职责的效率和效果。

6.31 与此类似,按摊余成本计量的资产所赚取的利息和按摊余成本计量的负债所发生的利息的有关信息,也具有预测价值和证实价值。

现行价值

公允价值

6.32 由于公允价值反映市场参与者对未来现金流量金额、时间分布和不确定性的当前预期,因此,按照公允价值计量资产和负债所提供的信息具有预测价值。这些预期可反映市场参与者当前的风险偏好。由于所提供的信息可为之前的预期提供反馈,因而也具有证实价值。

6.33 由于反映市场参与者当前预期的收益和费用可用作预测未来收益和费用的输入值,因而具有一定的预测价值。这些收益和费用还有助于评估主体管理层履行其使用主体经济资源职责的效率和效果。

6.34 第6.14段所述各因素可导致资产或负债的公允价值发生变动。这些因素具有不同特征,单独识别这些因素产生的收益和费用,可为财务报表使用者提供有用信息［参见第7.14（2）段］。

6.35 如果主体在某市场中取得一项资产,并利用另一市场（主体将在该市场出售该资产）中的价格确定其公允价值,两个市场价格之间的差额在首次确定公允价值时被确认为收益。

6.36 如果交易发生的市场,同时也是计量公允价值时所用价格的来源市场,通常情况下出售资产或转移负债的对价金额与其公允价值相近。这种情况下,如果按照公允价值计量资产或负债,则出售资产或转移负债时产生的净收益或净费用金额通常很小,除非交易成本的影响较是重大的。

使用价值和履约价值

6.37 使用价值提供关于资产使用和资产最终处置中预计现金流量的现值的有关信息。该信息可用来评估未来净现金流入的前景,因此可能具有预测价值。

6.38 履约价值可提供关于履行负债所需的预计现金流量的现值的有关信息。因此,履约价值具有预测价值,尤其是在主体将履行此负债而非通过协商来转移或清偿负债的情况下。

6.39 对使用价值或履约价值的估计更新以及对未来现金流量的金额、时间分布和不确定性估计的有关信息,可为之前对使用价值或履约价值的估计提供反馈,因此也具有证实价值。

现行成本

6.40 由于现行成本可反映在计量日取得或创建同等资产的成本，或者产生或承担同等负债所收取的对价，因此按照现行成本计量的资产和负债的信息具有相关性。

6.41 与历史成本类似，现行成本可提供关于已消耗资产的成本或履行负债产生的收益的有关信息。该信息可用来计算当前的毛利，还可用作预测未来毛利的输入值。与历史成本不同的是，现行成本反映的是资产消耗或负债履约时的价格。如价格发生重大变动，基于现行成本预测的毛利要比基于历史成本预测的毛利更加有用。

6.42 为报告资产消耗的现行成本（或履行负债的现行收益），主体应将报告期间内账面价值的变动分为资产消耗的现行成本（或履行负债的现行收益）和价格变化影响。价格变化的影响有时被称为"持有利得"或"持有损失"。

表 6.1　　　　　　　　特定计量基础所提供的信息一览表

资产

	财务状况表			
	历史成本	公允价值（市场参与者假设）	使用价值（特定主体假设）①	现行成本
账面价值	未消耗或未收取和可收回的历史成本（包括交易成本）。（包括融资组成部分的应计利息。）	出售资产时将收取的价格（不扣除处置时的交易成本）。	资产使用和资产最终处置产生的未来现金流量的现值（扣除处置时交易成本的现值）。	未消耗或未收取和可收回的现行成本（包括交易成本）。
	财务业绩表			
事项	历史成本	公允价值（市场参与者假设）	使用价值（特定主体假设）	现行成本
初始确认②	—	所获取资产已支付对价与公允价值之间的差额③。所获取资产的交易成本。	所获取资产已支付对价与使用价值之间的差额。所获取资产的交易成本。	—

续表

事项	财务业绩表			
	历史成本	公允价值（市场参与者假设）	使用价值（特定主体假设）	现行成本
资产的出售或消耗[4][5]	与已出售或已消耗资产的历史成本等额的费用。 收到的收益。 （可按总额或净额列报。） 出售资产产生的交易成本费用。	与已出售或已消耗资产的公允价值等额的费用。 收到的收益。 （可按总额或净额列报。） 出售资产产生的交易成本费用。	与已出售或已消耗资产的使用价值等额的费用。 收到的收益。 （可按总额或净额列报。）	与已出售或已消耗资产的现行成本等额的费用。 收到的收益。 （可按总额或净额列报。） 出售资产产生的交易成本费用。
利息收益	利息收益，按历史利率计算，如为可变利息，则需更新。	在公允价值变动产生的收益和费用中反映。 （可单独识别。）	在使用价值变动产生的收益和费用中反映。 （可单独识别。）	利息收益，按当前利率计算。
减值	因历史成本不再可收回而产生的费用。	在公允价值变动产生的收益和费用中反映。 （可单独识别。）	在使用价值变动产生的收益和费用中反映。 （可单独识别。）	因现行成本不再可收回而产生的费用。

续表

事项	财务业绩表			
	历史成本	公允价值（市场参与者假设）	使用价值（特定主体假设）	现行成本
价值变动	不确认，减值除外。 对金融资产，预计现金流量变动产生的收益和费用。	在公允价值变动产生的收益和费用中反映。	在使用价值变动产生的收益和费用中反映。	反映价格变动影响的收益和费用（持有利得和持有损失）。

①本栏汇总了使用价值作为计量基础所提供的信息。但如第6.75段指出，使用价值可能无法作为定期重新计量的可行的计量基础。
②收益或费用可能来自对未按市场条件取得的资产的初始确认。
③如果取得资产所在的市场与计量资产公允价值时所用价格的来源市场不同，则会产生收益或费用。
④资产的消耗通常通过销售成本、折旧或摊销来报告。
⑤收取的收益通常与收取的对价相等，但取决于相关负债所使用的计量基础。

负债

事项	财务状况表			
	历史成本	公允价值（市场参与者假设）	履约价值（特定主体假设）	现行成本
账面价值	承担负债未履行部分所收取的对价（扣除交易成本），如估计现金流出超出该对价，则超出部分相应增加账面价值。 （包括融资组成部分产生的应计利息。）	转移负债未履行部分所支付的价格（不包括转移时产生的交易成本）。	履行负债中未履行部分时产生的未来现金流量的现值（包括履行或转移负债时产生的交易成本现值）。	当前为承担未履行负债部分收取的对价（扣除交易成本），如估计现金流出超出该对价，则超出部分相应增加账面价值。

国际财务报告准则

续表

事项	财务业绩表			
	历史成本	公允价值（市场参与者假设）	履约价值（特定主体假设）	现行成本
初始确认①	—	已收取对价与负债公允价值之间的差额。② 产生或承担负债时的交易成本。	已收取对价与负债履约价值之间的差额。 产生或承担负债时的交易成本。	—
履行负债	与已履行负债的历史成本等额的收益（反映历史对价）。 履行负债时产生成本的费用。 （可按净额或总额列报。）	与已履行负债的公允价值等额的收益。 履行负债时产生成本的费用。 （可按净额或总额列报。如果以总额列报，则可单独列报历史对价。）	与已履行负债的履约价值等额的收益。 履行负债时产生成本的费用。 （可按净额或总额列报。如果以总额列报，则可单独列报历史对价。）	与已履行负债的现行成本等额的收益（反映现行对价）。 履行负债时产生成本的费用。 （可按净额或总额列报。如果以总额列报，则可单独列报历史对价。）
负债的转移	与已转移负债的历史成本等额的收益（反映历史对价）。 转移负债时支付成本（包括交易成本）的费用。 （可按净额或总额列报。）	与已转移负债的公允价值等额的收益。 转移负债时支付成本（包括交易成本）的费用。 （可按净额或总额列报。）	与已转移负债的履约价值等额的收益。 转移负债时支付成本（包括交易成本）的费用。 （可按净额或总额列报。）	与已转移负债的现行成本等额的收益（反映现行对价）。 转移负债时支付成本（包括交易成本）的费用。 （可按净额或总额列报。）

续表

事项	财务业绩表			
	历史成本	公允价值（市场参与者假设）	履约价值（特定主体假设）	现行成本
利息费用	利息费用，按历史利率计算，如为可变利息，则需更新。	在公允价值变动产生的收益和费用中反映。 （可单独识别。）	在履约价值变动产生的收益和费用中反映。 （可单独识别。）	利息费用，按当前利率计算。
使负债成为致损负债的事项的影响	与估计现金流量流出超出负债历史成本的部分等额的费用，或该超出部分的后续变动。	在公允价值变动产生的收益和费用中反映。 （可单独识别。）	在履约价值变动产生的收益和费用中反映。 （可单独识别。）	与估计现金流量流出超出负债现行成本的部分等额的费用，或该超出部分的后续变动。
价值变动	不确认，除非出现致损负债。 金融负债——估计现金流量变动产生的收益和费用。	在公允价值变动产生的收益和费用中反映。	在履约价值变动产生的收益和费用中反映。	反映价格变动的影响的收益和费用（持有利得和持有损失）。

①收益或费用可能来自对未按市场条件产生或承担的负债的初始确认。
②如果产生或承担负债所在的市场与计量负债公允价值时所用价格的来源市场不同，则会出现收益或费用。

选择计量基础时考虑的因素

6.43 在选择资产或负债以及相关收益和费用的计量基础时，有必要考虑该计量基础在财务状况表和财务业绩表中产生的信息的性质（参见第6.23段至第6.42段和表6.1），以及其他因素（参见第6.44段至第6.86段）。

6.44 在大多数情况下，不能基于单一因素选择计量基础。每个因素的相对重要性取决于具体事实和情况。

6.45 计量基础提供的信息必须对财务报表使用者而言有用。为此，信息必须具有相关性并且如实反映其意在反映的现象。此外，应尽可能提供具有可比性、可验证性、及时性和可理解性的信息。

6.46 根据第2.21段的解释，应用基本质量特征最高效和最有成效的流程是识别与经济现象最具有相关性的信息。如果此类信息无法获得或无法以如实反映该经济现象的方式提供，则需要考虑次相关的信息。第6.49段至第6.76段进一步讨论了在选择计量基础时质量特征发挥的作用。

6.47 第6.49段至第6.76段的讨论侧重在对已确认资产或负债项目，选择一项计量基础时应考虑的因素。其中的部分讨论还适用于报表附注中对已确认或未确认项目计量基础的选择。

6.48 第6.77段至第6.82段讨论了初始确认时选择计量基础应考虑的其他因素。如果初始计量基础与后续计量基础不一致，则由于计量基础发生变化，可能在首次后续计量时就会确认收益和费用。确认此类收益和费用可能导致描述了事实上并未发生的交易和事项。因此，选择资产或负债以及相关收益和费用的计量基础时，需要兼顾初始计量和后续计量。

相关性

6.49 资产或负债以及相关收益和费用的计量基础所提供信息的相关性，受以下方面影响：

（1）资产或负债的特征（参见第6.50段至第6.53段）；以及

（2）资产或负债产生未来现金流量的方式（参见第6.54段至第6.57段）。

资产或负债的特征

6.50 计量基础提供的信息的相关性，一定程度上取决于资产或负债的特征，尤其取决于现金流量的波动性，以及资产或负债的价值对市场因素或其他风险的敏感程度。

6.51 如果资产或负债的价值对市场因素或其他风险敏感，则其历史成本与现行价值可能显著不同。因此，如果有关价值变动的信息对财务报表使用者而言很重要，历史成本可能无法提供具有相关性的信息。例如，对于属于衍生工具的金融资产或金融负债，摊余成本无法提供具有相关性的信息。

6.52 此外，如果使用历史成本，价值的变动并非在价值变化时报告，而是在处置、减值或履约等事项发生时才报告。而这可能被错误地解读为所有被确认收益和费用均在此类事项发生时产生，而非在持有资产或负债的期间产生。另外，由于以历史成本计量不能及时提供有关价值变动的信息，所报告的收益和费用不能及时地反映报告期内主体持有资产或负债而承担的风险的全面影响，该信息可能缺少预测价值和证实价值。

6.53 资产或负债的公允价值变动反映了市场参与者的预期变动和其风险偏好变动。由于所计量的资产或负债的特征和主体业务活动的性质不同，反映这些变动的信息可能无法总是为财务报表使用者提供预测价值或证实价值。当主体的业务活动不涉及出售资产或转移负债时，例如，主体仅出于使用或收取合同现金流量的目的持有资产，或主体将自己履行负债时，反映变动的信息便可能无法提供预测价值或证实价值。

未来现金流量的产生

6.54 根据第1.14段所述，有些经济资源可直接产生现金流量；而在其他情况下，需要综合使用经济资源来间接产生现金流量。如何使用经济资源以及资产和负债如何产生现金流量，一定程度上取决于主体业务活动的性质。

6.55 当主体的业务活动涉及使用多项经济资源，且需要通过综合使用这些经济资源来生产和向客户营销商品或服务，从而间接产生现金流量时，历史成本或现行成本很可能可以提供有关该活动的具有相关性的信息。例如，不动产、厂场和设备通常需要与主体的其他经济资源一起综合使用；同样，如果不广泛利用主体的其他经济资源（例如，在生产和营销活动中），存货通常就无法向客户售出。第6.24段至第6.31段以及第6.40段至第6.42段解释了以历史成本或现行成本计量此类资产如何提供具有相关性的信息，这些信息用于计算报告期内所实现的毛利。

6.56 对于直接产生现金流量的资产和负债，例如，可在不产生重大经济惩罚（如没有重大业务中断）的情况下独立出售的资产，能够提供最具有相关性信息的计量基础很可能是现行价值，它包含了对未来现金流量的金额、时间分布和不确定性的当前估计。

6.57 当主体的业务活动涉及管理金融资产和金融负债，意在收取合同现金流量时，摊余成本可提供可用于计算资产所赚取的利息和负债所发生的利息之间差额的相关信息。然而，在评估摊余成本能否提供有用信息时，还有必要考虑金融资产或金融负债的特征。当现金流量取决于本金和利息以外的因素时，摊余成本不太可能提供具有相关性的信息。

如实反映

6.58 当资产和负债以某种方式相关时,对此类资产和负债使用不同的计量基础会导致计量不一致(会计错配)。如果财务报表包含计量不一致,这些财务报表在某些方面可能无法如实反映主体财务状况和财务业绩。因此,在某些情况下,与使用不同的计量基础产生的信息相比,对相关资产和负债使用相同的计量基础会为财务报表使用者提供更有用的信息。当某项资产或负债产生的现金流量与另一资产或负债产生的现金流量直接相关时,尤其如此。

6.59 根据第2.13段和第2.18段,尽管完美的如实反映应当做到准确无误,但这并不意味着计量方法必须在所有方面完全精确。

6.60 当一项计量无法通过观察活跃市场的价格直接确定,而必须通过估计来确定,便会产生计量的不确定性。与特定计量基础有关的计量不确定性的程度,可能会影响该计量基础提供的信息能否如实反映主体的财务状况和财务业绩。高度的计量不确定性不一定会妨碍主体使用一种计量基础提供具有相关性的信息。然而,在某些情况下,计量不确定性的程度如此之高,会使某一计量基础提供的信息无法充分实现如实反映(参见第2.22段)。在这种情况下,考虑选择同样能够提供具有相关性信息的另一计量基础可能更为适当。

6.61 计量的不确定性不同于结果的不确定性和存在的不确定性:

(1) 当某资产或负债产生的经济利益流入或流出的金额或时间分布存在不确定性时,即为结果的不确定性。

(2) 当一项资产或负债是否存在具有不确定性时,即为存在的不确定性。第5.12段至第5.14段讨论了存在的不确定性对如下决策的影响:主体在一项资产或负债是否存在尚不确定时,是否确认该项资产或负债。

6.62 结果的不确定性或存在的不确定性有时可能导致计量的不确定性,但不是必然的。例如,如果资产的公允价值能够通过观察活跃市场的价格直接确定,即使因为不确定该资产最终会产生多少现金而存在结果的不确定性,但与计量该公允价值相关的计量的不确定性并不存在。

提升性质量特征和成本限制

6.63 可比性、可理解性和可验证性这些提升性质量特征以及成本限制对计量基础的选择会产生影响。下文将阐述这些影响。第6.69段至第6.76段还讨论了对特定计量基础的影响。及时性这一提升性质量特征对计量没有特别的影响。

6.64 正如成本会限制其他财务报告决策一样,成本亦会限制计量基础的选择。因此,在选择计量基础时,重要的是考虑以该计量基础向财务报表使用者提供的信息的效益,是否可能证明提供和使用该信息的成本是合理的。

6.65 无论是在同一报告主体的不同期间,还是不同主体的同一期间内,对于相同的项目，一致地使用相同的计量基础，都有助于使财务报表更可比。

6.66 计量基础变化可能会使财务报表的可理解性降低。但是，如果其他因素的重要性超过可理解性的降低（例如，如果该变化可产生更多具有相关性的信息），则可能这种变化就是合理的。如果作出变化，需要向财务报表使用者提供解释性信息，以使其能够了解该变化的影响。

6.67 可理解性部分取决于使用了多少种不同的计量基础以及使用的计量基础是否随时间变化。一般而言，如果在一套财务报表中使用较多的计量基础，则所产生的信息将变得更加复杂，因而可理解性更低，且财务状况表和财务业绩表中的总计或小计的信息含量降低。然而，如果是为了提供有用的信息而有必要如此，使用更多的计量基础可能是恰当的。

6.68 如果计量基础的计量结果可以被独立检验，检验既可以是直接的（例如通过观察价格）也可以是间接的（例如通过检查模型的输入值），则可验证性得到提升。如果某项计量无法验证，则财务报表使用者可能需要解释性信息，以便了解该计量是如何确定的。在某些这种情况下，可能有必要对使用另一种不同的计量基础进行详细说明。

历史成本

6.69 在很多情况下，历史成本计量比现行价值计量更简单，因此成本更低。此外，使用历史成本计量基础确定的计量一般易于理解，并且在许多情况下可以验证。

6.70 然而，对消耗进行估计以及对减值损失或致损负债进行识别和计量可能是主观的。因此，资产或负债的历史成本有时同现行价值一样难以计量或验证。

6.71 使用历史成本计量基础，在不同时间取得的相同资产或产生的相同负债，在财务报表中会以不同金额报告。这会降低同一报告主体在不同期间和不同主体在同一期间的可比性。

现行价值

6.72 由于公允价值是从市场参与者的角度而非特定主体的角度来确定的，并且与取得资产或产生负债的时间无关，原则上，同一市场上的不同主体，以公允价值计量的相同的资产或负债，其计量的金额应该相同。这可以提高同一报告主体的不同期间和不同主体同一期间的可比性。相反，由于使用价值和履约价值是从特定主体的角度确定的，因此，不同主体的相同资产或负债的计量会有所不同。这些差异可能会降低可比性，尤其是在这些资产或负债以类似方式产生现金流量的情况下。

6.73 如果资产或负债的公允价值能够通过观察活跃市场中的价格直接确定，则公允价值计量过程成本低且简单易懂；并且公允价值可以通过直接观察来验证。

6.74 当无法直接在活跃的市场中观察到公允价值时，估计公允价值可能需要用到估值技术（有时包括使用基于现金流量的计量技术），在确定使用价值和履约价值时通常也需要。以下情况取决于所使用的技术：

(1) 估计估值输入值和应用估值技术可能成本高昂且复杂。

(2) 过程中的输入值可能是主观的，并且输入值和过程本身的有效性可能难以验证。这会导致相同资产或负债的计量可能有所不同，从而降低可比性。

6.75 在很多情况下，对于与其他资产结合使用的单项资产，无法有效确定使用价值。相反，使用价值是基于一组资产确定的，可能需要分配至各单项资产。这个过程具有主观性和武断性。此外，对单项资产使用价值的估计，可能无法恰当反映其与该组中其他资产协同效应的影响。因此，对与其他资产结合使用的资产，确定其使用价值可能是一个成本高昂的过程，其复杂性和主观性降低了可验证性。由于这些原因，使用价值可能无法作为这些资产定期重新计量的可行的计量基础。但是，使用价值偶尔会用于资产的重新计量，例如，在减值测试中根据使用价值来确定历史成本是否可完全收回。

6.76 使用现行成本计量基础，不同期间取得的相同资产或产生的相同负债，在财务报表中将以相同金额报告。这会提高同一报告主体在不同期间和不同主体在同一期间财务报表的可比性。但是，确定现行成本可能是复杂的、主观的和成本高昂的。例如，如第 6.22 段所述，可能需要通过调整新资产的现行价格来估计资产的现行成本，以反映主体持有资产的现行年限和状况。此外，由于技术和商业实务的变化，许多资产无法找到相同的替代资产。因此，为了估计与现有资产同等的资产的现行成本，需要对新资产的现行价格进行进一步的主观调整。此外，将现行成本账面价值的变动拆分为消耗的现行成本与价格变动的影响（参见第 6.42 段）可能会很复杂，且需要进行武断的假设。由于这些困难，现行成本计量可能缺乏可验证性和可理解性。

初始计量的特殊因素

6.77 针对无论是初始确认还是后续计量，第 6.43 段至第 6.76 段讨论了选择计量基础时考虑的因素。第 6.78 段至第 6.82 段讨论初始确认时考虑的一些额外因素。

6.78 初始确认时，除非交易成本是重大的，否则由于基于市场条件进行交易的事件而取得的资产或产生的负债，其成本通常与该事件发生日的公允价值类似。然而，即使这两个金额相似，也需要描述在初始确认时使用的计量基础。如果后续将使用历史成本，则在初始确认时，历史成本计量基础通常也是适当的。类似地，如果后续将使用现行价值，则在初始确认时，现行价值计量基础通常也是适当的。使用相同的计量基础进行初始确认和后续计量，避免了在第一次后续计量时就因计量基础变化而确认收益或费用（参见第 6.48 段）。

6.79 当主体基于市场条件进行交易，以转移另一项资产或负债的方式取得资产或产生负债时，所取得资产或所产生负债的初始计量将决定交易是否会产生收益或费用。当资产或负债按成本计量时，在初始确认时不产生收益或费用，除非因被转让资产或负债的终止确认而产生收益或费用，或资产发生减值或负债致损。

6.80 取得资产或产生负债可能不是基于市场条件进行的交易。例如：

(1) 交易价格可能会受到各方之间的关系或其中一方的财务困境或其他强制力

的影响；

（2）资产可能由政府免费授予该主体或由另一方向该主体捐赠；

（3）依据法律或法规强制承担的负债；或者

（4）不当行为导致支付赔偿或罚款的负债。

6.81 在此类情况下，按历史成本计量取得的资产或产生的负债，可能无法如实反映主体的资产和负债以及交易或其他事项所产生的收益或费用。因此，如第 6.6 段所述，按认定成本计量取得的资产或产生的负债可能是适当的。认定成本和支付或收到的对价之间的差额确认为初始确认时的收益或费用。

6.82 取得资产或发生负债时，如果事项不属于基于市场条件进行的交易，则需要对该交易或其他事项的所有相关方面进行甄别和考虑。例如，可能需要确认其他资产、其他负债、权益求偿权持有者的投入或向权益求偿权持有者的分配，以如实反映该交易或其他事项对主体财务状况的影响实质（参见第 4.59 段至第 4.62 段），以及对主体财务业绩的相关影响实质。

一种以上计量基础

6.83 有时，基于对第 6.43 段至第 6.76 段所述因素的考虑可能会得出结论认为，对于一项资产或负债以及相关收益或费用需要一种以上的计量基础，以提供如实反映主体财务状况和财务业绩的具有相关性的信息。

6.84 在大多数情况下，提供该信息的最可理解的方式如下：

（1）针对财务状况表中的资产或负债以及财务业绩表中的相关收益和费用使用单一计量基础；以及

（2）在附注中提供采用另一种计量基础的额外信息。

6.85 但是，在某些情况下，通过使用以下计量基础，使得该信息更具相关性或更能如实反映主体的财务状况及其财务业绩：

（1）针对财务状况表中的资产或负债使用现行价值计量基础；以及

（2）针对损益表①中的相关收益和费用使用另一计量基础（参见第 7.17 段至第 7.18 段）。

选择计量基础时，有必要考虑第 6.43 段至第 6.76 段中讨论的因素。

6.86 在此类情况下，对资产或负债的现行价值变动期间产生的收益总额或费用总额进行区分和分类（参见第 7.14 段至第 7.19 段），以便：

（1）将采用针对损益表选择的计量基础计量的收入或费用计入损益表；以及

（2）将所有剩余收益或费用计入其他综合收益。因此，与该资产或负债相关的累计其他综合收益等于以下两者之间的差额：

①财务状况表中的资产或负债的账面价值；以及

---

① 《概念框架》并未明确财务业绩表由一张报表还是两张报表构成。《概念框架》使用术语"损益表"来指代单独一张报表以及单一一张财务业绩表中的某个单独部分。

②假设采用针对损益表选择的计量基础确定的资产或负债的账面价值。

权益的计量

6.87 权益的总账面价值（权益总额）并非直接计量。该总账面价值等于所有已确认资产的总账面价值减去所有已确认负债的总账面价值。

6.88 由于通用目的财务报表并非意在反映一个主体的价值，因此权益的总账面价值通常不等于：

（1）该主体的权益求偿权的总市值；

（2）对基于持续经营假设的主体整体出售可获得的金额；或者

（3）可通过出售主体的全部资产和清偿主体的全部负债获得的金额。

6.89 尽管不对权益总额进行直接计量，但直接计量某些个别权益类别（参见第4.65段）和某些权益的组成部分（参见第4.66段）的账面价值可能是适当的。然而，由于权益总额是作为余值进行计量的，因此，至少一种权益类别无法直接计量。类似的，至少权益的一个组成部分无法直接计量。

6.90 单个类别的权益或权益的组成部分的账面价值通常为正值，但在某些情况下可为负值。

类似地，权益总额通常为正值，但也可为负值，这取决于确认了哪些资产和负债以及这些资产和负债是如何计量的。

基于现金流量的计量技术

6.91 计量有时难以直接观察。在某些此类情况下，估计计量的方式之一是使用基于现金流量的计量技术。但此类技术并非计量基础，而是采用计量基础时使用的技术。因此，当使用此类技术时，有必要明确使用了哪种计量基础以及此类技术反映适用于该计量基础的因素的程度。例如，如果计量基础是公允价值，则适用该计量基础的因素见第6.14段。

6.92 在采用修改的计量基础时，可使用基于现金流量的计量技术，例如，对履约价值进行修改，以剔除主体未能履行负债的可能性（自身信用风险）的影响。修改计量基础有时会生成对财务报表使用者更具相关性的信息，或者降低其编报和理解的成本。但是，财务报表使用者往往更难理解修改的计量基础。

6.93 结果的不确定性［参见第6.61（1）段］源自未来现金流量金额或时间分布的不确定性。这些不确定性是资产和负债的重要特征。当参考对不确定的未来现金流量的估计来计量资产或负债时，应考虑的一项因素是这些现金流量的估计金额或估计时间分布的可能波动［参见第6.14（2）段］。在从可能的现金流量范围内选择单一金额时，需考虑这些波动。有时选择的金额本身就是可能产生的金额，但情况并非总是如此。提供最具相关性信息的金额通常是从该范围的中间部分（中心估计）选择的。不同的中心估计提供不同的信息。例如：

（1）期望值（概率加权平均值，也称为统计均值）反映结果的整个区间，并对可能性更高的结果赋予更多的权重。期望值并非意在预测资产或负债产生的现金或其他经济利益的最终流入或流出。

（2）很可能发生的最大金额（类似于统计中值）表明产生后续损失和后续收益的概率均不超过50%。

（3）最有可能的结果（统计众数）为资产或负债产生的单一最有可能的最终流入或流出。

6.94 中心估计取决于对未来现金流量和其金额或时间分布的波动性的估计。该估计并未涵盖承担不确定性的价格［即，第6.14（4）段中描述的因素］，最终结果可能与中心估计不同。

6.95 没有一种中心估计能够提供可能结果区间的完整信息，因此，使用者可能需要了解关于可能结果区间的信息。

国际财务报告准则

财务报告
概念框架

起始段落

第 7 章——列示和披露

列示和披露作为沟通工具 ···	7.1
列示和披露的目标和原则 ··	7.4
分类 ···	7.7
资产和负债的分类 ···	7.9
抵销 ···	7.10
权益的分类 ···	7.12
收益和费用的分类 ···	7.14
损益和其他综合收益 ··	7.15
汇总 ···	7.20

列示和披露作为沟通工具

7.1 报告主体通过在财务报表中列示和披露信息来沟通有关其资产、负债、权益、收益和费用的信息。

7.2 财务报表信息的有效沟通使信息更具相关性,有助于如实反映主体的资产、负债、权益、收益和费用,同时还提高了财务报表信息的可理解性和可比性。实现财务报表信息的有效沟通,需要做到:

(1)专注于列示和披露的目标和原则,而不是规则;

(2)通过将类似项目归类、将不相似项目分开的方式,对信息进行分类;以及

(3)以既不过于细致、也不过度概略的方式,对信息进行汇总,从而不模糊信息。

7.3 正如成本会限制其他财务报告决策一样,成本亦会限制关于列示和披露的决策。因此,在作出关于列示和披露的决策时,重要的是考虑通过列示或披露特定信息向财务报表使用者提供的效益,是否很可能证明提供和使用该信息的成本是合理的。

列示和披露的目标和原则

7.4 为促进财务报表中信息的有效沟通,在准则中制定列示和披露要求时,需要在以下两方面之间取得平衡:

(1)在提供如实反映主体资产、负债、权益、收益和费用的具有相关性的信息时,赋予主体以灵活性;和

(2)要求报告主体保持信息可比,无论是同一报告主体的不同期间,还是不同主体的同一期间。

7.5 将列示和披露的目标纳入准则,有助于财务报表中信息的有效沟通,因为,这些目标有助于主体识别有用的信息,并决定如何以最有效的方式沟通这些信息。

7.6 考虑以下原则也有助于财务报表中信息的有效沟通:

(1)针对特定主体的信息比标准化描述(有时被称为"模板文字")更有用;以及

(2)通常没有必要在财务报表不同部分中重复同样的信息,这会降低财务报表的可理解性。

分类

7.7 分类是出于列示和披露目的,根据共有特征对资产、负债、权益、收益或费用进行归类。这些特征包括但不限于项目的性质、其在主体业务活动中的角色

（或功能），以及其计量方式。

7.8 将不相似的资产、负债、权益、收益或费用归为一类，会削弱信息的相关性，降低可理解性和可比性，并且可能无法如实反映其意在反映的内容。

资产和负债的分类

7.9 分类可用于为资产或负债选择的核算单元（参见第4.48段至第4.55段）。但有时将一项资产或负债分为具有不同特征的几个组成部分，并将这些组成部分划分为不同类别，可能更为适当。如果将这些组成部分划分为不同类别会提高最终提供的财务信息的有用性，则这样分类是适当的。例如，将一项资产或负债分为流动和非流动组成部分，并将这些组成部分划分为不同类别，可能是适当的。

抵销

7.10 抵销是指主体将一项资产和一项负债作为单独的核算单元予以确认和计量，但在财务状况表中将其组合为单一净额列报。抵销将不相似的项目归类在一起，因此通常是不适当的。

7.11 抵销资产和负债不同于将一系列权利和义务作为单一核算单元进行处理（参见第4.48段至第4.55段）。

权益的分类

7.12 为了提供有用的信息，如果某些权益求偿权具有不同的特征，可能有必要将其划分为不同类别（参见第4.65段）。

7.13 类似地，为了提供有用的信息，如果权益某些组成部分受到特定法律、监管或其他要求的限制，则可能有必要将权益组成部分划分为不同类别。例如，在某些国家或地区，只有当主体拥有足够的可分配的累积盈余（参见第4.66段）时，才允许主体向权益求偿权持有者进行分配。分别列示或披露这些累积盈余可能会提供有用的信息。

收益和费用的分类

7.14 分类适用于：
（1）为资产或负债所选择的核算单元产生的收益和费用；或者
（2）收益和费用的组成部分，如果这些组成部分具有不同特征且被单独识别。例如，资产现行价值的变动可能包括价值变动和应计利息的影响（参见表6.1）。如果这样做能够提高相应财务信息的有用性，那么，区分这些组成部分就是适当的。

损益和其他综合收益

7.15 收益和费用分类为：

（1）在损益表①；或者

（2）在损益表之外，作为其他综合收益。

7.16 损益表是报告期内主体财务业绩信息的主要来源。该报表包含损益总计，高度概括描述了该主体在此期间的财务业绩。许多财务报表使用者将这一合计数纳入分析，作为分析的起点或作为该期间主体财务业绩的主要指标。尽管如此，为了解主体在此期间的财务业绩，还需要对所有已确认的收益和费用——包括计入其他综合收益的收益和费用——进行分析，并对财务报表中包含的其他信息进行分析。

7.17 由于损益表是关于主体在此期间内财务业绩的主要信息来源，因此，所有收益和费用原则上都包含在该报表中。然而，在制定准则时，理事会可能会在特殊情况下决定，将资产或负债现行价值的变动所产生的收益或费用计入其他综合收益，以使损益表提供更具相关性的信息，或者更能如实反映该主体在该期间的财务业绩。

7.18 以历史成本计量为基础产生的收益和费用（参见表6.1）包含在损益表中；一项资产或负债现行价值变化的一部分，被单独识别作为收益和费用时，也包含在损益表中。例如，如果一项金融资产以现行价值计量，并且利息收益被从价值的其他变动中区分出来，该利息收益包含在损益表中。

7.19 原则上，如果将在一个期间内计入其他综合收益的收益和费用在未来期间内从其他综合收益重分类至损益表，能够使损益表提供更具相关性的信息，或更加如实反映该主体未来期间的财务业绩，则应进行重分类。但是，如果存在下列情况，例如，对重分类的期间或金额的甄别缺少明晰的依据，理事会在制定准则时，可决定包含在其他综合收益中的收益和费用不在之后的期间重分类。

汇总

7.20 汇总是将具有共有特征的资产、负债、权益、收益或费用加总并包含在同一类别中。

7.21 通过汇集大量的细节，汇总使信息更加有用。但是，汇总会隐藏其中一些细节。因此，需要在海量细节和过分简化之间找到一个平衡点，以便具有相关性的信息不会被掩盖。

7.22 财务报表的不同部分可能需要不同程度的汇总。例如，财务状况表和财务业绩表通常会提供汇总信息，附注中则提供更详细的信息。

---

① 《概念框架》并未明确财务业绩表由一张报表还是两张报表构成。《概念框架》使用术语"损益表"来指代单独一张报表、以及单一一张财务业绩表中的某个单独部分。同样地，《概念框架》使用术语"损益合计"来指代单独一张报表的合计、以及单一一张财务业绩表中某部分的小计。

第 8 章——资本和资本保全概念

起始段落

资本概念 ··	**8.1**
资本保全概念和利润的确定 ···	**8.3**
资本保全调整 ··	**8.10**

> 第8章内容继续沿用了2010版《概念框架》的内容，未做改动。此部分内容在1989年发布的《财务报表的编制和列报框架》中首次出现。

资本概念

8.1 大多数主体在编制财务报表时采用资本的财务概念。按照资本的财务概念，资本视同投入的货币或投入的购买力，是主体净资产或权益的同义语。按照资本的实物概念，资本视同营运能力，被看作是以每日产出等为基础的主体的生产能力。

8.2 主体选择适当的资本概念，要以其财务报表使用者的需要为基础。因此，如果财务报表的使用者主要关心保全名义投入资本或投入资本购买力，就应当采用资本的财务概念。如果使用者主要关心的是主体的营运能力，就应当采用资本的实物概念。资本概念的运用会有一些计量上的困难，但是，所选择的资本概念，表明了在确定利润时所要达到的目标。

资本保全概念和利润的确定

8.3 第8.1段资本的概念，引出了下列资本保全的概念：

（1）*财务资本保全*。根据这一概念，在扣除本期内对所有者的分配和所有者的出资以后，期末净资产的财务（或货币）金额必须大于期初净资产的财务（或货币）金额，才算赚得利润。财务资本保全的计量，可以用名义货币单位或不变购买力单位。

（2）*实物资本保全*。根据这一概念，在扣除本期内对所有者的分配和所有者的出资以后，主体的期末实物生产能力（或营运能力），或主体期末达到上述实物生产能力所需的资源或资金，必须大于期初实物生产能力，才算赚得利润。

8.4 资本保全的概念关系到主体如何定义其力求保全的资本。因为它提供了计量利润的参照点，从而也就规定了资本概念与利润概念的联系。它是区分主体资本回报和资本返还的前提。资产的流入必须大于保全资本所需要的金额，才可以作为利润，也才可以作为资本回报。利润是从收益中扣除费用（包括恰当的资本保全调整）后的余额。如果费用大于收益，这一余额就是亏损。

8.5 实物资本保全概念要求采用现行成本计量基础。但是，财务资本保全概念不要求采用特定的计量基础。根据这一概念选择的计量基础，取决于主体力求保全的财务资本的类型。

8.6 两种资本保全概念的主要区别，在于对主体资产和负债价格变动影响的处理。一般说来，如果主体期末拥有的资本与期初一样多，主体就保全了自己的资本。凡是大于期初保全资本所需要的金额，都是利润。

8.7 根据以名义货币单位定义资本的财务资本保全概念，利润表示本期内名义货币资本的增加。因此，本期持有资产的价格上升，传统意义上称作持有利得，基于财务资本保全概念，就是利润。但是，在通过交换交易方式处置资产之前，持有利得不能确认为利润。如果是以不变购买力单位来定义财务资本保全概念，利润就表示本期内投入购买力的增加。这样，在资产价格的上升中，只有超出一般物价水平上升的那一部分才能作为利润，其余增加部分只能作为资本保全调整，因此后者是权益的一部分。

8.8 根据以实物生产能力定义资本的实物资本保全概念，利润表示实物资本在本期内的增加。所有影响主体资产和负债的价格变动，都应当作为主体实物生产能力计量上的变动，从而都应当作为资本保全调整，即作为权益的一部分，而不作为利润。

8.9 计量基础和资本保全概念的选择，决定了编制财务报表所采用的会计模型。不同的会计模型表现出不同程度的相关性和可靠性，如同在其他方面一样，管理层必须在相关性和可靠性之间寻求一种平衡。本《概念框架》适用于一系列会计模型，并且为根据所选模型建立的财务报表提供编报指南。目前，理事会不打算指定使用某一特定会计模型，除非是对于特殊情况，例如以恶性通货膨胀经济中的货币进行报告的主体。不过，这一意向将根据世界形势的发展加以审议。

资本保全调整

8.10 资产和负债的重估或重述，引起权益的增加或减少。虽然这些增加或减少符合收益和费用的定义，但是根据资本保全的相应概念，它们不列入收益表，而是作为资本保全调整或重估价盈余计入权益。

附录
术语表

下列术语定义摘录或产生自《财务报告概念框架》相关段落。

汇总	将具有共同特征的资产、负债、权益、收益或费用加总并包含在同一类别中。	第7.20段
资产	主体由于过去的事项而控制的现时经济资源。	第4.3段
账面价值	资产、负债或权益在财务状况表中确认的金额。	第5.1段
分类	出于列示和披露的目的,根据共有特征对资产、负债、权益、收益或费用进行归类。	第7.7段
汇总财务报表	由两个或两个以上不都是存在母子公司关系的主体构成的报告主体的财务报表。	第3.12段
合并财务报表	由母公司及其子公司构成的报告主体的财务报表。	第3.11段
经济资源的控制权	主导经济资源的使用并且获得该资源可能产生的经济利益的现时能力。	第4.20段
终止确认	从主体的财务状况表中移除全部或部分已确认的资产或负债。	第5.26段
经济资源	具备产生经济利益潜力的权利。	第4.4段
提升性质量特征	使有用信息更加有用的质量特征。提升性质量特征包括可比性、可验证性、及时性和可理解性。	第2.4段、第2.23段
权益	主体资产扣除所有负债后的剩余利益。	第4.63段
权益求偿权	对主体资产扣除所有负债后的剩余利益的求偿权。	第4.64段
待执行合同	双方同等程度地未履行的合同或合同的一部分,即,双方均未履行任何义务,或双方均履行了部分义务且履约程度相当。	第4.56段
存在的不确定性	关于资产或负债存在与否的不确定性。	第4.13段、第4.35段

国际财务报告准则

费用	引起权益减少的资产减少或负债增加,但不包括对权益求偿权持有者的分配。	第4.69段
基本质量特征	财务信息必须具备的对通用目的财务报告主要使用者有用的质量特征,包括相关性和如实反映。	第2.4段、第2.5段
通用目的财务报告	提供关于报告主体经济资源、对主体的求偿权及这些经济资源与求偿权的变动,且对财务报表主要使用者作出有关向主体提供资源决策有用的财务信息的报告。	第1.2段、第1.12段
通用目的财务报表	通用目的财务报告的特定形式,提供关于报告主体资产、负债、权益、收益和费用的信息。	第3.2段
收益	引起权益增加的资产增加或负债减少,但不包括权益求偿权持有者的投入。	第4.68段
负债	主体由于过去的事项而承担的转移经济资源的现时义务。	第4.26段
重要性信息	通用目的财务报告提供了关于特定报告主体的财务信息,如果省略或误报某信息会影响通用目的财务报告的主要使用者基于这些报告所作出的决策,则该信息为重要性信息。	第2.11段
计量	对资产或负债以及相关收益和费用应用特定计量基础产生的结果。	第6.1段
计量基础	被计量项目的一项已识别特征,如历史成本、公允价值或履约价值。	第6.1段
计量的不确定性	财务报告中的货币金额不可直接观察,而是必须进行估计,则计量不确定性相应产生。	第2.19段
抵销	将作为单独核算单元予以确认和计量的资产和负债在财务状况表中组合为单一净额。	第7.10段
结果的不确定性	关于由资产或负债产生的经济利益流入或流出的金额或时间分布的不确定性。	第6.61段
产生经济利益的潜力	经济资源内已存在的且至少在一种情况下能够为主体产生高于所有其他方可能从中获得的经济利益的特征。	第4.14段

(通用目的财务报告的)主要使用者	现有和潜在投资者、贷款人和其他债权人。	第1.2段
审慎性	在不确定性条件下进行判断时的谨慎性。审慎性的运用是指不高估资产或收益，不低估负债或费用。同样的，运用审慎性也不允许低估资产或收益，或者高估负债或费用。	第2.16段
确认	将符合资产、负债、权益、收益和费用定义的财务报表要素项目纳入财务状况表或财务业绩表的过程。确认涉及以文字和金额表述一个项目（单独或与其他项目汇总在一起）并将该金额纳入财务状况表或财务业绩表的一项或多项合计中。	第5.1段
报告主体	被要求或主动选择编制财务报表的主体。	第3.10段
非合并财务报表	仅包含母公司的报告主体的财务报表。	第3.11段
核算单元	适用确认标准和计量概念的一项权利或一组权利、一项义务或一组义务，或者一组权利和义务。	第4.48段
有用财务信息	有助于财务报表主要使用者作出有关向主体提供资源的决策的财务信息。为具备有用性，财务信息必须具有相关性并且如实反映其意在反映的内容。	第1.2段、第2.4段
(通用目的财务报告的)使用者	参见（通用目的财务报告的）主要使用者。	

《财务报告概念框架》由理事会于 2018 年 3 月批准发布

《财务报告概念框架》由国际会计准则理事会 14 位理事中的 13 位批准发布。Tarca 女士因近期才在理事会任职而弃权。

Hans Hoogervorst	主席
Suzanne Lloyd	副主席
Nick Anderson	
Martin Edelmann	
Françoise Flores	
Amaro Luiz De Oliveira Gomes	
Gary Kabureck	
Jianqiao Lu	
Takatsugu Ochi	
Darrel Scott	
Thomas Scott	
Chungwoo Suh	
Ann Tarca	
Mary Tokar	

《财务报告概念框架》结论基础

目　　录

	起始段落
《概念框架》的现状和目的	
项目历史	BC0.1
目的	BC0.18
现状	BC0.21
过渡至 2018 版《概念框架》	BC0.27
业务活动	BC0.29
长期投资的影响	BC0.34
第 1 章——通用目的财务报告的目标	
引言	BC1.1
主要使用者	BC1.9
对决策的有用性	BC1.27
关于报告主体经济资源、对主体的求偿权以及经济资源与求偿权变动的信息	BC1.44
第 2 章——有用财务信息的质量特征	
引言	BC2.1
财务报告的目标和有用财务信息的质量特征	BC2.5
基本质量特征和提升性质量特征	BC2.9
基本质量特征	BC2.12
提升性质量特征	BC2.58
未包含的质量特征	BC2.70
有用财务报告的成本限制	BC2.73
第 3 章——财务报表和报告主体	
重点关注财务报表	BC3.1
财务报表的目标和范围	BC3.3
财务报表中采用的角度	BC3.9
持续经营假设	BC3.11
报告主体	BC3.12

第 4 章——财务报表要素
  引言 ………………………………………………………………… **BC4.1**
  定义——资产和负债的共性问题 ………………………………… **BC4.3**
  资产的定义 ………………………………………………………… **BC4.23**
  负债的定义 ………………………………………………………… **BC4.44**
  资产和负债 ………………………………………………………… **BC4.69**
  权益的定义 ………………………………………………………… **BC4.89**
  收益和费用的定义 ………………………………………………… **BC4.93**
  其他可能的定义 …………………………………………………… **BC4.97**

第 5 章——确认和终止确认
  确认 ………………………………………………………………… **BC5.1**
  终止确认 …………………………………………………………… **BC5.23**

第 6 章——计量
  引言 ………………………………………………………………… **BC6.1**
  混合计量 …………………………………………………………… **BC6.5**
  计量基础和所提供信息 …………………………………………… **BC6.12**
  选择计量基础时考虑的因素 ……………………………………… **BC6.34**
  权益的计量 ………………………………………………………… **BC6.52**

第 7 章——列示和披露
  引言 ………………………………………………………………… **BC7.1**
  权益的分类 ………………………………………………………… **BC7.4**
  收益和费用的分类 ………………………………………………… **BC7.6**

第 8 章——资本和资本保全概念 …………………………………………… **BC8.1**

《财务报告概念框架》结论基础

本结论基础与《财务报告概念框架》（以下简称《概念框架》）一并发布，但不构成其组成部分。本结论基础汇总了国际会计准则理事会（以下简称"理事会"）在制定《概念框架》时的考虑。理事会个别理事认为某些因素重要性要高于其他因素。

《概念框架》的现状和目的

	起始段落
项目历史	**BC0.1**
2018 版修订内容——方法和范围	BC0.10
目的	**BC0.18**
现状	**BC0.21**
过渡至 2018 版《概念框架》	**BC0.27**
业务活动	**BC0.29**
长期投资的影响	**BC0.34**
作为业务活动的长期投资	BC0.37
长期投资者的信息需求	BC0.40

项目历史

BC0.1 理事会的前身国际会计准则委员会于1989年发布了《编报财务报表的框架》（以下简称"1989版《框架》"）。

BC0.2 理事会和美国国家准则制定机构——美国财务会计准则委员会（以下简称"委员会"）于2004年开始了对双方概念框架进行修订的联合项目。

BC0.3 项目第一阶段为制定相关章节来描述通用目的财务报告目标和有用财务信息质量特征。在此过程中，理事会和委员会于2006年发布了讨论文件（以下简称"2006年讨论文件"），于2008年发布了征求意见稿（以下简称"2008年征求意见稿"）[①]。在考虑了上述两份文件收到的反馈意见和向外征询所得信息后，理事会和委员会于2010年发布了修订版《财务报告概念框架》（以下简称"2010版《概念框架》"）中的两章修订内容，分别关于财务报告目标和有用财务信息质量特征。相关章节发布后立即生效。1989版《框架》的其余内容沿用至2010版《概念框架》，未做改动。

BC0.4 理事会与委员会除完成了通用目的财务报告的目标和有用财务信息质量特征的相关章节制定工作外，还完成了如下工作：

（1）先后就报告主体的概念发布了讨论文件和征求意见稿（2010年征求意见稿）[②]；

（2）讨论了财务报表要素的定义；以及

（3）针对计量事项进行了讨论并举行了公开圆桌会议。

BC0.5 因理事会和委员会在2010年集中精力于其他项目，暂停了概念框架项目，因此上述工作并未给《概念框架》带来进一步的修订。

BC0.6 2011年，理事会就其议程开展公开征询。大多数反馈意见者认为应将概念框架项目作为理事会的优先项目。于是，理事会于2012年重启了概念框架项目。

BC0.7 在2010年之前，理事会与委员会原计划分八个独立阶段完成概念框架项目，但仅完成了一个阶段，即关于目标与质量特征的内容。2012年重启该项目时，理事会决定为修订版《概念框架》制定一整套完整的提案，而非继续之前分阶段的方法。制定完整的《概念框架》使理事会和利益相关方能够更加清晰地了解《概念框架》不同方面之间的联系。

BC0.8 理事会在制定修订版《概念框架》的过程中，于2013年发布了讨论文

[①] 见《对财务报告概念框架改进的初步意见：财务报告目标和对决策有用的财务报告信息的质量特征（讨论文件）》（2006年发布）和《财务报告概念框架改进：第1章和第2章（征求意见稿）》（2008年发布）。

[②] 见《对财务报告概念框架改进的初步意见——报告主体（讨论文件）》（2008年发布）和《财务报告概念框架——报告主体（征求意见稿）》（2010年发布）。

件（以下简称"2013 年讨论文件"），于 2015 年发布了征求意见稿（以下简称"2015 年征求意见稿"）。① 理事会在考虑了上述两份文件收到的反馈意见和向外征询所得信息后，于 2018 年完成了概念框架项目，并发布了修订版《财务报告概念框架》（以下简称"2018 版《概念框架》"）。

BC0.9 2012 年项目重启后，理事会未与委员会合作开展工作。2018 版《概念框架》对通用目的财务报告和有用财务信息质量特征的相关章节仅进行了有限修改。而委员会未对其《财务会计概念公告》进行相应修改。

2018 版修订内容——方法和范围

BC0.10 尽管 2010 版《概念框架》已经帮助理事会制定国际财务报告准则（以下简称"准则"），但是：

（1）某些重要方面未涉及；

（2）某些方面的指引不够清晰；以及

（3）某些方面已经过时。

BC0.11 理事会在制定 2018 版《概念框架》的过程中，对 2010 版《概念框架》查漏补缺，并对其进行了澄清和更新，但并未从根本上重新考虑 2010 版《概念框架》的所有方面。尤其是虽然理事会重新考虑了财务报告目标和有用财务信息质量特征相关章节的部分方面，但未从根本上重新考虑这些章节。选择上述方法时，理事会注意到，在制定 2010 版《概念框架》的过程中，这些章节已遵循了大量的应循程序。

BC0.12 理事会通常针对重点项目建立咨询小组。对于《概念框架》项目，理事会将会计准则咨询论坛（ASAF）作为其咨询小组。会计准则咨询论坛为理事会的咨询机构，由国家会计准则制定机构和关心财务报告的地区性组织组成。理事会在制定 2018 版《概念框架》期间就多个议题与会计准则咨询论坛展开了讨论。

BC0.13 理事会在制定 2018 版《概念框架》的过程中，力求在提供高层级的概念和提供足够详细内容之间达到平衡，以使其对理事会和其他人更加有用。但部分利益相关方表示，在某些方面，理事会的提议仅描述了准则制定过程中进行判断时需要考虑的因素，因而他们认为提议未对基本概念进行审查且未能提供充分指引。但理事会不认同此观点。理事会认为《概念框架》是帮助其制定准则的实用工具。理事会得出结论认为，当由于应用概念产生的结果不唯一或各个结果相互冲突而需要理事会进行判断时，如果《概念框架》在描述概念时未对进行上述判断所需考虑的因素进行解释，那么《概念框架》就失去了它的意义。

BC0.14 理事会在制定 2018 版《概念框架》过程中，重点关注近期准则制定项目中所涉及的概念，这样做的目的在于反映理事会在相关事项上的最前沿思想，而非为其准则制定决策或当前实务提供依据。

---

① 参见《财务报告概念框架审阅（讨论文件）》（2013 年发布）和《财务报告概念框架（征求意见稿）》（2015 年发布）。

BC0.15 由于理事会不希望推迟《概念框架》中其他亟需的改进之处，因此 2018 版《概念框架》未讨论同时具有负债和权益特征的金融工具的分类事宜。目前，理事会正在具有权益特征的金融工具这一研究项目中探索如何区分负债与权益。必要时，作为该项目的一项可能结果，理事会将更新《概念框架》（参见 BC4.45 段）。

BC0.16 2018 版《概念框架》中对资本和资本保全的讨论沿用了 2010 版《概念框架》的内容，未做改动。该讨论内容最初出现于 1989 版《框架》当中（参见 BC8.1 段至 BC8.4 段）。未来，理事会可能会在认为必要时考虑修订该讨论内容。

BC0.17 理事会在制定 2018 版《概念框架》的过程中，未讨论：权益法、以外币计价的金额的折算、或对恶性通货膨胀下计量单元的重述。理事会得出结论认为，这些问题最好是在考虑修订与这些议题相关的准则项目中解决。

目的（第 SP1.1 段）

BC0.18 2010 版《概念框架》包含了一份《概念框架》可能用途的长清单。理事会在 2018 版《概念框架》中精简了该清单，识别出《概念框架》的三种主要用途，包括：协助理事会制定准则，协助编制者在某一特定交易或事项无适用准则时（或者某项准则允许会计政策选择）时制定会计政策，以及协助各方理解和解读准则。

BC0.19 理事会考虑了是否应指明《概念框架》的主要目的仅为协助理事会制定准则。理事会最终没有这样做，原因在于理事会认识到《概念框架》给其他方带来的帮助并不会妨碍理事会制定目标明确且具有一致性的概念以帮助其制定准则。

BC0.20 尽管在某一特定交易或事项无适用准则、或者某项准则允许选择会计政策时，编制者可运用《概念框架》制定其会计政策，但《概念框架》的部分内容仅适用于理事会。

2018 版《概念框架》指出，这种情况下，理事会可在制定准则时作出特别决定（例如，参见第 7.17 段）。

现状（第 SP1.2 段至第 SP1.3 段）

BC0.21 1989 版《框架》和 2010 版《概念框架》均指出《概念框架》并非准则，不可超越具体准则。理事会在 2018 版《概念框架》中重申了这一事实。

BC0.22 理事会发现，《概念框架》的地位在实务中运行情况良好。且《概念框架》不可超越准则中的要求这一明确表述，防止了主体试图超越那些主体可能认为与《概念框架》相矛盾的不适当的准则。

BC0.23 部分利益相关方认为理事会制定准则不应偏离《概念框架》。理事会不同意此观点。在某些情况下，理事会可能需要偏离《概念框架》的部分方面。承认这一点有助于《概念框架》的制定，但须明确仅在需要满足通用目的财务报告目标时，此类偏离才是适当的。这一需求之所以可能会出现是由于概念思维或经济环境会发生变化，新准则或修订的准则需要反映这些变化。

BC0.24 2015年征求意见稿中部分反馈意见者对于概念框架对未来准则提议的影响表示担忧。他们尤其担忧针对资产和负债的定义的修订提议。作为回应，理事会对修订后的资产和负债定义，以及支持这些定义的指引进行了测试（参见BC4.19段至BC4.22段）。测试的目标之一是为了帮助理事会和利益相关方评估修订后概念对未来准则的影响。此外，理事会还测试了修订后概念和现有准则间的不一致之处。

BC0.25 测试的目标并非要识别理事会是否应跟随《概念框架》制定修订相应准则的提议。对《概念框架》的修订不会自动导致对准则的修订。对准则所做修订意在解决财务报告的缺陷。任何凸显准则不一致性的对《概念框架》的修订，理事会都必须在制定工作计划时从其他优先性的角度进行考虑。①

BC0.26 中小主体国际财务报告准则®包括一个与中小主体财务报表的概念和基本原则相关的部分。该部分以1989版《框架》为基础。理事会在下次审阅中小主体国际财务报告准则时，将会考虑是否需要对此部分进行修改。

过渡至2018版《概念框架》

BC0.27 理事会和国际财务报告准则解释委员会将在其发布之后立即采用2018版《概念框架》。制定国际财务报告准则解释公告初稿时，如果国际财务报告准则解释委员会发现准则（包括以1989版《框架》或2010版《概念框架》为基础制定的准则）与2018版《概念框架》中的概念之间存在不一致，则解释委员会将按照基金会《应循程序手册》要求，上报至理事会。②

BC0.28 修订后的概念可为理事会制定或修订准则提供指引。但对《概念框架》的修订不会自动导致对现有准则的修订（参见BC0.25段）。因此，《概念框架》的修订不会对大多数报告主体的财务报表立即产生影响。仅在某一特定交易或事项无适用准则、或者某项准则允许会计政策选择时，财务报表编制者需要使用《概念框架》制定会计政策的情况下，才会受修订的直接影响。③ 为帮助这类主体成功过渡至2018版《概念框架》，理事会于2018年发布了《对国际财务报告准则中〈概念框架〉的

---

① 参见国际财务报告准则基金会《应循程序手册》第4.23段。
② 参见国际财务报告准则基金会《应循程序手册》第7.8段。
③ 如果某一特定交易、其他事项或情况无适用准则，则根据《国际会计准则第8号——会计政策、会计估计变更和差错》第11段，主体必须在针对该特定交易制定和应用会计政策时考虑《概念框架》。如果某项准则允许会计政策选择，则主体根据《国际会计准则第1号——财务报表列报》的总体要求选择会计政策，即财务报表必须能够公允反映主体的财务状况、财务业绩和现金流量。《国际会计准则第1号》第15段描述了公允反映和《概念框架》中概念之间的联系。

引用的修订》。该文件把准则中对 1989 版《框架》的引用（如适用）替换为对 2018 版《概念框架》的引用，同时更新相关摘录引用。

业务活动

BC0.29 理事会在制定 2018 版《概念框架》的过程中，得出结论认为，由于主体业务活动的性质会影响某些类型财务信息的相关性，因此其在制定或修订准则时可能需要考虑该因素。

BC0.30 部分利益相关方认为考虑主体业务活动的性质必然导致主观性，会有损于财务报表的可比性，理事会不同意该观点。实际上，大多数情况下主体业务活动的性质均可从客观角度确定。因此，如果主体从事同一类型的业务活动，理事会预计这些业务活动将以类似的方式反映在主体的财务报表中。

BC0.31 理事会考虑是否应从准则制定的所有方面考虑主体业务活动的性质，是否应将业务活动作为一个总概念纳入《概念框架》。理事会得出结论认为，主体业务活动的性质并非以同样的方式、同样的程度影响财务报告的所有方面，因此，业务活动不应作为一个总概念纳入《概念框架》。因此 2018 版《概念框架》中不包含关于主体业务活动如何影响财务报告决策的一般讨论，而是结合如下背景对该因素进行了讨论：

（1）核算单元的选择［参见第 4.51（1）④段］；

（2）针对资产或负债和相关收益和费用的计量基础的选择（参见第 6.54 段至第 6.57 段）。在某些情况下，这会使部分收益或费用项目计入其他综合收益（参见第 6.83 段至第 6.86 段中关于一种以上计量基础的讨论）；

（3）对资产、负债、权益、收益或费用的分类（参见第 7.7 段）。

BC0.32 2018 版《概念框架》对业务活动的概念进行了讨论，以协助理事会制定相关准则。业务活动的概念在特定准则中可以得到进一步的解释和扩展。《国际财务报告准则第 9 号——金融工具》中对业务模式的讨论就是理事会应用业务活动概念的一个例子。

BC0.33 理事会决定在 2018 版《概念框架》中，使用"业务活动"这一术语来替代"业务模式"。"业务模式"这一术语为国际综合报告委员会、金融稳定理事会强化信息披露工作组及多个监管机构等不同组织所使用，其含义较为广泛。如 2018 版《概念框架》仍采用"业务模式"，会与上述定义相混淆。

长期投资的影响

BC0.34 长期投资相关内容得到了政府和其他方的广泛关注。政府指出鼓励长期投资是促进经济增长的重要手段。

BC0.35 理事会考虑了准则在促进长期投资中的作用，并指出：

（1）理事会通过制定相关准则要求报告主体编制具有透明度的财务报告，在促进包括长期投资在内的投资方面作出了重要贡献。具有透明度的财务报告是保持金融市场健康有效运行的先决条件，有助于市场参与者作出更加有效和明智的资源配置和其他经济决策，进而提高资本提供者（投资者和贷款人）的投资兴趣。具有透明度的财务报告还为评估主体管理层的受托责任提供有用的输入值。

（2）但准则的作用并不在于鼓励或阻止任何类型的投资。相反，准则制定决策的初衷在于满足主体提供有用信息的需求。

BC0.36 理事会在制定2018版《概念框架》的过程中，考虑了《概念框架》是否可为理事会提供充分、适当的工具，以协助其在制定准则时考虑以下两点：

（1）长期投资业务活动（参见BC0.37段至BC0.39段）；以及

（2）长期投资者的信息需求（参见BC0.40段至BC0.43段）。

作为业务活动的长期投资

BC0.37 理事会考虑了某些利益相关方的建议，即应将长期投资作为特定类型的业务活动（或业务模式），并对开展该业务活动的主体制定特定的计量、列示和披露要求。这些利益相关方建议：

（1）主体不应对其长期投资及相关负债使用现行价值计量基础；或者

（2）如主体对此类投资和负债使用了现行价值计量基础，则重新计量产生的收益和费用应计入其他综合收益，而非计入损益表。

BC0.38 根据2018版《概念框架》第6.54段至第6.57段的讨论，主体当前开展的业务活动的性质会影响资产或负债产生未来现金流量的方式。因此，为资产或负债和相关收益或费用选择计量基础时，应将主体业务活动的性质考虑在内。此外，在某些情况下，考虑主体业务活动的性质会使主体部分收益或费用项计入其他综合收益（参见第6.85段至第6.86段）。理事会得出结论认为，如果未来项目中考虑如何对业务活动包括长期投资的主体的长期投资或其负债进行会计处理，则2018版《概念框架》对此因素的讨论会为理事会作出适当的准则制定决策提供充足的工具。

BC0.39 理事会决定在2018版《概念框架》中不应明确提及长期投资业务活动，原因如下：

（1）明确提及任何特定的业务活动都会使得《概念框架》不适当地包含过多详细信息；以及

（2）《概念框架》未提及任何其他业务活动。

长期投资者的信息需求

BC0.40 部分利益相关方建议《概念框架》应重点关注长期投资者的信息需求，

同时指出他们的信息需求与短期投资者的需求存在差异。这些利益相关方认为：

（1）理事会过于关注短期投资者的需求。

（2）理事会过于关注潜在投资者的需求，对现有长期投资者的需求关注不足。现有长期投资者持有报告主体的所有权，且承担所有权的剩余风险。因此，这些利益相关方认为长期投资者需要能够协助其评估管理层对主体经济资源受托责任的信息。

（3）理事会过度使用现行价值计量基础，尤其是反映市场参与者假设的计量基础（如公允价值），而这些计量基础所提供信息对短期投资者的相关性高于对创造长期价值感兴趣的投资者。

（4）过度使用现行价值计量基础（尤其针对长期投资）且将未实现收益计入损益表可能会：

①导致股利分配过度或不稳定，不符合长期投资者的最佳利益；

②导致管理层薪酬（包括奖金）过高；以及

③助长短期效益主义和金融工程，打击长期投资的积极性。

BC0.41 理事会不同意 BC0.40 段所述观点，原因如下：

（1）理事会对短期投资者需求的重视程度并不高于对长期投资者需求的重视程度。理事会认为长期投资者和短期投资者都是财务报表的主要使用者。理事会还认为短期投资者的信息需求同样也是长期投资者的信息需求。

（2）《概念框架》同时将现有和潜在投资者视作财务报表的主要使用者。理事会通过与财务报表使用者就《概念框架》项目和许多其他项目展开的讨论，发现没有理由认为现有投资者的信息需求不同于潜在投资者的信息需求。此外，2018 版《概念框架》对通用目的财务报告的目标的讨论进行了修订，强调了向投资者提供信息以帮助其评估管理层对主体经济资源受托责任的重要性。2018 版《概念框架》明确指出向主体提供资源的决策包括对管理层影响主体经济资源使用的行动行使表决权或施加影响。因此，2018 版《概念框架》澄清，在确定财务信息的有用性时已考虑现有投资者（包括长期投资者）的需求（参见 BC1.36 段至 BC1.37 段）。

（3）当理事会决定要求或允许使用现行价值计量基础时，并不是因为其认为此计量基础对短期投资者尤为有用。相反，是针对哪类信息最可能对财务报表使用者（包括长期和短期投资者）有用的评估结果驱使理事会作出这样的决定。根据 2018 版《概念框架》"第 6 章——计量"中的概念，理事会将继续按此制定决策。

（4）理事会认为，会计信息（如利润）不是且不应是股利和奖金分配的唯一决定因素。分配政策受许多其他因素影响，如主体的融资需求、当前和预计流动性、主体面临的风险、法律约束和（奖金分配情况下）薪酬政策与激励安排。具体影响因素会因不同主体、不同国家和时间的推移而有所不同。要求理事会在制定准则过程中考虑上述因素，既不可行也不现实。

BC0.42 综上所述，理事会得出结论认为，就主要使用者及其信息需求以及通用目的财务报告的目标而言，2018 版《概念框架》包含了充分适当的讨论，可以适当解决长期投资者的需求。

BC0.43 可想而知,长期投资者可能需要主体提供短期投资者不需要的部分信息,例如,长期投资者需要更多信息,以支持其关于对管理层行动行使表决权或施加影响的决定。但理事会得出结论认为,为帮助其识别特定准则应要求主体提供哪些信息,《概念框架》中无需特别提及长期投资者需求。理事会在制定准则时,会不时地从投资者(包括长期投资者)中获取意见和反馈,以确保其了解投资者需要哪些信息。

起始段落

第1章——通用目的财务报告的目标

引言	**BC1.1**
2018年修订	BC1.2
通用目的财务报告（2010版）	BC1.4
报告主体的财务报告（2010版）	BC1.8
主要使用者	**BC1.9**
主要使用者（2010版）	BC1.9
是否应识别主要使用者群体？（2010版）	BC1.14
为何现有和潜在的投资者、贷款人及其他债权人被视为主要使用者？（2010版）	BC1.15
主要使用者群体（2018版）	BC1.18
是否应建立主要使用者层级？（2010版）	BC1.21
主要使用者群体以外的其他使用者的信息需求（2010版）	BC1.22
管理层的信息需求（2010版）	BC1.22
监管机构的信息需求（2010版）	BC1.23
对决策的有用性	**BC1.27**
对决策的有用性（2010版）	BC1.27
受托责任（2018版）	BC1.32
术语"受托责任"（2018版）	BC1.41
不同类型主体的财务报告目标（2010版）	BC1.42
关于报告主体的经济资源、对主体的求偿权以及经济资源与求偿权变动的信息	**BC1.44**
财务业绩信息的重要性（2010版）	BC1.44
财务状况与偿债能力（2010版）	BC1.47

> 2018 年，理事会对《概念框架》第 1 章进行了有限修订，在本章的原结论基础中新增了对理事会在制定这些修订时所考虑因素的描述。理事会在结论基础的各部分标题后增加了年份，以表明各部分的制定年份。除了新增和更新交叉索引以及进行微小但必要的编辑修改之外，反映理事会 2010 年编制本章时所考虑因素的结论基础部分在 2018 年未予更新。

引言

BC1.1 第 1 章第一版由理事会与委员会联合制定，并于 2010 年发布（参见 BC0.3 段）。因此，本结论基础引用了委员会的部分文献。

2018 年修订

BC1.2 理事会在 2012 年重新启动《概念框架》项目时，并未从根本上重新考虑第 1 章（参见 BC0.11 段）。尽管 2013 年讨论文件的部分反馈意见者同意这种方法，但许多人认为理事会应重新考虑第 1 章的一个或多个方面。根据这些意见，理事会考虑是否对以下方面进行修改：

（1）主要使用者（参见 BC1.18 段至 BC1.20 段）；以及

（2）受托责任（参见 BC1.32 段至 BC1.41 段）。

BC1.3 对于理事会 2018 年作出的有限修改，委员会未相应对《概念公告第 8 号：财务报告概念框架》的第 1 章"通用目的财务报告的目标"进行任何修改。理事会得出结论认为，其对第 1 章进行改进所取得的价值要高于与委员会版本在这些方面存在不一致所带来的不利影响。

通用目的财务报告（2010 版）

BC1.4 《概念框架》确立了财务报告（而非仅仅财务报表）的目标，这与理事会的职责相符。财务报表是财务报告的核心部分，且理事会所处理的大多数事项均涉及财务报表。尽管委员会《概念公告第 1 号———企业财务报告的目标》的范围是财务报告，但委员会的其他概念公告则着重关注财务报表。理事会的前身于 1989 年发布的理事会《编报财务报表的框架》（1989 版《框架》）仅涉及财务报表。因此，对理事会和委员会而言，2010 版《概念框架》涵盖的范围比之前的框架涵盖的范围更为广泛。①

---

① 除第 1 章和第 2 章外，2018 版《概念框架》侧重于（通用目的）财务报表，而非（通用目的）财务报告（参见第 3.1 段）。

BC1.5 某些利益相关方认为，科技进步可能导致通用目的财务报告变得过时。新科技［例如，可扩展商业报告语言（XBRL）］，在将来可能使报告主体为不同的使用者编制或提供的必要信息组合成不同的财务报告，以满足他们各自的信息需求变得可行。

BC1.6 为不同的使用者提供不同报告或者向使用者提供用以组合其自定义报告所需的各类信息将导致高昂的成本。要求财务信息使用者自行组合其所需的报告可能并不合理，因为许多使用者为此可能需要掌握更多的会计知识。因此，理事会得出结论认为，目前通用目的财务报告在满足各类使用者的信息需求方面仍是最高效和最有效的方式。

BC1.7 在2006年讨论文件中，理事会采用了"通用目的外部财务报告"这一术语。"外部"意在说明内部使用者（例如，管理层）并非理事会所设定的通用目的财务报告的预期受益人。在重新审议的过程中，理事会得出结论认为该术语是冗余的。因此，第1章的标题为"通用目的的财务报告"。

报告主体的财务报告（2010版）

BC1.8 2008年征求意见稿的某些反馈意见者认为，报告主体与其权益投资者或权益投资者中的特定部分不可分离。上述观点源于一个过去的时期，在这个时期，大多数企业均为独资或合伙企业，由对在经营过程中形成的债务承担无限责任的所有者管理。随着时间的推移，企业与其所有者逐渐分离。当今，绝大多数企业由于下列各项因素而令其法律实质与其所有者相分离：组织的法律形式、具有众多承担有限法律责任的投资者以及独立于所有者的职业经理人。因此，理事会得出结论认为，财务报告应通过针对主体（及其经济资源和求偿权）的会计处理，而非对主体的主要使用者及其在报告主体中权益的会计处理来反映这种分离。①

主要使用者（第1.5段和第1.8段至第1.10段）

主要使用者（2010版）

BC1.9 第1.2段所述的财务报告目标提及现有和潜在的投资者、贷款人及其他债权人。第1.5段中对主要使用者的描述提及无法要求报告主体直接向其提供信息的现有和潜在的投资者、贷款人及其他债权人。第1.10段指出，"监管机构以及除投资者、贷款人及其他债权人以外的公众人士"可能认为通用目的的财务报告中的信息是有用的，但他们并非通用目的的财务报告主要提供的对象。

---

① 另参见2018版《概念框架》第3.8段和BC3.9段至BC3.10段。

BC1.10 1989 版《框架》第 9 段指出，使用者包括"现有的和潜在的投资者、雇员、贷款人、供应商和其他商业债权人"（并在随后述及投资者需求时添加了"顾问"）。第 1.2 段中的使用者意在涵盖上述所有人员。1989 版《框架》第 9 段同时列出了诸如客户、政府及其代理机构和公众等其他潜在的使用者。这些使用者与第 1.10 段中所列的可能对财务报告感兴趣的非主要使用者相类似。

BC1.11 1989 版《框架》第 10 段指出，"由于投资者是主体风险资本的提供者，提供满足他们需要的财务报表，也可以满足财务报表其他使用者的大部分需求"。该表述可能被理解为其关注重点仅局限于投资者。但是，第 12 段明确指出，财务报表的目标是提供"有助于广泛使用者作出经济决策"的信息。因此，1989 版《框架》将投资者的需求作为广泛使用者的需求代表予以着重关注，但并未明确识别主要使用者群体。

BC1.12 委员会的《概念公告第 1 号》提及"作出理性投资、信贷和类似决策的现有和潜在投资者与债权人及其他使用者"（第 34 段），并指出"主要投资者群体包括权益证券持有者和债务证券持有者"，以及"主要债权人群体包括提供信贷的商品和服务供应商、拥有求偿权的客户和雇员、贷款机构、贷款者个人以及债务证券持有者"（第 35 段）。与 1989 版《框架》重点强调风险资本提供者不同的是，《概念公告第 1 号》同时提及"寻求安全投资的各方以及愿意接受风险以获得高回报率的各方"（第 35 段）。但是，与 1989 版《框架》相类似，《概念公告第 1 号》指出，术语"投资者"和"债权人""还可包括证券分析师和顾问、经纪人、律师、监管机构以及向投资者和债权人提供建议或代表其利益的其他各方，或关注投资者和债权人的进展情况的其他各方"（第 35 段）。

BC1.13 第 1.3 段、第 1.5 段和第 1.10 段不同于 1989 版《框架》和《概念公告第 1 号》的原因有两个：一是为了消除 1989 版《框架》与《概念公告第 1 号》之间的差异；二是更为直接地着重关注那些对提供资源作出决策的使用者（但并不排除顾问）。相关原因在 BC1.15 段至 BC1.17 段和 BC1.21 段至 BC1.26 段中详述。

是否应识别主要使用者群体？（2010 版）

BC1.14 2006 年讨论文件和 2008 年征求意见稿建议识别财务报告的主要使用者群体。2008 年征求意见稿的某些反馈意见者指出，尚未向主体提供资源且不考虑向主体提供资源的其他使用者出于各种原因也会使用财务报告。尽管理事会可以理解此类使用者的信息需求，但得出结论认为，如果不界定主要使用者群体，《概念框架》将存在过于抽象或含糊的风险。

为何现有和潜在的投资者、贷款人及其他债权人被视为主要使用者？（2010 版）

BC1.15 2006 年讨论文件和 2008 年征求意见稿的某些反馈意见者建议，主要使用者群体应局限于主体的现有股东或控制主体的大股东。其他反馈意见者则认为，主要使用者应为现有股东和债权人，且财务报告应着重关注他们的需求。

BC1.16　理事会认为主要使用者群体应为报告主体的现有和潜在投资者、贷款人及其他债权人，原因如下：

（1）现有和潜在的投资者、贷款人及其他债权人最迫切地需要获得财务报告中的信息，并且他们大多数无法要求主体直接向其提供信息。

（2）理事会和委员会的职责使其必须着重关注资本市场的参与者的需求，资本市场的参与者不仅包括现有的投资者，还包括潜在的投资者及现有和潜在的贷款人和其他债权人。

（3）有些国家或地区的公司治理模型基于股东而界定，而有些国家或地区则基于所有类型的利益相关方，能够满足特定主要使用者需求的信息可能也会满足这两类公司治理模型所在国家或地区的使用者的需求。

BC1.17　某些反馈意见者认为，特定的主要使用者群体范围太过宽泛，这将导致财务报告包含过多的信息。但是，"过多"仅是一种主观判断。在制定与财务报告目标相符的财务报告要求时，理事会和委员会将借助有用财务信息的质量特征和成本限制来作出规范，以免提供过多信息。

主要使用者群体（2018版）

BC1.18　2013年讨论文件和2015年征求意见稿的反馈意见者对主要使用者群体描述的意见，与理事会在最初制定第1章时所考虑和利益相关方所表达的意见相似：

（1）部分反馈意见者认为主要使用者群体的界定过于狭窄，认为应扩大范围，将雇员、客户、供应商、监管机构及其他方纳入其中。

（2）相反，其他反馈意见者则认为，主要使用者群体的界定过于宽泛，认为理事会应将主要使用者界定为主体权益求偿权的持有者（或可界定为主体最后剩余权益求偿权的持有者）。他们认为权益求偿权的持有者的信息需求与其他资本提供者不同（且可能更广泛），因为他们面临更广泛的风险。

BC1.19　鉴于反馈意见者的意见，理事会重新考虑了对主要使用者群体的描述。但是，理事会得出结论认为，将主要使用者群体界定为报告主体的现有和潜在投资者、贷款人及其他债权人的理由仍然是成立的（参见BC1.16段）。此外，根据2018版《概念框架》第1.8段，关注主要使用者的共同信息需求并不妨碍报告主体为主要使用者的某一特定群体提供对他们来说最有用的额外信息。因此，理事会得出结论认为，无需修改对主要使用者群体的描述。

BC1.20　此外，理事会还决定，2018版《概念框架》无需将长期投资者作为具有特定信息需求的主要使用者的一个特定群体（参见BC0.40段至BC0.41段）。

是否应建立主要使用者层级？（2010版）

BC1.21　2008年征求意见稿的某些反馈意见者对主要使用者群体的构成表示支

持，并同时建议理事会建立主要使用者层级，因为投资者、贷款人及其他债权人具有不同的信息需求。但是，理事会认为，个别使用者的信息需求和愿望可能与在报告主体中拥有同类权益的其他使用者的信息需求和愿望有所不同，且可能发生冲突。通用目的财务报告意在为使用者提供通用信息，无法涵盖所有信息要求。理事会将致力于确定一个意在以符合成本效益的方式满足大多数使用者需求的信息集合。

主要使用者群体以外的其他使用者的信息需求（2010 版）

管理层的信息需求（2010 版）

BC1.22 某些利益相关方就通用目的财务报告与管理层需求之间的相互影响提出质疑。理事会指出，向主要使用者提供的某些信息有可能满足管理层的部分需求而非全部需求。但是，管理层有能力获得额外的财务信息，因此，通用目的财务报告无需明确地针对管理层。

监管机构的信息需求（2010 版）

BC1.23 某些利益相关方表示，维持资本市场的金融稳定（某个国家或地区的经济或金融体系的稳定）应作为财务报告的一项目标，并指出财务报告应着重关注负责维持金融稳定的监管机构和财政政策决策者的需求。

BC1.24 其他利益相关方反对制定有关维持金融稳定的目标。他们认为财务报表应尽可能不存偏见地反映报告主体的实际经济状况，而这样的列报不一定不符合金融稳定目标。通过反映实际经济状况，财务报表可能有助于使用者作出更明智的决策，从而为金融稳定提供支持（即便这并非财务报表的主要目标）。①

BC1.25 但是，金融稳定目标的拥护者对制定该目标所产生的结果另有想法。他们并未鼓励理事会要求主体提供可供监管机构和财政政策决策者使用的相关信息，而是建议理事会考虑新准则对全球经济和金融体系稳定性的影响，并至少不时地将关注重点从投资者、贷款人及其他债权人的信息需求更多地转向该目标。

BC1.26 理事会承认，投资者、贷款人及其他债权人的利益通常与监管机构的利益重叠。但是，将财务报告目标扩展至包括维持金融稳定有时可能会导致各类目标发生冲突，而理事会并不具备解决这些冲突的能力。例如，某些人士可能认为维持金融稳定的最好方式是要求报告主体不报告或推迟报告资产或负债的某些价值变动。几乎可以肯定的是，上述要求将导致投资者、贷款人及其他债权人无法获得其所需的信息。避免冲突的唯一方法是消除或淡化有关向投资者、贷款人及其他债权人提供信息的现行目标。理事会得出结论认为，消除这一目标将与其满足资本市场参与者信息需

---

① 金融危机顾问小组（FCAG）持有这一观点。金融危机顾问小组由约 20 名资深领导人组成，这些领导人不仅对国际金融市场具有广泛经验，而且十分关注财务报告信息的透明度。金融危机顾问小组于 2009 年成立，意在就金融危机及全球监管环境的潜在变化对准则制定工作的影响向理事会和委员会提供建议。

对决策的有用性（第1.2段至第1.4段）

对决策的有用性（2010版）

BC1.27 理事会和委员会先前的框架均侧重于将提供对经济决策有用的信息作为财务报告的基本目标。这些框架还指出，对经济决策有用的财务信息也有助于评估管理层如何履行其受托责任。

BC1.28 作为第1章基础的2006年讨论文件指出，财务报告的目标应侧重于有关资源配置的决策。尽管2006年讨论文件的大多数反馈意见者同意提供对决策有用的信息是合适的目标，但他们认为，投资者、贷款人及其他债权人还需要借助财务报告信息作出除资源配置决策以外的其他决策。例如，股东在针对留用或更换董事进行表决以及对管理层成员的薪酬进行表决时，需要获得相关信息作为决策的依据。股东的决策过程可能包括，通过与竞争对手主体的管理层在类似情况下的表现相比，来评价该主体管理层的绩效。

BC1.29 理事会同意上述反馈意见者的观点，并指出在大多数情况下，为资源配置决策而提供的信息也有助于对管理层的绩效进行评估。因此，在作为第1章基础的2008年征求意见稿中，理事会建议，财务报告的目标是提供关于报告主体的、有助于作为资本提供者的现有和潜在的投资者、贷款人及其他债权人作出相关决策的财务信息。同时，2008年征求意见稿还对财务报表在为主体资源受托责任的相关决策提供支持时所起的作用进行了说明。

BC1.30 2008年征求意见稿在两个单独的章节中分别就"财务报告的目标"及"决策有用性"进行了探讨。理事会将这两个章节合并纳入第1章，因为决策有用性是财务报告的目标。因此，这两个章节阐述了相同的观点并提供了过度详尽的细节。因合并这两个章节而删除了涉及评估现金流量前景的有用性和评估受托责任的有用性的两个单独部分。理事会并无意暗示评估未来现金流量前景或评估管理层受托责任的质量两者之间哪一个更重要。在作出关于向主体提供资源的决策时，该两者同等重要；而关于受托责任的信息对于那些能够就管理层的行动进行表决或施加影响的资源提供者而言也十分重要。

BC1.31 理事会决定不在本章内使用2010版《概念框架》中的"受托责任"这

---

① 另参见BC0.34段至BC0.43段获取理事会2018年关于准则对促进长期投资的作用的讨论，见2018版《概念框架》SP1.5段中关于《概念框架》对基金会和理事会任务的贡献的说明，即基金会和理事会以制定能够提高金融市场的透明度、公众受托责任和效率的准则为己任。

一术语，因为可能很难将其翻译成其他语言。取而代之的是，理事会对受托责任的含义进行了描述。相应地，2010 版《概念框架》中的财务报告的目标承认：使用者既对资源配置进行决策，也对管理层是否高效且有效地利用了所提供的资源进行决策。

受托责任（2018 版）

BC1.32　2010 年第 1 章发布后，某些利益相关方对其进行了解读，特别是针对删除"受托责任"这一术语，他们解读为这样做忽视了财务报表使用者需要信息来帮助他们评估管理层受托责任的事实。根据 BC1.30 段，理事会无意忽视这一需求。尽管如此，理事会还是得出结论认为，2010 版《概念框架》中的这一措辞不够清晰。

BC1.33　因此，在 2018 版《概念框架》中，理事会改进了措辞以澄清其初衷。理事会重新引入"受托责任"这一术语，并在描述通用目的财务报告的目标时，强调了提供评估管理层对主体经济资源的受托责任所需信息的重要性。这一强调有助于突出管理层对使用者向其托管的经济资源的责任。

BC1.34　为了更加突出重要性，2018 版《概念框架》认定评估管理层受托责任所需的信息可能部分地可与帮助使用者评估主体未来净现金流入前景所需的信息区分开来。必须同时具备这两类信息才能达到财务报告的总体目标，即提供对作出向主体提供资源相关决策（资源配置决策）有用的信息。

BC1.35　理事会还考虑了一些利益相关方建议的其他方法。如果采用这些方法，提供信息以帮助评估管理层的受托责任将被视作财务报告目标的一部分，或视作同样重要的另一目标。理事会否决了这些方法，因为：

（1）评估管理层的受托责任本身并不是目的；它是作出资源配置决策所需的输入值。例如，管理层受托责任的履行不尽如人意的结论可能会导致更换管理层这一决策，以增加未来回报。

（2）引入另一财务报告目标可能会引起混淆。

BC1.36　此外，在 2018 版《概念框架》中，理事会澄清了管理层的受托责任评估如何促成资源配置决策。理事会通过扩展对资源配置决策的解释来进行了澄清。2015 年征求意见稿的反馈意见指出，部分反馈意见者将资源配置决策解读为仅指有关买入、出售或持有的决策。因此，他们认为资源配置决策不包括持有投资时作出的决策，例如，重新任命或更换管理层的决策，评估管理层薪酬是否合理的决策，或批准管理层提出的业务战略的决策。

BC1.37　理事会并不打算将资源配置决策狭义地解读为仅指有关买入、出售或持有的决策。因此，2018 版《概念框架》明确指出，资源配置决策涉及关于以下内容的决策：

（1）买入、出售或持有权益和债务工具；

（2）提供或清偿贷款和其他形式的信贷；或者

(3) 对管理层①影响主体经济资源使用的行动行使表决权或施加影响。

财务报表使用者在作出任何上述决策时，需要评估未来净现金流入的金额、时间分布和不确定性以及管理层对主体经济资源的受托责任。

BC1.38 BC1.37（3）段提到了管理层影响主体经济资源使用的行动。此类行动的决策中的一个例子是对董事会成员表决的决策。该表决最终将影响董事会采取的影响该主体经济资源使用的后续行动。但是，财务报告并不意在提供信息，以帮助该信息的主要使用者行使针对管理层的其他行动的表决权，例如，针对不直接影响主体经济资源使用的公众政策发表声明。

BC1.39 2015年征求意见稿的某些反馈意见者表示，在某些情况下，评估管理层受托责任所需的信息与评估主体未来净现金流入前景所需的信息不同。特别是，这些反馈意见者主要关注计量基础的选择：

(1) 部分反馈意见者认为，在某些情况下，评估受托责任时历史成本计量比现行价值计量更有用，因为他们认为历史成本计量更易于验证，并更易于与管理层实际进行的交易直接联系起来；以及

(2) 相反，其他反馈意见则认为，在某些情况下，现行价值计量可能对评估受托责任更有用，因为他们认为此类计量可以提供相较于当前其他可选行动方案，管理层的业绩如何的有关信息。

BC1.40 在2018版《概念框架》对财务报告目标的描述中强调受托责任的重要性时，理事会并无意暗示对任何特定计量基础的偏好。在2018版《概念框架》"第6章——计量"中讨论了选择计量基础时需要考虑的因素。

术语"受托责任"（2018版）

BC1.41 修订后的第1章重新引入了"受托责任"这一术语，并阐释对管理层的受托责任的评估涉及评估主体管理层和治理层履行其使用该主体经济资源的责任的效率和效果（参见第1.4段和第1.22段至第1.23段）。该评估使财务报表的使用者能够确保管理层就其行为负责。理事会使用的术语"受托责任"与对该术语的一般理解是一致的，即，认真负责地管理其受托管理的某物。②对第1章的这些改进提供了更明晰的阐述，因而理事会得出结论认为，改进的益处要大于2010版《概念框架》中提出的翻译困难。

不同类型主体的财务报告目标（2010版）

BC1.42 理事会考虑了通用目的财务报告的目标是否应视主体的类型而有所不同。可能需加以区分的不同类型主体包括：

(1) 小型主体与大型主体；

---

① "管理层"是指主体的管理层和治理层［参见2018版《概念框架》第1.4（2）段］。

② 韦氏在线词典提供了对受托责任的定义（https://www.merriam-webster.com/dictionary/stewardship）。

（2）有上市（公开交易的）债务或权益金融工具的主体，与没有此类金融工具的主体；以及

（3）股权集中的主体与股权分散的主体。

BC1.43 财务报告的外部使用者拥有类似的目标（无论其投资于何种类型的主体）。因此，理事会得出结论认为，通用目的财务报告的目标对所有主体而言均是相同的。但是，成本限制及不同主体间业务活动的差异有时可能会导致理事会允许或要求不同类型的主体以不同的方式进行报告。

关于报告主体的经济资源、对主体的求偿权以及经济资源与求偿权变动的信息（第1.12段至第1.21段）

财务业绩信息的重要性（2010版）

BC1.44 长期以来，许多利益相关方一直认为通过综合收益及其组成部分反映的报告主体的财务业绩是最重要的信息。[①]《概念公告第1号》（第43段）指出：

财务报告主要通过计量综合收益及其组成部分来反映关于企业业绩的信息。投资者、债权人及关注企业净现金流入前景评估的其他各方，对上述信息尤为感兴趣。

与此相反，1989版《框架》认为报告主体的财务状况信息与财务业绩信息同样重要。

BC1.45 为了有助于作出决策，财务报告必须提供有关报告主体的经济资源、求偿权以及经济资源与求偿权在某个期间内的变动的信息。如果报告主体不对其经济资源和求偿权进行识别和计量，则无法提供有关其财务业绩（由综合收益、损益或其他类似的项目体现）的合理完整的信息。因此，理事会得出结论认为，将某一类信息指定为财务报告的关注重点是不恰当的。

BC1.46 在探讨主体的财务状况时，2008年征求意见稿提及"经济资源和对经济资源的求偿权"。本章采用"主体的经济资源和对报告主体的求偿权"的表述（参见第1.12段）。作出该修订的原因是，在许多情况下，对主体的求偿权并非是针对特定资源的索偿。此外，许多求偿权将通过未来净现金流入所形成的资源而得到履行。因此，尽管所有求偿权均为针对主体提出的索偿，但并非所有求偿权均针对主体的现有资源。

财务状况与偿债能力（2010版）

BC1.47 某些利益相关方认为，财务状况表的主要目的应是提供有助于评估报

[①]《概念公告第1号》提及"盈余及其组成部分"。但是，委员会发布的《概念公告第6号——财务报表要素》以术语"综合收益"取代了术语"盈余"。而"盈余"这一术语被作为综合收益的组成部分保留下来。

国际财务报告准则

告主体偿债能力的信息。问题并不在于财务报告中的信息是否应当有助于评估偿债能力，显而易见，答案是肯定的。投资者、贷款人及其他债权人均十分关注评估偿债能力，而通用目的财务报告的目标即提供有助于上述各方作出决策的信息。

BC1.48 但是，某些利益相关方认为，财务状况表应针对贷款人、其他债权人及监管机构的信息需求编制，并可能因此对投资者及其他使用者造成损害。这样做将有悖于财务报告应满足主要使用者的共同信息需求这一目标。因此，理事会否决了关于财务状况表（或其他特定财务报表）应针对某些特定使用者的需求进行编制的观点。

起始段落

第 2 章——有用财务信息的质量特征

引言	**BC2.1**
2018 年修订	**BC2.2**
财务报告的目标和有用财务信息的质量特征（2010 版）	**BC2.5**
基本质量特征和提升性质量特征（2010 版）	**BC2.9**
基本质量特征	**BC2.12**
相关性	BC2.12
预测价值和证实价值（2010 版）	BC2.15
预测价值与相关统计术语之间的差异（2010 版）	BC2.17
重要性（2010 版）	BC2.18
重要性（2018 版）	BC2.20
如实反映	BC2.21
术语"可靠性"被取代（2010 版）	BC2.22
术语"如实反映"被保留（2018 版）	BC2.28
实质重于形式（2010 版）	BC2.32
实质重于形式（2018 版）	BC2.33
审慎性和中立性（2010 版）	BC2.34
审慎性（2018 版）	BC2.37
计量的不确定性（2018 版）	BC2.46
如实反映能否通过实证方式衡量？（2010 版）	BC2.50
应用基本质量特征（2018 版）	BC2.52
提升性质量特征	**BC2.58**
可比性（2010 版）	BC2.58
可验证性（2010 版）	BC2.60
及时性（2010 版）	BC2.63
可理解性（2010 版）	BC2.66
未包含的质量特征（2010 版）	**BC2.70**
有用财务报告的成本限制（2010 版）	**BC2.73**

> *2018 年，理事会对《概念框架》第 2 章进行了有限修订，在本章的原结论基础中新增了对理事会在制定这些修订时所考虑因素的描述。理事会在结论基础的各部分标题后增加了年份，以表明各部分的制定年份。除了新增和更新交叉索引以及进行微小但必要的编辑修改之外，反映理事会 2010 年编制本章时所考虑因素的结论基础部分在 2018 年未予更新。*

引言

BC2.1 本章节的第一版由理事会与委员会联合制定，并于 2010 年发布在 2010 版《概念框架》第 3 章（参见 BC0.3 段）。因此，本结论基础引用了委员会的部分文献。

2018 年修订

BC2.2 理事会在 2012 年重启《概念框架》项目时，并未从根本上重新考虑关于有用财务信息的质量特征这一章节（参见 BC0.11 段）。尽管 2013 年讨论文件的部分反馈意见者同意这种方法，但许多人认为理事会应重新考虑本章节的一个或多个方面。根据这些意见，理事会考虑是否对以下方面进行修改：

（1）重要性（参见 BC2.20 段）；

（2）可靠性和计量不确定性（参见 BC2.28 段至 BC2.31 段和 BC2.46 段至 BC2.49 段）；

（3）实质重于形式（参见 BC2.33 段）；

（4）审慎性（参见 BC2.37 段至 BC2.45 段）；以及

（5）应用基本质量特征（参见 BC2.52 段至 BC2.57 段）。

BC2.3 此外，理事会将关于有用财务信息的质量特征这一章节号改为第 2 章。理事会还对第 2 章进行了部分编辑修订，主要是为了更准确地使用术语"如实反映"，即讨论财务信息是否如实反映其意在反映的内容（例如，经济现象），而非讨论财务信息本身是否被如实反映。

BC2.4 对于理事会 2018 年作出的有限修改，委员会未相应对《概念公告第 8 号——财务报告概念框架》的第 3 章"有用财务信息的质量特征"进行任何修改。理事会得出结论认为，其对第 2 章进行改进所取得的价值要高于与委员会版本在这些方面存在不一致所带来的不利影响。

财务报告的目标和有用财务信息的质量特征（2010 版）

BC2.5 财务报告的各个方面（包括确认、终止确认、计量、分类、列示和披露）均存在多种替代方法。在制定准则时，理事会将选择一种最有助于实现财务报告目标的方法。如果不存在适用的准则或在采用特定准则的过程中需要运用判断或进行选择，财务信息编制者也必须选择某种方法来实现财务报告的目标。

BC2.6 第 1 章规定，通用目的财务报告的目标是提供关于报告主体的、有助于现有和潜在投资者、贷款人及其他债权人作出有关向主体提供资源的决策的财务信息。本《概念框架》所关注的决策者是现有和潜在投资者、贷款人及其他债权人。

BC2.7 该目标本身就需要运用大量判断，且基本上未就如何作出上述判断提供任何指引。第 2 章描述了为应用该目标而进行判断的第一个步骤，该步骤识别及描述了为实现财务报告的目标，财务信息应当具备的质量特征。本章也对成本（对财务报告的普遍限制）进行了探讨。

BC2.8 后续章节使用质量特征来指导如何作出关于确认、计量和财务报告的其他方面的选择。

基本质量特征和提升性质量特征（2010 版）（第 2.4 段）

BC2.9 第 2 章将最关键的基本质量特征与提升性质量特征加以区分，其中，提升性质量特征不太关键但最好能具备。2006 年讨论文件并未明确区分这两类质量特征。由于 2006 年讨论文件的反馈意见者对质量特征之间的相互关系感到困惑，因此，理事会随后作出上述区分。

BC2.10 2008 年征求意见稿的某些反馈意见者指出，所有质量特征均应被视为具有同等重要性，并且基本质量特征与提升性质量特征之间的区分较为武断。其他反馈意见者认为，最重要的质量特征因具体情况而异，因此区分质量特征是不恰当的。

BC2.11 理事会不认为该区分是武断的。不具备相关性和如实反映这两个基本质量特征的财务信息是无用的。并且，即使提高此类财务信息的可比性、可验证性、及时性和可理解性，也无法使其变得有用。但是，具有相关性和能够如实反映其意在反映的内容的财务信息，即使不具备任何提升性质量特征也仍然是有用的。

基本质量特征（第2.5段至第2.22段）

相关性（第2.6段至第2.11段）

BC2.12 显然，仅当财务信息能够导致作出不同决策时，它对决策才是有用的。《概念框架》使用术语"相关性"描述这一能力。相关性是有用财务信息的基本质量特征。

BC2.13 《概念框架》中相关性的定义与委员会《概念公告第2号——会计信息的质量特征》中相关性的定义一致。1989版《框架》中相关性的定义为，仅当信息实际上造成使用者作出不同决策时，该信息才是相关的。但是，使用者考虑很多来源的各种信息，即使在相关事实发生之后，有关特定经济现象的信息对决策的影响程度即使并非完全无法确定，也是很难确定的。

BC2.14 与之相反，信息是否能够导致作出不同的决策（2010版《概念框架》所定义的相关性）是可以确定的。发布征求意见稿和其他应循程序文件的主要目的之一，是就提议的准则所要求的信息是否能够影响使用者的决策来征求使用者的意见。理事会也通过与使用者召开会议就提议的准则、潜在的议程决定、采用近期实施的准则对报告信息的影响以及其他事项进行讨论来评估相关性。

预测价值和证实价值（2010版）（第2.7段至第2.10段）

BC2.15 投资者、贷款人及其他债权人所作的许多决策均是以有关权益投资、贷款及其他债务工具回报的金额及时间分布所隐含的或明确的预测为基础。因此，仅当信息有助于使用者作出新预测、证实或更正先前的预测或两者兼有（即，符合预测价值和证实价值的定义）时，该信息才能够对其中一项决策产生影响。

BC2.16 1989版《框架》将预测价值和证实价值视为相关性的组成部分，而《概念公告第2号》则提及预测价值和反馈价值。理事会得出结论认为，证实价值和反馈价值意在表述相同的含义。理事会和委员会同意双方将使用相同的术语（证实价值）以避免产生这两个概念框架意图不同的表象。

预测价值与相关统计术语之间的差异（2010版）

BC2.17 《概念框架》所使用的预测价值与统计上使用的可预测性和持续性不同。如果信息能够用于对过去或当前事件的最终结果作出预测，则其具有预测价值。与之相反，统计学家使用可预测性指代可预测出某一数列中的下一个数字的准确性，并使用持续性指代某一数列持续以过往的变动方式变动的趋势。

重要性（2010 版）（第 2.11 段）

BC2.18 《概念公告第 2 号》和 1989 版《框架》对重要性作出了类似的讨论和定义。《概念公告第 2 号》将重要性描述为对财务报告的一种限制，仅能与质量特征（特别是相关性和如实反映）一并考虑。另一方面，1989 版《框架》将重要性作为相关性的一个方面来讨论，且并未指出重要性具有与其他质量特征相联系的作用。

BC2.19 2006 年讨论文件和 2008 年征求意见稿指出，重要性是财务报告中的一项普遍限制，因为它与所有的质量特征相关。但是，2008 年征求意见稿的部分反馈意见者认为，尽管重要性具有普遍性，但其并非是对报告主体报告信息能力的限制，而是相关性的一个方面，因为不重要的信息并不影响使用者的决策。此外，准则制定机构在制定准则时并不考虑重要性，因为重要性是主体特定的考虑因素。理事会和委员会同意这些观点，并得出结论认为，重要性是适用于个别主体层面相关性的一个方面。

重要性（2018 版）

BC2.20 理事会在修订 2018 版《概念框架》时得出结论认为，2010 版《概念框架》已清楚描述了重要性概念。因此，根据《概念框架》第 1.5 段，理事会并未修改对重要性的描述，仅澄清描述中提及的使用者为通用目的财务报告的主要使用者。该澄清强调，关于重要性的决策意在反映主要使用者的需求，而非任何其他使用者群体的需求。

如实反映（第 2.12 段至第 2.19 段）

BC2.21 2010 版《概念框架》第 3 章对如实反映的讨论与先前框架的讨论存在两个重大差异。第一，使用了术语"如实反映"而非"可靠性"。第二，《概念公告第 2 号》或 1989 版《框架》中作为可靠性不同方面的实质重于形式、审慎性（稳健性）和可验证性不属于 2010 版《概念框架》中如实反映所考虑的方面。尽管因 BC2.32 段和 BC2.34 段阐述的原因，2010 版《概念框架》中删除了实质重于形式和审慎性，但在 2018 版《概念框架》中重新引入了这两个概念，并进行了澄清。自 2010 版开始，将可验证性描述为提升性质量特征而非基本质量特征的一部分（参见第 2.30 段至第 2.32 段）。

术语"可靠性"被取代（2010 版）

BC2.22 《概念公告第 2 号》和 1989 版《框架》使用术语"可靠性"来描述如今被称为"如实反映"的内容。

BC2.23 《概念公告第 2 号》将如实反映、可验证性及中立性列为可靠性的内容，并将完整性作为如实反映的一部分进行讨论。

BC2.24 1989 版《框架》指出：当信息不存在重大差错及偏见，且如实反映了其意在反映或被合理预期其反映的情况而能够被使用者所依赖时，信息就具备了可靠性。

1989 版《框架》还讨论了如实反映的不同方面，即实质重于形式、中立性、审慎性和完整性。

BC2.25 遗憾的是，上述两个框架均未明确传达可靠性的含义。反馈意见者对众多提议准则的反馈意见表明，缺乏对术语"可靠性"的共识。某些意见着重于可验证性或不存在重大差错而实质上未实现如实反映。其他意见则更着重于如实反映，可能与中立性相结合。某些意见显然认为可靠性主要是指精确度。

BC2.26 由于理事会未能成功解释可靠性在上述情况下意在表达的含义，理事会寻求使用另一术语来更清晰地传达其意在表述的含义。术语"如实反映"（即，在财务报告中如实反映经济现象）应运而生。该术语包含了原框架下作为可靠性不同方面的主要特征。

BC2.27 2006 年讨论文件和 2008 年征求意见稿的许多反馈意见者反对理事会以"如实反映"取代"可靠性"的初步决定。某些反馈意见者认为，理事会应当更好地解释可靠性的含义，而非取代该术语。但是，许多表达该意见的反馈意见者所提出的可靠性含义与理事会的初衷不同。特别是，许多反馈意见者对可靠性的描述更接近理事会提出的可验证性概念而非可靠性概念。这些意见使理事会坚定了其以"如实反映"取代"可靠性"的决定。

术语"如实反映"被保留（2018 版）

BC2.28 理事会在制定 2018 版《概念框架》的过程中，考虑是否恢复"可靠性"这一术语，将其作为"如实反映"质量特征的一个标签。利益相关方对此的观点如下：

（1）与"如实反映"相比，术语"可靠性"更加清晰、更易理解。

（2）2010 版《概念框架》隐含着这样的结论，如果主体提供了足够多的解释性信息，则所有经济现象都可以得到如实反映。这样解读如实反映可能导致允许主体确认不能可靠计量的项目。因此，在识别可纳入财务报表的信息类型时，如实反映不能用作有效的筛选条件。

（3）1989 版《框架》承认在相关性和可靠性间存在权衡。相关性越高则可靠性越低，反之，可靠性越高则相关性越低。某些反馈意见者认为 2010 版《概念框架》未对两者进行权衡（参见 BC2.52 段至 BC2.57 段）。

（4）2018 版《概念框架》的一个关键概念是：财务报表应具备可信度，即财务报表使用者需确信他们可信赖财务报表如实反映了其意在反映的内容。仅将此概念视为提升性定性特征（可验证性，参见 BC2.60 段至 BC2.62 段）无法体现其重要性。

BC2.29 理事会发现可靠性在准则中有如下两种含义：

（1）表示计量不确定性的可容忍程度。此含义在 1989 版《框架》的确认标准中得到反映（在 2010 年修订 1989 版《框架》时未对此术语进行复核）：仅在很可能产生经济利益流入或流出，且相应的成本或价值能够可靠计量的情况下，才对满足要素定义的项目进行确认。

（2）表示有用财务信息的质量特征。该质量特征之前称为"可靠性"，现称为"如实反映"。准则中很少采用此含义。

BC2.30 将术语"可靠性"改为"如实反映"的目的在于，避免 BC2.29 段中两种"可靠性"含义的混淆。从 2013 年讨论文件和 2015 年征求意见稿收到的反馈意见中似乎发现，许多反馈意见者仍认为"可靠性"代表计量的不确定性可容忍程度，而非 1989 版《框架》中所述的质量特征。因此，理事会保留了术语"如实反映"，作为之前被称作"可靠性"的质量特征的标签。然而，2010 版《概念框架》未充分讨论计量的不确定性在财务报告中的作用，为消除这一顾虑，理事会在 2018 版《概念框架》中讨论了计量的不确定性如何影响财务信息的有用性（参见第 2.19 段、第 2.22 段和 BC2.46 段至 BC2.49 段）。此外，2018 版《概念框架》还讨论了计量的不确定性在作出有关确认和计量决策时的作用（参见第 5.19 段至第 5.23 段和第 6.60 段）。

BC2.31 在 2018 年有关审慎性和实质重于形式的讨论进行修订后（参见 BC2.37 段至 BC2.45 段和 BC2.33 段），1989 版《框架》对可靠性质量特征的描述和 2018 版《概念框架》对如实反映质量特征的描述基本一致。表 2.1 对两者进行了对比。

表 2.1 1989 版《框架》中的可靠性和 2018 版《概念框架》中的如实反映

1989 版《框架》可靠性	2018 版《概念框架》如实反映
如实反映了其意在反映的情况而能够被使用者所依赖	如实反映其意在反映的经济现象（参见第 2.12 段）
完整性	完整性（参见第 2.14 段）
中立性	中立性（参见第 2.15 段）
无重大差错或偏见	无差错，且具中立性（参见第 2.18 段和第 2.15 段）
实质重于形式	实质重于形式（参见第 2.12 段）
审慎性	审慎性（参见第 2.16 段至 2.17 段）

实质重于形式（2010 版）（第 2.12 段）

BC2.32 2010 版《概念框架》未将实质重于形式作为如实反映的一个单独组成部分，因为理事会认为此举多余。如实反映是指财务信息反映经济现象的实质而非仅反映其法律形式。反映相关经济现象的法律形式而非其经济实质并不构成如实反映。

实质重于形式（2018 版）

BC2.33 理事会在制定 2018 版《概念框架》的过程中，注意到部分利益相关方曾推测，理事会在 2010 版《概念框架》中删除了对实质重于形式的引用，说明理事会不再要求描述经济现象的本质。而理事会事实上并无此意。因此，为避免进一步的误解，并突出理事会的本意，理事会在 2018 版《概念框架》第 2.12 段中重新明确了如实反映经济现象本质的必要性。理事会在 2018 版《概念框架》第 4.59 段至第 4.62 段进一步解释了如何如实反映合同权利和合同义务的实质。

审慎性和中立性（2010 版）（第 2.15 段）

BC2.34 2010 版《概念框架》第 2 章未将审慎性或保守主义作为如实反映的一个方面，因为理事会得出结论认为，纳入其中任一项均将与中立性不一致。但 2006 年讨论文件和 2008 年征求意见稿的部分反馈意见者不同意该观点。他们认为，框架应包括保守主义或审慎性或者同时包括两者。他们认为偏见不应总被认为是不可取的，尤其是在偏见能产生对某些使用者更具有相关性的信息的情况下。

BC2.35 为减少某些被认为过度乐观的管理层估计的影响，有意反映对资产、负债、收益或权益的保守估计的做法有时是可取的。但是，即使 1989 版《框架》禁止进行蓄意错报，劝谏保持审慎性仍可能会导致偏见。在某一期间内低估资产或高估负债经常导致高估后续期间的财务业绩。这样的结果不能被称为具有审慎性或中立性。

BC2.36 2008 年征求意见稿的其他反馈意见者认为中立性是不可能实现的。他们认为，具有相关性的信息必然带有目的，而有目的的信息并不中立。换言之，因为财务报告是影响决策的工具，因此无法保持中立。显然，所报告的财务信息预期将对该信息使用者的行为产生影响，而仅凭许多使用者基于所报告的信息采取类似行动这一事实，并不能说明其缺乏中立性。理事会并不试图鼓励或预测使用者采取的具体行动。如果财务信息带有偏见，鼓励使用者采取或避免预先决定的行动，则该信息并不中立。

审慎性（2018 版）（第 2.16 段至第 2.17 段）

BC2.37 理事会在制定 2018 版《概念框架》的过程中，注意到不同利益相关方在使用"审慎性"时指代的内容各有不同。主要包括以下方面：

（1）部分利益相关方在使用审慎性时，所指代的是在不确定性条件下进行判断时的谨慎性，但并非在作出关于收益或资产的判断时比作出关于费用或负债判断时更加谨慎（"谨慎的审慎性"——参见 BC2.39 段至 BC2.40 段）。

（2）其他利益相关方在使用审慎性时，所指代的是保持系统不对称性——费用相比收益确认阶段更早（"不对称审慎性"——参见 BC2.41 段至 BC2.45 段）。利益相关方就如何实现系统不对称性以及实现程度表达了一系列看法。例如，一些利益相关方主张使用具有如下要求的审慎性概念：

①支持收益或资产确认的证据需比支持费用或负债确认的证据更具说服力；或者

②需选择损失确认阶段早于利得确认阶段的计量基础。

BC2.38 对审慎性的理解与对术语"中立性"的理解挂钩。理事会识别了中立性的如下两个方面：

（1）会计政策应用的中立性——以中立（即不带偏见）的方式应用所选择的会计政策（参见 BC2.39 段）；以及

（2）会计政策选择的中立性——为了提供具有相关性的信息以如实反映其意在反映的内容而对会计政策进行选择（参见 BC2.44 段）。如实反映要求所描述的内容具有中立性。

如果财务信息不具有倾向性，并未通过权衡轻重、片面强调、故意弱化或其他操纵方式来提高使用者乐于或不乐于接受财务信息的可能性，则该财务信息具有中立性。①

BC2.39 一些利益相关方认为保持审慎性（被定义为在不确定性条件下进行判断时的谨慎性）有助于在应用会计政策时保持中立性，理事会对此表示认同。因此，"谨慎的审慎性"［参见 BC2.37（1）段］有助于实现对资产、负债、权益、收益和费用的如实反映。明确这一点预计将：

（1）有助于编制者、审计师和监管机构纠正管理层因乐观情绪而产生的自然偏见，例如，该含义强调在估计计量过程中选择不可直接观察的输入值时必须保持谨慎；以及

（2）有助于理事会制定严格的准则，降低应用报告主体会计政策时产生管理层偏见的风险。

BC2.40 理事会发现，2010 版《概念框架》删除术语"审慎性"令人困惑，且有可能加剧在使用此术语时的不同理解。使用者仍继续使用此术语，但并未明确此术语的含义。此外，一些利益相关方认为，由于删除术语"审慎性"，按照国际财务报告准则所编制的财务信息不具备中立性，且实际上是不审慎的。因此理事会得出结论认为，通过重新引入此术语和明确解释"审慎性"的含义（即在两方面均应保持谨慎性以使资产和负债既不被高估也不被低估）可以减少困惑。因此，理事会在 2018 版《概念框架》中重新引入了术语"审慎性"，并明确审慎性的定义为在不确定性条件下进行判断时运用谨慎。

BC2.41 2015 年征求意见稿的某些反馈意见者建议理事会进一步将"不对称审慎性"［参见 BC2.37（2）段］作为有用财务信息的必要质量特征，原因如下：

（1）不对称审慎性可反映投资者对下行风险的关注度大于对上行潜力的关注度这一观点；

（2）许多准则中都包含不对称审慎性的相关内容，《概念框架》应承认这一事实，以便在制定准则时，一致应用不对称审慎性；

（3）通过限制对股东的分配，不对称审慎性可将当前股东取得的收益会损害未来股东利益的风险降到最低；以及

---

① 参见 2018 版《概念框架》第 2.15 段。

(4) 通过限制管理层薪酬，不对称审慎性可降低管理层的乐观程度，促进长期增长。

BC2.42 理事会未在 2018 版《概念框架》中纳入不对称审慎性，因为对资产和负债的会计处理不对称或对收益和费用的会计处理不对称的系统性要求，有时可能会与财务信息应具备相关性并如实反映的需求发生冲突。理事会指出，根据其确切性质，在所有情况下应用不对称审慎性的要求可能会：

(1) 禁止确认所有未实现利得。在某些情况下，例如，在计量许多金融工具时，确认未实现利得对向财务报告使用者提供具有相关性的信息是必须的。

(2) 禁止确认所有无可观察市场价格的未实现利得。在某些情况下，以现行价值计量一项资产或负债（可能需要确认未实现利得）可向财务报告使用者提供具有相关性的信息，即使无法通过观察活跃市场价格直接确定该现行价值。

(3) 允许主体使用针对该资产选择的计量基础以低于无偏见估计的金额计量资产或以高于无偏见估计的金额计量负债。这种方法无法产生具有相关性的信息且无法如实反映。

BC2.43 此外，理事会还指出，财务报告中的信息可能会被用作确定向股东的分配和管理层薪酬的输入值，但这些信息仅是考虑的因素之一［参见 BC0.41（4）段］。

BC2.44 然而，尽管否决了系统性不对称的要求，理事会仍得出结论认为，并非所有不对称性均与中立性相悖。选择中立的会计政策意味着不应把目标设定为提高使用者乐于或不乐于接受财务信息的可能性。选择中立会计政策：

(1) 不要求主体在财务状况表中确认主体的价值。2018 版《概念框架》第 1.7 段指出，通用目的财务报告并非意在反映一个报告主体的价值。

(2) 不要求确认所有资产和负债。2018 版《概念框架》"第 5 章——确认和终止确认"讨论了资产和负债的确认标准。

(3) 不要求以现行价值计量所有资产和负债。2018 版《概念框架》"第 6 章——计量"讨论了选择计量基础时需要考虑的因素。考虑这些因素不会导致作出这样的要求。

(4) 不禁止对以历史成本计量的资产进行减值测试。以历史成本计量（包括减值测试）符合中立性，前提是该计量基础的选择不存在偏见。不存在偏见是指选择计量基础时不会通过权衡轻重、片面强调、故意弱化或其他方式操纵信息，以提高使用者乐于或不乐于接受财务信息的可能性。

BC2.45 因此，2018 版《概念框架》承认准则可能包含不对称要求。这是理事会决定要求主体提供如实反映其意在反映内容的最具有相关性的信息的结果，而非采用不对称审慎性的结果。早于 2018 版《概念框架》制定的几项准则都反映了此类决策。例如，《国际会计准则第 37 号——准备、或有负债和或有资产》针对或有负债和或有资产设定的确认条件不同。

计量的不确定性（2018 版）（第 2.19 段）

BC2.46 根据 BC2.28（2）段，2013 年讨论文件的一些反馈意见者担心在确定纳入财务报表的信息类型时，如实反映这一质量特征并不能成为一个有效的筛选条件。他们认为 2010 版《概念框架》没有阐明高度的计量不确定性会导致财务信息的有用性降低。

BC2.47 2010 版《概念框架》第 QC16 段已经阐明，如果估计的不确定性太大，则可能无法提供有用信息：

如实反映本身不一定能够产生有用的信息。例如，一个报告主体可能通过政府补助获得不动产、厂场和设备。显然，报告该主体以零成本取得资产能够如实反映其成本，但该信息可能并非十分有用。另一个更具体的例子是为反映资产价值的减值而对资产账面价值的减记金额进行估计。如果报告主体恰当地运用了适当的流程，恰当地描述了该估计值并对显著影响该估计值的不确定性作了说明，则该估计值即为如实反映。然而，如果该估计值的不确定性太大，它就不会特别有用。换言之，资产得到如实反映的相关性是值得质疑的。如果不存在其他更能如实反映的方式，则该估计值可能提供了最佳的可用信息。

BC2.48 尽管如此，估计的不确定性水平及其有用性之间的联系显然不是很明显，许多 2010 版《概念框架》的读者似乎忽略了这一点。因此，2015 年征求意见稿讨论了计量的不确定性如何影响财务信息的相关性。2015 年征求意见稿的反馈意见者对计量的不确定性的讨论表示欢迎。然而，某些反馈意见者认为，计量的不确定性是如实反映这一基本质量特征的一个方面，而不是相关性的一个方面。理事会同意这些观点并且认为：

（1）计量的不确定性使信息不易验证。正如 2018 版《概念框架》第 2.30 段所解释的那样，可验证性能帮助使用者确信有关信息如实反映了其意在反映的经济现象。计量的不确定性的水平越高，就越无法向使用者保证特定估计可以如实反映经济现象。因此，计量的不确定性会影响经济现象是否可被如实反映。

（2）2018 版《概念框架》第 2.20 段至第 2.21 段说明了应用基本质量特征的最高效且最有效的流程。根据该说明，相关性这一质量特征是考虑哪些特定的信息对使用者而言能称之为是有用的。另一方面，如实反映这一质量特征是考虑这些信息是否能提供如实的反映。因此，与估计流程相关的计量的不确定性不会影响相关性，但是会影响该计量是否能以实现如实反映的方式进行。

（3）即使信息受到高度计量的不确定性的影响，也可能是相关的。例如，如果相关的现象存在重大风险和不确定性，那么采用高度不确定的计量可能是提供关于该现象具有相关性信息的唯一方式。

BC2.49 因此，2018 版《概念框架》将计量的不确定性描述为影响是否可能提供如实反映的因素。此外，理事会还指出，在对如实反映的讨论中解决计量的不确定性问题更加符合两个基本质量特征（相关性和如实反映）之间权衡的理念（参见第

2.22 段和 BC 2.52 段至 BC2.56 段）。

如实反映能否通过实证方式衡量？（2010 版）

BC2.50 实证会计的研究者通过研究主体权益或债务工具市价变动的相关性，已经累积了相当多的证据来支持相关且如实反映的财务信息。但是，此类研究并未提供通过实证方式将如实反映和相关性分开衡量的技术方法。

BC2.51 针对提供有关财务指标如何如实反映的统计信息，先前两个框架讨论了其可取性。这并非无前例可循。其他统计信息有时在财务报告中得以反映。例如，某些主体披露衍生金融工具的风险价值及类似头寸。理事会预计，在某些情况下，仍有必要对财务报告运用统计概念。遗憾的是，理事会和委员会尚未找到量化财务报告中如实反映程度的方法。

应用基本质量特征（2018 版）（第2.20 段至第2.22 段）

BC2.52 在制定 2018 版《概念框架》时，理事会讨论了是否需要在应用基本质量特征时进行权衡。

BC2.53 1989 版《框架》包含在相关性和可靠性（两者均被视为有用财务信息的质量特征）之间进行权衡的理念。2010 版《概念框架》虽未提到这种权衡，但却提到信息在同时具备相关性和如实反映两方面的特征时才是有用信息。2010 版《概念框架》还进一步指出，如实反映不相关现象和未如实反映相关现象均无法帮助使用者作出有用的决策。2010 版《概念框架》第 QC16 段中对估计不确定性的讨论①隐含地指出，可能需要在相关性和如实反映之间作出权衡（参见 BC2.47 段）。

BC2.54 2013 年讨论文件的某些反馈意见者对 2010 版《概念框架》缺少对质量特征之间权衡的理念展开讨论表示担忧。他们的主要担忧似乎与信息的相关性和该信息的计量不确定性的可容忍水平之间的关系有关。

BC2.55 根据 2018 版《概念框架》BC2.48 段至 BC2.49 段，理事会将计量的不确定性描述为可能影响是否可能提供如实反映的因素。此外，理事会在第 2.22 段中澄清，按照第 2.20 段至第 2.21 段的流程，可能需要在相关性和如实反映之间进行权衡。需要进行这种权衡的一种情况是，具有高度的计量不确定性导致对某估计值能否充分如实反映经济现象存疑。第 2.22 段的内容以 2010 版《概念框架》第 QC16 段对计量的不确定性的讨论（参见 BC2.47 段）为基础。

BC2.56 理事会得出结论认为，明确承认相关性和计量不确定性之间的权衡会有助于解释为什么在某些情况下具有高度计量不确定性的估计值可能会提供有用的信息，例如，唯一具有相关性的信息是一个高度不确定的估计值的情况。

BC2.57 此外，理事会更新了描述基本质量特征应用过程时使用的术语。为了

---

① 结合 2010 版《概念框架》第 QC16 段，估计不确定性是指 2018 版《概念框架》中的计量不确定性。

与2018版《概念框架》第2.6段中的相关性描述保持一致,并避免与经济资源定义中使用的"有可能"一词混淆(参见BC4.8段至BC4.9段),理事会在第2.21段中将"有可能"一词替换为"能够"。

提升性质量特征

可比性(2010版)(第2.24段至第2.29段)

BC2.58 1989版《框架》和《概念公告第2号》均将可比性作为一个重要概念,但这两个框架对其重要程度持不同意见。1989版《框架》指出,可比性与相关性和如实反映同等重要。① 而《概念公告第2号》将可比性描述为两项或以上信息之间关系的质量,可比性虽然重要,但其重要程度次于相关性和如实反映。

BC2.59 如果具有相关性且如实反映的信息能够易于与其他主体报告的类似信息或与同一主体在其他期间报告的类似信息相比较,则该信息是最有用的。需要制定准则的最重要原因之一是提高所报告财务信息的可比性。但是,相关且如实反映其意在反映的内容的信息即使不易于比较却仍然有用。然而,可比信息若不相关则是无用信息,而且若未能如实反映其意在反映的内容则会产生误导。因此,将可比性作为提升性质量特征而非基本质量特征。

可验证性(2010版)(第2.30段至第2.32段)

BC2.60 使用可验证的信息能够增强使用者的信心。缺乏可验证性并不一定导致信息无用,但是使用者可能会因该信息未能如实反映其意在反映的内容的风险更高而更为谨慎。

BC2.61 1989版《框架》并未明确将可验证性作为可靠性的一个方面,但是《概念公告第2号》将可验证性作为可靠性的一个方面。但是,由于1989版《框架》中可靠性的定义包含"能被使用者所信赖"的表述,这意味着使用者需要就信息获取保证,因此,这两个框架的差异可能并不像表面上那样大。

BC2.62 2006年讨论文件指出,所报告的财务信息必须是可验证的,从而令使用者能够确信该信息不存在重大差错及偏见并且可以信赖其反映了意在反映的内容。因此,可验证性被视为如实反映的一个方面。某些反馈意见者指出,将可验证性作为如实反映的一个方面可能导致将不易于验证的信息排除在外。此类反馈意见者认为,许多就提供相关财务信息而言非常重要的前瞻性估计(例如,预计现金流量、使用年限及残值)均无法直接验证。但是,排除有关此类估计的信息将大大降低财务报

---

① 1989版《框架》使用了术语"可靠性"而非"如实反映",但两者的含义类似。

及时性（2010 版）（第2.33 段）

BC2.63 1989 版《框架》将及时性作为削弱信息相关性的限制因素进行讨论。《概念公告第 2 号》将及时性描述为相关性的一个方面。但是，在这两个框架中讨论的及时性实质上是相同的。

BC2.64 2006 年讨论文件将及时性描述为相关性的一个方面。但是，某些反馈意见者指出，及时性并非在与预测价值和证实价值相同的意义上成为相关性的一部分。理事会也认同及时性不同于相关性的其他组成部分这一观点。

BC2.65 及时性十分可取，但与相关性和如实反映相比，关键程度略低。及时的信息仅在其具有相关性且如实反映其意在反映的内容时才有用。相反，具有相关性且如实反映的信息，即使未能如期及时报告，仍然可能是有用的（特别是出于证实目的）。

可理解性（2010 版）（第2.34 段至第2.36 段）

BC2.66 1989 版《框架》和《概念公告第 2 号》均包含可理解性，该质量特征令使用者能够理解信息从而有助于作出决策。两个框架均包含类似的描述，即为了使财务信息具备可理解性，使用者应当具备合理的财务知识水平并愿意通过合理的努力对财务信息进行研究。

BC2.67 尽管对可理解性和使用者了解财务报告的责任有多次讨论，但误解一直存在。例如，某些意见认为，即使新会计方法会令报告主体报告对决策有用的财务信息，但鉴于某些使用者可能无法理解，因此不应采用新会计方法。这些意见意味着可理解性较相关性更为重要。

BC2.68 如果考虑可理解性是基本原则，则避免报告关于非常复杂事项的信息可能是适当的，即使该信息具有相关性且能够实现如实反映。将可理解性划分为提升性质量特征意在表明应尽可能清晰地列报和说明难以理解的信息。

BC2.69 为了澄清另一经常被误解的要点，2010 版《概念框架》指出，使用者有责任通过合理的努力对所报告的财务信息进行实际研究而非（之前框架所述的）仅仅是愿意这样做。此外，2010 版《概念框架》指出，使用者可能需要寻求顾问的协助来了解特别复杂的经济现象。

未包含的质量特征（2010 版）

BC2.70 透明度、高质量、内部一致性、真实和公允反映或公允列报及可信性被建议归为可取的财务信息质量特征。但是，透明度、高质量、内部一致性、真实和公允反映或公允列报是用于描述具有相关性和如实反映质量特征，且通过可比性、可验证性、及时性和可理解性得以提升的信息的不同措辞。可信性与此类似，但其还隐含了报告主体管理层的可信赖度。

BC2.71 利益相关方有时提出关于准则制定决策标准的其他建议，并且理事会有时会引述这些标准作为部分决策的依据。这些标准包括简明性、可操作性、实用性或实务性以及可接受性。

BC2.72 这些标准并非质量特征，而是对提供有用财务信息的效益和成本进行整体权衡的一部分。例如，采用较简单的方法耗费的成本可能会低于采用较复杂的方法。在某些情况下，较简单方法所产生的信息实质上可能与较复杂方法所产生的信息相同，但在一定程度上不及较复杂方法所产生的信息精确。在这种情况下，准则制定机构会在权衡成本效益时降低如实反映程度并降低实施成本。

有用财务报告的成本限制（2010 版）（第 2.39 段至第 2.43 段）

BC2.73 成本是准则制定机构以及财务信息的提供者和使用者在考虑可能实施的新财务报告准则要求的效益时应谨记的普遍限制。成本并非信息的质量特征，而是用以提供信息的过程的特征。

BC2.74 理事会一直并且将继续尝试制定更具结构性的方法，以获得与收集和处理提议准则要求主体提供信息的成本相关的信息。所使用的主要方法是要求利益相关方（有时通过实地测试及问卷等正式方法）提交在可行范围内予以量化的特定提案的成本及效益的相关信息。这些要求产生了有用的信息，直接导致对提议要求的修订，以在不显著减少相关效益的情况下降低成本。

国际财务报告准则

起始段落

第 3 章——财务报表和报告主体

重点关注财务报表 …………………………………………………	**BC3.1**
财务报表的目标和范围 ……………………………………………	**BC3.3**
有关风险的信息 ………………………………………………	BC3.7
财务报表中采用的角度 ……………………………………………	**BC3.9**
持续经营假设 ………………………………………………………	**BC3.11**
报告主体 ……………………………………………………………	**BC3.12**
报告主体的描述和边界 ………………………………………	BC3.13
汇总财务报表 …………………………………………………	BC3.20
合并与非合并财务报表 ………………………………………	BC3.22
共同控制和重大影响 …………………………………………	BC3.26

概念框架
结论基础

重点关注财务报表（第3.1段）

BC3.1 第1章明确了通用目的财务报告的目标。第2章讨论了有助于实现该目标的有用财务信息的质量特征。这类质量特征同时适用于财务报表提供的财务信息和其他财务报告提供的财务信息。

BC3.2 财务报表是财务报告的核心部分，理事会讨论的大部分问题都涉及财务报表。此外，如果讨论与其他形式的财务报告相关的问题，会使2018版《概念框架》大幅延期完成，从而导致相关改进被迫推迟。因此，2018版《概念框架》第3章至第8章重点关注财务报表提供的信息，而不讨论管理层评述、中期财务报告、新闻稿和供分析的补充材料等其他形式的财务报告。①

财务报表的目标和范围（第3.2段至第3.3段）

BC3.3 理事会基于对通用目的财务报告目标的描述（参见2018版《概念框架》第1.2段）和《国际会计准则第1号——财务报表列报》第9段对财务报表目标的描述，对2018版《概念框架》中的财务报表目标进行了描述。《国际会计准则第1号》第9段的描述如下：

财务报表是主体财务状况和财务业绩的结构性列报。财务报表的目标是提供有关主体财务状况、财务业绩和现金流量的有用信息，以帮助广大使用者作出经济决策。财务报表亦反映管理层对受托管理资源的受托责任。为实现这一目标……

BC3.4 在2018版《概念框架》中，对财务报表目标的描述有别于《国际会计准则第1号》中的描述，具体如下：

（1）将财务报表要素联系起来。在2018版《概念框架》中，对目标的描述是指：

①资产、负债和权益，而非财务状况；以及

②收益和费用，而非财务业绩。

（2）在2018版《概念框架》中描述的目标并不包括提供有关现金流量的信息。尽管有关现金流量的信息对于财务报表使用者而言很重要，但2018版《概念框架》并未将现金流入和现金流出作为财务报表的要素。

（3）2018版《概念框架》扩展了对目标的描述，包括了为财务报表主要使用者作出有关向主体提供资源的决策提供有用信息的诸项考虑。相关信息在评估报告主体

---

① 2010年，理事会发布《国际财务报告准则实务公告第1号——管理层评述》，这是针对管理层评论列报的宽泛而非约束性的框架，管理层评论随附于根据准则编制的财务报表。

未来净现金流入前景和评估管理层对主体经济资源的受托责任时需为有用信息。

BC3.5 对财务报表中提供信息的描述是指财务状况表和财务业绩表。2015年征求意见稿的一些反馈意见者认为该描述还应涉及现金流量表和权益变动表。他们认为仅明确提及财务状况表和财务业绩表可能被解读为，暗示这两种报表比提供有关现金流量或有关权益求偿权持有者的投入和对此类持有者的分配的报表更重要。

BC3.6 2018版《概念框架》第3.3（3）段讨论了有关现金流量的信息和有关权益求偿权持有者的投入和对其分配的信息。理事会认为这类信息的重要性程度并不低于财务状况表和财务业绩表所提供的信息。2018版《概念框架》之所以仅提及这两类报表是因为只有它们提供了被确认的要素（资产、负债、权益、收益和费用）的汇总。此外，有必要将此类报表识别作为确认发生之地，否则将无法清晰地描述确认。相比之下，现金流入和流出以及权益求偿权持有者的投入和对其的分配并非财务报表的要素，因此提供此类项目信息的报表无法提供被确认要素的汇总。

有关风险的信息［第3.3（3）①段至第3.3（3）②段］

BC3.7 2018版《概念框架》阐明，财务报表提供有关符合财务报表要素定义的已确认和未确认项目产生的风险的信息。2013年讨论文件的一些反馈意见者表达了对未明确定义"风险"一词的顾虑。因此，他们认为"有关风险的信息"可能被理解为任何类型的信息，包括最好在财务报表以外报告的信息。事实上，一些反馈意见者认为有关主体如何管理风险的信息不应纳入财务报表。

BC3.8 然而，理事会注意到，在评估主体产生现金流量的能力和评估管理层对主体经济资源的受托责任时，有关主体已确认和未确认资产和负债的风险的信息很可能是有用信息。因此，这类信息有助于实现财务报表的目标。

财务报表中采用的角度（第3.8段）

BC3.9 2018版《概念框架》阐明，财务报表应从报告主体整体出发（通常称为"主体角度"），而非从主体现有或潜在投资者、贷款人或其他债权人的任意特定群体的角度来提供信息。这反映了理事会认为应将报告主体与其投资者、贷款人或其他债权人区分开来（参见BC1.8段）的观点。

BC3.10 理事会采用主体角度的原因在于这符合第1.2段中的通用目的财务报告的目标，即，为现有或潜在投资者、贷款人或其他债权人提供有用信息，而非为这些出资方中的特定群体提供信息。如果提供相关信息是为满足主要使用者中的特定群体的需求，则可能有必要为各组特定群体提供不同的财务报表。而这可能会引起困惑，并降低财务报告的可信度。另外，根据BC1.6段，为不同的主要使用者群体提供不同报告的成本可能会较高。

持续经营假设（第3.9段）

BC3.11 对持续经营假设的描述基本沿用自2010版《概念框架》，只是将"大大缩小经营规模"替换为"终止交易"，使该描述更加接近《国际会计准则第1号——财务报表列报》和《国际会计准则第10号——报告期后事项》中的描述。

报告主体（第3.10段至第3.18段）

BC3.12 2010版《概念框架》未讨论报告主体的定义；亦未描述如何确定报告主体的范围。理事会在制定2018版《概念框架》中的报告主体概念时，考虑了与美国财务会计准则委员会联合制定的2010年征求意见稿的反馈意见以及2015年征求意见稿的反馈意见。

报告主体的描述和边界（第3.10段和第3.13段至第3.14段）

BC3.13 2018版《概念框架》对报告主体进行了一般描述，而非规定哪些主体必须、应该或是可以编制通用目的财务报表，而且理事会也无权规定。

BC3.14 理事会在确定2018版《概念框架》中对报告主体的描述时，考虑了是否能够通过纳入2010年征求意见稿中报告主体的某些重要特征的资料来改善对报告主体的描述。尤其是在2010年征求意见稿中，理事会：①

（1）将报告主体描述为限定领域内的经济活动，若现有和潜在权益投资者、贷款人或其他债权人在决定是否向主体提供资源和评估该主体的管理层和治理层是否高效且有效地使用所提供的资源时无法直接获得所需信息，报告主体的财务信息有可能成为有用信息；以及

（2）明确识别报告主体的三个必要但非始终充分的特征：
①主体的经济活动正在开展、已经开展或将要开展；
②主体的经济活动能够与其他主体的经济活动以及该主体所处的经济环境客观区分开来；以及
③在决定是否向主体提供资源和评估管理层和治理层是否高效且有效地使用所提供的资源时，有关主体经济活动的财务信息有可能成为有用信息。

BC3.15 理事会得出结论认为，BC3.14（2）③段提及的特征会在确定报告主体的边界时发挥作用（参见BC3.18段）。然而，理事会并未使用2010年征求意见稿中

---

① 参见2010年3月发布的《财务报告概念框架：报告主体（征求意见稿）》。

的其他资料来扩展2018版《概念框架》中对报告主体的描述，原因如下：

（1）如果主体从未开展过且不会开展经济活动，其财务报表不太可能为财务报表使用者提供有用信息；以及

（2）"限定领域"和"可客观区分"两个词含义模糊不清，不能为确定报告主体提供明确指引。

BC3.16 在2015年征求意见稿中，理事会提议在确定报告主体的边界时，应确保其财务报表能够为现有和潜在投资者、贷款人或其他债权人提供具有相关性的信息，并如实反映该主体的经济活动。此外，理事会还进一步提议，财务报表应描述纳入报告主体的一系列经济活动。

BC3.17 2015年征求意见稿的某些反馈意见者表达了顾虑，即，该提案未充分限制报告主体的范围，因此财务报表可能反映了主观臆断的资产和负债范围，使得所提供的信息不完整从而具有误导性。他们尤其担忧属于某主体一部分的报告主体可能会选择对不完整的一系列经济活动进行报告，例如，从其财务报表中剔除其应分担的间接费用。此外，如果报告主体是某主体的一部分，则可能很难确定应将哪些求偿权纳入财务报表。

BC3.18 鉴于以上顾虑，理事会修订了对确定报告主体边界的讨论。2018版《概念框架》解释道，如果报告主体不是法律主体，且不是仅由具有母子公司关系的法律主体构成，则在确定其边界时应关注使用者的信息需求。根据第2.4段，使用者需要的是具有相关性并且如实反映其意在反映的内容的信息。理事会得出结论认为，在确定报告主体的边界时，如实反映质量特征中的完整性和中立性尤为重要。例如，如果在确定报告主体的边界时包含主观臆断的或不完整的经济活动，则该报告主体财务报表中提供的信息会不完整，而且可能不中立。因此，如果以这种方式确定边界，则生成的信息无法满足使用者的信息需求。理事会还得出结论认为，为了帮助使用者了解一套财务报表中包含的内容，这些财务报表必须描述报告主体边界的确定方法和报告主体的范围。

BC3.19 如果报告主体是法律主体或仅由具有母子公司关系的法律主体构成，则通常能够简单直接地确定报告主体的边界。在此类情况下，报告主体的边界取决于一个或一组法律主体的边界。以这种方式确定报告主体的边界能够满足使用者的信息需求。

汇总财务报表（第3.12段）

BC3.20 2010年征求意见稿指出，在同一控制的情况下，汇总财务报表可能提供报告主体的有用信息。许多反馈意见者支持就此进行讨论，但不同意将汇总财务报表局限于同一控制下的主体。

BC3.21 理事会得出结论认为，汇总财务报表在某些情况下能够为财务报表使用者提供有用信息。因此，2018版《概念框架》第3.12段确认了汇总财务报表的概念。但是，2018版《概念框架》并未讨论主体何时能够或如何编制汇总财务报表。理事会得出结论认为，如果未来理事会决定就该议题制定准则，最好届时进行讨论。

合并与非合并财务报表（第3.11 段和第3.15 段至第3.18 段）

BC3.22 2018 版《概念框架》讨论了合并与非合并财务报表中提供的财务信息的有用性。根据第 3.2 段，财务报表的目标是为财务报表的主要使用者提供有用的财务信息。对于合并财务报表，主要使用者的信息需求可能因其重点关注母公司（参见 BC3.23 段至 BC3.24 段）还是重点关注子公司（参见 BC3.25 段）而有所不同。

BC3.23 理事会在制定 2018 版《概念框架》的过程中得出结论认为，母公司及其子公司的资产、负债、权益、收益和费用的信息，对于母公司现有和潜在投资者、贷款人或其他债权人而言为有用信息（参见第 3.15 段）。合并财务报表即提供此类信息。

BC3.24 理事会还得出结论认为，母公司自身关于资产、负债、权益、收益和费用的信息，对于母公司现有和潜在投资者、贷款人或其他债权人而言可能是另一种有用信息（见第 3.17 段）。因此，2018 版《概念框架》指出，母公司可能被要求或选择：

(1) 在编制合并财务报表的基础上进一步编制非合并财务报表；或者

(2) 在合并财务报表附注中提供母公司自身资产、负债、权益、收益和费用的信息。

BC3.25 财务报表意在满足尽可能多的主要使用者的普遍信息需求，因此不必包含仅对主要使用者中的特殊群体（如，子公司的投资者、贷款人或其他债权人）有用的信息。例如，某些有关子公司资产、负债、权益、收益和费用的信息对于该子公司财务报表而言可能是重要信息，但对于母公司的合并财务报表而言可能并非重要信息。子公司自身的财务报表意在为其财务报表的主要使用者提供有关该子公司资产、负债、权益、收益和费用的信息。

共同控制和重大影响

BC3.26 理事会在制定 2018 版《概念框架》的过程中考虑了该版《概念框架》是否应对共同控制和重大影响的概念加以解释。根据 2010 年征求意见稿，共同控制和重大影响不会产生控制。理事会仍同意这一结论，但认为不必在该版《概念框架》中纳入共同控制和重大影响的概念。因此，2018 版《概念框架》并未提及上述概念。理事会在制定 2018 版《概念框架》的过程中，未讨论这些概念是否应继续在准则制定中发挥作用。

第4章——财务报表要素

	起始段落
引言	**BC4.1**
定义——资产和负债的共性问题	**BC4.3**
经济资源的单独定义	BC4.6
删除预期流入流出的概念	BC4.8
过去事项	BC4.15
测试修订后的定义	BC4.19
资产的定义	**BC4.23**
经济资源	BC4.24
重点关注权利	BC4.28
商誉	BC4.32
可辨认性和可分离性	BC4.34
其他价值来源	BC4.35
立即消耗的商品或服务	BC4.37
所有其他方可获得的经济利益	BC4.38
控制	BC4.40
所有权的风险和报酬	BC4.41
驳回的建议	BC4.43
负债的定义	**BC4.44**
义务	BC4.47
无实际能力避免	BC4.49
解释"无实际能力避免"	BC4.54
术语	BC4.56
一方的义务即为另一方的权利	BC4.59
经济资源的转移	BC4.62
由于过去事项而形成的现时义务	BC4.64
资产和负债	**BC4.69**

非互惠交易 ·· BC4.69
　　　或有负债和或有资产 ·· BC4.71
　　　核算单元 ·· BC4.74
　　　待执行合同 ·· BC4.78
　　　报告合同权利和义务的实质 ·· BC4.88
权益的定义 ·· **BC4.89**
收益和费用的定义 ·· **BC4.93**
　　　基于资产和负债变动的收益和费用的定义 ···································· BC4.93
　　　收益和费用的类型 ·· BC4.96
其他可能的定义 ··· **BC4.97**

引言

BC4.1 2010 版《概念框架》和之前的 1989 版《框架》对财务报表的下列要素进行了定义：

(1) 资产——由于过去事项而由主体控制的、预期会导致未来经济利益流入主体的资源；

(2) 负债——主体由于过去事项而承担的现时义务，该义务的履行预期会导致含有经济利益的资源流出主体；

(3) 权益——主体资产扣除主体所有负债以后的剩余利益；

(4) 收益——会计期间内经济利益的增加，其形式表现为因资产流入、资产增加或是负债减少而引起的权益增加，但不包括与权益参与者出资有关的权益增加；

(5) 费用——会计期间内经济利益的减少，其形式表现为因资产流出、资产消耗或是发生负债而引起的权益减少，但不包括与对权益参与者的分配有关的权益减少。

BC4.2 在 2018 版《概念框架》中，理事会修改了这些定义。

定义——资产和负债的共性问题

BC4.3 理事会发现，2010 版《概念框架》中的资产和负债的定义对解决准则制定过程中的许多问题很有用。但是，这些定义的某些方面在实务中会造成疑惑，因为：

(1) 在资产和负债的定义中明确提及经济利益流入流出模糊了经济资源或义务与由此产生的经济利益流入流出之间的区别；以及

(2) 一些读者将术语"预期"解读为概率阈值。另外，一些读者不清楚定义中的术语"预期"和确认条件中的"很可能"之间的关系。

BC4.4 为了解决这些问题，并且出于 BC4.6 段至 BC4.18 段中给出的理由，理事会将定义修改如下：

(1) 资产指主体由于过去的事项而控制的现时经济资源；

(2) 负债指主体由于过去的事项而承担的转移经济资源的现时义务；以及

(3) 经济资源指具备产生经济利益潜力的权利。

BC4.5 BC4.23 段至 BC4.43 段讨论了关于资产定义的支持性指引，BC4.44 段至 BC4.68 段则对负债的定义进行了讨论。

经济资源的单独定义（第4.4段）

BC4.6 与2010版《概念框架》中定义相比，2018版的主要结构性变化是引入了经济资源的单独定义。将未来经济利益流入流出从资产和负债的定义部分移至经济资源的支持性定义部分。

BC4.7 理事会认为，这种单独定义有助于消除BC4.3（1）段中提到的混淆。进一步明确强调资产（或负债）是一种经济资源（或义务），而不是经济资源（或义务）可能产生的经济利益的最终流入（或流出）。同时也简化了相关定义，使资产和负债更能够相互呼应。

删除预期流入流出的概念（第4.14段和第4.37段）

BC4.8 2018版《概念框架》用资产（或负债）"具备产生经济利益的潜力"（或"具有要求转移经济资源的潜力"）的概念取代了2010版《概念框架》中资源"预期"流入或流出的概念。对这一概念的引用出现在经济资源的定义以及负债定义的支持性指引中。

BC4.9 理事会替换了预期资源流入或流出的概念，理由如下：

（1）删除"预期"，将重点放在经济资源或义务的定义上。保留"预期"或"很可能流出或流入"的概念可能会排除很多明显属于资产和负债的项目，例如买入的或签出的价外期权、保险合同和发生特定的不确定未来事项时转移经济资源的义务（参见BC4.63段）。

（2）预期流量的概念是无益的，因为对该术语的解释可能会存在很大差异，并且通常与概率阈值的概念相关联。

BC4.10 2013年讨论文件使用了"能够"产生经济利益而非"具备潜力"。然而，2018版《概念框架》第2.6段至第2.7段在讨论相关性时已经使用了"能够"一词，因此使用"能够"一词既用来描述哪种信息是相关的，又在定义经济资源时采用了不同的含义，可能会产生混淆。为避免这种混淆，理事会在定义经济资源时引入了"具备潜力"这一术语。

BC4.11 "具备产生经济利益的潜力"（或类似的"具有要求转移经济资源的潜力"）包含以下要点：

（1）可能在未来产生经济利益是不足够的，这些经济利益必须来源于经济资源中已存在的某种特征。例如，购入的期权有可能为持有者带来经济利益，但仅仅是因为该期权已经包含了允许持有者行使该期权的权利。

（2）该定义并未意图设定最小概率阈值。重要的是，至少在一种情况下，经济资源会产生经济利益。

BC4.12 某些利益相关方指出，理事会应该保留预期资源流入或流出的概念。他们表示，如果预期不会有经济利益流入或至少没有合理可能，那么财务报表的使用者和编制者就不会将某个项目视为资产。这些反馈意见者认为，修订后的定义将明显扩大资产和负债的范围，这可能导致：

（1）存在识别所有可能的资产和负债的压力，如果资产或负债最终未被确认或被计量为零，则会为了极少的利益而造成重大的操作性负担；

（2）更多不确定、不太可能或难以计量的项目将被确认为资产和负债，除非确认标准更加严格；

（3）原则上所有资产和负债都应予以确认的假设，即使在预期不会产生流入或流出的情况下；以及

（4）由于不可能产生流入或流出而不确认资产和负债的情况下，在附注中提供这些资产和负债的无相关性的信息的压力。

BC4.13 理事会得出结论认为，删除"预期"的概念（被某些人解读为概率阈值）不会造成重大的操作性负担。在实务中，主体同时考虑资产和负债的定义以及确认标准，以识别主体可能需要确认的资产和负债，或者可能需要在附注中披露信息的资产和负债。

BC4.14 此外，理事会得出结论认为，利益相关方关于在经济利益流入或流出的可能性低时是否确认资产或负债的这一担忧，最好在确认决策阶段解决，而非在定义阶段（参见第 4.15 段、第 4.38 段、第 5.15 段至第 5.17 段和 BC5.15 段至 BC5.20 段）。这与多年来理事会应用 2010 版《概念框架》的方式一致。

过去事项（第 4.26 段和第 4.42 段至第 4.47 段）

BC4.15 2018 版《概念框架》中：

（1）保留了资产和负债定义中的"由于过去事项"的表述；且

（2）保留了负债定义中"现时"一词，并在资产定义中加入了"现时"一词。

BC4.16 理事会在制定 2018 版《概念框架》的过程中，考虑了是否有必要在资产和负债定义中都加入"现时"和"由于过去事项"两项表述。

BC4.17 将"由于过去事项"的表述加入资产和负债的定义后，理事会未发现任何重大问题。而且主体还可通过识别过去事项，确定如何在其财务报表中报告该事项，例如如何分类和列报由于过去事项产生的收益、费用或现金流量。BC4.64 段至 BC4.68 段讨论了"由于过去事项"的表述对修订后的负债定义而言尤其重要的原因。因此，理事会在资产和负债定义中保留了该表述。

BC4.18 如果过去事项产生了资产或负债，仅凭这一事实无法确定该资产或负债目前是否仍然存在，还须考虑主体是否仍然控制现时经济资源或是否仍承担现时义务。因此，理事会在负债定义中继续保留"现时"一词，并将该词纳入资产的定义。在资产的定义中加入"现时"一词强调了资产和负债定义之间的相互呼应。

测试修订后的定义

BC4.19 2016 年，理事会分析了 2015 年征求意见稿提议的资产和负债定义修订

的影响，意在实现如下两个目标：
(1) 帮助理事会和利益相关方评估提案对未来准则的影响；以及
(2) 帮助发现所提议定义和支持性指引中的问题。

BC4.20 具体行动包括：
(1) 对23个示例应用提议定义和支持性指引，分析所得结果；
(2) 确认提议定义和支持性指引如何帮助理事会就其部分当前项目作出决定；以及
(3) 在2016年9月举办的世界准则制定机构会议上，同与会者就示例展开讨论。

BC4.21 选择和制定示例是为了对2015年征求意见稿的反馈意见者所提的问题进行检验。这些示例包括满足资产或负债定义但经济利益流入或流出可能性低或结果有高度不确定性的权利和义务。这些示例的分析不仅解释了存在某项资产或负债的原因，还解释了根据第5章所述的确认标准，不一定能在财务报表中确认该资产或负债的原因。示例中还包括2015年征求意见稿的反馈意见者所认为的提议定义和支持性指引的影响不明确或可能不符合准则要求的特定交易。示例分析还阐述了在很多情况下应用提议定义和支持性指引如何得出符合准则要求的结论及其原因。

BC4.22 2016年9月世界准则制定机构会议上，与会者的反馈强调了提议指引表述不够清晰的方面。理事会在制定修订后定义和支持性指引的过程中，考虑了这些反馈以及针对提案收到的其他反馈。

资产的定义

BC4.23 本部分讨论了资产定义的以下方面：
(1) 经济资源（参见BC4.24段至BC4.27段）；
(2) 重点关注权利（参见BC4.28段至BC4.39段）；以及
(3) 控制（参见BC4.40段至BC4.43段）。

经济资源（第4.4段和第4.14段至第4.18段）

BC4.24 BC4.6段至BC4.7段解释了理事会引入经济资源这一单独定义的决定，BC4.8段至BC4.14段讨论了理事会从资产定义中删除"预期流入流出"的概念且不将该概念纳入经济资源定义的决定。

BC4.25 理事会得出结论认为，资产的定义应指经济资源，而非由此产生的经济利益。虽然资产的价值在于其产生未来经济利益的潜力，但处于主体控制之下的是包含这种潜力的现时权利，而非未来经济利益。

BC4.26 理事会考虑是否用术语"资源"而非"经济资源"。2013年讨论文件的部分反馈意见者认为，"经济资源"一词过于局限，仅涵盖了具有市场价值的资源。理事会意在使术语"经济资源"涵盖具备产生经济利益潜力的所有资源，而非仅涵盖当前市场存在的资源。根据2018版《概念框架》第4.11段至第4.12段，理事会选择"经济资源"这一术语是因为该术语有助于强调所讨论的资源并非实物对象，而是对实物对象的权利。

BC4.27 在一些经济体内，理事会的《概念框架》被应用至公众部门和非营利性企业等金融市场外的其他领域。因此，一些利益相关方认为资产的定义应包括能产生现金流量之外利益的资源，如为报告主体、其他方或更广泛社会带来的社会或环境服务或利益。同样地，一些利益相关方认为，为满足更广泛利益相关方群体的预期或维护公众支持，负债的定义应包括转移上述利益的义务和出于审慎或道德的目的而形成的义务。然而，理事会目前的关注重点为营利性主体，因此其得出结论认为，资产的定义的关注重点仍为具备产生经济利益潜力的资源，负债定义的关注重点仍为转移经济资源的义务。

重点关注权利（第4.6段至第4.13段）

BC4.28 理事会在2018版《概念框架》发布之前使用术语"资源"来定义资产。2018版《概念框架》中，改为使用术语"经济资源"，并将经济资源以及资产定义为一项权利。为强调上述修订带来的影响，2018版《概念框架》阐明，例如不动产、厂场和设备等实物对象，经济资源并非这些实物对象本身，而是对此类对象享有的一系列权利。第4.11段列举了这些权利。

BC4.29 理事会在制定2018版《概念框架》的过程中，考虑了2013年讨论文件和2015年征求意见稿的部分反馈意见者的建议，即不应仅将资产定义为权利，而应定义为权利或资源。这些反馈意见者认为：

（1）将某些资产（例如有形资产）描述为资源要比描述为权利更为恰当。反馈意见者认为，将有形资产作为一系列权利进行会计处理这一概念不符合实际，尤其在将这一概念与"分拆"权利并将其作为单独资产确认的想法相结合时。

（2）除非《概念框架》解释识别核算单元的驱动因素，否则主体在针对由多个权利构成的单一资产时，是将其作为整体确认，还是将构成该资产的某些权利单独确认这一问题上，很难给出一致的解释。

（3）关注较大的一组权利中的某些权利会给确认与终止确认条件和核算单元带来更大压力。为确认是否存在新的资产或负债，主体需要思考诸多问题，而这样做无法为财务报表使用者带来明确利益。这些反馈意见者认为关注权利这一方法给准则的制定和应用，尤其是在终止确认决策方面，带来了挑战。

BC4.30 理事会注意到，许多资产是根据合同、法规或类似方式确立的，例如金融资产、承租人对租赁机器的使用权，以及专利等许多无形资产。同样地，实物对象的所有权来源于法律授予的权利。此外，尽管程度不同，源自实物对象的完全法定所有权的权利和源自合同赋予的实物对象99%（或50%或甚至1%）使用寿命的使用权都属于某种权利。且由于存在法律差异或发生法律变化，特定的一组权利是否可能构成完全法定所有权，在不同的经济体或者不同时点结论不同。

BC4.31 因此，理事会认为定义两种不同类型的资产并无好处，即一种在财务报表中描述为资源（例如，对实物对象的完全法定所有权），另一种描述为权利（对全部或部分资源享有的所有其他权利）。尽管如此，2018版《概念框架》第4.12段指出，将一系列权利描述为实物对象通常能够以最简洁和可理解的方式如实反映这些权利。

商誉

BC4.32 理事会在制定2018版《概念框架》的过程中，未重新考虑《国际财务报告准则第3号——企业合并》结论基础部分BC313段至BC323段中的结论。这几个段落解释了"核心"商誉的构成，同时表明了核心商誉满足资产的定义。

BC4.33 理事会在制定2018版《概念框架》最终版的过程中得出结论认为，不宜在《概念框架》中提及商誉这一特定资产。因此，2018版《概念框架》未提及商誉。

可辨认性和可分离性

BC4.34 《国际会计准则第38号——无形资产》要求无形资产应具备可辨认性，以便于与商誉进行区分。《国际会计准则第38号》指出，如果一项资产可与主体区分开来，或来自合同或其他法定权利，则该资产具有可辨认性。因此，理事会在制定2018版《概念框架》的过程中，讨论了资产的定义是否应要求资产具备可辨认性以及可分离性两个问题。理事会得出结论认为，如果资产具备可分离性或来自合同或其他法定权利，则更易辨认、计量和描述该资产。而这会影响确认该资产是否会提供具有相关性的信息以及该资产是否会得到如实反映的判断。但理事会得出结论认为，不应将可辨认性和可分离性作为资产定义的一部分。

其他价值来源

BC4.35 理事会在制定2018版《概念框架》的过程中，对主体通过合同、法规和类似方式以外的其他方式获得的专有技术等项目进行了讨论。理事会得出结论认为此类项目可以是资产。理事会考虑了术语"权利"是否足够涵盖上述项目，或者理事会是否应将经济资源定义为"权利或其他价值来源"。

BC4.36 理事会得出结论认为，"其他价值来源"这一概念过于模糊，无法用于正式定义。相反，2018版《概念框架》中指出，术语"权利"不仅包含通过合同、法规和类似方式获得的权利，还包括通过其他方式获得的权利，如通过取得或创建不公开的专有技术获得的权利。第4.22段进一步解释了即使该专有技术不受注册专利的保护，主体仍可控制该专有技术的使用权的原因。对概念的这一解释并非全新内容，而是基于2010版《概念框架》第4.12段。

立即消耗的商品或服务（第 4.8 段）

BC4.37 2018 版《概念框架》澄清，某些商品或服务在收到之时立即被消耗，主体具有从这些商品或服务获得经济利益的即时权利。该权利在此类商品或服务被主体消耗前短暂存在。这一点与《国际财务报告准则第 2 号——以股份为基础的支付》中将所获得的员工服务视为立即被消耗的资产的观点相一致。

所有其他方可获得的经济利益（第 4.9 段）

BC4.38 2018 版《概念框架》指出，所有其他方无需耗费重大成本均可获得的权利通常不属于持有该权利的主体的资产。理事会在 2018 版《概念框架》加入了这一解释，以澄清将资产定义为权利不会迫使主体识别其可能持有的大量权利并将其确认为资产。

BC4.39 对于所有其他方均可获得的权利通常不属于特定主体的资产的原因，存在多种不同解释。原因之一为，此类权利（如，道路公共使用权）有可能为该主体产生的经济利益通常不会超出所有其他方可从中获得的经济利益。另一原因（或是额外原因）为，此类权利不由主体控制，即主体无法拒绝其他方获取由此类权利产生的经济利益。

控制（第4.19 段至第4.25 段）

BC4.40 2018 版《概念框架》在资产定义中保留了经济资源应"由主体控制"的概念。《概念框架》中引入了控制的定义。理事会在《国际财务报告准则第 15 号——客户合同收入》中对资产的控制的定义以及《国际财务报告准则第 10 号——合并财务报表》中对主体的控制的定义的基础上设立控制的定义。① 虽然上述准则中对控制的定义存在差异，但其所用的基本概念相同，即主体能够主导资产（或主体资产）的使用，同时能够获得经济利益（或回报）。2018 版《概念框架》在资产的定义和母公司对其子公司的控制描述中均用到了控制的概念。

所有权的风险和报酬

BC4.41 理事会对资产的定义是否应包含所有权的风险和报酬概念进行了考虑。部分准则将风险敞口（或与可变回报风险敞口相关的概念）视为控制的一个方面或一项指征：

（1）《国际财务报告准则第 10 号》指出"投资者能够控制被投资者，是指投资者通过参与被投资者的相关活动而承担或享有可变回报，并且能够运用对被投资者的权力影响其回报金额"。

---

① 参见《国际财务报告准则第 15 号》第 33 段和《国际财务报告准则第 10 号》第 5 段至第 7 段。

(2)《国际财务报告准则第 15 号》指出，对资产的控制已被转移至客户的指征之一为"客户承担并享有该资产所有权的重大风险和报酬"。《国际财务报告准则第 15 号》结论基础部分指出，如果主体承担资产所有权的风险和报酬，那么主体可能对该资产具有控制权。

BC4.42 2018 版《概念框架》用一般术语解释了控制与所有权的风险和报酬之间的关系。然而，2018 版《概念框架》并未使用短语"所有权的风险和报酬"，而是使用"经济利益金额的重大波动的敞口"（参见第 4.24 段）。

驳回的建议

BC4.43 理事会在制定 2018 版《概念框架》的过程中，对有关控制的定义和处理方式的其他建议进行了考虑，但最终驳回了这些建议，这些建议包括：

（1）建议不在资产定义中提及控制，因经济资源的定义中已隐含主体拥有控制该资源的权利。理事会认同这一观点，但认为在资产定义明确提及控制有助于定义和支持性指引的构建。

（2）建议将必须存在控制这一要求作为确认条件，而非资产定义的内容。部分利益相关方认为，这样做可将两个互相独立的问题分开（即，是否存在资产以及谁拥有该资产）。但由于这样做不太可能改变哪些资产需要进行确认的事实，且理事会在实务中未发现任何问题，因此决定不将有关控制的表述移至资产确认条件下。

（3）建议理事会应修订控制的定义，采用表述"几乎所有"的经济利益。理事会认为，"几乎所有"的经济利益这一表述是多余的，且如果主体仅确认其控制的权利，该表述可能产生混淆。例如，如果主体控制了获得一栋建筑物所产生经济利益的 20% 的权利，则该主体的资产即为获得该建筑物所产生经济利益的 20% 的权利。因为主体的资产并非对整栋建筑物的权利，因此不需要获得该建筑物产生的所有或几乎所有经济利益的权利。准则制定过程中可能出现是否需要在准则中使用"几乎所有"等标准这一问题，例如当某一准则要求主体将一组权利作为单一资产（单一核算单元）进行会计处理时。

负债的定义（第 4.26 段至第 4.47 段）

BC4.44 在 2018 版《概念框架》中，负债指主体由于过去事项而承担的转移经济资源的现时义务。与之前定义相比，主要变动如下：

（1）删除了预期经济利益流出的表述。出于 BC4.8 段至 BC4.14 段所讨论的原因，上述表述被支持性指引取代，即转移经济资源的义务必须具有要求主体将经济资源转移至另一方（参见第 4.37 段）的潜力。

（2）采用新术语"经济资源"替代术语"含有经济利益的资源"（参见 BC4.6 段至 BC4.7 段）。

BC4.45 如 BC0.15 段所述，2018 版《概念框架》未讨论同时具有负债和权益特征的金融工具的分类问题。目前理事会正在其针对具有权益特征的金融工具的研究项目中探索如何区分负债与权益。必要时，理事会将更新《概念框架》作为该项目得出的一个可能结果。理事会在最终确定 2018 版《概念框架》的过程中，尽量不添加在研究项目完成后需要重新审视的新概念或新指引。

BC4.46 理事会在制定 2018 版《概念框架》的过程中得出结论认为，确定负债存在须同时满足以下三个条件：

（1）主体承担义务（参见 BC4.47 段至 BC4.61 段）；

（2）该义务为转移经济资源（参见 BC4.62 段至 BC4.63 段）；以及

（3）该义务为由于过去事项而形成的现时义务（参见 BC4.64 段至 BC4.68 段）。

义务（第4.28 段至第4.35 段）

BC4.47 在应用之前的负债定义时，被各方普遍接受的观点是当义务是无条件的且法律上可执行时（在这种情况下，主体显然没有避免转移的能力）主体承担转移经济资源的现时义务。但在某些情况下，主体具有避免未来转移的某种有限能力。由于该能力被限制在何种程度将导致主体承担"现时义务"并不明确，因此在准则的制定和应用过程中曾出现问题。

BC4.48 2018 版《概念框架》将义务定义为职责或责任，这点与 2010 版《概念框架》一致，但为澄清术语"义务"的含义，2018 版《概念框架》指出，如果主体承担其无实际能力避免的职责或责任，则主体承担义务。

无实际能力避免（第 4.29 段至第 4.34 段）

BC4.49 理事会对以下情况发生时可能产生的问题进行考虑，制定了"无实际能力避免"的标准：

（1）主体虽然没有法律上可执行的转移经济资源的义务，但其避免该转移的能力受到其惯例、已发布政策或特定声明的限制（此类义务有时被称为"推定义务"）；或

（2）已存在主体转移经济资源的要求，但该要求的结果取决于主体自身所采取的行动。

BC4.50 尽管 2013 年讨论文件分别考虑了上述两种情况，但某些反馈意见者认为这两种情况中的相关问题类似，即主体避免转移的能力被限制。2018 版《概念框架》中"无实际能力避免"的标准同时适用于上述两种情况。然而，评估主体是否有避免特定转移的实际能力的因素将取决于主体职责或责任的性质，理事会将在制定准则时考虑这些因素。

BC4.51 对于主体可通过未来行动避免经济资源转移的情况，不同准则下的处理方法不同。为确定何时出现转移经济资源的现时义务，理事会在准则中识别出以下三种观点：

(1) 观点1——主体必须不具备避免未来转移的能力。例如，根据《国际财务报告解释公告第21号——征税》的解释，《国际会计准则第37号——准备、或有负债和或有资产》规定如果现时义务存在，主体必须不具备避免未来转移经济资源的能力（甚至是理论上的能力）。

(2) 观点2——主体必须不具备避免未来转移的实际能力。例如，根据《国际会计准则第34号——中期财务报告》，如果一项租赁的可变租赁付款额取决于主体能否达到特定的年销量水平，那么如果预计能够达到该销量水平，且主体除支付未来租赁付款额外无其他现实选择，则主体在达到该销量水平前即承担该义务。

(3) 观点3——无需限制主体避免未来转移的能力。如果其他条件都满足，则作为过去事项产生的结果足以判断主体可能必须转移经济资源。例如，根据《国际会计准则第19号——雇员福利》，如果主体为换取雇员已提供的服务而向雇员支付取决于未来雇佣情况的福利（非已行权的福利），则主体须确认负债。《国际会计准则第19号》未要求主体评估其是否有实际能力避免支付上述福利。

BC4.52 在2018版《概念框架》中，理事会采用了"观点2"，理由如下：

(1) 理事会驳回了观点1，因为当主体只在理论上具有避免转移经济资源的能力而没有避免该转移的实际能力时，如果主体的义务列表中遗漏了该转移的义务，将使得对许多财务报表使用者而言有用的信息被排除在外。这种遗漏导致过分强调法律形式，未充分关注如实反映该义务的实质，而在实务中该实质与法律上可执行的义务具有同等约束力。此外，如果主体只在理论上有采取避免义务的行动的权利，但没有行使该权利的实际能力，那么该义务仍然可以有效地约束主体，如同其不具备该理论上的权利一样。

(2) 理事会驳回了意见3，因为"义务"这一术语隐含有对主体避免转移经济资源的能力的某种限制。

BC4.53 理事会驳回了多个利益相关方提出的采用基于未来流出概率的阈值的建议。这些反馈意见者建议，如果主体很可能或可能合理确定主体将转移一项经济资源，则应视作该主体承担一项义务。他们认为，该阈值能够提供对当期费用最相关的计量方法。尽管如此，由于BC4.9（1）段、BC4.52（2）段和BC4.94（4）段给出的理由，2018版《概念框架》中的义务定义侧重于义务是否存在。而支持性指引侧重于主体有义务做什么，而非可能结果的可能性。

解释"无实际能力避免"

BC4.54 理事会得出结论认为，评估主体是否具备避免某一特定转移的实际能力取决于该主体的职责或责任的性质。应用"无实际能力避免"的标准时需运用判断。一些利益相关方担心，允许财务报表编制者应用这一标准将导致实务处理多样化，并且在某些情况下，主体将在某些利益相关方认为该主体没有承担真正的义务时确认负债。但是，理事会指出，通常财务报表编制者是在有进一步的规定和指引的情况下应用这一标准。如有必要，在制定准则时，理事会将就该标准应用于特定案例制定指引。

BC4.55 2018 版《概念框架》第 4.34 段将那些行为导致的经济后果比转移经济资源更为不利作为主体没有避免转移的实际能力的例子。举例的目的在于不仅表明进行转移在经济上是有利的，而且不转移的不利经济后果过于严重以至于主体没有避免转移的实际能力。尽管该主体理论上具有避免转移的权利，但没有行使该权利的实际能力。

术语

BC4.56 理事会考虑了下列术语是否比"无实际能力避免"更易解读：
（1）"无现实选择"；或者
（2）"几乎或根本无法（在实务中）避免"。

BC4.57 这两个术语的含义类似于"无实际能力避免"。理事会之所以选择使用"无实际能力避免"，是因为这能最有效地表明需要识别主体有义务做什么，而非关注于很可能的结果。此外，理事会借鉴了"实际能力"一词，一些准则在评估主体是否控制资产时使用了这一术语，出于类似目的，在 2018 版《概念框架》第 4.20 段和第 4.22 段使用了术语"现时能力"。

BC4.58 早于 2018 版《概念框架》制定的一些准则使用术语"推定义务"来指代引起义务的某些情况或使用术语"经济强制"来指代某些不引起义务的情况。2018 版《概念框架》没有使用这些术语来区分义务存在和不存在的情况，因为理事会得出结论认为，这些术语未被证明有助于其目的且没有必要这样做。

一方的义务即为另一方的权利

BC4.59 根据 2018 版《概念框架》第 4.30 段，如果一方负有转移经济资源的义务，则另一方（或多方）就有接收该经济资源的权利。理事会决定，这一声明将帮助主体应用负债的定义，因为相比确定一方是否承担义务，有时可能更容易确定另一方（或多方）是否拥有权利。

BC4.60 如果报告主体的义务不是法律上可执行的义务，而是由报告主体的惯例、已发布政策或特定声明产生的，或者取决于主体的未来行为，理事会考虑在这类情况下，是否另一方拥有能够控制的资产。理事会得出结论认为，在这类情况下，交易对手确实控制了资产。根据第 4.23 段，如果主体是将从经济资源中获得经济利益的一方，则该主体控制该经济资源。

BC4.61 一般原则是，对于每项义务而言都存在获得经济资源的相应权利，理事会在制定 2018 版《概念框架》的过程中讨论了环境义务是否属于例外情况。理事会得出结论认为，对于此类义务，相应的权利由整个社会（即该地区的居民）控制。他们有权获得恢复其环境所需的服务。因此，2018 版《概念框架》确定针对该一般原则没有例外情况。

经济资源的转移（第4.36 段至第4.41 段）

BC4.62 根据2018 版《概念框架》，负债的第二个条件是该义务必须具有要求主体转移经济资源的潜力。BC4.8 段至 BC4.14 段解释了为什么理事会用负债具有要求转移经济资源的潜力这一概念取代了预期资源流出的概念。

BC4.63 发生特定的不确定未来事项时要求转移经济资源的义务有可能要求转移经济资源，因此可以引发负债，例如，BC4.64 段至 BC4.68 段中讨论的由于过去事项而形成的现时义务就是这类情况。这种义务有时被称为"随时履约义务"。2018 版《概念框架》没有使用这一术语，因为理事会认为没必要这样做。

由于过去事项而形成的现时义务（第4.42 段至第4.47 段）

BC4.64 2010 版《概念框架》中的负债定义要求现时义务是过去事项的结果，但没有具体说明如何确定哪个事项形成了现有义务（有时称为"义务事项"）。然而，2018 版《概念框架》解释了如何解读"由于过去事项而形成的"。

BC4.65 一些义务是由于单一义务事项而形成的，例如收到货物。其他义务会通过连续的义务事项随着时间的推移累积，例如开展连续的活动。

BC4.66 在某些情况下，一系列事项会形成一项义务。例如，如果在一段时期内达到最低标准（例如最低收入金额、最低雇员人数或最低资产金额），并且报告主体在之后的某一特定日期仍继续运营，则会形成义务。在这种情况下，确定哪些事项（满足最低标准或在特定日期继续运营）是义务事项可能特别困难。如果义务的定义仅包含无条件的义务［参见 BC4.51（1）段讨论的观点 1］，明确提及过去事项便是多余的，这是因为根据观点 1，义务事项指的是使义务变为无条件义务的事项，在本段给出的例子中，该义务事项是指在之后的特定日期继续运营。

BC4.67 然而，理事会最终采用了更广义的"无实际能力避免"表述［参见 BC4.51（2）段讨论的观点 2］。在应用这个概念时，一系列事项中的部分事项发生就可能导致主体承担义务：即，如果主体没有避免尚未发生的事项的实际能力，则主体可能需要承担义务。因此，最重要是的解释若要使主体承担"由于过去事项而形成的"的现时义务，一系列事项中的哪些事项必须发生。

BC4.68 理事会得出结论认为，"由于过去事项而形成的"意味着：

（1）主体已获得经济利益或已采取行动。

（2）因此，主体将要或可能必须因此转移本不必转移的经济资源。该活动增加了该主体将要或可能必须转移的经济资源的规模。

资产和负债

非互惠交易

BC4.69 理事会考虑了 2018 版《概念框架》是否应明确讨论非互惠交易中产生的资产和负债,例如,捐赠、所得税及其他税费。理事会指出,2018 版《概念框架》中的指引是在没有假设所有交易都是互惠交易的情况下制定的。事实上,一些指引(特别是支持负债定义的指引)是在深入考虑非互惠交易的情况下制定的。

BC4.70 理事会得出结论认为,支持资产和负债定义的指引既适用于互惠交易,也适用于非互惠交易。针对这两种交易,首先都要确定交易产生的权利和义务。因此,2018 版《概念框架》不包含针对非互惠交易的特定指引。

或有负债和或有资产

BC4.71 2018 版《概念框架》并未使用"或有负债"和"或有资产"两个术语。根据早于 2018 版《概念框架》制定的《国际会计准则第 37 号——准备、或有负债和或有资产》,"或有负债"是包含三类不符合该准则的确认条件的项目的集合:

(1)第一类项目是存在不确定性的可能义务,且该义务只能通过不完全在主体控制范围之内的不确定未来事项的发生与否来确定。2018 版《概念框架》第 4.35 段和第 5.14 段将这类项目作为存在的不确定性(即一项负债存在与否具有不确定性)的案例进行了分析。

(2)第二类项目是由于过去事项而形成的现时义务,但该义务因履行此类义务而导致经济资源流出的可能性不大而不予确认。2018 版《概念框架》第 4.37 段至第 4.38 段和第 5.15 段至第 5.17 段将这类项目作为经济利益流出可能性低的负债的案例进行了分析。

(3)最后一类项目是由于过去事项而形成的现时义务,但该义务因金额无法足够可靠地计量而不予确认。2018 版《概念框架》第 2.19 段、第 2.22 段和第 5.19 段至第 5.23 段将此类项目作为具有高度计量不确定性的负债的案例进行了分析。

BC4.72 2018 版《概念框架》中未使用"或有负债"这一术语,原因如下:

(1)《国际会计准则第 37 号》中的定义所涵盖的三类项目不构成单一的自然类别。类别(1)中的项目可能是负债,但受到存在的不确定性的影响。类别(2)和(3)中的项目是负债,但在应用"第 5 章——确认和终止确认"中所述的确认标准后,确认与否均有可能。

(2)或有负债不是财务报表中有别于负债和权益之外的另一要素。此外,一些"或有负债"是负债,但另一些则不是。

(3)"或有负债"这一术语的常见使用方式与《国际会计准则第 37 号》中的不同。它通常指如果发生某些不确定的未来事项,可能会导致经济资源流出的项目。是否可能发生义务事项取决于具体情况。如果发生了义务事项,则该项目可能是负债,但受到存在的不确定性、结果不确定性、计量不确定性的影响或这些不确定性任意组合的综合影响。对该负债可能确认也可能不确认。

BC4.73 类似考虑同样适用于"或有资产"。

核算单元(第 4.48 段至第 4.55 段)

BC4.74 如果未选择确认或计量要求适用的核算单元,则不可能制定针对特定项目的确认要求或计量基础。同样,如果不考虑应用确认或计量要求的方式来选择核算单元,可能不会产生有用信息。因此,2018 版《概念框架》指出,必须同时考虑核算单元及针对特定项目的确认和计量要求。

BC4.75 理事会在制定 2018 版《概念框架》的过程中,考虑了确认时使用的核算单元是否会与计量时使用的核算单元有所不同。理事会认为,数个项目可能符合单独确认的条件,但计量时则作为一个整体。例如,符合单独确认条件的一组项目:
(1)可在估计其可收回金额时作为单一核算单元进行计量;或者
(2)作为实务变通,有时可作为一项投资组合进行计量。
因此,理事会得出结论认为,有时针对确认和计量选择不同的核算单元可能是适当的。

BC4.76 就核算单元作出的决策与制定准则过程中作出的确认和计量决策是相关联的。因此,理事会得出结论认为,需要在制定准则的过程中而非在《概念框架》中作出有关选择核算单元的决策。

BC4.77 2018 版《概念框架》包括对在确定使用哪种核算单元时应考虑的因素的讨论。由于这些因素的相对重要性取决于主体进行会计处理的项目的具体特征,因此理事会并未对其进行优先级排序。理事会认为,针对大范围的准则,确定最有用核算单元的所考虑因素,不存在可以统一使用的单一排序。

待执行合同(第 4.56 段至第 4.58 段)

BC4.78 2018 版《概念框架》提供了有关待执行合同修订后的且更为广泛的支持性指引。澄清的内容如下:
(1)待执行合同确立了交换经济资源的合并权利和义务;
(2)交换经济资源的合并权利和义务是相互依存,不能分开的;以及
(3)合并权利和义务构成了单一资产或负债。

BC4.79 虽然某些利益相关方认为待执行合同会产生一项权利(取得一种经济资源)和一项单独义务(转移另一种经济资源),但理事会指出该权利和义务相互高度依赖,即,取得第一种资源的权利以履行转移第二种资源的义务为条件,转移第二

种资源的义务以取得第一种资源为条件。

BC4.80 理事会进一步指出，即使利益相关方在不同的时间转移经济资源，但经济资源交换会与首次转移同时发生。例如，主体可能按照合同向客户销售商品并在之后某日收到客户的付款。当主体向客户转移商品时，其会同时获得取得客户付款的权利。与此同时，客户收到商品并承担了支付义务。双方交换经济资源的合并权利和义务在首次转移时得以履行，同时被新权利（在本例中，为取得付款的权利）或义务（在本例中，为付款的义务）取代。

BC4.81 因此，理事会得出结论认为，待执行合同包含交换经济资源的合并权利和义务，而不是取得一种经济资源的权利和转移另一经济资源的单独义务。

BC4.82 理事会考虑了交换经济资源的合并权利和义务是否赋予报告主体单独资产（交换资源的权利，相当于购入期权）和单独负债（交换资源的义务，相当于签出期权）。

BC4.83 交换经济资源的购入期权赋予持有方进行交换或取消交换而免受处罚的权利。相反，如果持有方行使该权利，则签出期权的发行方承担进行交换的义务。但是，如果主体既是相关经济资源交换的购入期权的持有方又是该交换的签出期权的发行方，则：

（1）如果交易对手行使主体签出期权下的权利，则主体在其购入期权下取消交易的权利因其承担的交换义务而失效；以及

（2）如果主体行使其购入期权下的权利，则交易对手在主体签出期权下取消交易的权利因其承担的交换义务而失效。

BC4.84 因此，如果主体同时是根据同一条款进行的同一相关交易的购入期权持有方和签出期权发行方，双方均无避免交换经济资源的权利。因此对于待执行合同，合同条款仅会产生一种结果，即除非双方均同意终止合同，否则将发生交换。而且，主体交换经济资源的权利和义务是相互依赖不可分开的。因此，无法将合同拆分为一个以上的单一资产或负债。如果交换是根据目前有利于报告主体的条款进行的，则合同为一项资产；如果交换是根据目前不利于报告主体的条款进行的，则合同为一项负债。

BC4.85 2015年征求意见稿的某些反馈意见者就待执行合同的结论如何影响对租赁合同产生的资产和负债的会计处理，或者如何影响于交易日对金融资产的会计处理，询问理事会的结论：

（1）根据《国际财务报告准则第16号——租赁》结论基础部分的解释，在租赁期开始日，承租人获得了在一段期间内使用相关资产的权利，而出租人通过向承租人提供可用资产交付了该权利。一旦出租人履行了交付该权利的义务，租赁合同不再属于待执行合同。承租人控制了使用权资产并承担支付租赁付款额的义务。

（2）《国际财务报告准则第9号——金融工具》允许对以常规方式购买或出售的金融资产采用"交易日会计"。交易日会计视作金融资产已于承诺（交易）日交付，而非在结算之前将购买或出售合同作为金融衍生工具核算。《国际财务报告准则第9

号》允许将交易日会计作为管理和记录短期交易的简单实用的方法。换言之，之所以采用这一方法是因为考虑了成本限制，即考虑交易日会计和结算日会计（《国际财务报告准则第9号》允许的另一方法）的相对成本和效益。

BC4.86　2018 版《概念框架》并未明确讨论待执行合同资产和负债的确认，因为 2018 版《概念框架》并未针对任何其他类型的资产和负债提出具体确认要求。同其他资产或负债的确认要求一样，理事会将在制定准则过程中提出针对待执行合同的确认要求。

BC4.87　鉴于利益相关方的担忧，理事会考虑了有关待执行合同的修订概念是否可能导致需要确认更多待执行合同产生的资产和负债。现行实务中，在许多情况下，并未针对待执行合同确认资产或负债。理事会预计这一情况将保持不变。适用于所有其他资产和负债的计量考虑因素（参见"第6章——计量"）同样适用于待执行合同产生的单一资产或负债。当待执行合同适用历史成本计量基础时，该合同通常以零金额计量（与未对该合同进行确认的实务影响相同），除非该合同为亏损合同。例如，针对购入存货的待执行合同的历史成本为零（假设无交易成本），除非该合同为亏损合同。

报告合同权利和义务的实质（第4.59 段至第4.62 段）

BC4.88　如第 2.12 段所解释的，2018 版《概念框架》明确规定，为了如实反映经济现象，主体应报告该现象的实质。2018 版《概念框架》包含有关报告合同权利和合同义务的实质的概念。这些概念以理事会在实施准则制定项目过程中制定的概念为基础。理事会确定，将相关概念纳入 2018 版《概念框架》将有助于确保这些概念在准则中的应用更加统一。

权益的定义（第 4.63 段至第 4.67 段）

BC4.89　2018 版《概念框架》仍然：
（1）对负债和权益进行非此即彼的区分；
（2）将权益定义为主体资产扣除所有负债后的剩余利益；以及
（3）未讨论当主体的权益包含不同类别的权益求偿权和不同的权益组成部分时，哪些形式的列示和披露是适当的（参见第 7.12 段至第 7.13 段）。

BC4.90　理事会考虑了仍然对负债和权益进行非此即彼的区分是否足以为财务报表使用者提供关于针对主体的求偿权的有用信息。负债与权益之间非此即彼的区分的内在局限性在于它试图对不同程度上具有不同特征的求偿权作出单一区分。取消这种非此即彼的区分并针对所有求偿权定义单一要素，有助于对每种求偿权单独确定以描述其具体特征。但是，除非所有求偿权均直接计量，否则任何方法都需要确定至少一个通过资产和负债账面价值来间接计量的剩余类别求偿权。此外，如果不对整个主体进行估值，就不可能直接计量所有求偿权，这超出了通用目的财务报告的既定目标。因此，将求偿权至少分为两类是不可避免的。

BC4.91 2013年讨论文件的某些反馈意见者建议，直接定义权益并引入另一要素（第三类求偿权）可能可以更好地描述同时具有负债和权益特征的求偿权。但是，理事会得出结论认为，引入另一要素会使分类和后续会计处理更加复杂。此外，可能有必要确定第三类求偿权的变动是应该符合收益的定义还是费用的定义。与引入新要素类似的结果还可以通过在负债或权益中分别列报不同类别来实现。

BC4.92 理事会将在其"具有权益特征的金融工具"研究项目中进一步探索如何区分负债和权益。该研究项目：

（1）将考虑区分负债和权益的方法，包括可能需要修改《概念框架》中负债或权益的定义的方法。理事会将在适当的时候使用该项目的结论来决定是否在其现行议程中增加一个修改相关准则、修改《概念框架》或同时修改两者的项目。理事会在决定启动现行项目前均须执行应循程序以将项目添加到其议程。

（2）不太可能改变第4.28段至第4.35段中的支持性指引，该指引关注识别报告主体是否负有转移经济资源的义务，其目的不在于帮助区分负债和权益（参见BC4.45段）。

收益和费用的定义（第4.68段至第4.72段）

基于资产和负债变动的收益和费用的定义

BC4.93 2010版《概念框架》基于资产和负债的变动对收益和费用进行定义。2013年讨论文件的部分反馈意见者对此提出质疑。他们认为，这种方法使财务状况表不恰当地优先于财务业绩表，并且没有充分认识到对财务业绩表的交易进行会计处理和配比收益和费用的重要性。

BC4.94 理事会不同意这种观点并得出结论认为：

（1）认为理事会完全或主要侧重于财务状况表的假定是不正确的。财务报表意在提供有关主体财务状况和财务业绩的信息（参见第3.3段）。因此，理事会在作出有关确认、计量及列示和披露的决策时，会考虑所得到的信息能否提供有关主体财务状况和财务业绩的有用信息。理事会未意在将有关财务状况或财务业绩的某一类信息作为财务报告的关注重点。

（2）有关交易的信息对财务报表的使用者而言为具有相关性的信息。因此，很多财务报告目前都以交易为基础，并将继续如此。

（3）导致产生收益和费用的交易也会导致资产和负债发生变动。因此，识别收益和费用后必然会识别哪些资产和负债已经发生变动。理事会和其他准则制定机构多年来发现，相较于首先定义收益和费用，然后将资产和负债描述为确认收益和费用的附带结果，首先定义资产和负债并将收益和费用定义为资产和负债的变动，这一方式更为有效、高效和精确。

（4）资产和负债的定义不仅仅是会计技术问题。它们指的是实际的经济现象（经济资源和转移经济资源的义务）。描述资产、负债和权益的财务状况表能够为使用者提供关于主体财务状况的更具相关性和更易理解的信息，而仅仅汇总配比收益和费用过程的附带产生的金额则不能，这些金额不一定能够描述经济现象。

（5）基于配比收益和费用的方法无法定义收益和费用涉及的期间。根据2018版《概念框架》第5.5段，如果收益和费用相互关联，他们通常会被同时确认，原因是相关资产和负债也会同时发生变动。然而，配比收益和费用的意图并不能证明在财务状况表中确认不符合资产或负债定义的项目是合理的。

BC4.95 理事会注意到，收益和费用的定义方面没有发现重大问题。因此，2018版《概念框架》所做的修订均为使收益和费用的定义与资产和负债定义的修订保持一致的必要修订。

收益和费用的类型

BC4.96 2010版《概念框架》中对收益和费用的讨论大多围绕列示和披露。2018版《概念框架》"第7章——列示和披露"对列示和披露进行了讨论。2010版《概念框架》的其他讨论涉及各种类型的收益和费用，例如，收入、利得和损失。而2018版《概念框架》未包含这部分内容。最初纳入这部分内容的目的在于强调收益包括收入和利得，费用包括损失。但理事会认为，现在这种强调是不必要的，在《概念框架》中划分收益和费用的子分类是无益的。理事会认为删除这部分内容不会引起实务的任何变化。

其他可能的定义

BC4.97 理事会在制定2018版《概念框架》的过程中，考虑了是否将权益求偿权持有者的投入、对权益求偿权持有者的分配以及现金流入和现金流出作为财务报表要素。由于理事会得出结论认为这些定义的缺失并未造成重大问题，因此2018版《概念框架》未包含此类定义。

起始段落

第5章——确认和终止确认

确认 ………………………………………………………………	**BC5.1**
相关性 …………………………………………………………	BC5.12
存在的不确定性 ………………………………………………	BC5.13
经济利益流入或流出可能性低 …………………………………	BC5.15
如实反映 ………………………………………………………	BC5.21
终止确认 ……………………………………………………………	**BC5.23**

确认（第5.6段至第5.25段）

BC5.1 2010版《概念框架》中的确认标准指出，若符合要素定义的项目满足下列要求，则主体应确认该项目：

（1）与该项目有关的未来经济利益将很可能流入或流出主体；以及

（2）该项目的成本或价值能够可靠计量。

BC5.2 上述确认标准带来以下问题：

（1）早于2018版《概念框架》制定的部分准则中采用了可能性确认标准，但并未一致地应用。这些准则使用了不同的可能性标准，其中包括"很可能""比不可能更可能"、"几乎确定"和"合理可能"。

（2）对部分确认问题应用可能性标准，可能会造成具有相关性的信息缺失或对主体财务状况或财务业绩的误导性陈述。例如，应用可能性标准可能会阻止部分衍生金融工具的确认。此外，可能性确认还可能导致主体在交易未产生经济收益时确认收益。例如，假设主体以在未来发生某不太可能发生的事项时承担支付固定金额的义务来换取现金。如果主体因考虑其收到现金时未来经济利益流出可能性较低而未确认负债，则主体将立即确认利得。为避免上述问题，早于2018版《概念框架》制定的准则（如《国际财务报告准则第9号——金融工具》）未采用可能性确认标准。

（3）对可靠性的表述不清晰，可能会引起不恰当的结果。尽管1989版《框架》将可靠性作为质量特征，但2010版《概念框架》不再使用术语"可靠性"指代质量特征，且未对可靠性进行定义（参见BC2.21段至BC2.31段）。"可靠"计量在实务中通常被解读为符合计量不确定性可容忍程度的计量，亦可能被解读为具有可验证性和无误性。因此，可靠计量的确认标准可能被解读为不得确认任何计量不确定性高的项目，即使确认该项目可提供有用信息。

BC5.3 2018版《概念框架》指出仅在确认一项资产或负债可以为财务报表使用者提供有用信息的情况下才可确认该资产或负债，有用信息指：

（1）资产或负债以及由此产生的收益、费用或权益变动的具有相关性的信息；以及

（2）对资产或负债以及由此产生的收益、费用或权益变动的如实反映。

BC5.4 2010版《概念框架》和2018版《概念框架》中的方法具有类似的目标，但具体实施存在差异：

（1）2010版《概念框架》针对确认不太可能提供具有有用财务信息质量特征的信息的案例制定了实用但主观的筛选方法，即通过可能性和可靠性进行筛选。

（2）2018版《概念框架》直接使用质量特征，并为质量特征的应用方法提供了指引。该指引解释了确认在什么情况下可能会产生缺乏质量特征的信息，包括应用2010版《概念框架》可能得出不是很可能引起经济利益流入流出或不可能进行可靠

计量的结论的某些（并非所有）情况。

BC5.5 理事会考虑了 2018 版《概念框架》是否应包括对所有符合资产定义或负债定义的项目都应确认的假设（或总体原则）。该假设可能意味着，如果理事会认为确认特定项目不会提供有用信息，则可能必须在特定准则中纳入此原则的例外情况。

BC5.6 理事会拒绝采用上述方法，因为理事会预计，在某些情况下其仍可得出结论认为，确认特定资产或负债不会提供有用信息，或确认这些资产或负债产生的成本将超过其获得的效益。《概念框架》需要为理事会提供指引，以帮助其决定如何在准则中设定确认要求。所有符合资产或负债定义的项目均应确认的这一假设或总体原则过于局限，无法提供上述指引。

BC5.7 某些利益相关方担心 2018 版《概念框架》所述的确认方法无法提供足够的指导，因为该方法过于抽象和主观。这些利益相关方建议理事会制定更加具体和强有力的确认标准，确保理事会能够制定出要求一致的准则，为使用者提供有用信息。

BC5.8 在考虑该担忧时，理事会发现 1989 版《框架》和 2010 版《概念框架》设定了同样抽象和主观的标准，即可能性和可靠性。2018 版《概念框架》中经修订的确认方法与有用财务信息质量特征直接挂钩，且提供了比之前方法更加清晰和完善的指引。理事会认为，在《概念框架》中设定更加严格的确认标准并不会有助于理事会在准则中设定以不超过其效益的成本来产生对财务报表使用者有用信息的确认要求。

BC5.9 某些利益相关方不赞同经修订的确认方法，他们担忧该方法可能扩大确认的资产和负债的范围。

BC5.10 理事会在修订确认标准过程中，希望制定有助于其能基于更加一致的原则作出决策的工具，扩大或缩小确认的资产或负债的范围并非其目的。BC5.15 段至 BC5.20 段阐述了理事会对经济利益流入或流出可能性低的情况的特定担忧的应对措施，BC5.21 段至 BC5.22 段阐述了理事会对计量不确定性的特定担忧的应对措施。

BC5.11 此外，理事会还注意到，根据 2018 版《概念框架》第 SP1.2 段，《概念框架》中的任何内容均不可超越准则中的规定，因此，2018 版《概念框架》中经修订的确认标准不会对财务报表编制者如何应用早于 2018 版《概念框架》发布的准则中制定的确认标准造成影响。

相关性（第5.12 段至第5.17 段）

BC5.12 经修订的确认标准的支持性指引中提供了表明确认资产或负债可能无法向财务报表使用者提供具有相关性信息的因素的示例。其中两个因素与以下情况相关：

（1）资产或负债存在与否存在不确定性（参见 BC5.13 段至 BC5.14 段）；或者

（2）存在资产或负债，但经济利益流入或流出的可能性低（参见 BC5.15 段至 BC5.20 段）。

存在的不确定性（第 5.14 段）

BC5.13 有时资产或负债存在与否存在不确定性（即，存在的不确定性）。理事会得出结论认为，应将存在的不确定性与结果的不确定性和计量的不确定性分开考虑。尽管存在的不确定性可能会引起结果的不确定性和计量的不确定性，但在概念上存在的不确定性与另外两者是不同的，且对确认决策的影响也不同。对不同类型的不确定性加以区分有助于确定哪些信息最有可能与财务报表使用者相关，以及如何实现如实反映。

BC5.14 因具体的方法依具体事实和情况而定，所以关于如何在作出确认决策时考虑存在的不确定性，2018 版《概念框架》未提供具体指引。

经济利益流入或流出可能性低（第 5.15 段至第 5.17 段）

BC5.15 2013 年讨论文件和 2015 年征求意见稿的许多反馈意见者认为确认标准应继续使用可能性标准。他们认为：

（1）可能性标准已被证明是应用质量特征的可行方式。针对经济利益流入流出可能性低的项目提议的支持性指引不够清晰，可能会造成困惑和不一致。

（2）删除可能性标准并从资产和负债定义中删除"预期"表述，可能会扩大主体对经济利益流入或流出可能性低的资产和负债的确认范围。确认此类资产和负债无法提供有用信息。此外，财务报表编制者可能必须为此广泛搜索权利和义务。（BC4.8 段至 BC4.14 段对将"预期"流入流出概念的删除进行了讨论）

（3）如果确认了未来经济流入和流出可能性低的资产和负债，则可能必须按照基于预期值的金额确认。此类计量具有难度，会给财务报表编制者带来负担。有时提供关于可能结果的范围和分布的信息要比提供一个基于预期值的计量更加有用。此类计量可能会造成精确计量的假象。

BC5.16 某些反馈意见者建议对部分资产或负债（如专利或研发支出）而非所有资产或负债（例如，衍生金融资产）应用可能性筛选条件，或对部分交易而非所有交易（例如，不对现金取得资产应用）应用可能性筛选条件。这些反馈意见者建议，仅为允许确认部分金融工具而从确认标准中删除可能性标准这一决策不合理。在准则中纳入针对特定金融工具的例外情况即可实现该目的。

BC5.17 理事会指出，可能性标准可能是筛选其确认无法提供具有相关性的信息的资产和负债的一种可行方法。但在某些确认可以提供具有相关性的信息的情况下，采用该方法会导致未确认资产和负债。此外，也难以设定出适用于所有准则和所有确认事项的可能性标准。

BC5.18 理事会还注意到，无论对经济利益流入或流出可能性低的资产或负债应用哪种计量基础，该基础都可能反映出可能性低的事实，即要求的计量基础仅反映经济利益最大流入或最大流出是不太可能的。

BC5.19 因此 2018 版《概念框架》未纳入可能性标准。但在某些情况下，经济利益流入或流出的可能性低可以作为确认无法提供具有相关性的信息的指标。具体原因参见第 5.16 段至第 5.17 段。

BC5.20 某些利益相关方担心术语"可能性低"过于主观，难以一致地解释。但理事会对可能性低的情况的讨论意在表明在其中的某些情况下理事会可能会得出结论认为部分信息可能不相关，其目标并非确定可能性标准并以该标准判断信息相关与否。

如实反映（第 5.18 段至第 5.25 段）

BC5.21 根据 BC5.2 段至 BC5.4 段的讨论，2018 版《概念框架》中的确认标准并不包括仅在资产或负债的成本或价值能够可靠计量时方可确认资产或负债的要求。理事会得出结论认为，计量的不确定性程度高不一定会妨碍计量提供关于资产或负债的有用信息，所以很难设定适用于所有准则和所有确认事项的计量的不确定性的单一标准。因此，2018 版《概念框架》讨论了计量的不确定性被视为可能影响是否可通过对资产或负债的确认来提供如实反映的因素，并在必要时通过解释性信息予以支持。本讨论以"第 2 章——有用财务信息的质量特征"（参见第 2.19 段、第 2.22 段和 BC2.46 段至 BC2.49 段）中关于计量不确定性的讨论为基础。

BC5.22 2013 年讨论文件和 2015 年征求意见稿的某些反馈意见者认为，在确认负债或费用时对计量不确定性的可容忍程度高于确认资产或收益。他们将此称为审慎性的应用（不对称审慎性，采用 BC2.37 段中的术语）。理事会得出结论认为，计量不确定性的程度是否可提供如实反映取决于具体事实和情况，因此只有在制定准则时才能确定（参见第 5.9 段）。BC2.44 段至 BC2.45 段进一步讨论了关于确认和计量的决策的对称性。

终止确认（第 5.26 段至第 5.33 段）

BC5.23 2010 版《概念框架》未定义终止确认；也未阐述何时发生终止确认。

BC5.24 关于终止确认的讨论通常会比较以下两种终止确认方法：

（1）控制法——终止确认指确认的相反过程。因此，当资产或负债不再符合确认标准（或不再存在，或不再属于该主体的资产或负债）时，该主体终止确认资产或负债。

（2）风险和报酬法——主体继续确认资产或负债，直至该主体不再承担该资产或负债产生的大部分风险和报酬。即使在主体处置已转移部分的当日资产或负债不符合确认条件，该持续确认仍然适用，前提是在该日该主体仅取得了保留部分并且此前未确认该部分。①

BC5.25 为解决控制法和风险和报酬法之间的某些明显冲突，理事会在 2018 版《概念框架》中对以下内容进行了解释：

（1）如果主体显然转移了资产但保留了该资产可能产生的经济利益金额的重大积极或消极变化的风险敞口，这有时表明该主体可能仍然控制该资产；以及

（2）如果主体将资产转移给代该主体持有资产的另一方（代理人），则转移方仍然控制该资产。

BC5.26 理事会在制定 2018 版《概念框架》的过程中得出结论认为，终止确认的会计要求的目标是如实反映以下两方面内容：

（1）引起终止确认的交易或其他事项发生之后保留的资产和负债（包括作为交易或其他事项一部分的已取得、已发生或已创建的资产或负债）；以及

（2）由该交易或其他事项引起的主体资产和负债的变动。

BC5.27 理事会认为，控制法更侧重于 BC5.26（1）段所述的目标，而风险和报酬法则更侧重于 BC5.26（2）段所述的目标。如果主体转移整个资产或整个负债并且不再承担该资产或负债的敞口，那么控制法与风险和报酬法的结果相同。此外，在这种情况下，实现 BC5.26 段所述的两个目标都很直接。

BC5.28 相比之下，如果主体仅转移部分资产或负债或保留部分变化的敞口，理事会在准则制定上就面临着困难。在此类情况下，控制法与风险和报酬法不会总是得出相同结果，而且 BC5.26 段中的两个目标有时会相互冲突。理事会认为这两个目标都是有效的。因此，2018 版《概念框架》中，理事会没有具体说明使用控制法还是风险和报酬法。

BC5.29 相反，理事会采用了涉及以下内容的方法：

（1）终止确认已转移部分。

（2）继续确认保留部分（如有）。

（3）必要时采用下列一个或多个步骤，以实现 BC5.26 段的一项或两项目标：

①在财务状况表中单独列示任何保留部分；

②在财务业绩表中单独列示由于终止确认已转移部分而确认的收益和费用；以及

③提供解释性信息。

（4）如果对已转移部分的终止确认不足以实现 BC5.26 段的两个目标，即使有单独列报或解释性信息的支持，最后应考虑继续确认已转移部分是否能够实现这些目标。需通过提供单独列报或解释性信息来支持继续确认，因为财务报表将纳入不符合财务报表要素的项目，作为资产和负债以及相关的收益和费用。

---

① 2018 版《概念框架》第 5.28 段解释了已转移部分和保留部分包含的内容。

BC5.30 理事会考虑了对终止确认的会计要求目标的描述是否应明确提及除如实反映质量特征之外的相关性质量特征。理事会指出，BC5.26段的目标确定了在考虑终止确认时需要如实地反映哪些经济现象。理事会认为，关于这些经济现象的信息与财务报表使用者有关。因此，理事会得出结论认为，明确提及相关性并不会改变其实现这两个目标的方式。

《财务报告概念框架》结论基础

起始段落

第 6 章——计量

引言 ··	**BC6.1**
混合计量 ···	**BC6.5**
计量基础和所提供的信息 ···	**BC6.12**
历史成本 ··	BC6.19
现行价值 ··	BC6.23
交易成本 ··	BC6.30
选择计量基础时考虑的因素 ··	**BC6.34**
对财务状况表和财务业绩表的影响 ·······································	BC6.36
相关性 ··	BC6.37
如实反映 ··	BC6.43
提升性质量特征 ···	BC6.46
初始计量的特殊因素 ··	BC6.49
一种以上计量基础 ···	BC6.50
权益的计量 ···	**BC6.52**

引言

BC6.1 理事会在制定 2018 版《概念框架》的过程中，未就何时适用特定计量基础提供详细指引，因为特定计量基础的适用性取决于具体事实和情况。但 2018 版《概念框架》：

（1）描述了计量基础和所提供的信息；以及

（2）讨论了选择计量基础时考虑的因素。

BC6.2 2015 年征求意见稿的某些反馈意见者质疑，简单描述计量基础并讨论选择计量基础时考虑的因素是否能为理事会制定准则中的计量要求提供充分指引。这些反馈意见者建议理事会对计量进行进一步研究，并且：

（1）推迟发布修订版《概念框架》，直至研究完成；

（2）发布不含有计量章节的修订版《概念框架》；或者

（3）制定关于计量的概览性的暂行指引以供使用，直到能够制定更完整的概念和原则。

BC6.3 理事会驳回了这些建议。2010 版《概念框架》几乎未提供计量指引，这是需要解决的重大欠缺。理事会得出结论认为，2018 版《概念框架》中的指引将有助于制定准则中的计量要求。

BC6.4 此外，理事会考虑了 2018 版《概念框架》是否需要确定一个单独的总体计量目标。理事会得出结论认为，单独的计量目标不太可能提供有用的额外指引来帮助其制定计量要求。相反，2018 版《概念框架》描述了计量如何为通用目的财务报表的目标提供帮助（参见第 6.45 段）。

混合计量（第 6.2 段）

BC6.5 理事会在制定 2018 版《概念框架》的过程中，考虑了《概念框架》是否应倡导采用单一计量基础。使用单一计量基础的主要优点是：

（1）计入财务报表的金额可以更有意义地相加、相减和比较；以及

（2）财务报表的复杂性降低，可理解性提高。

BC6.6 此外，如果理事会要确定能够满足财务报表使用者信息需求的财富或资本概念，那么就需要一个单一计量基础来计量财富或资本。但是，根据 BC8.1 段至 BC8.4 段的讨论，理事会决定不更新关于资本和资本保全的讨论，且不试图确定能够满足财务报表使用者信息需求的财富或资本概念。

BC6.7 2013 年讨论文件和 2015 年征求意见稿均表明，针对所有资产、负债、收益和费用的单一计量基础可能并不总能向财务报表使用者提供最具相关性的信息。

几乎所有评论此问题的反馈意见者均支持所建议的方法。

BC6.8 然而，少数反馈意见者不同意上述方法并建议从下列各项中选取一个作为单一计量基础：

（1）历史成本；

（2）公允价值；

（3）现行进入价值（例如，现行成本，参见 2018 版《概念框架》第 6.21 段至第 6.22 段）；或者

（4）剥夺（豁免）价值［参见 BC6.29（1）段］。

BC6.9 建议采用单一计量基础的大多数反馈意见者承认，实务中无法实现这一点，至少在短期内是如此。不过，他们表示，理事会应描述制定准则时将默认使用的计量基础。然后，理事会应就任何使用其他计量基础的决策提供解释。

BC6.10 理事会得出结论认为，在不同的情况下，采用不同的计量基础可能会提供与财务报表使用者相关的信息。另外，在不同的情况下，特定的计量基础可能：

（1）比其他计量基础更易于理解和实施；

（2）可验证性更强，不易出错或计量不确定性水平低于其他计量基础；或者

（3）实施成本低于其他计量基础。

BC6.11 因此，2018 版《概念框架》指出，考虑有用财务信息的质量特征和成本限制的情况下，可能会针对不同的资产、负债、收益和费用选择不同的计量基础。

计量基础和所提供的信息（第 6.4 段至第 6.42 段）

BC6.12 2018 版《概念框架》识别了两类计量基础。BC6.19 段至 BC6.22 段讨论了历史成本基础，BC6.23 段至 BC6.29 段讨论了现行价值计量基础。

BC6.13 2013 年讨论文件将基于现金流量的计量作为单独类别的计量基础。而 2018 版《概念框架》并未如此，原因在于理事会得出结论认为，基于现金流量的计量本身并不是计量基础。相反，在应用指定计量基础时基于现金流量的计量技术可被用于估计计量。2018 版《概念框架》的第 6.91 段至第 6.95 段讨论了如何以这种方式使用这些技术。

BC6.14 理事会考虑并驳回了将计量基础按照其提供的信息分为下列两类的想法：提供有关主体业务活动投入的成本的输入值（如历史成本和现行成本等进入价值）以及提供有关主体业务活动产出的成本的信息（如公允价值、使用价值或履约价值等退出价值）。理事会发现，在描述或选择用于特定准则的计量基础时这一区别并没有帮助，这是因为同一市场的进入价值和退出价值之间的差异通常很小，交易成本除外（参见 BC6.30 段至 BC6.33 段）。

BC6.15 2018 版《概念框架》描述了理事会在制定准则时很可能考虑选择的计量基础。根据第 6.3 段，一项准则可能需要描述如何实施该准则中选择的计量基础。

BC6.16 此外，2018 版《概念框架》讨论了特定计量基础提供的信息。识别此类信息将有助于确定在特定情况下特定计量基础是否很可能向财务报表使用者提供有用信息。

BC6.17 2015 年征求意见稿的一些反馈意见者表示，对计量基础的讨论存在偏见。部分反馈意见者认为，该讨论更偏向历史成本；相反，其他反馈意见者认为该讨论更偏向现行价值。理事会在制定 2018 版《概念框架》过程中，试图对各计量基础和所提供的信息进行无偏见的描述。理事会并未意在偏向任何一种计量基础。

BC6.18 在"第 6 章——计量"中，术语"价值"一般指资产或负债的经济价值，而非账面价值（参见第 5.1 段）和公允价值等特定现行价值。例如，由于货币的时间价值等因素，经济价值可能不同于未来现金支付或未来现金收入的情况。

历史成本（第6.4 段至第6.9 段和第6.24 段至第6.31 段）

BC6.19 根据 2018 版《概念框架》，资产的历史成本为初始购建该资产发生的成本的价值，包括购建该资产支付的对价加上交易成本。负债的历史成本为初始发生或承担负债时收取的对价减去交易成本后的价值。在制定准则时，理事会将决定是否明确规定如何确定这些初始价值。

BC6.20 资产的全部或部分消耗会导致对消耗的部分资产的终止确认。如果该资产以历史成本计量，则终止确认通过该资产的折旧或摊销反映。同样，负债的全部或部分履行会导致对履行的部分负债的终止确认。

BC6.21 当资产发生减值或负债致损，如果不对初始确认时确定的成本进行更新，则无法提供具有相关性的信息。因此，2018 版《概念框架》指出应通过更新资产的历史成本以反映部分历史成本不再可收回的事实，即，应更新该资产的账面价值以反映减值。同样，应更新负债的历史成本以反映导致负债致损的变动，即，为发生或承担该负债而收取的对价不再足以反映履行该负债的义务。但是，历史成本并不反映未发生减值的资产或未致损的负债的价值变动。

BC6.22 金融资产或金融负债的摊余成本反映未来现金流量的折现后的估计值，折现率自初始确认后并不更新，除非该资产或负债按可变利率计息。对于发放或收到的贷款，如果定期收取或支付利息，则该贷款的摊余成本通常近似于最初支付或收取的金额。此外，如果发放的贷款发生减值，则其账面价值减少。因此，2018 版《概念框架》将金融资产和金融负债的摊余成本分类为历史成本的一种形式。

现行价值（第6.10 段至第6.22 段和第6.32 段至第6.42 段）

BC6.23 2018 版《概念框架》将现行价值计量识别为利用能够反映计量日具体情况的已更新信息提供有关资产、负债及相关收益和费用的金额信息。其阐明了现行价值计量基础包括公允价值、使用价值（资产）、履约价值（负债）和现行成本。

BC6.24 2018 版《概念框架》对公允价值的描述与《国际财务报告准则第 13

号——公允价值计量》的描述一致。对使用价值和履约价值的描述基于《国际会计准则第 36 号——资产减值》中使用价值的定义，该定义是在 2018 版《概念框架》之前制定的准则中有关主体特定价值的最明确的定义。对现行成本的描述基于多个学术来源中对现行成本的描述。

BC6.25　早于 2018 版《概念框架》制定的部分准则使用了使用价值，但并未将其作为单独计量基础。在此类准则中，使用价值被用于确定按历史成本计量且可能发生减值的资产的可收回金额。在此背景下，如果以使用价值确定减值资产的可收回金额，在减值损失予以确认之后的时点，该资产的账面价值等于其使用价值。然而，2018 版《概念框架》将使用价值作为单独计量基础，原因在于：

（1）其在概念上与历史成本不同，尽管使用价值被用于确定可收回历史成本；以及

（2）理事会可能决定，在某些情况下，主体应使用主体特定现行价值（即使用价值）而非公允价值计量资产。

BC6.26　2018 版《概念框架》解释了使用价值和履约价值反映与公允价值相同的因素，但两者使用的是针对主体的假设，而非市场参与者的假设。

BC6.27　因此，使用价值和履约价值反映承担现金流量的内在不确定性的价格，即风险溢价。纳入此类风险溢价可产生具有相关性的信息，原因在于其能够反映具有不同程度的不确定性的项目之间的经济差异。《国际会计准则第 36 号》中对使用价值的描述隐含了纳入风险溢价的意图。①

BC6.28　虽然国际财务报告准则并未广泛采用现行成本，但是很多学术文献主张在财务报告中使用现行成本。因此，2018 版《概念框架》纳入了现行成本。

BC6.29　2018 版《概念框架》并未描述以下现行价值计量基础：

（1）资产的剥夺价值或负债的豁免价值。资产的剥夺价值指主体在被剥夺被计量资产的情况下将遭受的损失。类似地，负债的豁免价值指主体在被豁免被计量负债的情况下将享有的利益。由于剥夺价值或豁免价值比其他计量基础更复杂且只有少数经济体使用，故理事会并未对其进行讨论。因此，理事会得出结论认为，在制定准则时不太可能使用剥夺价值或豁免价值。

（2）可变现净值。可变现净值指资产销售的预计对价扣除预计销售成本。理事会得出结论认为，不必单独描述可变现净值，因为它基于另一现行价值计量。

（3）免除履约成本。免除履约成本指通过与交易对手协商而不再承担义务的预计成本（包括交易成本）。相较于履约，主体被免除履约的情况比较少见，因此理事会得出结论认为，不必在 2018 版《概念框架》中描述该计量基础。

交易成本

BC6.30　在以下两种情况时可产生交易成本：

---

① 参见《国际会计准则第 36 号——资产减值》第 55 段至第 56 段、第 A1 段和第 A15 段至第 A21 段。

(1) 取得资产或发生/承担负债；以及

(2) 出售或处置资产或清偿或转移负债。

BC6.31 界定哪些成本为交易成本超出了《概念框架》的范围。在特定准则，交易成本通常指除交易对价之外的增量成本，即如果被计量的特定资产（或负债）未取得（或发生）或未被出售或处置（或转移或履行）的情况下不会发生的成本。

BC6.32 在取得资产或产生负债时产生的交易成本为取得资产或产生负债的交易的一项特征。因此：

(1) 资产或负债的历史成本和现行成本反映此类交易成本。虽然此类交易成本不属于交易价格，但主体若不发生此类交易成本可能无法取得该资产或发生该负债。

(2) 如果计量意在描述资产或负债的公允价值、履约价值或使用价值，则该计量不反映此类交易成本。此类成本并不影响该资产或负债的现行价值。

BC6.33 在出售或处置资产或者清偿或转移负债时将发生的交易成本，是可能的未来交易的一项特征。因此：

(1) 如果主体预计交易成本将发生，则使用价值和履约价值反映该交易成本；

(2) 公允价值并不反映此类交易成本；以及

(3) 历史成本和现行成本并不反映在出售或处置资产或者清偿或转移负债时将发生的交易成本，因为此类计量基础为进入价值，而进入价值反映的是取得资产或发生负债的成本。

选择计量基础时考虑的因素（第6.43段至第6.86段）

BC6.34 为满足财务报表的目标，特定计量基础提供的信息必须是对财务报表使用者而言有用的信息。为此，计量基础须提供具有相关性并且如实反映其意在反映的内容的信息。2018版《概念框架》讨论了相关性和如实反映如何影响计量基础的选择。

BC6.35 理事会考虑了是否需要规定在选择计量基础时考虑相关因素的顺序（例如，采用层级或决策树），但最后得出结论认为，这样做不可行且不可取。各项因素的相对重要性取决于具体事实和情况。事实上，在很多情况下，在选择计量基础时需要考虑多项因素。

对财务状况表和财务业绩表的影响（第6.43段）

BC6.36 2018版《概念框架》指出，在选择计量基础时，必须考虑计量基础在财务状况表和财务业绩表中产生的信息的性质。2015年征求意见稿的某些反馈意见者表示，《概念框架》应更加关注特定计量方法对财务业绩表的影响。他们认为，对于财务报表使用者而言，财务业绩表比财务状况表更有用。然而，理事会得出结论认为，这些报表中产生的信息的相对重要性取决于使用者在分析中如何使用这些信息，而使用者在分析中如何使用这些信息取决于具体的事实和情况。

相关性（第6.49段至第6.57段）

BC6.37 2018版《概念框架》讨论了下列会影响计量基础产生信息的相关性的因素：

（1）资产或负债的特征；以及

（2）如何产生未来现金流量（参见BC6.38段至BC6.42段）。

BC6.38 第1.14段指出，有些经济资源直接产生现金流量，而其他经济资源则需综合使用才能产生现金流量。基于这一点，2018版《概念框架》确定了在选择计量基础时需要考虑的一个因素，即资产或负债如何产生未来现金流量。

BC6.39 2018版《概念框架》指出，资产或负债如何产生未来现金流量在一定程度上取决于主体业务活动的性质。例如，取决于主体业务活动的性质，同一资产可能作为存货出售、出租给另一主体，或用于该主体的业务。理事会指出，采用同一方法计量以不同的方式产生现金流量的资产或负债，会使不同的事项看起来相同，从而降低可比性。①

BC6.40 尽管2015年征求意见稿的某些反馈意见者担心，如果在选择计量基础时考虑主体业务活动的性质会产生主观性，但多数反馈意见者支持采用这种方法。此外，理事会指出，在多数情况下，主体业务活动的性质是一个事实，而不是一种观点或管理层意图。否则，理事会将需要考虑如何解决主观性问题。

BC6.41 出于BC0.39段给出的原因，2018版《概念框架》并未明确提及长期投资等任何特定的业务活动。

BC6.42 为了帮助选择计量基础，2018版《概念框架》还就历史成本或现行价值计量基础何时能够提供有关金融资产和金融负债的具有相关性的信息提供了指引。该指引基于理事会在制定《国际财务报告准则第9号——金融工具》时确定的概念。《国际财务报告准则第9号》的结论基础部分解释了理事会为何决定使用这些概念。

如实反映（第6.58段至第6.62段）

BC6.43 2018版《概念框架》将以下两项作为能够影响特定计量基础提供的信息是否能够如实反映其所描述的经济现象的因素：

（1）资产和负债是否在某种程度上相关；以及

（2）计量的不确定性（参见BC6.44段至BC6.45段）。

BC6.44 2013年讨论文件的某些反馈意见者建议，在选择计量基础时考虑的因素之一即为与该计量基础相关的计量的不确定性程度。某些反馈意见者使用术语

---

① 2018版《概念框架》第2.27段指出："可比性不是完全统一。为了使信息可比，相同的事项必须采用相同的处理方法，而不同的事项必须采用不同的处理方法。"

"可靠性"来描述该因素。根据 BC2.28 段至 BC2.31 段的讨论，理事会并未重新引入"可靠性"一词。根据 2018 版《概念框架》第 2.22 段的解释，如果估计过程中计量的不确定性程度高，则可能表明有关该经济现象的其他信息可能更加有用（参见 BC2.55 段至 BC2.56 段）。此外，"第 6 章——计量"讨论了计量的不确定性如何影响计量基础的选择。

BC6.45 2015 年征求意见稿的某些反馈意见者指出，按照他们对审慎性的理解运用审慎性，可能隐含表示负债计量不确定性的可容忍程度总是高于资产[参见 BC2.37（2）段、BC2.41 段至 BC2.45 段和 BC2.55 段至 BC2.56 段]。但理事会不同意这一观点并得出结论认为，计量的不确定性的可容忍程度取决于具体事实和情况，而且只有在制定准则时才能够确定。

提升性质量特征（第6.63 段至第6.76 段）

BC6.46 2018 版《概念框架》确定了四个能够提高财务信息有用性的"提升性质量特征"——可比性、可验证性、及时性和可理解性。理事会在制定 2018 版《概念框架》的过程中，认为除了"第 2 章——有用财务信息的质量特征"中的讨论之外，及时性对计量基础的选择没有特别的影响。2018 版《概念框架》讨论了可比性、可验证性和可理解性对计量基础选择产生的一般影响。

BC6.47 理事会在制定 2018 版《概念框架》的过程中，考虑了反馈意见者提出的以下建议：
（1）可验证性在选择计量基础时应发挥更重要的作用；以及
（2）如果理事会在制定准则时阻止财务报表编制者选择计量基础，则可比性可进一步提升。

BC6.48 理事会得出结论认为，对可验证性的讨论适当地反映了可验证性在作为选择计量基础的一项考虑因素时的作用。此外，理事会得出结论认为，因为第 2.29 段表明允许对同一经济现象采用不同的会计处理方法将削弱可比性，所以不必进一步讨论制定允许编制者选择替代性计量基础的准则的缺点。

初始计量的特殊因素（第6.77 段至第6.82 段）

BC6.49 2015 年征求意见稿讨论了交易具有相似价值的项目和交易具有不同价值的项目两种情况。2015 年征求意见稿的反馈意见者指出，"相似价值"和"不同价值"的含义不清。为消除此种担忧，2018 版《概念框架》引入了交易条件是否为市场条件的描述。

一种以上计量基础（第6.83 段至第6.86 段）

BC6.50 2018 版《概念框架》讨论了为向财务报表使用者提供有用信息而须针对资产或负债以及相关收益和费用使用一种以上计量基础的情况。

BC6.51 提供此类信息的方式之一是针对财务状况表中的资产或负债使用一种现行价值计量基础，而对损益表中的相关收益或费用使用另一计量基础。在这种情况下，包括在损益表中的收益或费用与资产或负债的现行价值变动之间的差异会计入其他综合收益。根据第 7.17 段的讨论，理事会仅可能在极少情况下要求以这种方式提供信息，只有当这样做能够使损益表提供更具相关性的信息，或是更能如实反映主体当期的财务业绩的情况下。

权益的计量（第 6.87 段至第 6.90 段）

BC6.52 尽管权益总额并非直接计量，但通过直接计量个别类别的权益或权益组成部分来提供有用信息的做法可能是适当的。2018 版《概念框架》讨论了这一想法。

BC6.53 2015 年征求意见稿的一些反馈意见者不同意直接计量个别类别的权益或权益组成部分这一建议，原因在于：

（1）因为权益是指剩余利益，因此不宜直接计量某一类别的权益或权益的某一组成部分；以及

（2）将权益分为不同类别和组成部分会导致项目的披露对报告主体整体而言无财务影响，因此这样做不符合采用报告主体的角度的观点。

BC6.54 尽管权益的账面价值总额（权益总额）是以剩余利益进行计量，但理事会指出，权益是指一种求偿权，即主体资产扣除所有负债后的剩余利益。直接计量某些类别的权益或权益的某些组成部分并不与该定义相悖，这不同于直接计量权益总额。即使直接计量了某些个别类别的权益或权益组成部分，权益总额仍等于所有已确认资产的账面价值总额减去所有已确认负债的账面价值总额。因此，如果主体拥有一个以上类别的权益或一个以上的权益组成部分，则至少应将其中一个以剩余利益进行计量。

BC6.55 理事会还得出结论认为，直接计量某些个别类别的权益或权益的某些组成部分不会与财务报表中采用的主体角度相悖。直接计量可能会为财务报表使用者提供有助于决定是否向主体提供资源的信息。此类信息是从主体的角度提供的，反映了针对主体持有的权益求偿权。此类信息并不是从特定求偿权持有者的角度提供的。

第 7 章——列示和披露

	起始段落
引言 ···	**BC7.1**
权益的分类 ··	**BC7.4**
收益和费用的分类 ··	**BC7.6**
术语 ···	BC7.6
列示与披露收益和费用的指引方法 ··································	BC7.9
描述损益 ···	BC7.15
损益和其他综合收益 ··	BC7.21
将项目重分类至损益 ··	BC7.26

引言

BC7.1 2010版《概念框架》未包含列示和披露主题。理事会于2011年就其议程开展公开征询意见，反馈意见者认为应将列报和披露主题作为理事会的优先项目。确定的具体问题之一是提供关于主体财务业绩的信息，包括其他综合收益的使用。

BC7.2 作为对上述反馈的回应，2018版《概念框架》中首次加入了如下内容：

（1）关于描述如何在财务报表中列示和披露信息的概念。此类概念有助于指导理事会在准则中制定列示和披露要求，并帮助主体在财务报表中提供信息。

（2）为理事会提供收益和费用分类的指引，帮助理事会确定应将收益或费用计入损益还是计入损益之外的其他综合收益（参见第7.15段至第7.18段）。

（3）为理事会提供是否应将计入其他综合收益的收益和费用在之后期间重分类至损益及应在何时重分类的指引（参见第7.19段）。

BC7.3 理事会发布2018版《概念框架》时正致力于：

（1）制定披露动议，计划多个实施和研究项目，意在通过提供基于《概念框架》中列示和披露概念制定的额外指引以改善财务报表披露。

（2）关于主要财务报表的研究项目。该项目研究对财务业绩表、现金流量表、也可能包括财务状况表和所有者权益变动表的结构和内容可能的针对性改进。

权益的分类（第7.12段至第7.13段）

BC7.4 2018版《概念框架》仅就何时适合单独列报不同类别的权益求偿权和不同的权益组成部分提供了概要指引。该指引的制定基础为第7.7段至第7.8段所述的分类的概念。

BC7.5 理事会可能在具有权益特征的金融工具的研究项目中探索如何改善所有者权益变动表或列示或披露要求，其中可能包含理事会于2013年讨论文件中探索的部分改善方法。

收益和费用的分类（第7.14段至第7.19段）

术语

BC7.6 理事会在2018版《概念框架》引入了术语"财务业绩表"，来描述损益表或相关部分以及显示其他综合收益的报表或相关部分。

BC7.7 2018 版《概念框架》之所以使用术语"财务业绩表",是因为该术语能够与准则中的术语"财务状况表"统一,且比理事会有时使用的术语"综合收益表"更加清晰。

BC7.8 2007 年,理事会发布了一项规定,即将确认在损益之外的收益和费用计入综合收益表。理事会同时还引入了术语"其他综合收益"来描述未计入损益的收益和费用。某些反馈意见者认为,术语"其他综合收益"既缺乏针对性,又不易于财务报表使用者理解。尽管如此,理事会仍得出结论认为,如不使用该术语或使用其他术语可能会造成混淆。因此,理事会在 2018《概念框架》中仍采用了这一术语。

列示与披露收益和费用的指引方法

BC7.9 多年来,理事会确定了多个可以或必须计入损益之外的收益和费用项目。这些决定均出于特定项目中的特定原因,而非出于某个统一应用的概念性原因。

BC7.10 1989 版《框架》和 2010 版《概念框架》未提及计入损益之外的收益或费用,也未提及其他综合收益。

BC7.11 理事会认为在《概念框架》中加入有关此主题的讨论十分必要。但其认为《概念框架》不应讨论应在一张还是两张财务业绩表中列示收益和费用,这应在制定准则时确定。自 2007 年起,该决定在《国际会计准则第 1 号——财务报表列报》中得以体现。

BC7.12 理事会在制定 2018 版《概念框架》的过程中考虑了以下问题:

(1) 如何定义或描述损益(参见 BC7.15 段至 BC7.20 段);

(2) 如何确定将哪些收益和费用计入损益,哪些计入其他综合收益(参见 BC7.21 段至 BC7.25 段);以及

(3) 是否以及何时将计入其他综合收益的金额重分类至损益(参见 BC7.26 段至 BC7.33 段)。

BC7.13 2013 年讨论文件和 2015 年征求意见稿的许多反馈意见者认为,关于列示收益和费用的建议指引不够充分,无法为理事会制定准则提供清晰的基础。许多反馈意见者要求理事会进一步讨论财务业绩报告问题。

BC7.14 但理事会认为缺乏有关收益和费用的列示指引是 2010 版《概念框架》的一项重大缺陷。理事会得出结论认为其已取得了重大进展,为收益和费用的列示制定了概要指引,这一指引将协助理事会在准则中制定披露要求。因此,理事会决定在 2018 版《概念框架》加入此指引,而非在单独的项目中就损益和其他综合收益表的使用进行探讨。该决定不妨碍进一步讨论财务业绩报告问题。

描述损益(第 7.16 段)

BC7.15 2018 版《概念框架》:

(1) 将损益表描述为报告期间主体财务业绩信息的主要来源;以及

（2）将损益合计或损益小计描述为报告期间主体财务业绩信息的高度汇总。

BC7.16 许多财务报表使用者将损益合计或损益小计作为起点或主体财务业绩主要指标加入分析，上述描述内容符合这一事实。

BC7.17 仅按照第 7.16 段所述方式描述损益表可能不太满足反馈意见者对"损益"进行定义或更精确描述的要求，但根据之前的工作结果，理事会得出结论认为，很难找到一项或较少数量的几项特征是所有计入损益表的项目所共有的，但却是最适合计入其他综合收益的项目所不具备的。因此理事会得出结论认为不太可能就损益或其他综合收益制定出严格的概念性定义。

BC7.18 同时，理事会得出结论认为，其无法制定最适合计入损益的所有种类项目的规范清单。这样的清单不可能完整，且这样做会必然导致主体将最适合计入损益的部分（可能是大部分）项目计入其他综合收益。

BC7.19 许多利益相关方不断要求理事会界定损益，其中的少数利益相关方为如何制定定义或如何区分计入损益和计入其他综合收益的收益和费用提供建议。但未就可行方法达成共识。

BC7.20 根据本结论基础 BC7.17 段至 BC7.19 段，理事会得出结论认为不可能为损益或其他综合收益制定出严格的概念性定义，也不可能制定最适合计入损益的所有种类项目的规范清单。尽管如此，理事会在 2018 年《概念框架》首次引入了关于对理事会来说何时适合将收益或费用计入其他综合收益的指引。理事会认为，提供有关该议题的指引是一项重大改进。

损益和其他综合收益（第7.17 段）

BC7.21 正如 BC7.17 段所述，理事会没有识别出最适合于计入损益表的所有项目的一个或一组共同特征。

BC7.22 此外，理事会探讨了对将会或可能计入其他综合收益的一小组类别项目进行定义的可能性。理事会在 2013 年讨论文件中讨论了一种方法，但未取得反馈意见者的有力支持。

BC7.23 理事会在 2018 版《概念框架》中基于对损益表的描述制定了收益和费用的分类方法。根据 BC7.15 段，该描述指出损益表是有关报告期间主体财务业绩信息的主要来源。如果损益表是该信息的主要来源，若无有力理由便将收益和费用排除在损益表之外，会降低损益表的有用性。

BC7.24 因此，理事会在 2018 版《概念框架》中提出了以下原则，即，所有收益和费用均应计入损益表。此举意在强调损益表是收益和费用默认的计入位置。因此，仅在例外情况下才会作出将收益和费用排除在损益表之外并计入其他综合收益的决定。例外情况为，理事会得出结论认为要求或允许将特定收益或费用项目排除在损益表之外可以使损益表提供更具相关性的信息，或更能如实反映主体在该期间的财务业绩。

BC7.25 2018 版《概念框架》未包含理事会如何得出上述结论的具体指引。理事会预计会在制定准则过程中作出这一决定，并在这些准则的结论基础部分解释得出相关结论的理由。主体不得自行决定（参见《国际会计准则第 1 号》第 88 段）。

将项目重分类至损益（第7.19 段）

BC7.26 理事会考虑了是否应将计入其他综合收益的收益和费用在之后期间重分类至损益。这种重分类有时被称为"重分类调整"。

BC7.27 早于 2018 版《概念框架》制定的部分准则要求进行重分类，而部分准则不允许进行重分类。出现这一差异的原因在于，理事会在不同时期对此问题采用了不同方法。有时，理事会的方法是将财务业绩表视为单一业绩报表，即各项收益或费用在此报表中都应仅出现一次。为了与上述方法保持一致，理事会通常在准则中规定不得进行重分类。有时，理事会的方法是所有收益和费用都应在某一时点被计入损益。为实现此目标，则会要求重分类。

BC7.28 必须避免由于理事会的组成及其选择的方法发生变化导致理事会关于重分类的决定随着时间的推移而变化。因此，2018 年《概念框架》提出了理事会制定重分类决策时适用的原则。

BC7.29 理事会得出结论认为，如果损益表是报告期间主体财务业绩信息的主要来源，那么损益表中随时间累计的金额需尽可能完整。因此，仅在存在有力理由的特定情况下，才可将收益和费用永久排除在损益表之外。

BC7.30 因此，2018 版《概念框架》中列出了一项原则，即，计入其他综合收益的收益和费用将在之后期间重分类至损益。重分类发生的报告期间，即，为重分类可使损益表提供更具相关性的信息或更能如实反映主体在该期间的财务业绩的期间。

BC7.31 第 6.83 段至第 6.86 段描述了在财务状况表中使用一种计量基础，在损益表中使用另一种计量基础的方法。使用这种方法时，重分类是确保在资产或负债持有期间计入损益表的收益或费用的累计金额与使用针对财务状况表选择的计量基础确定的金额一致的唯一方式。

BC7.32 在某些情况下，无法识别出将收益和费用重分类至损益会产生 BC7.30 段的结果的期间。此时，如无适当且非随意的重分类基础，则重分类不会提供有用信息。

BC7.33 2018 版《概念框架》未提供有关重分类何时无法提供有用信息的特定指引。理事会预计会在制定准则时作出这一决定，并在这些准则的结论基础部分解释得出相关结论的理由。主体不得自行决定。

第 8 章——资本和资本保全概念

BC8.1 理事会认为，在制定 2018《概念框架》的过程中更新对资本和资本保全的讨论不可行，而且可能会严重推迟 2018 版《概念框架》的完成时间。

BC8.2 理事会认为，不宜将有关资本和资本保全的讨论从 2018 版《概念框架》中全部删除，因为这些概念对于财务报告十分重要，而且会影响收益和费用的定义、计量基础的选择以及列示和披露的决定。

BC8.3 因此，2018 版《概念框架》"第 8 章——资本和资本保全概念"的内容沿用了 2010 版《概念框架》的内容，未做改动。该内容最初出现于 1989 版《框架》当中。

BC8.4 如果理事会未来认为有修订必要，将会重新考虑资本和资本保全的概念。

Conceptual Framework
for Financial Reporting

CONCEPTUAL FRAMEWORK FOR FINANCIAL REPORTING

CONTENTS

from paragraph

STATUS AND PURPOSE OF THE *CONCEPTUAL FRAMEWORK*	**SP1.1**
CHAPTER 1—THE OBJECTIVE OF GENERAL PURPOSE FINANCIAL REPORTING	
INTRODUCTION	1.1
OBJECTIVE, USEFULNESS AND LIMITATIONS OF GENERAL PURPOSE FINANCIAL REPORTING	1.2
INFORMATION ABOUT A REPORTING ENTITY'S ECONOMIC RESOURCES, CLAIMS AGAINST THE ENTITY AND CHANGES IN RESOURCES AND CLAIMS	1.12
Economic resources and claims	1.13
Changes in economic resources and claims	1.15
Financial performance reflected by accrual accounting	1.17
Financial performance reflected by past cash flows	1.20
Changes in economic resources and claims not resulting from financial performance	1.21
INFORMATION ABOUT USE OF THE ENTITY'S ECONOMIC RESOURCES	1.22
CHAPTER 2—QUALITATIVE CHARACTERISTICS OF USEFUL FINANCIAL INFORMATION	
INTRODUCTION	2.1
QUALITATIVE CHARACTERISTICS OF USEFUL FINANCIAL INFORMATION	2.4
Fundamental qualitative characteristics	2.5
Enhancing qualitative characteristics	2.23
THE COST CONSTRAINT ON USEFUL FINANCIAL REPORTING	2.39
CHAPTER 3—FINANCIAL STATEMENTS AND THE REPORTING ENTITY	
FINANCIAL STATEMENTS	3.1
Objective and scope of financial statements	3.2
Reporting period	3.4
Perspective adopted in financial statements	3.8
Going concern assumption	3.9
THE REPORTING ENTITY	3.10
Consolidated and unconsolidated financial statements	3.15
CHAPTER 4—THE ELEMENTS OF FINANCIAL STATEMENTS	
INTRODUCTION	4.1

DEFINITION OF AN ASSET	4.3
Right	4.6
Potential to produce economic benefits	4.14
Control	4.19
DEFINITION OF A LIABILITY	4.26
Obligation	4.28
Transfer of an economic resource	4.36
Present obligation as a result of past events	4.42
ASSETS AND LIABILITIES	4.48
Unit of account	4.48
Executory contracts	4.56
Substance of contractual rights and contractual obligations	4.59
DEFINITION OF EQUITY	4.63
DEFINITIONS OF INCOME AND EXPENSES	4.68
CHAPTER 5—RECOGNITION AND DERECOGNITION	
THE RECOGNITION PROCESS	5.1
RECOGNITION CRITERIA	5.6
Relevance	5.12
Faithful representation	5.18
DERECOGNITION	5.26
CHAPTER 6—MEASUREMENT	
INTRODUCTION	6.1
MEASUREMENT BASES	6.4
Historical cost	6.4
Current value	6.10
INFORMATION PROVIDED BY PARTICULAR MEASUREMENT BASES	6.23
Historical cost	6.24
Current value	6.32
FACTORS TO CONSIDER WHEN SELECTING A MEASUREMENT BASIS	6.43
Relevance	6.49
Faithful representation	6.58
Enhancing qualitative characteristics and the cost constraint	6.63
Factors specific to initial measurement	6.77
More than one measurement basis	6.83
MEASUREMENT OF EQUITY	6.87

CASH-FLOW-BASED MEASUREMENT TECHNIQUES	6.91
CHAPTER 7—PRESENTATION AND DISCLOSURE	
PRESENTATION AND DISCLOSURE AS COMMUNICATION TOOLS	7.1
PRESENTATION AND DISCLOSURE OBJECTIVES AND PRINCIPLES	7.4
CLASSIFICATION	7.7
Classification of assets and liabilities	7.9
Classification of equity	7.12
Classification of income and expenses	7.14
AGGREGATION	7.20
CHAPTER 8—CONCEPTS OF CAPITAL AND CAPITAL MAINTENANCE	
CONCEPTS OF CAPITAL	8.1
CONCEPTS OF CAPITAL MAINTENANCE AND THE DETERMINATION OF PROFIT	8.3
CAPITAL MAINTENANCE ADJUSTMENTS	8.10
APPENDIX—DEFINED TERMS	

Approval by the Board of the *Conceptual Framework for Financial Reporting* issued in March 2018

CONCEPTUAL FRAMEWORK FOR FINANCIAL REPORTING

STATUS AND PURPOSE OF THE *CONCEPTUAL FRAMEWORK*

SP1.1   The *Conceptual Framework for Financial Reporting* (*Conceptual Framework*) describes the objective of, and the concepts for, general purpose financial reporting. The purpose of the *Conceptual Framework* is to:

   (a)   assist the International Accounting Standards Board (Board) to develop IFRS Standards (Standards) that are based on consistent concepts;

   (b)   assist preparers to develop consistent accounting policies when no Standard applies to a particular transaction or other event, or when a Standard allows a choice of accounting policy; and

   (c)   assist all parties to understand and interpret the Standards.

SP1.2   The *Conceptual Framework* is not a Standard. Nothing in the *Conceptual Framework* overrides any Standard or any requirement in a Standard.

SP1.3   To meet the objective of general purpose financial reporting, the Board may sometimes specify requirements that depart from aspects of the *Conceptual Framework*. If the Board does so, it will explain the departure in the Basis for Conclusions on that Standard.

SP1.4   The *Conceptual Framework* may be revised from time to time on the basis of the Board's experience of working with it. Revisions of the *Conceptual Framework* will not automatically lead to changes to the Standards. Any decision to amend a Standard would require the Board to go through its due process for adding a project to its agenda and developing an amendment to that Standard.

SP1.5   The *Conceptual Framework* contributes to the stated mission of the IFRS Foundation and of the Board, which is part of the IFRS Foundation. That mission is to develop Standards that bring transparency, accountability and efficiency to financial markets around the world. The Board's work serves the public interest by fostering trust, growth and long-term financial stability in the global economy. The *Conceptual Framework* provides the foundation for Standards that:

   (a)   contribute to transparency by enhancing the international comparability and quality of financial information, enabling investors and other market participants to make informed economic decisions.

   (b)   strengthen accountability by reducing the information gap between the providers of capital and the people to whom they have entrusted their money. Standards based on the *Conceptual Framework* provide information needed to hold management to account. As a source of globally comparable information, those Standards are also of vital importance to regulators around the world.

   (c)   contribute to economic efficiency by helping investors to identify opportunities and risks across the world, thus improving capital allocation. For businesses, the use of a single, trusted accounting language derived from Standards based on the *Conceptual Framework* lowers the cost of capital and reduces international reporting costs.

CONCEPTUAL FRAMEWORK FOR FINANCIAL REPORTING

from paragraph

CHAPTER 1—THE OBJECTIVE OF GENERAL PURPOSE FINANCIAL REPORTING

INTRODUCTION	1.1
OBJECTIVE, USEFULNESS AND LIMITATIONS OF GENERAL PURPOSE FINANCIAL REPORTING	1.2
INFORMATION ABOUT A REPORTING ENTITY'S ECONOMIC RESOURCES, CLAIMS AGAINST THE ENTITY AND CHANGES IN RESOURCES AND CLAIMS	1.12
Economic resources and claims	1.13
Changes in economic resources and claims	1.15
Financial performance reflected by accrual accounting	1.17
Financial performance reflected by past cash flows	1.20
Changes in economic resources and claims not resulting from financial performance	1.21
INFORMATION ABOUT USE OF THE ENTITY'S ECONOMIC RESOURCES	1.22

CONCEPTUAL FRAMEWORK FOR FINANCIAL REPORTING

Introduction

1.1 The objective of general purpose financial reporting forms the foundation of the *Conceptual Framework*. Other aspects of the *Conceptual Framework*—the qualitative characteristics of, and the cost constraint on, useful financial information, a reporting entity concept, elements of financial statements, recognition and derecognition, measurement, presentation and disclosure—flow logically from the objective.

Objective, usefulness and limitations of general purpose financial reporting

1.2 The objective of general purpose financial reporting[1] is to provide financial information about the reporting entity that is useful to existing and potential investors, lenders and other creditors in making decisions relating to providing resources to the entity.[2] Those decisions involve decisions about:

    (a) buying, selling or holding equity and debt instruments;

    (b) providing or settling loans and other forms of credit; or

    (c) exercising rights to vote on, or otherwise influence, management's actions that affect the use of the entity's economic resources.

1.3 The decisions described in paragraph 1.2 depend on the returns that existing and potential investors, lenders and other creditors expect, for example, dividends, principal and interest payments or market price increases. Investors', lenders' and other creditors' expectations about returns depend on their assessment of the amount, timing and uncertainty of (the prospects for) future net cash inflows to the entity and on their assessment of management's stewardship of the entity's economic resources. Existing and potential investors, lenders and other creditors need information to help them make those assessments.

1.4 To make the assessments described in paragraph 1.3, existing and potential investors, lenders and other creditors need information about:

    (a) the economic resources of the entity, claims against the entity and changes in those resources and claims (see paragraphs 1.12–1.21); and

    (b) how efficiently and effectively the entity's management and governing board[3] have discharged their responsibilities to use the entity's economic resources (see paragraphs 1.22–1.23).

1.5 Many existing and potential investors, lenders and other creditors cannot require reporting entities to provide information directly to them and must rely on general purpose financial

---

1 Throughout the *Conceptual Framework*, the terms 'financial reports' and 'financial reporting' refer to general purpose financial reports and general purpose financial reporting unless specifically indicated otherwise.
2 Throughout the *Conceptual Framework*, the term 'entity' refers to the reporting entity unless specifically indicated otherwise.
3 Throughout the *Conceptual Framework*, the term 'management' refers to management and the governing board of an entity unless specifically indicated otherwise.

reports for much of the financial information they need. Consequently, they are the primary users to whom general purpose financial reports are directed.[1]

1.6 However, general purpose financial reports do not and cannot provide all of the information that existing and potential investors, lenders and other creditors need. Those users need to consider pertinent information from other sources, for example, general economic conditions and expectations, political events and political climate, and industry and company outlooks.

1.7 General purpose financial reports are not designed to show the value of a reporting entity; but they provide information to help existing and potential investors, lenders and other creditors to estimate the value of the reporting entity.

1.8 Individual primary users have different, and possibly conflicting, information needs and desires. The Board, in developing Standards, will seek to provide the information set that will meet the needs of the maximum number of primary users. However, focusing on common information needs does not prevent the reporting entity from including additional information that is most useful to a particular subset of primary users.

1.9 The management of a reporting entity is also interested in financial information about the entity. However, management need not rely on general purpose financial reports because it is able to obtain the financial information it needs internally.

1.10 Other parties, such as regulators and members of the public other than investors, lenders and other creditors, may also find general purpose financial reports useful. However, those reports are not primarily directed to these other groups.

1.11 To a large extent, financial reports are based on estimates, judgements and models rather than exact depictions. The *Conceptual Framework* establishes the concepts that underlie those estimates, judgements and models. The concepts are the goal towards which the Board and preparers of financial reports strive. As with most goals, the *Conceptual Framework*'s vision of ideal financial reporting is unlikely to be achieved in full, at least not in the short term, because it takes time to understand, accept and implement new ways of analysing transactions and other events. Nevertheless, establishing a goal towards which to strive is essential if financial reporting is to evolve so as to improve its usefulness.

Information about a reporting entity's economic resources, claims against the entity and changes in resources and claims

1.12 General purpose financial reports provide information about the financial position of a reporting entity, which is information about the entity's economic resources and the claims against the reporting entity. Financial reports also provide information about the effects of transactions and other events that change a reporting entity's economic resources and claims. Both types of information provide useful input for decisions relating to providing resources to an entity.

Economic resources and claims

1.13 Information about the nature and amounts of a reporting entity's economic resources and claims can help users to identify the reporting entity's financial strengths and weaknesses.

---

1 Throughout the *Conceptual Framework*, the terms 'primary users' and 'users' refer to those existing and potential investors, lenders and other creditors who must rely on general purpose financial reports for much of the financial information they need.

That information can help users to assess the reporting entity's liquidity and solvency, its needs for additional financing and how successful it is likely to be in obtaining that financing. That information can also help users to assess management's stewardship of the entity's economic resources. Information about priorities and payment requirements of existing claims helps users to predict how future cash flows will be distributed among those with a claim against the reporting entity.

1.14 Different types of economic resources affect a user's assessment of the reporting entity's prospects for future cash flows differently. Some future cash flows result directly from existing economic resources, such as accounts receivable. Other cash flows result from using several resources in combination to produce and market goods or services to customers. Although those cash flows cannot be identified with individual economic resources (or claims), users of financial reports need to know the nature and amount of the resources available for use in a reporting entity's operations.

Changes in economic resources and claims

1.15 Changes in a reporting entity's economic resources and claims result from that entity's financial performance (see paragraphs 1.17–1.20) and from other events or transactions such as issuing debt or equity instruments (see paragraph 1.21). To properly assess both the prospects for future net cash inflows to the reporting entity and management's stewardship of the entity's economic resources, users need to be able to identify those two types of changes.

1.16 Information about a reporting entity's financial performance helps users to understand the return that the entity has produced on its economic resources. Information about the return the entity has produced can help users to assess management's stewardship of the entity's economic resources. Information about the variability and components of that return is also important, especially in assessing the uncertainty of future cash flows. Information about a reporting entity's past financial performance and how its management discharged its stewardship responsibilities is usually helpful in predicting the entity's future returns on its economic resources.

Financial performance reflected by accrual accounting

1.17 Accrual accounting depicts the effects of transactions and other events and circumstances on a reporting entity's economic resources and claims in the periods in which those effects occur, even if the resulting cash receipts and payments occur in a different period. This is important because information about a reporting entity's economic resources and claims and changes in its economic resources and claims during a period provides a better basis for assessing the entity's past and future performance than information solely about cash receipts and payments during that period.

1.18 Information about a reporting entity's financial performance during a period, reflected by changes in its economic resources and claims other than by obtaining additional resources directly from investors and creditors (see paragraph 1.21), is useful in assessing the entity's past and future ability to generate net cash inflows. That information indicates the extent to which the reporting entity has increased its available economic resources, and thus its capacity for generating net cash inflows through its operations rather than by obtaining additional resources directly from investors and creditors. Information about a reporting entity's financial performance during a period can also help users to assess management's stewardship of the entity's economic resources.

1.19 Information about a reporting entity's financial performance during a period may also indicate the extent to which events such as changes in market prices or interest rates have increased or decreased the entity's economic resources and claims, thereby affecting the entity's ability to generate net cash inflows.

Financial performance reflected by past cash flows

1.20 Information about a reporting entity's cash flows during a period also helps users to assess the entity's ability to generate future net cash inflows and to assess management's stewardship of the entity's economic resources. That information indicates how the reporting entity obtains and spends cash, including information about its borrowing and repayment of debt, cash dividends or other cash distributions to investors, and other factors that may affect the entity's liquidity or solvency. Information about cash flows helps users understand a reporting entity's operations, evaluate its financing and investing activities, assess its liquidity or solvency and interpret other information about financial performance.

Changes in economic resources and claims not resulting from financial performance

1.21 A reporting entity's economic resources and claims may also change for reasons other than financial performance, such as issuing debt or equity instruments. Information about this type of change is necessary to give users a complete understanding of why the reporting entity's economic resources and claims changed and the implications of those changes for its future financial performance.

Information about use of the entity's economic resources

1.22 Information about how efficiently and effectively the reporting entity's management has discharged its responsibilities to use the entity's economic resources helps users to assess management's stewardship of those resources. Such information is also useful for predicting how efficiently and effectively management will use the entity's economic resources in future periods. Hence, it can be useful for assessing the entity's prospects for future net cash inflows.

1.23 Examples of management's responsibilities to use the entity's economic resources include protecting those resources from unfavourable effects of economic factors, such as price and technological changes, and ensuring that the entity complies with applicable laws, regulations and contractual provisions.

CHAPTER 2—QUALITATIVE CHARACTERISTICS OF USEFUL FINANCIAL INFORMATION

from paragraph

INTRODUCTION	**2.1**
QUALITATIVE CHARACTERISTICS OF USEFUL FINANCIAL INFORMATION	**2.4**
Fundamental qualitative characteristics	**2.5**
Relevance	2.6
Materiality	2.11
Faithful representation	2.12
Applying the fundamental qualitative characteristics	2.20
Enhancing qualitative characteristics	**2.23**
Comparability	2.24
Verifiability	2.30
Timeliness	2.33
Understandability	2.34
Applying the enhancing qualitative characteristics	2.37
THE COST CONSTRAINT ON USEFUL FINANCIAL REPORTING	**2.39**

CONCEPTUAL FRAMEWORK FOR FINANCIAL REPORTING

Introduction

2.1 The qualitative characteristics of useful financial information discussed in this chapter identify the types of information that are likely to be most useful to the existing and potential investors, lenders and other creditors for making decisions about the reporting entity on the basis of information in its financial report (financial information).

2.2 Financial reports provide information about the reporting entity's economic resources, claims against the reporting entity and the effects of transactions and other events and conditions that change those resources and claims. (This information is referred to in the *Conceptual Framework* as information about the economic phenomena.) Some financial reports also include explanatory material about management's expectations and strategies for the reporting entity, and other types of forward-looking information.

2.3 The qualitative characteristics of useful financial information[1] apply to financial information provided in financial statements, as well as to financial information provided in other ways. Cost, which is a pervasive constraint on the reporting entity's ability to provide useful financial information, applies similarly. However, the considerations in applying the qualitative characteristics and the cost constraint may be different for different types of information. For example, applying them to forward-looking information may be different from applying them to information about existing economic resources and claims and to changes in those resources and claims.

Qualitative characteristics of useful financial information

2.4 If financial information is to be useful, it must be relevant and faithfully represent what it purports to represent. The usefulness of financial information is enhanced if it is comparable, verifiable, timely and understandable.

Fundamental qualitative characteristics

2.5 The fundamental qualitative characteristics are relevance and faithful representation.

Relevance

2.6 Relevant financial information is capable of making a difference in the decisions made by users. Information may be capable of making a difference in a decision even if some users choose not to take advantage of it or are already aware of it from other sources.

2.7 Financial information is capable of making a difference in decisions if it has predictive value, confirmatory value or both.

2.8 Financial information has predictive value if it can be used as an input to processes employed by users to predict future outcomes. Financial information need not be a prediction or forecast to have predictive value. Financial information with predictive value is employed by users in making their own predictions.

---

1 Throughout the *Conceptual Framework*, the terms 'qualitative characteristics' and 'cost constraint' refer to the qualitative characteristics of, and the cost constraint on, useful financial information.

2.9 Financial information has confirmatory value if it provides feedback about (confirms or changes) previous evaluations.

2.10 The predictive value and confirmatory value of financial information are interrelated. Information that has predictive value often also has confirmatory value. For example, revenue information for the current year, which can be used as the basis for predicting revenues in future years, can also be compared with revenue predictions for the current year that were made in past years. The results of those comparisons can help a user to correct and improve the processes that were used to make those previous predictions.

Materiality

2.11 Information is material if omitting it or misstating it could influence decisions that the primary users of general purpose financial reports (see paragraph 1.5) make on the basis of those reports, which provide financial information about a specific reporting entity. In other words, materiality is an entity-specific aspect of relevance based on the nature or magnitude, or both, of the items to which the information relates in the context of an individual entity's financial report. Consequently, the Board cannot specify a uniform quantitative threshold for materiality or predetermine what could be material in a particular situation.

Faithful representation

2.12 Financial reports represent economic phenomena in words and numbers. To be useful, financial information must not only represent relevant phenomena, but it must also faithfully represent the substance of the phenomena that it purports to represent. In many circumstances, the substance of an economic phenomenon and its legal form are the same. If they are not the same, providing information only about the legal form would not faithfully represent the economic phenomenon (see paragraphs 4.59–4.62).

2.13 To be a perfectly faithful representation, a depiction would have three characteristics. It would be complete, neutral and free from error. Of course, perfection is seldom, if ever, achievable. The Board's objective is to maximise those qualities to the extent possible.

2.14 A complete depiction includes all information necessary for a user to understand the phenomenon being depicted, including all necessary descriptions and explanations. For example, a complete depiction of a group of assets would include, at a minimum, a description of the nature of the assets in the group, a numerical depiction of all of the assets in the group, and a description of what the numerical depiction represents (for example, historical cost or fair value). For some items, a complete depiction may also entail explanations of significant facts about the quality and nature of the items, factors and circumstances that might affect their quality and nature, and the process used to determine the numerical depiction.

2.15 A neutral depiction is without bias in the selection or presentation of financial information. A neutral depiction is not slanted, weighted, emphasised, de-emphasised or otherwise manipulated to increase the probability that financial information will be received favourably or unfavourably by users. Neutral information does not mean information with no purpose or no influence on behaviour. On the contrary, relevant financial information is, by definition, capable of making a difference in users' decisions.

2.16 Neutrality is supported by the exercise of prudence. Prudence is the exercise of caution when making judgements under conditions of uncertainty. The exercise of prudence means that assets and income are not overstated and liabilities and expenses are not understated.[1] Equally, the exercise of prudence does not allow for the understatement of assets or income or the overstatement of liabilities or expenses. Such misstatements can lead to the overstatement or understatement of income or expenses in future periods.

2.17 The exercise of prudence does not imply a need for asymmetry, for example, a systematic need for more persuasive evidence to support the recognition of assets or income than the recognition of liabilities or expenses. Such asymmetry is not a qualitative characteristic of useful financial information. Nevertheless, particular Standards may contain asymmetric requirements if this is a consequence of decisions intended to select the most relevant information that faithfully represents what it purports to represent.

2.18 Faithful representation does not mean accurate in all respects. Free from error means there are no errors or omissions in the description of the phenomenon, and the process used to produce the reported information has been selected and applied with no errors in the process. In this context, free from error does not mean perfectly accurate in all respects. For example, an estimate of an unobservable price or value cannot be determined to be accurate or inaccurate. However, a representation of that estimate can be faithful if the amount is described clearly and accurately as being an estimate, the nature and limitations of the estimating process are explained, and no errors have been made in selecting and applying an appropriate process for developing the estimate.

2.19 When monetary amounts in financial reports cannot be observed directly and must instead be estimated, measurement uncertainty arises. The use of reasonable estimates is an essential part of the preparation of financial information and does not undermine the usefulness of the information if the estimates are clearly and accurately described and explained. Even a high level of measurement uncertainty does not necessarily prevent such an estimate from providing useful information (see paragraph 2.22).

Applying the fundamental qualitative characteristics

2.20 Information must both be relevant and provide a faithful representation of what it purports to represent if it is to be useful. Neither a faithful representation of an irrelevant phenomenon nor an unfaithful representation of a relevant phenomenon helps users make good decisions.

2.21 The most efficient and effective process for applying the fundamental qualitative characteristics would usually be as follows (subject to the effects of enhancing characteristics and the cost constraint, which are not considered in this example). First, identify an economic phenomenon, information about which is capable of being useful to users of the reporting entity's financial information. Second, identify the type of information about that phenomenon that would be most relevant. Third, determine whether that information is available and whether it can provide a faithful representation of the economic phenomenon. If so, the process of satisfying the fundamental qualitative characteristics ends at that point. If not, the process is repeated with the next most relevant type of information.

2.22 In some cases, a trade-off between the fundamental qualitative characteristics may need to be made in order to meet the objective of financial reporting, which is to provide useful information about economic phenomena. For example, the most relevant information about a phenomenon may be a highly uncertain estimate. In some cases, the level of measurement uncertainty involved in making that estimate may be so high that it may be questionable whether the estimate would provide a sufficiently faithful representation of that

---

1 Assets, liabilities, income and expenses are defined in Table 4.1. They are the elements of financial statements.

phenomenon. In some such cases, the most useful information may be the highly uncertain estimate, accompanied by a description of the estimate and an explanation of the uncertainties that affect it. In other such cases, if that information would not provide a sufficiently faithful representation of that phenomenon, the most useful information may include an estimate of another type that is slightly less relevant but is subject to lower measurement uncertainty. In limited circumstances, there may be no estimate that provides useful information. In those limited circumstances, it may be necessary to provide information that does not rely on an estimate.

Enhancing qualitative characteristics

2.23 Comparability, verifiability, timeliness and understandability are qualitative characteristics that enhance the usefulness of information that both is relevant and provides a faithful representation of what it purports to represent. The enhancing qualitative characteristics may also help determine which of two ways should be used to depict a phenomenon if both are considered to provide equally relevant information and an equally faithful representation of that phenomenon.

Comparability

2.24 Users' decisions involve choosing between alternatives, for example, selling or holding an investment, or investing in one reporting entity or another. Consequently, information about a reporting entity is more useful if it can be compared with similar information about other entities and with similar information about the same entity for another period or another date.

2.25 Comparability is the qualitative characteristic that enables users to identify and understand similarities in, and differences among, items. Unlike the other qualitative characteristics, comparability does not relate to a single item. A comparison requires at least two items.

2.26 Consistency, although related to comparability, is not the same. Consistency refers to the use of the same methods for the same items, either from period to period within a reporting entity or in a single period across entities. Comparability is the goal; consistency helps to achieve that goal.

2.27 Comparability is not uniformity. For information to be comparable, like things must look alike and different things must look different. Comparability of financial information is not enhanced by making unlike things look alike any more than it is enhanced by making like things look different.

2.28 Some degree of comparability is likely to be attained by satisfying the fundamental qualitative characteristics. A faithful representation of a relevant economic phenomenon should naturally possess some degree of comparability with a faithful representation of a similar relevant economic phenomenon by another reporting entity.

2.29 Although a single economic phenomenon can be faithfully represented in multiple ways, permitting alternative accounting methods for the same economic phenomenon diminishes comparability.

Verifiability

2.30 Verifiability helps assure users that information faithfully represents the economic phenomena it purports to represent. Verifiability means that different knowledgeable and independent observers could reach consensus, although not necessarily complete agreement,

CONCEPTUAL FRAMEWORK FOR FINANCIAL REPORTING

that a particular depiction is a faithful representation. Quantified information need not be a single point estimate to be verifiable. A range of possible amounts and the related probabilities can also be verified.

2.31 Verification can be direct or indirect. Direct verification means verifying an amount or other representation through direct observation, for example, by counting cash. Indirect verification means checking the inputs to a model, formula or other technique and recalculating the outputs using the same methodology. An example is verifying the carrying amount of inventory by checking the inputs (quantities and costs) and recalculating the ending inventory using the same cost flow assumption (for example, using the first-in, first-out method).

2.32 It may not be possible to verify some explanations and forward-looking financial information until a future period, if at all. To help users decide whether they want to use that information, it would normally be necessary to disclose the underlying assumptions, the methods of compiling the information and other factors and circumstances that support the information.

Timeliness

2.33 Timeliness means having information available to decision-makers in time to be capable of influencing their decisions. Generally, the older the information is the less useful it is. However, some information may continue to be timely long after the end of a reporting period because, for example, some users may need to identify and assess trends.

Understandability

2.34 Classifying, characterising and presenting information clearly and concisely makes it understandable.

2.35 Some phenomena are inherently complex and cannot be made easy to understand. Excluding information about those phenomena from financial reports might make the information in those financial reports easier to understand. However, those reports would be incomplete and therefore possibly misleading.

2.36 Financial reports are prepared for users who have a reasonable knowledge of business and economic activities and who review and analyse the information diligently. At times, even well-informed and diligent users may need to seek the aid of an adviser to understand information about complex economic phenomena.

Applying the enhancing qualitative characteristics

2.37 Enhancing qualitative characteristics should be maximised to the extent possible. However, the enhancing qualitative characteristics, either individually or as a group, cannot make information useful if that information is irrelevant or does not provide a faithful representation of what it purports to represent.

2.38 Applying the enhancing qualitative characteristics is an iterative process that does not follow a prescribed order. Sometimes, one enhancing qualitative characteristic may have to be diminished to maximise another qualitative characteristic. For example, a temporary reduction in comparability as a result of prospectively applying a new Standard may be worthwhile to improve relevance or faithful representation in the longer term. Appropriate disclosures may partially compensate for non-comparability.

The cost constraint on useful financial reporting

2.39 Cost is a pervasive constraint on the information that can be provided by financial reporting. Reporting financial information imposes costs, and it is important that those costs are justified by the benefits of reporting that information. There are several types of costs and benefits to consider.

2.40 Providers of financial information expend most of the effort involved in collecting, processing, verifying and disseminating financial information, but users ultimately bear those costs in the form of reduced returns. Users of financial information also incur costs of analysing and interpreting the information provided. If needed information is not provided, users incur additional costs to obtain that information elsewhere or to estimate it.

2.41 Reporting financial information that is relevant and faithfully represents what it purports to represent helps users to make decisions with more confidence. This results in more efficient functioning of capital markets and a lower cost of capital for the economy as a whole. An individual investor, lender or other creditor also receives benefits by making more informed decisions. However, it is not possible for general purpose financial reports to provide all the information that every user finds relevant.

2.42 In applying the cost constraint, the Board assesses whether the benefits of reporting particular information are likely to justify the costs incurred to provide and use that information. When applying the cost constraint in developing a proposed Standard, the Board seeks information from providers of financial information, users, auditors, academics and others about the expected nature and quantity of the benefits and costs of that Standard. In most situations, assessments are based on a combination of quantitative and qualitative information.

2.43 Because of the inherent subjectivity, different individuals' assessments of the costs and benefits of reporting particular items of financial information will vary. Therefore, the Board seeks to consider costs and benefits in relation to financial reporting generally, and not just in relation to individual reporting entities. That does not mean that assessments of costs and benefits always justify the same reporting requirements for all entities. Differences may be appropriate because of different sizes of entities, different ways of raising capital (publicly or privately), different users' needs or other factors.

from paragraph

CHAPTER 3—FINANCIAL STATEMENTS AND THE REPORTING ENTITY

FINANCIAL STATEMENTS	**3.1**
Objective and scope of financial statements	**3.2**
Reporting period	**3.4**
Perspective adopted in financial statements	**3.8**
Going concern assumption	**3.9**
THE REPORTING ENTITY	**3.10**
Consolidated and unconsolidated financial statements	**3.15**

CONCEPTUAL FRAMEWORK FOR FINANCIAL REPORTING

Financial statements

3.1 Chapters 1 and 2 discuss information provided in general purpose financial reports and Chapters 3–8 discuss information provided in general purpose financial statements, which are a particular form of general purpose financial reports. Financial statements[1] provide information about economic resources of the reporting entity, claims against the entity, and changes in those resources and claims, that meet the definitions of the elements of financial statements (see Table 4.1).

Objective and scope of financial statements

3.2 The objective of financial statements is to provide financial information about the reporting entity's assets, liabilities, equity, income and expenses[2] that is useful to users of financial statements in assessing the prospects for future net cash inflows to the reporting entity and in assessing management's stewardship of the entity's economic resources (see paragraph 1.3).

3.3 That information is provided:

(a) in the statement of financial position, by recognising assets, liabilities and equity;

(b) in the statement(s) of financial performance,[3] by recognising income and expenses; and

(c) in other statements and notes, by presenting and disclosing information about:

    (i) recognised assets, liabilities, equity, income and expenses (see paragraph 5.1), including information about their nature and about the risks arising from those recognised assets and liabilities;

    (ii) assets and liabilities that have not been recognised (see paragraph 5.6), including information about their nature and about the risks arising from them;

    (iii) cash flows;

    (iv) contributions from holders of equity claims and distributions to them; and

    (v) the methods, assumptions and judgements used in estimating the amounts presented or disclosed, and changes in those methods, assumptions and judgements.

Reporting period

3.4 Financial statements are prepared for a specified period of time (reporting period) and provide information about:

---

[1] Throughout the *Conceptual Framework*, the term 'financial statements' refers to general purpose financial statements.
[2] Assets, liabilities, equity, income and expenses are defined in Table 4.1. They are the elements of financial statements.
[3] The *Conceptual Framework* does not specify whether the statement(s) of financial performance comprise(s) a single statement or two statements.

（a） assets and liabilities—including unrecognised assets and liabilities—and equity that existed at the end of the reporting period, or during the reporting period; and

(b) income and expenses for the reporting period.

3.5 To help users of financial statements to identify and assess changes and trends, financial statements also provide comparative information for at least one preceding reporting period.

3.6 Information about possible future transactions and other possible future events (forward-looking information) is included in financial statements if it:

(a) relates to the entity's assets or liabilities—including unrecognised assets or liabilities—or equity that existed at the end of the reporting period, or during the reporting period, or to income or expenses for the reporting period; and

(b) is useful to users of financial statements.

For example, if an asset or liability is measured by estimating future cash flows, information about those estimated future cash flows may help users of financial statements to understand the reported measures. Financial statements do not typically provide other types of forward-looking information, for example, explanatory material about management's expectations and strategies for the reporting entity.

3.7 Financial statements include information about transactions and other events that have occurred after the end of the reporting period if providing that information is necessary to meet the objective of financial statements (see paragraph 3.2).

Perspective adopted in financial statements

3.8 Financial statements provide information about transactions and other events viewed from the perspective of the reporting entity as a whole, not from the perspective of any particular group of the entity's existing or potential investors, lenders or other creditors.

Going concern assumption

3.9 Financial statements are normally prepared on the assumption that the reporting entity is a going concern and will continue in operation for the foreseeable future. Hence, it is assumed that the entity has neither the intention nor the need to enter liquidation or to cease trading. If such an intention or need exists, the financial statements may have to be prepared on a different basis. If so, the financial statements describe the basis used.

The reporting entity

3.10 A reporting entity is an entity that is required, or chooses, to prepare financial statements. A reporting entity can be a single entity or a portion of an entity or can comprise more than one entity. A reporting entity is not necessarily a legal entity.

3.11 Sometimes one entity (parent) has control over another entity (subsidiary). If a reporting entity comprises both the parent and its subsidiaries, the reporting entity's financial statements are referred to as 'consolidated financial statements' (see paragraphs 3.15–3.16). If a reporting entity is the parent alone, the reporting entity's financial statements are referred to as 'unconsolidated financial statements' (see paragraphs 3.17–3.18).

3.12 If a reporting entity comprises two or more entities that are not all linked by a parent-subsidiary relationship, the reporting entity's financial statements are referred to as 'combined financial statements'.

3.13 Determining the appropriate boundary of a reporting entity can be difficult if the reporting entity:

(a) is not a legal entity; and

(b) does not comprise only legal entities linked by a parent-subsidiary relationship.

3.14 In such cases, determining the boundary of the reporting entity is driven by the information needs of the primary users of the reporting entity's financial statements. Those users need relevant information that faithfully represents what it purports to represent. Faithful representation requires that:

(a) the boundary of the reporting entity does not contain an arbitrary or incomplete set of economic activities;

(b) including that set of economic activities within the boundary of the reporting entity results in neutral information; and

(c) a description is provided of how the boundary of the reporting entity was determined and of what constitutes the reporting entity.

Consolidated and unconsolidated financial statements

3.15 Consolidated financial statements provide information about the assets, liabilities, equity, income and expenses of both the parent and its subsidiaries as a single reporting entity. That information is useful for existing and potential investors, lenders and other creditors of the parent in their assessment of the prospects for future net cash inflows to the parent. This is because net cash inflows to the parent include distributions to the parent from its subsidiaries, and those distributions depend on net cash inflows to the subsidiaries.

3.16 Consolidated financial statements are not designed to provide separate information about the assets, liabilities, equity, income and expenses of any particular subsidiary. A subsidiary's own financial statements are designed to provide that information.

3.17 Unconsolidated financial statements are designed to provide information about the parent's assets, liabilities, equity, income and expenses, and not about those of its subsidiaries. That information can be useful to existing and potential investors, lenders and other creditors of the parent because:

(a) a claim against the parent typically does not give the holder of that claim a claim against subsidiaries; and

(b) in some jurisdictions, the amounts that can be legally distributed to holders of equity claims against the parent depend on the distributable reserves of the parent.

Another way to provide information about some or all assets, liabilities, equity, income and expenses of the parent alone is in consolidated financial statements, in the notes.

3.18 Information provided in unconsolidated financial statements is typically not sufficient to meet the information needs of existing and potential investors, lenders and other creditors of the parent. Accordingly, when consolidated financial statements are required, unconsolidated financial statements cannot serve as a substitute for consolidated financial statements. Nevertheless, a parent may be required, or choose, to prepare unconsolidated financial statements in addition to consolidated financial statements.

from paragraph

CHAPTER 4—THE ELEMENTS OF FINANCIAL STATEMENTS

INTRODUCTION	4.1
DEFINITION OF AN ASSET	4.3
Right	4.6
Potential to produce economic benefits	4.14
Control	4.19
DEFINITION OF A LIABILITY	4.26
Obligation	4.28
Transfer of an economic resource	4.36
Present obligation as a result of past events	4.42
ASSETS AND LIABILITIES	4.48
Unit of account	4.48
Executory contracts	4.56
Substance of contractual rights and contractual obligations	4.59
DEFINITION OF EQUITY	4.63
DEFINITIONS OF INCOME AND EXPENSES	4.68

Introduction

4.1 The elements of financial statements defined in the *Conceptual Framework* are:

  (a) assets, liabilities and equity, which relate to a reporting entity's financial position; and

  (b) income and expenses, which relate to a reporting entity's financial performance.

4.2 Those elements are linked to the economic resources, claims and changes in economic resources and claims discussed in Chapter 1, and are defined in Table 4.1.

Table 4.1—The elements of financial statements

Item discussed in Chapter 1	Element	Definition or description
Economic resource	Asset	A present economic resource controlled by the entity as a result of past events. An economic resource is a right that has the potential to produce economic benefits.
Claim	Liability	A present obligation of the entity to transfer an economic resource as a result of past events.
	Equity	The residual interest in the assets of the entity after deducting all its liabilities.
Changes in economic resources and claims, reflecting financial performance	Income	Increases in assets, or decreases in liabilities, that result in increases in equity, other than those relating to contributions from holders of equity claims.
	Expenses	Decreases in assets, or increases in liabilities, that result in decreases in equity, other than those relating to distributions to holders of equity claims.
Other changes in economic resources and claims	–	Contributions from holders of equity claims, and distributions to them.
	–	Exchanges of assets or liabilities that do not result in increases or decreases in equity.

Definition of an asset

4.3 An asset is a present economic resource controlled by the entity as a result of past events.

4.4 An economic resource is a right that has the potential to produce economic benefits.

4.5 This section discusses three aspects of those definitions:

(a) right (see paragraphs 4.6–4.13);

(b) potential to produce economic benefits (see paragraphs 4.14–4.18); and

(c) control (see paragraphs 4.19–4.25).

Right

4.6 Rights that have the potential to produce economic benefits take many forms, including:

(a) rights that correspond to an obligation of another party (see paragraph 4.39), for example:

(i) rights to receive cash.

(ii) rights to receive goods or services.

(iii) rights to exchange economic resources with another party on favourable terms. Such rights include, for example, a forward contract to buy an economic resource on terms that are currently favourable or an option to buy an economic resource.

(iv) rights to benefit from an obligation of another party to transfer an economic resource if a specified uncertain future event occurs (see paragraph 4.37).

(b) rights that do not correspond to an obligation of another party, for example:

(i) rights over physical objects, such as property, plant and equipment or inventories. Examples of such rights are a right to use a physical object or a right to benefit from the residual value of a leased object.

(ii) rights to use intellectual property.

4.7 Many rights are established by contract, legislation or similar means. For example, an entity might obtain rights from owning or leasing a physical object, from owning a debt instrument or an equity instrument, or from owning a registered patent. However, an entity might also obtain rights in other ways, for example:

(a) by acquiring or creating know-how that is not in the public domain (see paragraph 4.22); or

(b) through an obligation of another party that arises because that other party has no practical ability to act in a manner inconsistent with its customary practices, published policies or specific statements (see paragraph 4.31).

4.8 Some goods or services—for example, employee services—are received and immediately consumed. An entity's right to obtain the economic benefits produced by such goods or services exists momentarily until the entity consumes the goods or services.

4.9 Not all of an entity's rights are assets of that entity—to be assets of the entity, the rights must both have the potential to produce for the entity economic benefits beyond the economic benefits available to all other parties (see paragraphs 4.14–4.18) and be controlled by the entity (see paragraphs 4.19–4.25). For example, rights available to all parties without significant cost—for instance, rights of access to public goods, such as public rights of way over land, or know-how that is in the public domain—are typically not assets for the entities that hold them.

4.10 An entity cannot have a right to obtain economic benefits from itself. Hence:

(a) debt instruments or equity instruments issued by the entity and repurchased and held by it—for example, treasury shares—are not economic resources of that entity; and

(b) if a reporting entity comprises more than one legal entity, debt instruments or equity instruments issued by one of those legal entities and held by another of those legal entities are not economic resources of the reporting entity.

4.11 In principle, each of an entity's rights is a separate asset. However, for accounting purposes, related rights are often treated as a single unit of account that is a single asset (see paragraphs 4.48–4.55). For example, legal ownership of a physical object may give rise to several rights, including:

(a) the right to use the object;

(b) the right to sell rights over the object;

(c) the right to pledge rights over the object; and

(d) other rights not listed in (a)–(c).

4.12 In many cases, the set of rights arising from legal ownership of a physical object is accounted for as a single asset. Conceptually, the economic resource is the set of rights, not the physical object. Nevertheless, describing the set of rights as the physical object will often provide a faithful representation of those rights in the most concise and understandable way.

4.13 In some cases, it is uncertain whether a right exists. For example, an entity and another party might dispute whether the entity has a right to receive an economic resource from that other party. Until that existence uncertainty is resolved—for example, by a court ruling—it is uncertain whether the entity has a right and, consequently, whether an asset exists. (Paragraph 5.14 discusses recognition of assets whose existence is uncertain.)

Potential to produce economic benefits

4.14 An economic resource is a right that has the potential to produce economic benefits. For that potential to exist, it does not need to be certain, or even likely, that the right will produce economic benefits. It is only necessary that the right already exists and that, in at least one circumstance, it would produce for the entity economic benefits beyond those available to all other parties.

4.15 A right can meet the definition of an economic resource, and hence can be an asset, even if the probability that it will produce economic benefits is low. Nevertheless, that low probability might affect decisions about what information to provide about the asset and how to provide that information, including decisions about whether the asset is recognised (see paragraphs 5.15–5.17) and how it is measured.

4.16 An economic resource could produce economic benefits for an entity by entitling or enabling it to do, for example, one or more of the following:

(a) receive contractual cash flows or another economic resource;

(b) exchange economic resources with another party on favourable terms;

(c) produce cash inflows or avoid cash outflows by, for example:

(i) using the economic resource either individually or in combination with other economic resources to produce goods or provide services;

	(ii)	using the economic resource to enhance the value of other economic resources; or
	(iii)	leasing the economic resource to another party;
(d)		receive cash or other economic resources by selling the economic resource; or
(e)		extinguish liabilities by transferring the economic resource.

4.17 Although an economic resource derives its value from its present potential to produce future economic benefits, the economic resource is the present right that contains that potential, not the future economic benefits that the right may produce. For example, a purchased option derives its value from its potential to produce economic benefits through exercise of the option at a future date. However, the economic resource is the present right—the right to exercise the option at a future date. The economic resource is not the future economic benefits that the holder will receive if the option is exercised.

4.18 There is a close association between incurring expenditure and acquiring assets, but the two do not necessarily coincide. Hence, when an entity incurs expenditure, this may provide evidence that the entity has sought future economic benefits, but does not provide conclusive proof that the entity has obtained an asset. Similarly, the absence of related expenditure does not preclude an item from meeting the definition of an asset. Assets can include, for example, rights that a government has granted to the entity free of charge or that another party has donated to the entity.

Control

4.19 Control links an economic resource to an entity. Assessing whether control exists helps to identify the economic resource for which the entity accounts. For example, an entity may control a proportionate share in a property without controlling the rights arising from ownership of the entire property. In such cases, the entity's asset is the share in the property, which it controls, not the rights arising from ownership of the entire property, which it does not control.

4.20 An entity controls an economic resource if it has the present ability to direct the use of the economic resource and obtain the economic benefits that may flow from it. Control includes the present ability to prevent other parties from directing the use of the economic resource and from obtaining the economic benefits that may flow from it. It follows that, if one party controls an economic resource, no other party controls that resource.

4.21 An entity has the present ability to direct the use of an economic resource if it has the right to deploy that economic resource in its activities, or to allow another party to deploy the economic resource in that other party's activities.

4.22 Control of an economic resource usually arises from an ability to enforce legal rights. However, control can also arise if an entity has other means of ensuring that it, and no other party, has the present ability to direct the use of the economic resource and obtain the benefits that may flow from it. For example, an entity could control a right to use know-how that is not in the public domain if the entity has access to the know-how and the present ability to keep the know-how secret, even if that know-how is not protected by a registered patent.

4.23 For an entity to control an economic resource, the future economic benefits from that resource must flow to the entity either directly or indirectly rather than to another party. This aspect of control does not imply that the entity can ensure that the resource will produce economic benefits in all circumstances. Instead, it means that if the resource produces economic benefits, the entity is the party that will obtain them either directly or indirectly.

4.24 Having exposure to significant variations in the amount of the economic benefits produced by an economic resource may indicate that the entity controls the resource. However, it is only one factor to consider in the overall assessment of whether control exists.

4.25 Sometimes one party (a principal) engages another party (an agent) to act on behalf of, and for the benefit of, the principal. For example, a principal may engage an agent to arrange sales of goods controlled by the principal. If an agent has custody of an economic resource controlled by the principal, that economic resource is not an asset of the agent. Furthermore, if the agent has an obligation to transfer to a third party an economic resource controlled by the principal, that obligation is not a liability of the agent, because the economic resource that would be transferred is the principal's economic resource, not the agent's.

Definition of a liability

4.26 A liability is a present obligation of the entity to transfer an economic resource as a result of past events.

4.27 For a liability to exist, three criteria must all be satisfied:

(a) the entity has an obligation (see paragraphs 4.28–4.35);

(b) the obligation is to transfer an economic resource (see paragraphs 4.36–4.41); and

(c) the obligation is a present obligation that exists as a result of past events (see paragraphs 4.42–4.47).

Obligation

4.28 The first criterion for a liability is that the entity has an obligation.

4.29 An obligation is a duty or responsibility that an entity has no practical ability to avoid. An obligation is always owed to another party (or parties). The other party (or parties) could be a person or another entity, a group of people or other entities, or society at large. It is not necessary to know the identity of the party (or parties) to whom the obligation is owed.

4.30 If one party has an obligation to transfer an economic resource, it follows that another party (or parties) has a right to receive that economic resource. However, a requirement for one party to recognise a liability and measure it at a specified amount does not imply that the other party (or parties) must recognise an asset or measure it at the same amount. For example, particular Standards may contain different recognition criteria or measurement requirements for the liability of one party and the corresponding asset of the other party (or parties) if those different criteria or requirements are a consequence of decisions intended to select the most relevant information that faithfully represents what it purports to represent.

4.31 Many obligations are established by contract, legislation or similar means and are legally enforceable by the party (or parties) to whom they are owed. Obligations can also arise, however, from an entity's customary practices, published policies or specific statements if the entity has no practical ability to act in a manner inconsistent with those practices, policies or statements. The obligation that arises in such situations is sometimes referred to as a 'constructive obligation'.

4.32 In some situations, an entity's duty or responsibility to transfer an economic resource is conditional on a particular future action that the entity itself may take. Such actions could include operating a particular business or operating in a particular market on a specified future date, or exercising particular options within a contract. In such situations, the entity has an obligation if it has no practical ability to avoid taking that action.

4.33 A conclusion that it is appropriate to prepare an entity's financial statements on a going concern basis also implies a conclusion that the entity has no practical ability to avoid a transfer that could be avoided only by liquidating the entity or by ceasing to trade.

4.34 The factors used to assess whether an entity has the practical ability to avoid transferring an economic resource may depend on the nature of the entity's duty or responsibility. For example, in some cases, an entity may have no practical ability to avoid a transfer if any action that it could take to avoid the transfer would have economic consequences significantly more adverse than the transfer itself. However, neither an intention to make a transfer, nor a high likelihood of a transfer, is sufficient reason for concluding that the entity has no practical ability to avoid a transfer.

4.35 In some cases, it is uncertain whether an obligation exists. For example, if another party is seeking compensation for an entity's alleged act of wrongdoing, it might be uncertain whether the act occurred, whether the entity committed it or how the law applies. Until that existence uncertainty is resolved—for example, by a court ruling—it is uncertain whether the entity has an obligation to the party seeking compensation and, consequently, whether a liability exists. (Paragraph 5.14 discusses recognition of liabilities whose existence is uncertain.)

Transfer of an economic resource

4.36 The second criterion for a liability is that the obligation is to transfer an economic resource.

4.37 To satisfy this criterion, the obligation must have the potential to require the entity to transfer an economic resource to another party (or parties). For that potential to exist, it does not need to be certain, or even likely, that the entity will be required to transfer an economic resource—the transfer may, for example, be required only if a specified uncertain future event occurs. It is only necessary that the obligation already exists and that, in at least one circumstance, it would require the entity to transfer an economic resource.

4.38 An obligation can meet the definition of a liability even if the probability of a transfer of an economic resource is low. Nevertheless, that low probability might affect decisions about what information to provide about the liability and how to provide that information, including decisions about whether the liability is recognised (see paragraphs 5.15–5.17) and how it is measured.

4.39 Obligations to transfer an economic resource include, for example:

(a) obligations to pay cash.

(b) obligations to deliver goods or provide services.

(c) obligations to exchange economic resources with another party on unfavourable terms. Such obligations include, for example, a forward contract to sell an economic resource on terms that are currently unfavourable or an option that entitles another party to buy an economic resource from the entity.

(d) obligations to transfer an economic resource if a specified uncertain future event occurs.

(e) obligations to issue a financial instrument if that financial instrument will oblige the entity to transfer an economic resource.

4.40 Instead of fulfilling an obligation to transfer an economic resource to the party that has a right to receive that resource, entities sometimes decide to, for example:

(a) settle the obligation by negotiating a release from the obligation;

(b) transfer the obligation to a third party; or

(c) replace that obligation to transfer an economic resource with another obligation by entering into a new transaction.

4.41 In the situations described in paragraph 4.40, an entity has the obligation to transfer an economic resource until it has settled, transferred or replaced that obligation.

Present obligation as a result of past events

4.42 The third criterion for a liability is that the obligation is a present obligation that exists as a result of past events.

4.43 A present obligation exists as a result of past events only if:

(a) the entity has already obtained economic benefits or taken an action; and

(b) as a consequence, the entity will or may have to transfer an economic resource that it would not otherwise have had to transfer.

4.44 The economic benefits obtained could include, for example, goods or services. The action taken could include, for example, operating a particular business or operating in a particular market. If economic benefits are obtained, or an action is taken, over time, the resulting present obligation may accumulate over that time.

4.45 If new legislation is enacted, a present obligation arises only when, as a consequence of obtaining economic benefits or taking an action to which that legislation applies, an entity will or may have to transfer an economic resource that it would not otherwise have had to transfer. The enactment of legislation is not in itself sufficient to give an entity a present obligation. Similarly, an entity's customary practice, published policy or specific statement of the type mentioned in paragraph 4.31 gives rise to a present obligation only when, as a consequence of obtaining economic benefits, or taking an action, to which that practice, policy or statement applies, the entity will or may have to transfer an economic resource that it would not otherwise have had to transfer.

4.46 A present obligation can exist even if a transfer of economic resources cannot be enforced until some point in the future. For example, a contractual liability to pay cash may exist now even if the contract does not require a payment until a future date. Similarly, a contractual obligation for an entity to perform work at a future date may exist now even if the counterparty cannot require the entity to perform the work until that future date.

4.47 An entity does not yet have a present obligation to transfer an economic resource if it has not yet satisfied the criteria in paragraph 4.43, that is, if it has not yet obtained economic benefits, or taken an action, that would or could require the entity to transfer an economic resource that it would not otherwise have had to transfer. For example, if an entity has entered into a contract to pay an employee a salary in exchange for receiving the employee's services, the entity does not have a present obligation to pay the salary until it has received the employee's services. Before then the contract is executory—the entity has a combined right and obligation to exchange future salary for future employee services (see paragraphs 4.56–4.58).

Assets and liabilities

Unit of account

4.48 The unit of account is the right or the group of rights, the obligation or the group of obligations, or the group of rights and obligations, to which recognition criteria and measurement concepts are applied.

4.49 A unit of account is selected for an asset or liability when considering how recognition criteria and measurement concepts will apply to that asset or liability and to the related income and expenses. In some circumstances, it may be appropriate to select one unit of account for recognition and a different unit of account for measurement. For example, contracts may sometimes be recognised individually but measured as part of a portfolio of contracts. For presentation and disclosure, assets, liabilities, income and expenses may need to be aggregated or separated into components.

4.50 If an entity transfers part of an asset or part of a liability, the unit of account may change at that time, so that the transferred component and the retained component become separate units of account (see paragraphs 5.26–5.33).

4.51 A unit of account is selected to provide useful information, which implies that:

(a) the information provided about the asset or liability and about any related income and expenses must be relevant. Treating a group of rights and obligations as a single unit of account may provide more relevant information than treating each right or obligation as a separate unit of account if, for example, those rights and obligations:

(i) cannot be or are unlikely to be the subject of separate transactions;

(ii) cannot or are unlikely to expire in different patterns;

(iii) have similar economic characteristics and risks and hence are likely to have similar implications for the prospects for future net cash inflows to the entity or net cash outflows from the entity; or

(iv) are used together in the business activities conducted by an entity to produce cash flows and are measured by reference to estimates of their interdependent future cash flows.

(b) the information provided about the asset or liability and about any related income and expenses must faithfully represent the substance of the transaction or other event from which they have arisen. Therefore, it may be necessary to treat rights or obligations arising from different sources as a single unit of account, or to separate the rights or obligations arising from a single source (see paragraph 4.62). Equally, to provide a faithful representation of unrelated rights and obligations, it may be necessary to recognise and measure them separately.

4.52 Just as cost constrains other financial reporting decisions, it also constrains the selection of a unit of account. Hence, in selecting a unit of account, it is important to consider whether the benefits of the information provided to users of financial statements by selecting that unit of account are likely to justify the costs of providing and using that information. In general, the costs associated with recognising and measuring assets, liabilities, income and expenses increase as the size of the unit of account decreases. Hence, in general, rights or obligations arising from the same source are separated only if the resulting information is more useful and the benefits outweigh the costs.

4.53 Sometimes, both rights and obligations arise from the same source. For example, some contracts establish both rights and obligations for each of the parties. If those rights and obligations are interdependent and cannot be separated, they constitute a single inseparable asset or liability and hence form a single unit of account. For example, this is the case with executory contracts (see paragraph 4.57). Conversely, if rights are separable from obligations, it may sometimes be appropriate to group the rights separately from the obligations, resulting in the identification of one or more separate assets and liabilities. In other cases, it may be more appropriate to group separable rights and obligations in a single unit of account treating them as a single asset or a single liability.

4.54 Treating a set of rights and obligations as a single unit of account differs from offsetting assets and liabilities (see paragraph 7.10).

4.55 Possible units of account include:

(a) an individual right or individual obligation;

(b) all rights, all obligations, or all rights and all obligations, arising from a single source, for example, a contract;

(c) a subgroup of those rights and/or obligations—for example, a subgroup of rights over an item of property, plant and equipment for which the useful life and pattern of consumption differ from those of the other rights over that item;

(d) a group of rights and/or obligations arising from a portfolio of similar items;

(e) a group of rights and/or obligations arising from a portfolio of dissimilar items—for example, a portfolio of assets and liabilities to be disposed of in a single transaction; and

(f) a risk exposure within a portfolio of items—if a portfolio of items is subject to a common risk, some aspects of the accounting for that portfolio could focus on the aggregate exposure to that risk within the portfolio.

Executory contracts

4.56 An executory contract is a contract, or a portion of a contract, that is equally unperformed—neither party has fulfilled any of its obligations, or both parties have partially fulfilled their obligations to an equal extent.

4.57 An executory contract establishes a combined right and obligation to exchange economic resources. The right and obligation are interdependent and cannot be separated. Hence, the combined right and obligation constitute a single asset or liability. The entity has an asset if the terms of the exchange are currently favourable; it has a liability if the terms of the exchange are currently unfavourable. Whether such an asset or liability is included in the financial statements depends on both the recognition criteria (see Chapter 5) and the measurement basis (see Chapter 6) selected for the asset or liability, including, if applicable, any test for whether the contract is onerous.

4.58 To the extent that either party fulfils its obligations under the contract, the contract is no longer executory. If the reporting entity performs first under the contract, that performance is the event that changes the reporting entity's right and obligation to exchange economic resources into a right to receive an economic resource. That right is an asset. If the other party performs first, that performance is the event that changes the reporting entity's right and obligation to exchange economic resources into an obligation to transfer an economic resource. That obligation is a liability.

Substance of contractual rights and contractual obligations

4.59 The terms of a contract create rights and obligations for an entity that is a party to that contract. To represent those rights and obligations faithfully, financial statements report their substance (see paragraph 2.12). In some cases, the substance of the rights and obligations is clear from the legal form of the contract. In other cases, the terms of the contract or a group or series of contracts require analysis to identify the substance of the rights and obligations.

4.60 All terms in a contract—whether explicit or implicit—are considered unless they have no substance. Implicit terms could include, for example, obligations imposed by statute, such as statutory warranty obligations imposed on entities that enter into contracts to sell goods to customers.

4.61 Terms that have no substance are disregarded. A term has no substance if it has no discernible effect on the economics of the contract. Terms that have no substance could include, for example:

(a) terms that bind neither party; or

(b) rights, including options, that the holder will not have the practical ability to exercise in any circumstances.

4.62 A group or series of contracts may achieve or be designed to achieve an overall commercial effect. To report the substance of such contracts, it may be necessary to treat rights and obligations arising from that group or series of contracts as a single unit of account. For example, if the rights or obligations in one contract merely nullify all the rights or obligations in another contract entered into at the same time with the same counterparty, the combined effect is that the two contracts create no rights or obligations. Conversely, if a single contract creates two or more sets of rights or obligations that could have been created through two or more separate contracts, an entity may need to account for each set as if it arose from separate contracts in order to faithfully represent the rights and obligations (see paragraphs 4.48–4.55).

Definition of equity

4.63 Equity is the residual interest in the assets of the entity after deducting all its liabilities.

4.64 Equity claims are claims on the residual interest in the assets of the entity after deducting all its liabilities. In other words, they are claims against the entity that do not meet the definition of a liability. Such claims may be established by contract, legislation or similar means, and include, to the extent that they do not meet the definition of a liability:

(a) shares of various types, issued by the entity; and

(b) some obligations of the entity to issue another equity claim.

4.65 Different classes of equity claims, such as ordinary shares and preference shares, may confer on their holders different rights, for example, rights to receive some or all of the following from the entity:

(a) dividends, if the entity decides to pay dividends to eligible holders;

(b) the proceeds from satisfying the equity claims, either in full on liquidation, or in part at other times; or

CONCEPTUAL FRAMEWORK FOR FINANCIAL REPORTING

(c) other equity claims.

4.66 Sometimes, legal, regulatory or other requirements affect particular components of equity, such as share capital or retained earnings. For example, some such requirements permit an entity to make distributions to holders of equity claims only if the entity has sufficient reserves that those requirements specify as being distributable.

4.67 Business activities are often undertaken by entities such as sole proprietorships, partnerships, trusts or various types of government business undertakings. The legal and regulatory frameworks for such entities are often different from frameworks that apply to corporate entities. For example, there may be few, if any, restrictions on the distribution to holders of equity claims against such entities. Nevertheless, the definition of equity in paragraph 4.63 of the *Conceptual Framework* applies to all reporting entities.

Definitions of income and expenses

4.68 Income is increases in assets, or decreases in liabilities, that result in increases in equity, other than those relating to contributions from holders of equity claims.

4.69 Expenses are decreases in assets, or increases in liabilities, that result in decreases in equity, other than those relating to distributions to holders of equity claims.

4.70 It follows from these definitions of income and expenses that contributions from holders of equity claims are not income, and distributions to holders of equity claims are not expenses.

4.71 Income and expenses are the elements of financial statements that relate to an entity's financial performance. Users of financial statements need information about both an entity's financial position and its financial performance. Hence, although income and expenses are defined in terms of changes in assets and liabilities, information about income and expenses is just as important as information about assets and liabilities.

4.72 Different transactions and other events generate income and expenses with different characteristics. Providing information separately about income and expenses with different characteristics can help users of financial statements to understand the entity's financial performance (see paragraphs 7.14–7.19).

from paragraph

CHAPTER 5—RECOGNITION AND DERECOGNITION
THE RECOGNITION PROCESS	**5.1**
RECOGNITION CRITERIA	**5.6**
Relevance	**5.12**
Existence uncertainty	5.14
Low probability of an inflow or outflow of economic benefits	5.15
Faithful representation	**5.18**
Measurement uncertainty	5.19
Other factors	5.24
DERECOGNITION	**5.26**

The recognition process

5.1 Recognition is the process of capturing for inclusion in the statement of financial position or the statement(s) of financial performance an item that meets the definition of one of the elements of financial statements—an asset, a liability, equity, income or expenses. Recognition involves depicting the item in one of those statements—either alone or in aggregation with other items—in words and by a monetary amount, and including that amount in one or more totals in that statement. The amount at which an asset, a liability or equity is recognised in the statement of financial position is referred to as its 'carrying amount'.

5.2 The statement of financial position and statement(s) of financial performance depict an entity's recognised assets, liabilities, equity, income and expenses in structured summaries that are designed to make financial information comparable and understandable. An important feature of the structures of those summaries is that the amounts recognised in a statement are included in the totals and, if applicable, subtotals that link the items recognised in the statement.

5.3 Recognition links the elements, the statement of financial position and the statement(s) of financial performance as follows (see Diagram 5.1):

    (a) in the statement of financial position at the beginning and end of the reporting period, total assets minus total liabilities equal total equity; and

    (b) recognised changes in equity during the reporting period comprise:

        (i) income minus expenses recognised in the statement(s) of financial performance; plus

        (ii) contributions from holders of equity claims, minus distributions to holders of equity claims.

5.4 The statements are linked because the recognition of one item (or a change in its carrying amount) requires the recognition or derecognition of one or more other items (or changes in the carrying amount of one or more other items). For example:

    (a) the recognition of income occurs at the same time as:

        (i) the initial recognition of an asset, or an increase in the carrying amount of an asset; or

        (ii) the derecognition of a liability, or a decrease in the carrying amount of a liability.

    (b) the recognition of expenses occurs at the same time as:

        (i) the initial recognition of a liability, or an increase in the carrying amount of a liability; or

        (ii) the derecognition of an asset, or a decrease in the carrying amount of an asset.

Diagram 5.1: How recognition links the elements of financial statements

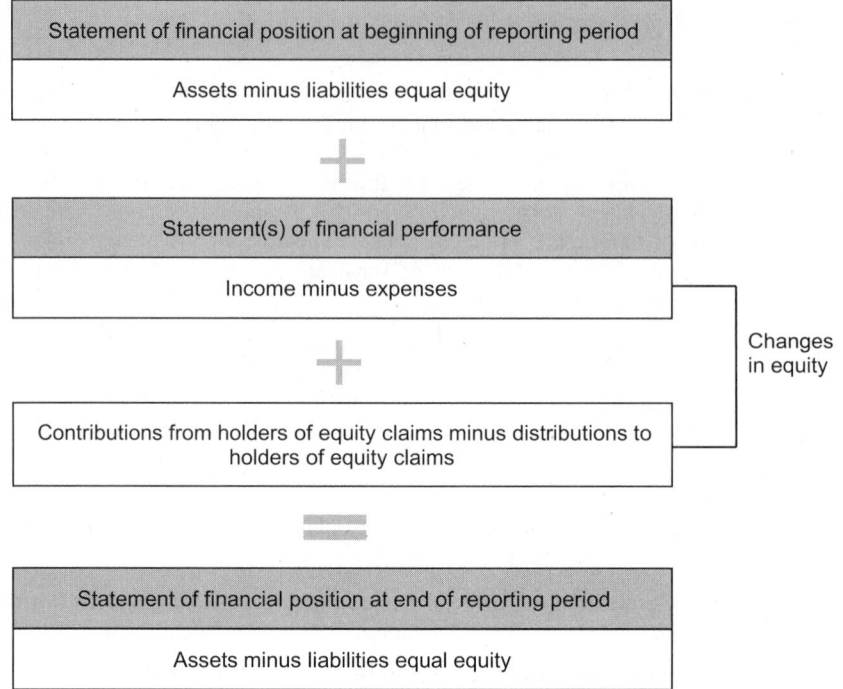

5.5 The initial recognition of assets or liabilities arising from transactions or other events may result in the simultaneous recognition of both income and related expenses. For example, the sale of goods for cash results in the recognition of both income (from the recognition of one asset—the cash) and an expense (from the derecognition of another asset—the goods sold). The simultaneous recognition of income and related expenses is sometimes referred to as the matching of costs with income. Application of the concepts in the *Conceptual Framework* leads to such matching when it arises from the recognition of changes in assets and liabilities. However, matching of costs with income is not an objective of the *Conceptual Framework*. The *Conceptual Framework* does not allow the recognition in the statement of financial position of items that do not meet the definition of an asset, a liability or equity.

Recognition criteria

5.6 Only items that meet the definition of an asset, a liability or equity are recognised in the statement of financial position. Similarly, only items that meet the definition of income or expenses are recognised in the statement(s) of financial performance. However, not all items that meet the definition of one of those elements are recognised.

5.7 Not recognising an item that meets the definition of one of the elements makes the statement of financial position and the statement(s) of financial performance less complete and can exclude useful information from financial statements. On the other hand, in some circumstances, recognising some items that meet the definition of one of the elements would not provide useful information. An asset or liability is recognised only if recognition of that asset or liability and of any resulting income, expenses or changes in equity provides users of financial statements with information that is useful, ie with:

(a) relevant information about the asset or liability and about any resulting income, expenses or changes in equity (see paragraphs 5.12–5.17); and

(b) a faithful representation of the asset or liability and of any resulting income, expenses or changes in equity (see paragraphs 5.18–5.25).

5.8 Just as cost constrains other financial reporting decisions, it also constrains recognition decisions. There is a cost to recognising an asset or liability. Preparers of financial statements incur costs in obtaining a relevant measure of an asset or liability. Users of financial statements also incur costs in analysing and interpreting the information provided. An asset or liability is recognised if the benefits of the information provided to users of financial statements by recognition are likely to justify the costs of providing and using that information. In some cases, the costs of recognition may outweigh its benefits.

5.9 It is not possible to define precisely when recognition of an asset or liability will provide useful information to users of financial statements, at a cost that does not outweigh its benefits. What is useful to users depends on the item and the facts and circumstances. Consequently, judgement is required when deciding whether to recognise an item, and thus recognition requirements may need to vary between and within Standards.

5.10 It is important when making decisions about recognition to consider the information that would be given if an asset or liability were not recognised. For example, if no asset is recognised when expenditure is incurred, an expense is recognised. Over time, recognising the expense may, in some cases, provide useful information, for example, information that enables users of financial statements to identify trends.

5.11 Even if an item meeting the definition of an asset or liability is not recognised, an entity may need to provide information about that item in the notes. It is important to consider how to make such information sufficiently visible to compensate for the item's absence from the structured summary provided by the statement of financial position and, if applicable, the statement(s) of financial performance.

Relevance

5.12 Information about assets, liabilities, equity, income and expenses is relevant to users of financial statements. However, recognition of a particular asset or liability and any resulting income, expenses or changes in equity may not always provide relevant information. That may be the case if, for example:

(a) it is uncertain whether an asset or liability exists (see paragraph 5.14); or

(b) an asset or liability exists, but the probability of an inflow or outflow of economic benefits is low (see paragraphs 5.15–5.17).

5.13 The presence of one or both of the factors described in paragraph 5.12 does not lead automatically to a conclusion that the information provided by recognition lacks relevance. Moreover, factors other than those described in paragraph 5.12 may also affect the conclusion. It may be a combination of factors and not any single factor that determines whether recognition provides relevant information.

Existence uncertainty

5.14 Paragraphs 4.13 and 4.35 discuss cases in which it is uncertain whether an asset or liability exists. In some cases, that uncertainty, possibly combined with a low probability of inflows or outflows of economic benefits and an exceptionally wide range of possible outcomes, may mean that the recognition of an asset or liability, necessarily measured at a single amount, would not provide relevant information. Whether or not the asset or liability is recognised, explanatory information about the uncertainties associated with it may need to be provided in the financial statements.

Low probability of an inflow or outflow of economic benefits

5.15   An asset or liability can exist even if the probability of an inflow or outflow of economic benefits is low (see paragraphs 4.15 and 4.38).

5.16   If the probability of an inflow or outflow of economic benefits is low, the most relevant information about the asset or liability may be information about the magnitude of the possible inflows or outflows, their possible timing and the factors affecting the probability of their occurrence. The typical location for such information is in the notes.

5.17   Even if the probability of an inflow or outflow of economic benefits is low, recognition of the asset or liability may provide relevant information beyond the information described in paragraph 5.16. Whether that is the case may depend on a variety of factors. For example:

(a)   if an asset is acquired or a liability is incurred in an exchange transaction on market terms, its cost generally reflects the probability of an inflow or outflow of economic benefits. Thus, that cost may be relevant information, and is generally readily available. Furthermore, not recognising the asset or liability would result in the recognition of expenses or income at the time of the exchange, which might not be a faithful representation of the transaction (see paragraph 5.25(a)).

(b)   if an asset or liability arises from an event that is not an exchange transaction, recognition of the asset or liability typically results in recognition of income or expenses. If there is only a low probability that the asset or liability will result in an inflow or outflow of economic benefits, users of financial statements might not regard the recognition of the asset and income, or the liability and expenses, as providing relevant information.

Faithful representation

5.18   Recognition of a particular asset or liability is appropriate if it provides not only relevant information, but also a faithful representation of that asset or liability and of any resulting income, expenses or changes in equity. Whether a faithful representation can be provided may be affected by the level of measurement uncertainty associated with the asset or liability or by other factors.

Measurement uncertainty

5.19   For an asset or liability to be recognised, it must be measured. In many cases, such measures must be estimated and are therefore subject to measurement uncertainty. As noted in paragraph 2.19, the use of reasonable estimates is an essential part of the preparation of financial information and does not undermine the usefulness of the information if the estimates are clearly and accurately described and explained. Even a high level of measurement uncertainty does not necessarily prevent such an estimate from providing useful information.

5.20   In some cases, the level of uncertainty involved in estimating a measure of an asset or liability may be so high that it may be questionable whether the estimate would provide a sufficiently faithful representation of that asset or liability and of any resulting income, expenses or changes in equity. The level of measurement uncertainty may be so high if, for example, the only way of estimating that measure of the asset or liability is by using cash-flow-based measurement techniques and, in addition, one or more of the following circumstances exists:

(a) the range of possible outcomes is exceptionally wide and the probability of each outcome is exceptionally difficult to estimate.

(b) the measure is exceptionally sensitive to small changes in estimates of the probability of different outcomes—for example, if the probability of future cash inflows or outflows occurring is exceptionally low, but the magnitude of those cash inflows or outflows will be exceptionally high if they occur.

(c) measuring the asset or liability requires exceptionally difficult or exceptionally subjective allocations of cash flows that do not relate solely to the asset or liability being measured.

5.21 In some of the cases described in paragraph 5.20, the most useful information may be the measure that relies on the highly uncertain estimate, accompanied by a description of the estimate and an explanation of the uncertainties that affect it. This is especially likely to be the case if that measure is the most relevant measure of the asset or liability. In other cases, if that information would not provide a sufficiently faithful representation of the asset or liability and of any resulting income, expenses or changes in equity, the most useful information may be a different measure (accompanied by any necessary descriptions and explanations) that is slightly less relevant but is subject to lower measurement uncertainty.

5.22 In limited circumstances, all relevant measures of an asset or liability that are available (or can be obtained) may be subject to such high measurement uncertainty that none would provide useful information about the asset or liability (and any resulting income, expenses or changes in equity), even if the measure were accompanied by a description of the estimates made in producing it and an explanation of the uncertainties that affect those estimates. In those limited circumstances, the asset or liability would not be recognised.

5.23 Whether or not an asset or liability is recognised, a faithful representation of the asset or liability may need to include explanatory information about the uncertainties associated with the asset or liability's existence or measurement, or with its outcome—the amount or timing of any inflow or outflow of economic benefits that will ultimately result from it (see paragraphs 6.60–6.62).

Other factors

5.24 Faithful representation of a recognised asset, liability, equity, income or expenses involves not only recognition of that item, but also its measurement as well as presentation and disclosure of information about it (see Chapters 6–7).

5.25 Hence, when assessing whether the recognition of an asset or liability can provide a faithful representation of the asset or liability, it is necessary to consider not merely its description and measurement in the statement of financial position, but also:

(a) the depiction of resulting income, expenses and changes in equity. For example, if an entity acquires an asset in exchange for consideration, not recognising the asset would result in recognising expenses and would reduce the entity's profit and equity. In some cases, for example, if the entity does not consume the asset immediately, that result could provide a misleading representation that the entity's financial position has deteriorated.

(b) whether related assets and liabilities are recognised. If they are not recognised, recognition may create a recognition inconsistency (accounting mismatch). That may not provide an understandable or faithful representation of the overall effect of the transaction or other event giving rise to the asset or liability, even if explanatory information is provided in the notes.

(c) presentation and disclosure of information about the asset or liability, and resulting income, expenses or changes in equity. A complete depiction includes all information necessary for a user of financial statements to understand the economic phenomenon depicted, including all necessary descriptions and explanations. Hence, presentation and disclosure of related information can enable a recognised amount to form part of a faithful representation of an asset, a liability, equity, income or expenses.

Derecognition

5.26 Derecognition is the removal of all or part of a recognised asset or liability from an entity's statement of financial position. Derecognition normally occurs when that item no longer meets the definition of an asset or of a liability:

(a) for an asset, derecognition normally occurs when the entity loses control of all or part of the recognised asset; and

(b) for a liability, derecognition normally occurs when the entity no longer has a present obligation for all or part of the recognised liability.

5.27 Accounting requirements for derecognition aim to faithfully represent both:

(a) any assets and liabilities retained after the transaction or other event that led to the derecognition (including any asset or liability acquired, incurred or created as part of the transaction or other event); and

(b) the change in the entity's assets and liabilities as a result of that transaction or other event.

5.28 The aims described in paragraph 5.27 are normally achieved by:

(a) derecognising any assets or liabilities that have expired or have been consumed, collected, fulfilled or transferred, and recognising any resulting income and expenses. In the rest of this chapter, the term 'transferred component' refers to all those assets and liabilities;

(b) continuing to recognise the assets or liabilities retained, referred to as the 'retained component', if any. That retained component becomes a unit of account separate from the transferred component. Accordingly, no income or expenses are recognised on the retained component as a result of the derecognition of the transferred component, unless the derecognition results in a change in the measurement requirements applicable to the retained component; and

(c) applying one or more of the following procedures, if that is necessary to achieve one or both of the aims described in paragraph 5.27:

(i) presenting any retained component separately in the statement of financial position;

(ii) presenting separately in the statement(s) of financial performance any income and expenses recognised as a result of the derecognition of the transferred component; or

(iii) providing explanatory information.

CONCEPTUAL FRAMEWORK FOR FINANCIAL REPORTING

5.29   In some cases, an entity might appear to transfer an asset or liability, but that asset or liability might nevertheless remain an asset or liability of the entity. For example:

(a)   if an entity has apparently transferred an asset but retains exposure to significant positive or negative variations in the amount of economic benefits that may be produced by the asset, this sometimes indicates that the entity might continue to control that asset (see paragraph 4.24); or

(b)   if an entity has transferred an asset to another party that holds the asset as an agent for the entity, the transferor still controls the asset (see paragraph 4.25).

5.30   In the cases described in paragraph 5.29, derecognition of that asset or liability is not appropriate because it would not achieve either of the two aims described in paragraph 5.27.

5.31   When an entity no longer has a transferred component, derecognition of the transferred component faithfully represents that fact. However, in some of those cases, derecognition may not faithfully represent how much a transaction or other event changed the entity's assets or liabilities, even when supported by one or more of the procedures described in paragraph 5.28(c). In those cases, derecognition of the transferred component might imply that the entity's financial position has changed more significantly than it has. This might occur, for example:

(a)   if an entity has transferred an asset and, at the same time, entered into another transaction that results in a present right or present obligation to reacquire the asset. Such present rights or present obligations may arise from, for example, a forward contract, a written put option, or a purchased call option.

(b)   if an entity has retained exposure to significant positive or negative variations in the amount of economic benefits that may be produced by a transferred component that the entity no longer controls.

5.32   If derecognition is not sufficient to achieve both aims described in paragraph 5.27, even when supported by one or more of the procedures described in paragraph 5.28(c), those two aims might sometimes be achieved by continuing to recognise the transferred component. This has the following consequences:

(a)   no income or expenses are recognised on either the retained component or the transferred component as a result of the transaction or other event;

(b)   the proceeds received (or paid) upon transfer of the asset (or liability) are treated as a loan received (or given); and

(c)   separate presentation of the transferred component in the statement of financial position, or provision of explanatory information, is needed to depict the fact that the entity no longer has any rights or obligations arising from the transferred component. Similarly, it may be necessary to provide information about income or expenses arising from the transferred component after the transfer.

5.33   One case in which questions about derecognition arise is when a contract is modified in a way that reduces or eliminates existing rights or obligations. In deciding how to account for contract modifications, it is necessary to consider which unit of account provides users of financial statements with the most useful information about the assets and liabilities retained after the modification, and about how the modification changed the entity's assets and liabilities:

(a)   if a contract modification only eliminates existing rights or obligations, the discussion in paragraphs 5.26–5.32 is considered in deciding whether to derecognise those rights or obligations;

(b) if a contract modification only adds new rights or obligations, it is necessary to decide whether to treat the added rights or obligations as a separate asset or liability, or as part of the same unit of account as the existing rights and obligations (see paragraphs 4.48–4.55); and

(c) if a contract modification both eliminates existing rights or obligations and adds new rights or obligations, it is necessary to consider both the separate and the combined effect of those modifications. In some such cases, the contract has been modified to such an extent that, in substance, the modification replaces the old asset or liability with a new asset or liability. In cases of such extensive modification, the entity may need to derecognise the original asset or liability, and recognise the new asset or liability.

from paragraph

CHAPTER 6—MEASUREMENT

INTRODUCTION	**6.1**
MEASUREMENT BASES	**6.4**
Historical cost	**6.4**
Current value	**6.10**
Fair value	6.12
Value in use and fulfilment value	6.17
Current cost	6.21
INFORMATION PROVIDED BY PARTICULAR MEASUREMENT BASES	**6.23**
Historical cost	**6.24**
Current value	**6.32**
Fair value	6.32
Value in use and fulfilment value	6.37
Current cost	6.40
FACTORS TO CONSIDER WHEN SELECTING A MEASUREMENT BASIS	**6.43**
Relevance	**6.49**
Characteristics of the asset or liability	6.50
Contribution to future cash flows	6.54
Faithful representation	**6.58**
Enhancing qualitative characteristics and the cost constraint	**6.63**
Historical cost	6.69
Current value	6.72
Factors specific to initial measurement	**6.77**
More than one measurement basis	**6.83**
MEASUREMENT OF EQUITY	**6.87**
CASH-FLOW-BASED MEASUREMENT TECHNIQUES	**6.91**

Introduction

6.1 Elements recognised in financial statements are quantified in monetary terms. This requires the selection of a measurement basis. A measurement basis is an identified feature—for example, historical cost, fair value or fulfilment value—of an item being measured. Applying a measurement basis to an asset or liability creates a measure for that asset or liability and for related income and expenses.

6.2 Consideration of the qualitative characteristics of useful financial information and of the cost constraint is likely to result in the selection of different measurement bases for different assets, liabilities, income and expenses.

6.3 A Standard may need to describe how to implement the measurement basis selected in that Standard. That description could include:

(a) specifying techniques that may or must be used to estimate a measure applying a particular measurement basis;

(b) specifying a simplified measurement approach that is likely to provide information similar to that provided by a preferred measurement basis; or

(c) explaining how to modify a measurement basis, for example, by excluding from the fulfilment value of a liability the effect of the possibility that the entity may fail to fulfil that liability (own credit risk).

Measurement bases

Historical cost

6.4 Historical cost measures provide monetary information about assets, liabilities and related income and expenses, using information derived, at least in part, from the price of the transaction or other event that gave rise to them. Unlike current value, historical cost does not reflect changes in values, except to the extent that those changes relate to impairment of an asset or a liability becoming onerous (see paragraphs 6.7(c) and 6.8(b)).

6.5 The historical cost of an asset when it is acquired or created is the value of the costs incurred in acquiring or creating the asset, comprising the consideration paid to acquire or create the asset plus transaction costs. The historical cost of a liability when it is incurred or taken on is the value of the consideration received to incur or take on the liability minus transaction costs.

6.6 When an asset is acquired or created, or a liability is incurred or taken on, as a result of an event that is not a transaction on market terms (see paragraph 6.80), it may not be possible to identify a cost, or the cost may not provide relevant information about the asset or liability. In some such cases, a current value of the asset or liability is used as a deemed cost on initial recognition and that deemed cost is then used as a starting point for subsequent measurement at historical cost.

6.7 The historical cost of an asset is updated over time to depict, if applicable:

(a) the consumption of part or all of the economic resource that constitutes the asset (depreciation or amortisation);

(b) payments received that extinguish part or all of the asset;

(c) the effect of events that cause part or all of the historical cost of the asset to be no longer recoverable (impairment); and

(d) accrual of interest to reflect any financing component of the asset.

6.8 The historical cost of a liability is updated over time to depict, if applicable:

(a) fulfilment of part or all of the liability, for example, by making payments that extinguish part or all of the liability or by satisfying an obligation to deliver goods;

(b) the effect of events that increase the value of the obligation to transfer the economic resources needed to fulfil the liability to such an extent that the liability becomes onerous. A liability is onerous if the historical cost is no longer sufficient to depict the obligation to fulfil the liability; and

(c) accrual of interest to reflect any financing component of the liability.

6.9 One way to apply a historical cost measurement basis to financial assets and financial liabilities is to measure them at amortised cost. The amortised cost of a financial asset or financial liability reflects estimates of future cash flows, discounted at a rate determined at initial recognition. For variable rate instruments, the discount rate is updated to reflect changes in the variable rate. The amortised cost of a financial asset or financial liability is updated over time to depict subsequent changes, such as the accrual of interest, the impairment of a financial asset and receipts or payments.

Current value

6.10 Current value measures provide monetary information about assets, liabilities and related income and expenses, using information updated to reflect conditions at the measurement date. Because of the updating, current values of assets and liabilities reflect changes, since the previous measurement date, in estimates of cash flows and other factors reflected in those current values (see paragraphs 6.14–6.15 and 6.20). Unlike historical cost, the current value of an asset or liability is not derived, even in part, from the price of the transaction or other event that gave rise to the asset or liability.

6.11 Current value measurement bases include:

(a) fair value (see paragraphs 6.12–6.16);

(b) value in use for assets and fulfilment value for liabilities (see paragraphs 6.17–6.20); and

(c) current cost (see paragraphs 6.21–6.22).

Fair value

6.12 Fair value is the price that would be received to sell an asset, or paid to transfer a liability, in an orderly transaction between market participants at the measurement date.

6.13 Fair value reflects the perspective of market participants—participants in a market to which the entity has access. The asset or liability is measured using the same assumptions that market participants would use when pricing the asset or liability if those market participants act in their economic best interest.

6.14 In some cases, fair value can be determined directly by observing prices in an active market. In other cases, it is determined indirectly using measurement techniques, for example, cash-flow-based measurement techniques (see paragraphs 6.91–6.95), reflecting all the following factors:

(a) estimates of future cash flows.

(b) possible variations in the estimated amount or timing of future cash flows for the asset or liability being measured, caused by the uncertainty inherent in the cash flows.

(c) the time value of money.

(d) the price for bearing the uncertainty inherent in the cash flows (a risk premium or risk discount). The price for bearing that uncertainty depends on the extent of that uncertainty. It also reflects the fact that investors would generally pay less for an asset (and generally require more for taking on a liability) that has uncertain cash flows than for an asset (or liability) whose cash flows are certain.

(e) other factors, for example, liquidity, if market participants would take those factors into account in the circumstances.

6.15 The factors mentioned in paragraphs 6.14(b) and 6.14(d) include the possibility that a counterparty may fail to fulfil its liability to the entity (credit risk), or that the entity may fail to fulfil its liability (own credit risk).

6.16 Because fair value is not derived, even in part, from the price of the transaction or other event that gave rise to the asset or liability, fair value is not increased by the transaction costs incurred when acquiring the asset and is not decreased by the transaction costs incurred when the liability is incurred or taken on. In addition, fair value does not reflect the transaction costs that would be incurred on the ultimate disposal of the asset or on transferring or settling the liability.

Value in use and fulfilment value

6.17 Value in use is the present value of the cash flows, or other economic benefits, that an entity expects to derive from the use of an asset and from its ultimate disposal. Fulfilment value is the present value of the cash, or other economic resources, that an entity expects to be obliged to transfer as it fulfils a liability. Those amounts of cash or other economic resources include not only the amounts to be transferred to the liability counterparty, but also the amounts that the entity expects to be obliged to transfer to other parties to enable it to fulfil the liability.

6.18 Because value in use and fulfilment value are based on future cash flows, they do not include transaction costs incurred on acquiring an asset or taking on a liability. However, value in use and fulfilment value include the present value of any transaction costs an entity expects to incur on the ultimate disposal of the asset or on fulfilling the liability.

6.19 Value in use and fulfilment value reflect entity-specific assumptions rather than assumptions by market participants. In practice, there may sometimes be little difference between the assumptions that market participants would use and those that an entity itself uses.

6.20 Value in use and fulfilment value cannot be observed directly and are determined using cash-flow-based measurement techniques (see paragraphs 6.91–6.95). Value in use and fulfilment value reflect the same factors described for fair value in paragraph 6.14, but from an entity-specific perspective rather than from a market-participant perspective.

Current cost

6.21 The current cost of an asset is the cost of an equivalent asset at the measurement date, comprising the consideration that would be paid at the measurement date plus the transaction costs that would be incurred at that date. The current cost of a liability is the consideration that would be received for an equivalent liability at the measurement date minus the transaction costs that would be incurred at that date. Current cost, like historical cost, is an entry value: it reflects prices in the market in which the entity would acquire the asset or would incur the liability. Hence, it is different from fair value, value in use and fulfilment value, which are exit values. However, unlike historical cost, current cost reflects conditions at the measurement date.

6.22 In some cases, current cost cannot be determined directly by observing prices in an active market and must be determined indirectly by other means. For example, if prices are available only for new assets, the current cost of a used asset might need to be estimated by adjusting the current price of a new asset to reflect the current age and condition of the asset held by the entity.

Information provided by particular measurement bases

6.23 When selecting a measurement basis, it is important to consider the nature of the information that the measurement basis will produce in both the statement of financial position and the statement(s) of financial performance. Table 6.1 summarises that information and paragraphs 6.24–6.42 provide additional discussion.

Historical cost

6.24 Information provided by measuring an asset or liability at historical cost may be relevant to users of financial statements, because historical cost uses information derived, at least in part, from the price of the transaction or other event that gave rise to the asset or liability.

6.25 Normally, if an entity acquired an asset in a recent transaction on market terms, the entity expects that the asset will provide sufficient economic benefits that the entity will at least recover the cost of the asset. Similarly, if a liability was incurred or taken on as a result of a recent transaction on market terms, the entity expects that the value of the obligation to transfer economic resources to fulfil the liability will normally be no more than the value of the consideration received minus transaction costs. Hence, measuring an asset or liability at historical cost in such cases provides relevant information about both the asset or liability and the price of the transaction that gave rise to that asset or liability.

6.26 Because historical cost is reduced to reflect consumption of an asset and its impairment, the amount expected to be recovered from an asset measured at historical cost is at least as great as its carrying amount. Similarly, because the historical cost of a liability is increased when it becomes onerous, the value of the obligation to transfer the economic resources needed to fulfil the liability is no more than the carrying amount of the liability.

6.27 If an asset other than a financial asset is measured at historical cost, consumption or sale of the asset, or of part of the asset, gives rise to an expense measured at the historical cost of the asset, or of part of the asset, consumed or sold.

6.28 The expense arising from the sale of an asset is recognised at the same time as the consideration for that sale is recognised as income. The difference between the income and the expense is the margin resulting from the sale. Expenses arising from consumption of an asset can be compared to related income to provide information about margins.

6.29 Similarly, if a liability other than a financial liability was incurred or taken on in exchange for consideration and is measured at historical cost, the fulfilment of all or part of the liability gives rise to income measured at the value of the consideration received for the part fulfilled. The difference between that income and the expenses incurred in fulfilling the liability is the margin resulting from the fulfilment.

6.30 Information about the cost of assets sold or consumed, including goods and services consumed immediately (see paragraph 4.8), and about the consideration received, may have predictive value. That information can be used as an input in predicting future margins from the future sale of goods (including goods not currently held by the entity) and services and hence to assess the entity's prospects for future net cash inflows. To assess an entity's prospects for future cash flows, users of financial statements often focus on the entity's prospects for generating future margins over many periods, not just on its prospects for generating margins from goods already held. Income and expenses measured at historical cost may also have confirmatory value because they may provide feedback to users of financial statements about their previous predictions of cash flows or of margins. Information about the cost of assets sold or consumed may also help in an assessment of how efficiently and effectively the entity's management has discharged its responsibilities to use the entity's economic resources.

6.31 For similar reasons, information about interest earned on assets, and interest incurred on liabilities, measured at amortised cost may have predictive and confirmatory value.

Current value

Fair value

6.32 Information provided by measuring assets and liabilities at fair value may have predictive value because fair value reflects market participants' current expectations about the amount, timing and uncertainty of future cash flows. These expectations are priced in a manner that reflects the current risk preferences of market participants. That information may also have confirmatory value by providing feedback about previous expectations.

6.33 Income and expenses reflecting market participants' current expectations may have some predictive value, because such income and expenses can be used as an input in predicting future income and expenses. Such income and expenses may also help in an assessment of how efficiently and effectively the entity's management has discharged its responsibilities to use the entity's economic resources.

6.34 A change in the fair value of an asset or liability can result from various factors identified in paragraph 6.14. When those factors have different characteristics, identifying separately income and expenses that result from those factors can provide useful information to users of financial statements (see paragraph 7.14(b)).

6.35 If an entity acquired an asset in one market and determines fair value using prices in a different market (the market in which the entity would sell the asset), any difference between the prices in those two markets is recognised as income when that fair value is first determined.

6.36 Sale of an asset or transfer of a liability would normally be for consideration of an amount similar to its fair value, if the transaction were to occur in the market that was the source for the prices used when measuring that fair value. In those cases, if the asset or liability is

Value in use and fulfilment value

6.37 Value in use provides information about the present value of the estimated cash flows from the use of an asset and from its ultimate disposal. This information may have predictive value because it can be used in assessing the prospects for future net cash inflows.

6.38 Fulfilment value provides information about the present value of the estimated cash flows needed to fulfil a liability. Hence, fulfilment value may have predictive value, particularly if the liability will be fulfilled, rather than transferred or settled by negotiation.

6.39 Updated estimates of value in use or fulfilment value, combined with information about estimates of the amount, timing and uncertainty of future cash flows, may also have confirmatory value because they provide feedback about previous estimates of value in use or fulfilment value.

Current cost

6.40 Information about assets and liabilities measured at current cost may be relevant because current cost reflects the cost at which an equivalent asset could be acquired or created at the measurement date or the consideration that would be received for incurring or taking on an equivalent liability.

6.41 Like historical cost, current cost provides information about the cost of an asset consumed or about income from the fulfilment of liabilities. That information can be used to derive current margins and can be used as an input in predicting future margins. Unlike historical cost, current cost reflects prices prevailing at the time of consumption or fulfilment. When price changes are significant, margins based on current cost may be more useful for predicting future margins than margins based on historical cost.

6.42 To report the current cost of consumption (or current income from fulfilment), it is necessary to split the change in the carrying amount in the reporting period into the current cost of consumption (or current income from fulfilment), and the effect of changes in prices. The effect of a change in prices is sometimes referred to as a 'holding gain' or a 'holding loss'.

CONCEPTUAL FRAMEWORK FOR FINANCIAL REPORTING

Table 6.1—Summary of information provided by particular measurement bases

Assets

	Statement of financial position			
	Historical cost	**Fair value (market-participant assumptions)**	**Value in use (entity-specific assumptions)[a]**	**Current cost**
Carrying amount	Historical cost (including transaction costs), to the extent unconsumed or uncollected, and recoverable. (Includes interest accrued on any financing component.)	Price that would be received to sell the asset (without deducting transaction costs on disposal).	Present value of future cash flows from the use of the asset and from its ultimate disposal (after deducting present value of transaction costs on disposal).	Current cost (including transaction costs), to the extent unconsumed or uncollected, and recoverable.
	Statement(s) of financial performance			
Event	**Historical cost**	**Fair value (market-participant assumptions)**	**Value in use (entity-specific assumptions)**	**Current cost**
Initial recognition[b]	—	Difference between consideration paid and fair value of the asset acquired.[c] Transaction costs on acquiring the asset.	Difference between consideration paid and value in use of the asset acquired. Transaction costs on acquiring the asset.	—
Sale or consumption of the asset[d], [e]	Expenses equal to historical cost of the asset sold or consumed. Income received. (Could be presented gross or net.) Expenses for transaction costs on selling the asset.	Expenses equal to fair value of the asset sold or consumed. Income received. (Could be presented gross or net.) Expenses for transaction costs on selling the asset.	Expenses equal to value in use of the asset sold or consumed. Income received. (Could be presented gross or net.)	Expenses equal to current cost of the asset sold or consumed. Income received. (Could be presented gross or net.) Expenses for transaction costs on selling the asset.

CONCEPTUAL FRAMEWORK FOR FINANCIAL REPORTING

Event	Statement(s) of financial performance			
	Historical cost	Fair value (market-participant assumptions)	Value in use (entity-specific assumptions)	Current cost
Interest income	Interest income, at historical rates, updated if the asset bears variable interest.	Reflected in income and expenses from changes in fair value. (Could be identified separately.)	Reflected in income and expenses from changes in value in use. (Could be identified separately.)	Interest income, at current rates.
Impairment	Expenses arising because historical cost is no longer recoverable.	Reflected in income and expenses from changes in fair value. (Could be identified separately.)	Reflected in income and expenses from changes in value in use. (Could be identified separately.)	Expenses arising because current cost is no longer recoverable.
Value changes	Not recognised, except to reflect an impairment. For financial assets—income and expenses from changes in estimated cash flows.	Reflected in income and expenses from changes in fair value.	Reflected in income and expenses from changes in value in use.	Income and expenses reflecting the effect of changes in prices (holding gains and holding losses).

(a) This column summarises the information provided if value in use is used as a measurement basis. However, as noted in paragraph 6.75, value in use may not be a practical measurement basis for regular remeasurements.

(b) Income or expenses may arise on the initial recognition of an asset not acquired on market terms.

(c) Income or expenses may arise if the market in which an asset is acquired is different from the market that is the source of the prices used when measuring the fair value of the asset.

(d) Consumption of the asset is typically reported through cost of sales, depreciation or amortisation.

(e) Income received is often equal to the consideration received but will depend on the measurement basis used for any related liability.

CONCEPTUAL FRAMEWORK FOR FINANCIAL REPORTING

Liabilities

	Statement of financial position			
	Historical cost	**Fair value (market-participant assumptions)**	**Fulfilment value (entity-specific assumptions)**	**Current cost**
Carrying amount	Consideration received (net of transaction costs) for taking on the unfulfilled part of the liability, increased by excess of estimated cash outflows over consideration received. (Includes interest accrued on any financing component.)	Price that would be paid to transfer the unfulfilled part of the liability (not including transaction costs that would be incurred on transfer).	Present value of future cash flows that will arise in fulfilling the unfulfilled part of the liability (including present value of transaction costs to be incurred in fulfilment or transfer).	Consideration (net of transaction costs) that would be currently received for taking on the unfulfilled part of the liability, increased by excess of estimated cash outflows over that consideration.
	Statement(s) of financial performance			
Event	**Historical cost**	**Fair value (market-participant assumptions)**	**Fulfilment value (entity-specific assumptions)**	**Current cost**
Initial recognition[a]	—	Difference between consideration received and the fair value of the liability.[b] Transaction costs on incurring or taking on the liability.	Difference between consideration received and the fulfilment value of the liability. Transaction costs on incurring or taking on the liability.	—
	Statement(s) of financial performance			
Event	**Historical cost**	**Fair value (market-participant assumptions)**	**Fulfilment value (entity-specific assumptions)**	**Current cost**
Fulfilment of the liability	Income equal to historical cost of the liability fulfilled (reflects historical consideration). Expenses for costs incurred in fulfilling the liability.	Income equal to fair value of the liability fulfilled. Expenses for costs incurred in fulfilling the liability.	Income equal to fulfilment value of the liability fulfilled. Expenses for costs incurred in fulfilling the liability.	Income equal to current cost of the liability fulfilled (reflects current consideration). Expenses for costs incurred in fulfilling the liability.

CONCEPTUAL FRAMEWORK FOR FINANCIAL REPORTING

	Statement(s) of financial performance			
Event	Historical cost	Fair value (market-participant assumptions)	Fulfilment value (entity-specific assumptions)	Current cost
	(Could be presented net or gross.)	(Could be presented net or gross. If gross, historical consideration could be presented separately.)	(Could be presented net or gross. If gross, historical consideration could be presented separately.)	(Could be presented net or gross. If gross, historical consideration could be presented separately.)
Transfer of the liability	Income equal to historical cost of the liability transferred (reflects historical consideration). Expenses for costs paid (including transaction costs) to transfer the liability. (Could be presented net or gross.)	Income equal to fair value of the liability transferred. Expenses for costs paid (including transaction costs) to transfer the liability. (Could be presented net or gross.)	Income equal to fulfilment value of the liability transferred. Expenses for costs paid (including transaction costs) to transfer the liability. (Could be presented net or gross.)	Income equal to current cost of the liability transferred (reflects current consideration). Expenses for costs paid (including transaction costs) to transfer the liability. (Could be presented net or gross.)
Interest expenses	Interest expenses, at historical rates, updated if the liability bears variable interest.	Reflected in income and expenses from changes in fair value. (Could be identified separately.)	Reflected in income and expenses from changes in fulfilment value. (Could be identified separately.)	Interest expenses, at current rates.
Effect of events that cause a liability to become onerous	Expenses equal to the excess of the estimated cash outflows over the historical cost of the liability, or a subsequent change in that excess.	Reflected in income and expenses from changes in fair value. (Could be identified separately.)	Reflected in income and expenses from changes in fulfilment value. (Could be identified separately.)	Expenses equal to the excess of the estimated cash outflows over the current cost of the liability, or a subsequent change in that excess.
Value changes	Not recognised except to the extent that the liability is onerous.	Reflected in income and expenses from changes in fair value.	Reflected in income and expenses from changes in fulfilment value.	Income and expenses reflecting the effect of changes in prices (holding gains and holding losses).

CONCEPTUAL FRAMEWORK FOR FINANCIAL REPORTING

Event	Statement(s) of financial performance			
	Historical cost	Fair value (market-participant assumptions)	Fulfilment value (entity-specific assumptions)	Current cost
	For financial liabilities—income and expenses from changes in estimated cash flows.			

(a) Income or expenses may arise on the initial recognition of a liability incurred or taken on not on market terms.

(b) Income or expenses may arise if the market in which a liability is incurred or taken on is different from the market that is the source of the prices used when measuring the fair value of the liability.

Factors to consider when selecting a measurement basis

6.43 In selecting a measurement basis for an asset or liability and for the related income and expenses, it is necessary to consider the nature of the information that the measurement basis will produce in both the statement of financial position and the statement(s) of financial performance (see paragraphs 6.23–6.42 and Table 6.1), as well as other factors (see paragraphs 6.44–6.86).

6.44 In most cases, no single factor will determine which measurement basis should be selected. The relative importance of each factor will depend on facts and circumstances.

6.45 The information provided by a measurement basis must be useful to users of financial statements. To achieve this, the information must be relevant and it must faithfully represent what it purports to represent. In addition, the information provided should be, as far as possible, comparable, verifiable, timely and understandable.

6.46 As explained in paragraph 2.21, the most efficient and effective process for applying the fundamental qualitative characteristics would usually be to identify the most relevant information about an economic phenomenon. If that information is not available or cannot be provided in a way that faithfully represents the economic phenomenon, the next most relevant type of information is considered. Paragraphs 6.49–6.76 provide further discussion of the role played by the qualitative characteristics in the selection of a measurement basis.

6.47 The discussion in paragraphs 6.49–6.76 focuses on the factors to be considered in selecting a measurement basis for recognised assets and recognised liabilities. Some of that discussion may also apply in selecting a measurement basis for information provided in the notes, for recognised or unrecognised items.

6.48 Paragraphs 6.77–6.82 discuss additional factors to consider in selecting a measurement basis on initial recognition. If the initial measurement basis is inconsistent with the subsequent measurement basis, income and expenses might be recognised at the time of the first subsequent measurement solely because of the change in measurement basis. Recognising such income and expenses might appear to depict a transaction or other event when, in fact, no such transaction or event has occurred. Hence, the choice of measurement

CONCEPTUAL FRAMEWORK FOR FINANCIAL REPORTING

basis for an asset or liability, and for the related income and expenses, is determined by considering both initial measurement and subsequent measurement.

Relevance

6.49 The relevance of information provided by a measurement basis for an asset or liability and for the related income and expenses is affected by:

(a) the characteristics of the asset or liability (see paragraphs 6.50–6.53); and

(b) how that asset or liability contributes to future cash flows (see paragraphs 6.54–6.57).

Characteristics of the asset or liability

6.50 The relevance of information provided by a measurement basis depends partly on the characteristics of the asset or liability, in particular, on the variability of cash flows and on whether the value of the asset or liability is sensitive to market factors or other risks.

6.51 If the value of an asset or liability is sensitive to market factors or other risks, its historical cost might differ significantly from its current value. Consequently, historical cost may not provide relevant information if information about changes in value is important to users of financial statements. For example, amortised cost cannot provide relevant information about a financial asset or financial liability that is a derivative.

6.52 Furthermore, if historical cost is used, changes in value are reported not when that value changes, but when an event such as disposal, impairment or fulfilment occurs. This could be incorrectly interpreted as implying that all the income and expenses recognised at the time of that event arose then, rather than over the periods during which the asset or liability was held. Moreover, because measurement at historical cost does not provide timely information about changes in value, income and expenses reported on that basis may lack predictive value and confirmatory value by not depicting the full effect of the entity's exposure to risk arising from holding the asset or liability during the reporting period.

6.53 Changes in the fair value of an asset or liability reflect changes in expectations of market participants and changes in their risk preferences. Depending on the characteristics of the asset or liability being measured and on the nature of the entity's business activities, information reflecting those changes may not always provide predictive value or confirmatory value to users of financial statements. This may be the case when the entity's business activities do not involve selling the asset or transferring the liability, for example, if the entity holds assets solely for use or solely for collecting contractual cash flows or if the entity is to fulfil liabilities itself.

Contribution to future cash flows

6.54 As noted in paragraph 1.14, some economic resources produce cash flows directly; in other cases, economic resources are used in combination to produce cash flows indirectly. How economic resources are used, and hence how assets and liabilities produce cash flows, depends in part on the nature of the business activities conducted by the entity.

6.55 When a business activity of an entity involves the use of several economic resources that produce cash flows indirectly, by being used in combination to produce and market goods or services to customers, historical cost or current cost is likely to provide relevant information about that activity. For example, property, plant and equipment is typically used in combination with an entity's other economic resources. Similarly, inventory typically cannot be sold to a customer, except by making extensive use of the entity's other economic resources (for example, in production and marketing activities). Paragraphs 6.24–6.31 and 6.40–6.42 explain how measuring such assets at historical cost or current cost can provide relevant information that can be used to derive margins achieved during the period.

6.56 For assets and liabilities that produce cash flows directly, such as assets that can be sold independently and without a significant economic penalty (for example, without significant business disruption), the measurement basis that provides the most relevant information is likely to be a current value that incorporates current estimates of the amount, timing and uncertainty of the future cash flows.

6.57 When a business activity of an entity involves managing financial assets and financial liabilities with the objective of collecting contractual cash flows, amortised cost may provide relevant information that can be used to derive the margin between the interest earned on the assets and the interest incurred on the liabilities. However, in assessing whether amortised cost will provide useful information, it is also necessary to consider the characteristics of the financial asset or financial liability. Amortised cost is unlikely to provide relevant information about cash flows that depend on factors other than principal and interest.

Faithful representation

6.58 When assets and liabilities are related in some way, using different measurement bases for those assets and liabilities can create a measurement inconsistency (accounting mismatch). If financial statements contain measurement inconsistencies, those financial statements may not faithfully represent some aspects of the entity's financial position and financial performance. Consequently, in some circumstances, using the same measurement basis for related assets and liabilities may provide users of financial statements with information that is more useful than the information that would result from using different measurement bases. This may be particularly likely when the cash flows from one asset or liability are directly linked to the cash flows from another asset or liability.

6.59 As noted in paragraphs 2.13 and 2.18, although a perfectly faithful representation is free from error, this does not mean that measures must be perfectly accurate in all respects.

6.60 When a measure cannot be determined directly by observing prices in an active market and must instead be estimated, measurement uncertainty arises. The level of measurement uncertainty associated with a particular measurement basis may affect whether information provided by that measurement basis provides a faithful representation of an entity's financial position and financial performance. A high level of measurement uncertainty does not necessarily prevent the use of a measurement basis that provides relevant information. However, in some cases the level of measurement uncertainty is so high that information provided by a measurement basis might not provide a sufficiently faithful representation (see paragraph 2.22). In such cases, it is appropriate to consider selecting a different measurement basis that would also result in relevant information.

6.61 Measurement uncertainty is different from both outcome uncertainty and existence uncertainty:

(a) outcome uncertainty arises when there is uncertainty about the amount or timing of any inflow or outflow of economic benefits that will result from an asset or liability.

(b) existence uncertainty arises when it is uncertain whether an asset or a liability exists. Paragraphs 5.12–5.14 discuss how existence uncertainty may affect decisions about whether an entity recognises an asset or liability when it is uncertain whether that asset or liability exists.

6.62 The presence of outcome uncertainty or existence uncertainty may sometimes contribute to measurement uncertainty. However, outcome uncertainty or existence uncertainty does not necessarily result in measurement uncertainty. For example, if the fair value of an asset can be determined directly by observing prices in an active market, no measurement uncertainty is associated with the measurement of that fair value, even if it is uncertain how much cash the asset will ultimately produce and hence there is outcome uncertainty.

Enhancing qualitative characteristics and the cost constraint

6.63 The enhancing qualitative characteristics of comparability, understandability and verifiability, and the cost constraint, have implications for the selection of a measurement basis. The following paragraphs discuss those implications. Paragraphs 6.69–6.76 discuss further implications specific to particular measurement bases. The enhancing qualitative characteristic of timeliness has no specific implications for measurement.

6.64 Just as cost constrains other financial reporting decisions, it also constrains the selection of a measurement basis. Hence, in selecting a measurement basis, it is important to consider whether the benefits of the information provided to users of financial statements by that measurement basis are likely to justify the costs of providing and using that information.

6.65 Consistently using the same measurement bases for the same items, either from period to period within a reporting entity or in a single period across entities, can help make financial statements more comparable.

6.66 A change in measurement basis can make financial statements less understandable. However, a change may be justified if other factors outweigh the reduction in understandability, for example, if the change results in more relevant information. If a change is made, users of financial statements may need explanatory information to enable them to understand the effect of that change.

6.67 Understandability depends partly on how many different measurement bases are used and on whether they change over time. In general, if more measurement bases are used in a set of financial statements, the resulting information becomes more complex and, hence, less understandable and the totals or subtotals in the statement of financial position and the statement(s) of financial performance become less informative. However, it could be appropriate to use more measurement bases if that is necessary to provide useful information.

6.68 Verifiability is enhanced by using measurement bases that result in measures that can be independently corroborated either directly, for example, by observing prices, or indirectly, for example, by checking inputs to a model. If a measure cannot be verified, users of financial statements may need explanatory information to enable them to understand how the measure was determined. In some such cases, it may be necessary to specify the use of a different measurement basis.

Historical cost

6.69 In many situations, it is simpler, and hence less costly, to measure historical cost than it is to measure a current value. In addition, measures determined applying a historical cost measurement basis are generally well understood and, in many cases, verifiable.

6.70 However, estimating consumption and identifying and measuring impairment losses or onerous liabilities can be subjective. Hence, the historical cost of an asset or liability can sometimes be as difficult to measure or verify as a current value.

6.71 Using a historical cost measurement basis, identical assets acquired, or liabilities incurred, at different times can be reported in the financial statements at different amounts. This can reduce comparability, both from period to period for a reporting entity and in a single period across entities.

Current value

6.72 Because fair value is determined from the perspective of market participants, not from an entity-specific perspective, and is independent of when the asset was acquired or the liability was incurred, identical assets or liabilities measured at fair value will, in principle, be measured at the same amount by entities that have access to the same markets. This can enhance comparability both from period to period for a reporting entity and in a single period across entities. In contrast, because value in use and fulfilment value reflect an entity-specific perspective, those measures could differ for identical assets or liabilities in different entities. Those differences may reduce comparability, particularly if the assets or liabilities contribute to cash flows in a similar manner.

6.73 If the fair value of an asset or liability can be determined directly by observing prices in an active market, the process of fair value measurement is low-cost, simple and easy to understand; and the fair value can be verified through direct observation.

6.74 Valuation techniques, sometimes including the use of cash-flow-based measurement techniques, may be needed to estimate fair value when it cannot be observed directly in an active market and are generally needed when determining value in use and fulfilment value. Depending on the techniques used:

(a) estimating inputs to the valuation and applying the valuation technique may be costly and complex.

(b) the inputs into the process may be subjective and it may be difficult to verify both the inputs and the validity of the process itself. Consequently, the measures of identical assets or liabilities may differ. That would reduce comparability.

6.75 In many cases, value in use cannot be determined meaningfully for an individual asset used in combination with other assets. Instead, the value in use is determined for a group of assets and the result may then need to be allocated to individual assets. This process can be subjective and arbitrary. In addition, estimates of value in use for an asset may inadvertently reflect the effect of synergies with other assets in the group. Hence, determining the value in use of an asset used in combination with other assets can be a costly process and its complexity and subjectivity reduces verifiability. For these reasons, value in use may not be a practical measurement basis for regular remeasurements of such assets. However, it may be useful for occasional remeasurements of assets, for example, when it is used in an impairment test to determine whether historical cost is fully recoverable.

CONCEPTUAL FRAMEWORK FOR FINANCIAL REPORTING

6.76   Using a current cost measurement basis, identical assets acquired or liabilities incurred at different times are reported in the financial statements at the same amount. This can enhance comparability, both from period to period for a reporting entity and in a single period across entities. However, determining current cost can be complex, subjective and costly. For example, as noted in paragraph 6.22, it may be necessary to estimate the current cost of an asset by adjusting the current price of a new asset to reflect the current age and condition of the asset held by the entity. In addition, because of changes in technology and changes in business practices, many assets would not be replaced with identical assets. Thus, a further subjective adjustment to the current price of a new asset would be required in order to estimate the current cost of an asset equivalent to the existing asset. Also, splitting changes in current cost carrying amounts between the current cost of consumption and the effect of changes in prices (see paragraph 6.42) may be complex and require arbitrary assumptions. Because of these difficulties, current cost measures may lack verifiability and understandability.

Factors specific to initial measurement

6.77   Paragraphs 6.43–6.76 discuss factors to consider when selecting a measurement basis, whether for initial recognition or subsequent measurement. Paragraphs 6.78–6.82 discuss some additional factors to consider at initial recognition.

6.78   At initial recognition, the cost of an asset acquired, or of a liability incurred, as a result of an event that is a transaction on market terms is normally similar to its fair value at that date, unless transaction costs are significant. Nevertheless, even if those two amounts are similar, it is necessary to describe what measurement basis is used at initial recognition. If historical cost will be used subsequently, that measurement basis is also normally appropriate at initial recognition. Similarly, if a current value will be used subsequently, it is also normally appropriate at initial recognition. Using the same measurement basis for initial recognition and subsequent measurement avoids recognising income or expenses at the time of the first subsequent measurement solely because of a change in measurement basis (see paragraph 6.48).

6.79   When an entity acquires an asset, or incurs a liability, in exchange for transferring another asset or liability as a result of a transaction on market terms, the initial measure of the asset acquired, or the liability incurred, determines whether any income or expenses arise from the transaction. When an asset or liability is measured at cost, no income or expenses arise at initial recognition, unless income or expenses arise from the derecognition of the transferred asset or liability, or unless the asset is impaired or the liability is onerous.

6.80   Assets may be acquired, or liabilities may be incurred, as a result of an event that is not a transaction on market terms. For example:

   (a)   the transaction price may be affected by relationships between the parties, or by financial distress or other duress of one of the parties;

   (b)   an asset may be granted to the entity free of charge by a government or donated to the entity by another party;

   (c)   a liability may be imposed by legislation or regulation; or

   (d)   a liability to pay compensation or a penalty may arise from an act of wrongdoing.

6.81   In such cases, measuring the asset acquired, or the liability incurred, at its historical cost may not provide a faithful representation of the entity's assets and liabilities and of any income or expenses arising from the transaction or other event. Hence, it may be appropriate to measure the asset acquired, or the liability incurred, at deemed cost, as described in paragraph 6.6. Any difference between that deemed cost and any consideration given or received would be recognised as income or expenses at initial recognition.

6.82 When assets are acquired, or liabilities incurred, as a result of an event that is not a transaction on market terms, all relevant aspects of the transaction or other event need to be identified and considered. For example, it may be necessary to recognise other assets, other liabilities, contributions from holders of equity claims or distributions to holders of equity claims to faithfully represent the substance of the effect of the transaction or other event on the entity's financial position (see paragraphs 4.59–4.62) and any related effect on the entity's financial performance.

More than one measurement basis

6.83 Sometimes, consideration of the factors described in paragraphs 6.43–6.76 may lead to the conclusion that more than one measurement basis is needed for an asset or liability and for related income and expenses in order to provide relevant information that faithfully represents both the entity's financial position and its financial performance.

6.84 In most cases, the most understandable way to provide that information is:

(a) to use a single measurement basis both for the asset or liability in the statement of financial position and for related income and expenses in the statement(s) of financial performance; and

(b) to provide in the notes additional information applying a different measurement basis.

6.85 However, in some cases, that information is more relevant, or results in a more faithful representation of both the entity's financial position and its financial performance, through the use of:

(a) a current value measurement basis for the asset or liability in the statement of financial position; and

(b) a different measurement basis for the related income and expenses in the statement of profit or loss[1] (see paragraphs 7.17–7.18).

In selecting those measurement bases, it is necessary to consider the factors discussed in paragraphs 6.43–6.76.

6.86 In such cases, the total income or total expenses arising in the period from the change in the current value of the asset or liability is separated and classified (see paragraphs 7.14–7.19) so that:

(a) the statement of profit or loss includes the income or expenses measured applying the measurement basis selected for that statement; and

(b) other comprehensive income includes all the remaining income or expenses. As a result, the accumulated other comprehensive income related to that asset or liability equals the difference between:

(i) the carrying amount of the asset or liability in the statement of financial position; and

---

[1] The *Conceptual Framework* does not specify whether the statement(s) of financial performance comprise(s) a single statement or two statements. The *Conceptual Framework* uses the term 'statement of profit or loss' to refer both to a separate statement and to a separate section within a single statement of financial performance.

CONCEPTUAL FRAMEWORK FOR FINANCIAL REPORTING

(ii) the carrying amount that would have been determined applying the measurement basis selected for the statement of profit or loss.

Measurement of equity

6.87 The total carrying amount of equity (total equity) is not measured directly. It equals the total of the carrying amounts of all recognised assets less the total of the carrying amounts of all recognised liabilities.

6.88 Because general purpose financial statements are not designed to show an entity's value, the total carrying amount of equity will not generally equal:

(a) the aggregate market value of equity claims on the entity;

(b) the amount that could be raised by selling the entity as a whole on a going concern basis; or

(c) the amount that could be raised by selling all of the entity's assets and settling all of its liabilities.

6.89 Although total equity is not measured directly, it may be appropriate to measure directly the carrying amount of some individual classes of equity (see paragraph 4.65) and some components of equity (see paragraph 4.66). Nevertheless, because total equity is measured as a residual, at least one class of equity cannot be measured directly. Similarly, at least one component of equity cannot be measured directly.

6.90 The total carrying amount of an individual class of equity or component of equity is normally positive, but can be negative in some circumstances. Similarly, total equity is generally positive, but it can be negative, depending on which assets and liabilities are recognised and on how they are measured.

Cash-flow-based measurement techniques

6.91 Sometimes, a measure cannot be observed directly. In some such cases, one way to estimate the measure is by using cash-flow-based measurement techniques. Such techniques are not measurement bases. They are techniques used in applying a measurement basis. Hence, when using such a technique, it is necessary to identify which measurement basis is used and the extent to which the technique reflects the factors applicable to that measurement basis. For example, if the measurement basis is fair value, the applicable factors are those described in paragraph 6.14.

6.92 Cash-flow-based measurement techniques can be used in applying a modified measurement basis, for example, fulfilment value modified to exclude the effect of the possibility that the entity may fail to fulfil a liability (own credit risk). Modifying measurement bases may sometimes result in information that is more relevant to the users of financial statements or that may be less costly to produce or to understand. However, modified measurement bases may also be more difficult for users of financial statements to understand.

6.93 Outcome uncertainty (see paragraph 6.61(a)) arises from uncertainties about the amount or timing of future cash flows. Those uncertainties are important characteristics of assets and liabilities. When measuring an asset or liability by reference to estimates of uncertain future cash flows, one factor to consider is possible variations in the estimated amount or timing of those cash flows (see paragraph 6.14(b)). Those variations are considered in selecting a single amount from within the range of possible cash flows. The amount selected is itself sometimes the amount of a possible outcome, but this is not always the case. The amount that provides the most relevant information is usually one from within the central part of the range (a central estimate). Different central estimates provide different information. For example:

(a) the expected value (the probability-weighted average, also known as the statistical mean) reflects the entire range of outcomes and gives more weight to the outcomes that are more likely. The expected value is not intended to predict the ultimate inflow or outflow of cash or other economic benefits arising from that asset or liability.

(b) the maximum amount that is more likely than not to occur (similar to the statistical median) indicates that the probability of a subsequent loss is no more than 50% and that the probability of a subsequent gain is no more than 50%.

(c) the most likely outcome (the statistical mode) is the single most likely ultimate inflow or outflow arising from an asset or liability.

6.94 A central estimate depends on estimates of future cash flows and possible variations in their amounts or timing. It does not capture the price for bearing the uncertainty that the ultimate outcome may differ from that central estimate (that is, the factor described in paragraph 6.14(d)).

6.95 No central estimate gives complete information about the range of possible outcomes. Hence users may need information about the range of possible outcomes.

from paragraph

CHAPTER 7—PRESENTATION AND DISCLOSURE
PRESENTATION AND DISCLOSURE AS COMMUNICATION TOOLS	**7.1**
PRESENTATION AND DISCLOSURE OBJECTIVES AND PRINCIPLES	**7.4**
CLASSIFICATION	**7.7**
Classification of assets and liabilities	**7.9**
Offsetting	7.10
Classification of equity	**7.12**
Classification of income and expenses	**7.14**
Profit or loss and other comprehensive income	7.15
AGGREGATION	**7.20**

Presentation and disclosure as communication tools

7.1 A reporting entity communicates information about its assets, liabilities, equity, income and expenses by presenting and disclosing information in its financial statements.

7.2 Effective communication of information in financial statements makes that information more relevant and contributes to a faithful representation of an entity's assets, liabilities, equity, income and expenses. It also enhances the understandability and comparability of information in financial statements. Effective communication of information in financial statements requires:

(a) focusing on presentation and disclosure objectives and principles rather than focusing on rules;

(b) classifying information in a manner that groups similar items and separates dissimilar items; and

(c) aggregating information in such a way that it is not obscured either by unnecessary detail or by excessive aggregation.

7.3 Just as cost constrains other financial reporting decisions, it also constrains decisions about presentation and disclosure. Hence, in making decisions about presentation and disclosure, it is important to consider whether the benefits provided to users of financial statements by presenting or disclosing particular information are likely to justify the costs of providing and using that information.

Presentation and disclosure objectives and principles

7.4 To facilitate effective communication of information in financial statements, when developing presentation and disclosure requirements in Standards a balance is needed between:

(a) giving entities the flexibility to provide relevant information that faithfully represents the entity's assets, liabilities, equity, income and expenses; and

(b) requiring information that is comparable, both from period to period for a reporting entity and in a single reporting period across entities.

7.5 Including presentation and disclosure objectives in Standards supports effective communication in financial statements because such objectives help entities to identify useful information and to decide how to communicate that information in the most effective manner.

7.6 Effective communication in financial statements is also supported by considering the following principles:

(a) entity-specific information is more useful than standardised descriptions, sometimes referred to as 'boilerplate'; and

(b) duplication of information in different parts of the financial statements is usually unnecessary and can make financial statements less understandable.

Classification

7.7 Classification is the sorting of assets, liabilities, equity, income or expenses on the basis of shared characteristics for presentation and disclosure purposes. Such characteristics include—but are not limited to—the nature of the item, its role (or function) within the business activities conducted by the entity, and how it is measured.

7.8 Classifying dissimilar assets, liabilities, equity, income or expenses together can obscure relevant information, reduce understandability and comparability and may not provide a faithful representation of what it purports to represent.

Classification of assets and liabilities

7.9 Classification is applied to the unit of account selected for an asset or liability (see paragraphs 4.48–4.55). However, it may sometimes be appropriate to separate an asset or liability into components that have different characteristics and to classify those components separately. That would be appropriate when classifying those components separately would enhance the usefulness of the resulting financial information. For example, it could be appropriate to separate an asset or liability into current and non-current components and to classify those components separately.

Offsetting

7.10 Offsetting occurs when an entity recognises and measures both an asset and liability as separate units of account, but groups them into a single net amount in the statement of financial position. Offsetting classifies dissimilar items together and therefore is generally not appropriate.

7.11 Offsetting assets and liabilities differs from treating a set of rights and obligations as a single unit of account (see paragraphs 4.48–4.55).

Classification of equity

7.12 To provide useful information, it may be necessary to classify equity claims separately if those equity claims have different characteristics (see paragraph 4.65).

7.13 Similarly, to provide useful information, it may be necessary to classify components of equity separately if some of those components are subject to particular legal, regulatory or other requirements. For example, in some jurisdictions, an entity is permitted to make distributions to holders of equity claims only if the entity has sufficient reserves specified as distributable (see paragraph 4.66). Separate presentation or disclosure of those reserves may provide useful information.

Classification of income and expenses

7.14 Classification is applied to:

(a) income and expenses resulting from the unit of account selected for an asset or liability; or

(b) components of such income and expenses if those components have different characteristics and are identified separately. For example, a change in the current

Profit or loss and other comprehensive income

7.15 Income and expenses are classified and included either:

(a) in the statement of profit or loss;[1] or

(b) outside the statement of profit or loss, in other comprehensive income.

7.16 The statement of profit or loss is the primary source of information about an entity's financial performance for the reporting period. That statement contains a total for profit or loss that provides a highly summarised depiction of the entity's financial performance for the period. Many users of financial statements incorporate that total in their analysis either as a starting point for that analysis or as the main indicator of the entity's financial performance for the period. Nevertheless, understanding an entity's financial performance for the period requires an analysis of all recognised income and expenses—including income and expenses included in other comprehensive income—as well as an analysis of other information included in the financial statements.

7.17 Because the statement of profit or loss is the primary source of information about an entity's financial performance for the period, all income and expenses are, in principle, included in that statement. However, in developing Standards, the Board may decide in exceptional circumstances that income or expenses arising from a change in the current value of an asset or liability are to be included in other comprehensive income when doing so would result in the statement of profit or loss providing more relevant information, or providing a more faithful representation of the entity's financial performance for that period.

7.18 Income and expenses that arise on a historical cost measurement basis (see Table 6.1) are included in the statement of profit or loss. That is also the case when income and expenses of that type are separately identified as a component of a change in the current value of an asset or liability. For example, if a financial asset is measured at current value and if interest income is identified separately from other changes in value, that interest income is included in the statement of profit or loss.

7.19 In principle, income and expenses included in other comprehensive income in one period are reclassified from other comprehensive income into the statement of profit or loss in a future period when doing so results in the statement of profit or loss providing more relevant information, or providing a more faithful representation of the entity's financial performance for that future period. However, if, for example, there is no clear basis for identifying the period in which reclassification would have that result, or the amount that should be reclassified, the Board may, in developing Standards, decide that income and expenses included in other comprehensive income are not to be subsequently reclassified.

---

[1] The *Conceptual Framework* does not specify whether the statement(s) of financial performance comprise(s) a single statement or two statements. The *Conceptual Framework* uses the term 'statement of profit or loss' to refer to a separate statement and to a separate section within a single statement of financial performance. Likewise, it uses the term 'total for profit or loss' to refer both to a total for a separate statement and to a subtotal for a section within a single statement of financial performance.

Aggregation

7.20 Aggregation is the adding together of assets, liabilities, equity, income or expenses that have shared characteristics and are included in the same classification.

7.21 Aggregation makes information more useful by summarising a large volume of detail. However, aggregation conceals some of that detail. Hence, a balance needs to be found so that relevant information is not obscured either by a large amount of insignificant detail or by excessive aggregation.

7.22 Different levels of aggregation may be needed in different parts of the financial statements. For example, typically, the statement of financial position and the statement(s) of financial performance provide summarised information and more detailed information is provided in the notes.

from paragraph

CHAPTER 8—CONCEPTS OF CAPITAL AND CAPITAL MAINTENANCE

CONCEPTS OF CAPITAL	8.1
CONCEPTS OF CAPITAL MAINTENANCE AND THE DETERMINATION OF PROFIT	8.3
CAPITAL MAINTENANCE ADJUSTMENTS	8.10

CONCEPTUAL FRAMEWORK FOR FINANCIAL REPORTING

> *The material included in Chapter 8 has been carried forward unchanged from the* Conceptual Framework for Financial Reporting *issued in 2010. That material originally appeared in the* Framework for the Preparation and Presentation of Financial Statements *issued in 1989.*

Concepts of capital

8.1 A financial concept of capital is adopted by most entities in preparing their financial statements. Under a financial concept of capital, such as invested money or invested purchasing power, capital is synonymous with the net assets or equity of the entity. Under a physical concept of capital, such as operating capability, capital is regarded as the productive capacity of the entity based on, for example, units of output per day.

8.2 The selection of the appropriate concept of capital by an entity should be based on the needs of the users of its financial statements. Thus, a financial concept of capital should be adopted if the users of financial statements are primarily concerned with the maintenance of nominal invested capital or the purchasing power of invested capital. If, however, the main concern of users is with the operating capability of the entity, a physical concept of capital should be used. The concept chosen indicates the goal to be attained in determining profit, even though there may be some measurement difficulties in making the concept operational.

Concepts of capital maintenance and the determination of profit

8.3 The concepts of capital in paragraph 8.1 give rise to the following concepts of capital maintenance:

(a) *Financial capital maintenance.* Under this concept a profit is earned only if the financial (or money) amount of the net assets at the end of the period exceeds the financial (or money) amount of net assets at the beginning of the period, after excluding any distributions to, and contributions from, owners during the period. Financial capital maintenance can be measured in either nominal monetary units or units of constant purchasing power.

(b) *Physical capital maintenance.* Under this concept a profit is earned only if the physical productive capacity (or operating capability) of the entity (or the resources or funds needed to achieve that capacity) at the end of the period exceeds the physical productive capacity at the beginning of the period, after excluding any distributions to, and contributions from, owners during the period.

8.4 The concept of capital maintenance is concerned with how an entity defines the capital that it seeks to maintain. It provides the linkage between the concepts of capital and the concepts of profit because it provides the point of reference by which profit is measured; it is a prerequisite for distinguishing between an entity's return on capital and its return of capital; only inflows of assets in excess of amounts needed to maintain capital may be regarded as profit and therefore as a return on capital. Hence, profit is the residual amount that remains after expenses (including capital maintenance adjustments, where appropriate) have been deducted from income. If expenses exceed income the residual amount is a loss.

CONCEPTUAL FRAMEWORK FOR FINANCIAL REPORTING

8.5 The physical capital maintenance concept requires the adoption of the current cost basis of measurement. The financial capital maintenance concept, however, does not require the use of a particular basis of measurement. Selection of the basis under this concept is dependent on the type of financial capital that the entity is seeking to maintain.

8.6 The principal difference between the two concepts of capital maintenance is the treatment of the effects of changes in the prices of assets and liabilities of the entity. In general terms, an entity has maintained its capital if it has as much capital at the end of the period as it had at the beginning of the period. Any amount over and above that required to maintain the capital at the beginning of the period is profit.

8.7 Under the concept of financial capital maintenance where capital is defined in terms of nominal monetary units, profit represents the increase in nominal money capital over the period. Thus, increases in the prices of assets held over the period, conventionally referred to as holding gains, are, conceptually, profits. They may not be recognised as such, however, until the assets are disposed of in an exchange transaction. When the concept of financial capital maintenance is defined in terms of constant purchasing power units, profit represents the increase in invested purchasing power over the period. Thus, only that part of the increase in the prices of assets that exceeds the increase in the general level of prices is regarded as profit. The rest of the increase is treated as a capital maintenance adjustment and, hence, as part of equity.

8.8 Under the concept of physical capital maintenance when capital is defined in terms of the physical productive capacity, profit represents the increase in that capital over the period. All price changes affecting the assets and liabilities of the entity are viewed as changes in the measurement of the physical productive capacity of the entity; hence, they are treated as capital maintenance adjustments that are part of equity and not as profit.

8.9 The selection of the measurement bases and concept of capital maintenance will determine the accounting model used in the preparation of the financial statements. Different accounting models exhibit different degrees of relevance and reliability and, as in other areas, management must seek a balance between relevance and reliability. This *Conceptual Framework* is applicable to a range of accounting models and provides guidance on preparing and presenting the financial statements constructed under the chosen model. At the present time, it is not the intention of the Board to prescribe a particular model other than in exceptional circumstances, such as for those entities reporting in the currency of a hyperinflationary economy. This intention will, however, be reviewed in the light of world developments.

Capital maintenance adjustments

8.10 The revaluation or restatement of assets and liabilities gives rise to increases or decreases in equity. While these increases or decreases meet the definition of income and expenses, they are not included in the income statement under certain concepts of capital maintenance. Instead these items are included in equity as capital maintenance adjustments or revaluation reserves.

Appendix
Defined terms

The following defined terms are extracted or derived from the relevant paragraphs of the Conceptual Framework for Financial Reporting.

aggregation	The adding together of assets, liabilities, equity, income or expenses that have shared characteristics and are included in the same classification.	CF.7.20
asset	A present economic resource controlled by the entity as a result of past events.	CF.4.3
carrying amount	The amount at which an asset, a liability or equity is recognised in the statement of financial position.	CF.5.1
classification	The sorting of assets, liabilities, equity, income or expenses on the basis of shared characteristics for presentation and disclosure purposes.	CF.7.7
combined financial statements	Financial statements of a reporting entity that comprises two or more entities that are not all linked by a parent-subsidiary relationship.	CF.3.12
consolidated financial statements	Financial statements of a reporting entity that comprises both the parent and its subsidiaries.	CF.3.11
control of an economic resource	The present ability to direct the use of the economic resource and obtain the economic benefits that may flow from it.	CF.4.20
derecognition	The removal of all or part of a recognised asset or liability from an entity's statement of financial position.	CF.5.26
economic resource	A right that has the potential to produce economic benefits.	CF.4.4
enhancing qualitative characteristic	A qualitative characteristic that makes useful information more useful. The enhancing qualitative characteristics are comparability, verifiability, timeliness and understandability.	CF.2.4, CF.2.23
equity	The residual interest in the assets of the entity after deducting all its liabilities.	CF.4.63

CONCEPTUAL FRAMEWORK FOR FINANCIAL REPORTING

equity claim	A claim on the residual interest in the assets of the entity after deducting all its liabilities.	CF.4.64
executory contract	A contract, or a portion of a contract, that is equally unperformed—neither party has fulfilled any of its obligations, or both parties have partially fulfilled their obligations to an equal extent.	CF.4.56
existence uncertainty	Uncertainty about whether an asset or liability exists.	CF.4.13, CF.4.35
expenses	Decreases in assets, or increases in liabilities, that result in decreases in equity, other than those relating to distributions to holders of equity claims.	CF.4.69
fundamental qualitative characteristic	A qualitative characteristic that financial information must possess to be useful to the primary users of general purpose financial reports. The fundamental qualitative characteristics are relevance and faithful representation.	CF.2.4, CF.2.5
general purpose financial report	A report that provides financial information about the reporting entity's economic resources, claims against the entity and changes in those economic resources and claims that is useful to primary users in making decisions relating to providing resources to the entity.	CF.1.2, CF.1.12
general purpose financial statements	A particular form of general purpose financial reports that provide information about the reporting entity's assets, liabilities, equity, income and expenses.	CF.3.2
income	Increases in assets, or decreases in liabilities, that result in increases in equity, other than those relating to contributions from holders of equity claims.	CF.4.68
liability	A present obligation of the entity to transfer an economic resource as a result of past events.	CF.4.26
material information	Information whose omission or misstatement could influence decisions that the primary users of general purpose financial reports make on the basis of those reports, which provide financial information about a specific reporting entity.	CF.2.11
measure	The result of applying a measurement basis to an asset or liability and related income and expenses.	CF.6.1
measurement basis	An identified feature—for example, historical cost, fair value or fulfilment value—of an item being measured.	CF.6.1

measurement uncertainty	Uncertainty that arises when monetary amounts in financial reports cannot be observed directly and must instead be estimated.	CF.2.19
offsetting	Grouping an asset and liability that are recognised and measured as separate units of account into a single net amount in the statement of financial position.	CF.7.10
outcome uncertainty	Uncertainty about the amount or timing of any inflow or outflow of economic benefits that will result from an asset or liability.	CF.6.61
potential to produce economic benefits	Within an economic resource, a feature that already exists and that, in at least one circumstance, would produce for the entity economic benefits beyond those available to all other parties.	CF.4.14
primary users (of general purpose financial reports)	Existing and potential investors, lenders and other creditors.	CF.1.2
prudence	The exercise of caution when making judgements under conditions of uncertainty. The exercise of prudence means that assets and income are not overstated and liabilities and expenses are not understated. Equally, the exercise of prudence does not allow for the understatement of assets or income or the overstatement of liabilities or expenses.	CF.2.16
recognition	The process of capturing for inclusion in the statement of financial position or the statement(s) of financial performance an item that meets the definition of one of the elements of financial statements—an asset, a liability, equity, income or expenses. Recognition involves depicting the item in one of those statements—either alone or in aggregation with other items—in words and by a monetary amount, and including that amount in one or more totals in that statement.	CF.5.1
reporting entity	An entity that is required, or chooses, to prepare general purpose financial statements.	CF.3.10
unconsolidated financial statements	Financial statements of a reporting entity that is the parent alone.	CF.3.11
unit of account	The right or the group of rights, the obligation or the group of obligations, or the group of rights and obligations, to which recognition criteria and measurement concepts are applied.	CF.4.48

CONCEPTUAL FRAMEWORK FOR FINANCIAL REPORTING

useful financial information	Financial information that is useful to primary users of general purpose financial reports in making decisions relating to providing resources to the reporting entity. To be useful, financial information must be relevant and faithfully represent what it purports to represent.	CF.1.2, CF.2.4
users (of general purpose financial reports)	See primary users (of general purpose financial reports).	–

Approval by the Board of the *Conceptual Framework for Financial Reporting* issued in March 2018

The *Conceptual Framework for Financial Reporting* was approved for issue by 13 of the 14 members of the International Accounting Standards Board. Ms Tarca abstained in view of her recent appointment to the Board.

Hans Hoogervorst	Chairman
Suzanne Lloyd	Vice-Chair
Nick Anderson	
Martin Edelmann	
Françoise Flores	
Amaro Luiz De Oliveira Gomes	
Gary Kabureck	
Jianqiao Lu	
Takatsugu Ochi	
Darrel Scott	
Thomas Scott	
Chungwoo Suh	
Ann Tarca	
Mary Tokar	

Basis for Conclusions
on the
Conceptual Framework
for Financial Reporting

CONCEPTUAL FRAMEWORK FOR FINANCIAL REPORTING

CONTENTS

from paragraph

STATUS AND PURPOSE OF THE *CONCEPTUAL FRAMEWORK*

HISTORY OF THE PROJECT	BC0.1
PURPOSE	BC0.18
STATUS	BC0.21
TRANSITION TO THE 2018 *CONCEPTUAL FRAMEWORK*	BC0.27
BUSINESS ACTIVITIES	BC0.29
IMPLICATIONS OF LONG-TERM INVESTMENT	BC0.34

CHAPTER 1—THE OBJECTIVE OF GENERAL PURPOSE FINANCIAL REPORTING

INTRODUCTION	BC1.1
PRIMARY USERS	BC1.9
USEFULNESS FOR MAKING DECISIONS	BC1.27
INFORMATION ABOUT A REPORTING ENTITY'S ECONOMIC RESOURCES, CLAIMS AGAINST THE ENTITY AND CHANGES IN RESOURCES AND CLAIMS	BC1.44

CHAPTER 2—QUALITATIVE CHARACTERISTICS OF USEFUL FINANCIAL INFORMATION

INTRODUCTION	BC2.1
THE OBJECTIVE OF FINANCIAL REPORTING AND THE QUALITATIVE CHARACTERISTICS OF USEFUL FINANCIAL INFORMATION	BC2.5
FUNDAMENTAL AND ENHANCING QUALITATIVE CHARACTERISTICS	BC2.9
FUNDAMENTAL QUALITATIVE CHARACTERISTICS	BC2.12
ENHANCING QUALITATIVE CHARACTERISTICS	BC2.58
QUALITATIVE CHARACTERISTICS NOT INCLUDED	BC2.70
THE COST CONSTRAINT ON USEFUL FINANCIAL REPORTING	BC2.73

CHAPTER 3—FINANCIAL STATEMENTS AND THE REPORTING ENTITY

FOCUS ON FINANCIAL STATEMENTS	BC3.1
OBJECTIVE AND SCOPE OF FINANCIAL STATEMENTS	BC3.3
PERSPECTIVE ADOPTED IN FINANCIAL STATEMENTS	BC3.9
GOING CONCERN ASSUMPTION	BC3.11

THE REPORTING ENTITY	BC3.12

CHAPTER 4—THE ELEMENTS OF FINANCIAL STATEMENTS

INTRODUCTION	BC4.1
DEFINITIONS—ISSUES COMMON TO BOTH ASSETS AND LIABILITIES	BC4.3
DEFINITION OF AN ASSET	BC4.23
DEFINITION OF A LIABILITY	BC4.44
ASSETS AND LIABILITIES	BC4.69
DEFINITION OF EQUITY	BC4.89
DEFINITIONS OF INCOME AND EXPENSES	BC4.93
OTHER POSSIBLE DEFINITIONS	BC4.97

CHAPTER 5—RECOGNITION AND DERECOGNITION

RECOGNITION	BC5.1
DERECOGNITION	BC5.23

CHAPTER 6—MEASUREMENT

INTRODUCTION	BC6.1
MIXED MEASUREMENT	BC6.5
MEASUREMENT BASES AND THE INFORMATION THEY PROVIDE	BC6.12
FACTORS TO CONSIDER WHEN SELECTING A MEASUREMENT BASIS	BC6.34
MEASUREMENT OF EQUITY	BC6.52

CHAPTER 7—PRESENTATION AND DISCLOSURE

INTRODUCTION	BC7.1
CLASSIFICATION OF EQUITY	BC7.4
CLASSIFICATION OF INCOME AND EXPENSES	BC7.6

CHAPTER 8—CONCEPTS OF CAPITAL AND CAPITAL MAINTENANCE

	BC8.1

Basis for Conclusions on the *Conceptual Framework for Financial Reporting*

This Basis for Conclusions accompanies, but is not part of the Conceptual Framework for Financial Reporting *(Conceptual Framework). It summarises the considerations of the International Accounting Standards Board (Board) in developing the* Conceptual Framework. *Individual Board members gave greater weight to some factors than to others.*

STATUS AND PURPOSE OF THE *CONCEPTUAL FRAMEWORK*

from paragraph

HISTORY OF THE PROJECT	**BC0.1**
Revision in 2018—approach and scope	**BC0.10**
PURPOSE	**BC0.18**
STATUS	**BC0.21**
TRANSITION TO THE 2018 *CONCEPTUAL FRAMEWORK*	**BC0.27**
BUSINESS ACTIVITIES	**BC0.29**
IMPLICATIONS OF LONG-TERM INVESTMENT	**BC0.34**
Long-term investment as a business activity	**BC0.37**
Information needs of long-term investors	**BC0.40**

CONCEPTUAL FRAMEWORK FOR FINANCIAL REPORTING

History of the project

BC0.1   In 1989, the Board's predecessor body, the International Accounting Standards Committee, issued the *Framework for the Preparation and Presentation of Financial Statements* (1989 *Framework*).

BC0.2   In 2004, the Board and the US national standard-setter, the Financial Accounting Standards Board (FASB), started a joint project to revise their conceptual frameworks.

BC0.3   The first phase of the project was to develop chapters that describe the objective of general purpose financial reporting and the qualitative characteristics of useful financial information. In developing these chapters, the Board and the FASB published a Discussion Paper in 2006 (2006 Discussion Paper) and an Exposure Draft in 2008 (2008 Exposure Draft).[1] After considering feedback on those documents and information gained from outreach, in 2010 the Board and the FASB issued two chapters of a revised *Conceptual Framework for Financial Reporting* (2010 *Conceptual Framework*). The chapters on the objective of general purpose financial reporting and qualitative characteristics of useful financial information came into effect as soon as they were issued. The remaining text of the 1989 *Framework* was carried forward to the 2010 *Conceptual Framework* unchanged.

BC0.4   In addition to finalising the chapters on the objective of general purpose financial reporting and qualitative characteristics of useful financial information, the Board and the FASB:

(a)   published a Discussion Paper and then an Exposure Draft (2010 Exposure Draft) on the concept of a reporting entity;[2]

(b)   discussed the definitions of the elements of financial statements; and

(c)   discussed and held public round-table meetings about measurement.

BC0.5   This work did not lead to further revisions at that time because in 2010 the Board and the FASB suspended work on the *Conceptual Framework* to concentrate on other projects.

BC0.6   In 2011, the Board carried out a public consultation on its agenda. Most respondents to that consultation identified the Conceptual Framework as a priority project for the Board. Consequently, in 2012 the Board restarted its Conceptual Framework project.

BC0.7   Before 2010, the Board and the FASB had planned to complete the project in eight separate phases, but completed only one phase—on objectives and qualitative characteristics. On restarting the project in 2012, the Board decided to develop a complete set of proposals for a revised *Conceptual Framework* instead of continuing with the phased approach. Developing the *Conceptual Framework* as a whole enabled the Board and stakeholders to see more clearly the links between different aspects of the *Conceptual Framework*.

BC0.8   In developing the revised *Conceptual Framework*, the Board published a Discussion Paper in 2013 (2013 Discussion Paper) and an Exposure Draft in 2015 (2015 Exposure Draft).[3] After considering feedback on these documents and information gained from outreach, in

---

1   See the Discussion Paper *Preliminary Views on an Improved Conceptual Framework for Financial Reporting: The Objective of Financial Reporting and Qualitative Characteristics of Decision-useful Financial Reporting Information* published in 2006 and the Exposure Draft *An Improved Conceptual Framework for Financial Reporting: Chapters 1 and 2* published in 2008.
2   See the Discussion Paper *Preliminary Views on an Improved Conceptual Framework for Financial Reporting—The Reporting Entity* published in 2008 and the Exposure Draft *Conceptual Framework for Financial Reporting—The Reporting Entity* published in 2010.
3   See the Discussion Paper *A Review of the Conceptual Framework for Financial Reporting* published in 2013 and the Exposure Draft *Conceptual Framework for Financial Reporting* published in 2015.

2018 the Board completed its Conceptual Framework project when it issued the revised *Conceptual Framework for Financial Reporting* (2018 *Conceptual Framework*).

BC0.9 The work since restarting the project in 2012 was not conducted jointly with the FASB. The 2018 *Conceptual Framework* includes limited changes to the chapters on the objective of general purpose financial reporting and qualitative characteristics of useful financial information. The FASB did not make corresponding changes to its Statements of Financial Accounting Concepts.

Revision in 2018—approach and scope

BC0.10 Although the 2010 *Conceptual Framework* had helped the Board when developing IFRS Standards (Standards):

(a) some important areas were not covered;

(b) the guidance in some areas was unclear; and

(c) some aspects were out of date.

BC0.11 In developing the 2018 *Conceptual Framework*, the Board built on the 2010 *Conceptual Framework*—filling in gaps, as well as clarifying and updating it, but not fundamentally reconsidering all aspects of the 2010 *Conceptual Framework*. In particular, although the Board reconsidered some aspects of chapters on the objective of financial reporting and qualitative characteristics of useful financial information, it did not reconsider those chapters fundamentally. In selecting that approach, the Board noted that these chapters went through extensive due process during the development of the 2010 *Conceptual Framework*.

BC0.12 The Board normally establishes a consultative group for major projects. For the Conceptual Framework project, the Board used the Accounting Standards Advisory Forum (ASAF) as its consultative group. The ASAF is an advisory group to the Board. It comprises national accounting standard-setters and regional bodies with an interest in financial reporting. The Board discussed a range of topics with the ASAF during the development of the 2018 *Conceptual Framework*.

BC0.13 In developing the 2018 *Conceptual Framework*, the Board sought a balance between providing high-level concepts and providing enough detail for the 2018 *Conceptual Framework* to be useful to the Board and others. Some stakeholders stated that in some areas the Board's proposals merely described the factors that the Board would consider in making judgements when developing Standards. They expressed the view that, as a result, the proposals did not examine fundamental concepts and were not sufficiently aspirational. The Board did not share that view. The Board viewed the *Conceptual Framework* as a practical tool to help it to develop Standards. The Board concluded that a *Conceptual Framework* would not fulfil this role if it described concepts without explaining the factors the Board needs to consider in making judgements when the application of concepts does not lead to a single answer, or leads to conflicting answers.

BC0.14 In developing the 2018 *Conceptual Framework*, the Board drew on some concepts developed in recent standard-setting projects. The Board's aim in doing so was to reflect the Board's most developed thinking on these matters, not to justify its standard-setting decisions or current practice.

BC0.15 The 2018 *Conceptual Framework* does not address classification of financial instruments with characteristics of both liabilities and equity because the Board did not want to delay other much-needed improvements to the *Conceptual Framework*. The Board is exploring how to distinguish liabilities from equity in its research project on Financial Instruments

BC0.16 with Characteristics of Equity. If necessary, the *Conceptual Framework* will be updated as one possible outcome of that project (see paragraph BC4.45).

BC0.16 The discussion of capital and capital maintenance in the 2018 *Conceptual Framework* is unchanged from the 2010 *Conceptual Framework*. That discussion originally appeared in the 1989 *Framework* (see paragraphs BC8.1–BC8.4). The Board may consider revising that discussion in the future if it considers that necessary.

BC0.17 In developing the 2018 *Conceptual Framework*, the Board did not address the equity method of accounting, the translation of amounts denominated in foreign currency or the restatement of the measuring unit in hyperinflation. The Board concluded that these issues would best be dealt with if it were to carry out projects to consider revising Standards on these topics.

Purpose (paragraph SP1.1)

BC0.18 The 2010 *Conceptual Framework* included a long list of possible uses of the *Conceptual Framework*. In 2018, the Board streamlined the list, identifying three main uses of the *Conceptual Framework*: assisting the Board in developing Standards, assisting preparers in developing accounting policies when no Standard applies to a particular transaction or other event (or when a Standard allows a choice of accounting policy) and assisting all parties in understanding and interpreting Standards.

BC0.19 The Board considered whether to focus the stated purpose of the *Conceptual Framework* by stating that its primary purpose would be only to assist the Board in developing Standards. The Board rejected this approach because acknowledging the assistance the *Conceptual Framework* can give to other parties would not prevent the Board from developing focused and consistent concepts that will help it to develop Standards.

BC0.20 Although preparers apply the *Conceptual Framework* in developing accounting policies when no Standard applies to a particular transaction or other event or when a Standard allows a choice of accounting policy, a few aspects of the *Conceptual Framework* can only be applied by the Board. In such cases, the 2018 *Conceptual Framework* indicates that the Board may make particular decisions in developing Standards (for example, see paragraph 7.17).

Status (paragraphs SP1.2–SP1.3)

BC0.21 The 1989 *Framework* and the 2010 *Conceptual Framework* stated that the *Conceptual Framework* is not a Standard and does not override any specific Standards. In the 2018 *Conceptual Framework*, the Board reconfirmed this status.

BC0.22 The Board found that the status of the *Conceptual Framework* has worked well in practice. Also, an explicit statement that the *Conceptual Framework* does not override any requirements in a Standard prevents entities from attempting to override inappropriately Standards those entities might view as contradicting the *Conceptual Framework*.

BC0.23 In some stakeholders' view, the Board should never develop Standards that depart from the *Conceptual Framework*. The Board disagreed with this view. In some circumstances, the Board might need to depart from aspects of the *Conceptual Framework*. It is helpful for the *Conceptual Framework* to acknowledge this, and to specify that such departures are appropriate only if needed to meet the objective of general purpose financial reporting.

BC0.24 Some respondents to the 2015 Exposure Draft expressed concerns about the implications of the proposals for future Standards. In particular, they expressed concerns about proposed changes to the definitions of an asset and a liability. In response, the Board tested the revised definitions of an asset and a liability and the guidance supporting those definitions (see paragraphs BC4.19–BC4.22). One of the aims of this test was to enable both the Board and stakeholders to assess implications of the revised concepts for future Standards. In addition, the Board tested for inconsistencies between the revised concepts and existing Standards.

BC0.25 The aim of these tests was not to identify whether the Board should develop proposals to amend any Standards following the revision of the *Conceptual Framework*. Amending a Standard is not an automatic consequence of that revision. Changes to Standards are made to address deficiencies in financial reporting. Any changes to the *Conceptual Framework* that highlight inconsistencies in the Standards must be considered by the Board in the light of other priorities when developing its work plan.[1]

BC0.26 The *IFRS for SMEs®* Standard includes a section on the concepts and basic principles underlying the financial statements of small and medium-sized entities. That section is based on the 1989 *Framework*. The Board will consider whether it should amend this section of the *IFRS for SMEs* Standard when it next reviews that Standard.

Transition to the 2018 *Conceptual Framework*

BC0.27 The Board and the IFRS Interpretations Committee will start using the 2018 *Conceptual Framework* immediately once it is issued. If, when developing a draft IFRIC® Interpretation, the IFRS Interpretation Committee is faced with an inconsistency between a Standard (including any Standard developed on the basis of the 1989 *Framework* or the 2010 *Conceptual Framework*) and the concepts in the 2018 *Conceptual Framework*, it will refer the issue to the Board, as required by the IFRS Foundation *Due Process Handbook*.[2]

BC0.28 The revised concepts will guide the Board when it develops or revises Standards. However, changes to the *Conceptual Framework* will not automatically lead to changes in existing Standards (see paragraph BC0.25). Accordingly, changes to the *Conceptual Framework* will have no immediate effect on the financial statements of most reporting entities. Preparers of financial statements could be directly affected by the changes only if they need to use the *Conceptual Framework* to develop an accounting policy when no Standard applies to a particular transaction or other event or when a Standard allows a choice of accounting policy.[3] To achieve transition to the 2018 *Conceptual Framework* for such entities, the Board issued *Amendments to References to the Conceptual Framework in IFRS Standards* in 2018. Where appropriate, that document replaces references in Standards to the 1989 *Framework* with references to the 2018 *Conceptual Framework* and updates related quotations.

---

1 See paragraph 4.23 of the IFRS Foundation *Due Process Handbook*.
2 See paragraph 7.8 of the IFRS Foundation *Due Process Handbook*.
3 If no Standard specifically applies to a transaction, other event or condition, paragraph 11 of IAS 8 *Accounting Policies, Changes in Accounting Estimates and Errors* requires entities to consider the *Conceptual Framework* in developing and applying an accounting policy for that transaction. If a Standard permits a choice of accounting policy, entities select an accounting policy subject to an overall requirement in IAS 1 *Presentation of Financial Statements* that financial statements must provide a fair presentation of the entity's financial position, financial performance and cash flows. The link between fair presentation and the concepts in the *Conceptual Framework* is described in paragraph 15 of IAS 1.

CONCEPTUAL FRAMEWORK FOR FINANCIAL REPORTING

Business activities

BC0.29 In developing the 2018 *Conceptual Framework*, the Board concluded that the nature of an entity's business activities can affect the relevance of some types of financial information and that the Board may need to consider that factor when developing or revising Standards.

BC0.30 The Board disagreed with the view expressed by some stakeholders that considering the nature of an entity's business activities necessarily leads to subjectivity and impairs comparability of financial statements. An entity's business activities are a matter of fact that can in most cases be determined objectively. Hence, if entities conduct the same type of business activities, the Board expects that those activities would be reflected in a similar manner in the entities' financial statements.

BC0.31 The Board considered whether the nature of business activities should be considered in all areas of standard-setting and should be embedded in the *Conceptual Framework* as an overarching concept. The Board concluded that the nature of an entity's business activities does not affect all areas of financial reporting in the same way and to the same extent and so it should not be included as an overarching concept. Accordingly, the 2018 *Conceptual Framework* does not include a general discussion of how an entity's business activities affect financial reporting decisions. Instead, the 2018 *Conceptual Framework* describes that factor in the context of:

(a) the selection of the unit of account (see paragraph 4.51(a)(iv)).

(b) the selection of a measurement basis for an asset or liability and for related income and expenses (see paragraphs 6.54–6.57). In some cases, this would lead to some items of income or expenses being included in other comprehensive income (see the discussion of more than one measurement basis in paragraphs 6.83–6.86).

(c) classification of assets, liabilities, equity, income or expenses (see paragraph 7.7).

BC0.32 The concept of business activities is discussed in the 2018 *Conceptual Framework* to assist the Board in developing Standards. In a particular Standard, the concept of business activities can be further explained and developed. The discussion of business model in IFRS 9 *Financial Instruments* is one example of how the Board has applied the concept of business activities.

BC0.33 The Board decided to use the term 'business activities' rather than the term 'business model' in the 2018 *Conceptual Framework*. The term 'business model' is used with a range of different meanings by various organisations, for example, the International Integrated Reporting Council, the Enhanced Disclosure Task Force of the Financial Stability Board and various regulators. Adopting the term 'business model' in the 2018 *Conceptual Framework* could have led to confusion with those definitions.

Implications of long-term investment

BC0.34 The subject of long-term investment has attracted a great deal of attention from governments and others. Governments have indicated that encouraging long-term investment is an important tool for promoting economic growth.

BC0.35 The Board considered the role of its Standards in promoting long-term investment and noted that:

(a) the Board makes an important contribution to the promotion of investment, including long-term investment, by producing Standards that require transparent financial reporting. This is a precondition for the healthy and efficient functioning of financial markets. Transparent financial reporting helps market participants to make more efficient and informed resource allocation and other economic decisions and thus makes investment more attractive to capital providers (investors and lenders). It also provides useful inputs for an assessment of stewardship.

(b) it is not, however, the role of the Standards to encourage or discourage any type of investments. Instead, standard-setting decisions are driven by the need for entities to provide useful information.

BC0.36 When developing the 2018 *Conceptual Framework*, the Board considered whether the *Conceptual Framework* will provide the Board with sufficient and appropriate tools to enable it, when developing Standards, to consider:

(a) the business activity of long-term investment (see paragraphs BC0.37–BC0.39); and

(b) the information needs of long-term investors (see paragraphs BC0.40–BC0.43).

Long-term investment as a business activity

BC0.37 The Board considered a suggestion made by some stakeholders that it should identify long-term investment as a particular type of business activity (or business model) and develop specific measurement and presentation and disclosure requirements for entities conducting that business activity. Some stakeholders expressing those views suggested that:

(a) entities should not use a current value measurement basis for their long-term investments and for their liabilities; or

(b) if a current value measurement basis is used for those investments and liabilities, income and expenses resulting from remeasurements should be included in other comprehensive income, not in the statement of profit or loss.

BC0.38 As discussed in paragraphs 6.54–6.57 of the 2018 *Conceptual Framework*, the nature of the business activities being conducted affects how an asset or liability contributes to future cash flows. Thus, the nature of an entity's business activities is considered in selecting a measurement basis for an asset or liability and for related income and expenses. Moreover, in some cases, considering the nature of an entity's activities may lead to some items of income and expenses being included in other comprehensive income (see paragraphs 6.85–6.86). The Board concluded that the discussion on this factor in the 2018 *Conceptual Framework* provides sufficient tools for the Board to make appropriate standard-setting decisions if future projects consider how to account for the long-term investments of entities whose business activities include long-term investment or for their liabilities.

BC0.39 For the following reasons, the Board decided that the 2018 *Conceptual Framework* should not refer explicitly to the business activity of long-term investment:

(a) referring explicitly to any particular business activity would, inappropriately, embed excessive detail in the *Conceptual Framework*; and

(b) the *Conceptual Framework* does not refer to any other business activity.

Information needs of long-term investors

BC0.40 Some stakeholders suggested that the *Conceptual Framework* should emphasise the information needs of long-term investors and that their information needs may differ from those of short-term investors. Views expressed by these stakeholders included the following:

(a) the Board focuses too much on the needs of short-term investors.

(b) the Board gives too much weight to the needs of potential investors and not enough weight to the needs of existing long-term investors. Existing long-term investors own the reporting entity and bear the residual risks of ownership. Hence, these stakeholders argue that long-term investors need information that helps them to assess management's stewardship of the entity's economic resources.

(c) the Board makes excessive use of current value measurement bases, particularly those reflecting market-participant assumptions, such as fair value, and those measurement bases provide information more relevant to short-term investors than to investors who are interested in long-term value creation.

(d) excessive use of current value measurement bases (especially for long-term investments) and recognition of unrealised gains in the statement of profit or loss may:

   (i) lead to excessive and volatile dividend distributions that are not in the best interest of long-term investors;

   (ii) lead to inflated management remuneration (including bonuses); and

   (iii) encourage short-termism and financial engineering and discourage long-term investment.

BC0.41 For the following reasons, the Board disagreed with the views expressed in paragraph BC0.40:

(a) the Board does not place more emphasis on the needs of short-term investors than on the needs of long-term investors. The Board considers both long-term investors and short-term investors to be primary users of financial statements. Moreover, the Board believes that there is no reason why short-term investors would need information that is not also needed by long-term investors.

(b) the *Conceptual Framework* identifies both existing and potential investors as primary users of financial statements. The Board's discussions with users in its project on the *Conceptual Framework* and in many other projects have identified no reasons why existing investors would need information that differs from the information needed by potential investors. Furthermore, the changes made by the 2018 *Conceptual Framework* to the discussion of the objective of general purpose financial reporting highlight the importance of providing information to help investors to assess management's stewardship of the entity's economic resources. The 2018 *Conceptual Framework* states explicitly that decisions relating to providing resources to the entity include decisions about exercising rights to vote on, or otherwise influence, management's actions that affect the use of the entity's economic resources. Thus, the 2018 *Conceptual Framework* clarifies that the needs of existing investors (including long-term investors) are considered when making decisions about the usefulness of financial information (see paragraphs BC1.36–BC1.37).

BASIS FOR CONCLUSIONS ON THE CONCEPTUAL FRAMEWORK FOR FINANCIAL REPORTING

    (c)   when the Board has decided to require or permit current value measurement bases, that has not been because of a belief that those measurement bases would be particularly useful to short-term investors. Instead, the Board's decisions have been driven by an assessment of what information is most likely to be useful to the primary users of financial statements, including both long-term and short-term investors. Under the concepts in Chapter 6—*Measurement* of the 2018 *Conceptual Framework*, this will continue to be the case.

    (d)   in the Board's view, accounting information (such as reported profit) is not, and should not be, the sole determinant of distributions of dividends and bonuses. Distribution policy is affected by many other factors, for example, the entity's financing needs, current and projected liquidity, the risks faced by the entity, legal constraints and (in the case of bonus decisions) remuneration policy and incentive arrangements. These factors differ by entity, by country and over time. It would be neither desirable nor feasible for the Board to consider them in standard-setting decisions.

BC0.42   For these reasons, the Board concluded that the 2018 *Conceptual Framework* contains sufficient and appropriate discussion of primary users and their information needs, and of the objective of general purpose financial reporting, to address appropriately the needs of long-term investors.

BC0.43   Conceivably, long-term investors may need entities to provide some information that is not also needed by short-term investors; for example, long-term investors may have more extensive needs for information to support decisions to vote on, or otherwise influence, management's actions. However, the Board concluded that to help it to identify what information particular Standards should require entities to provide, there is no need for the *Conceptual Framework* to contain a specific reference to the needs of long-term investors. When the Board develops Standards, it routinely seeks input and feedback from investors, including long-term investors, to help ensure that it understands what information they need.

CHAPTER 1—THE OBJECTIVE OF GENERAL PURPOSE FINANCIAL REPORTING

from paragraph

INTRODUCTION	BC1.1
Revision in 2018	BC1.2
General purpose financial reporting (2010)	BC1.4
Financial reporting of the reporting entity (2010)	BC1.8
PRIMARY USERS	BC1.9
Primary users (2010)	BC1.9
Should there be a primary user group? (2010)	BC1.14
Why are existing and potential investors, lenders and other creditors considered the primary users? (2010)	BC1.15
Primary user group (2018)	BC1.18
Should there be a hierarchy of users? (2010)	BC1.21
Information needs of other users who are not within the primary user group (2010)	BC1.22
Management's information needs (2010)	BC1.22
Regulators' information needs (2010)	BC1.23
USEFULNESS FOR MAKING DECISIONS	BC1.27
Usefulness for making decisions (2010)	BC1.27
Stewardship (2018)	BC1.32
The term 'stewardship' (2018)	BC1.41
The objective of financial reporting for different types of entities (2010)	BC1.42
INFORMATION ABOUT A REPORTING ENTITY'S ECONOMIC RESOURCES, CLAIMS AGAINST THE ENTITY AND CHANGES IN RESOURCES AND CLAIMS	BC1.44
The significance of information about financial performance (2010)	BC1.44
Financial position and solvency (2010)	BC1.47

BASIS FOR CONCLUSIONS ON THE CONCEPTUAL FRAMEWORK FOR FINANCIAL REPORTING

> *In 2018, the Board made limited changes to Chapter 1 of the* Conceptual Framework. *A description of the Board's considerations in developing those changes was added to the original Basis for Conclusions on this chapter. The Board added a date to the heading of each section of the Basis for Conclusions to indicate when that section was developed. Sections of the Basis for Conclusions that reflect the Board's considerations at the time of developing the chapter in 2010 were not updated in 2018 except to add and update cross-references and to make minor necessary editorial changes.*

Introduction

BC1.1 The first version of Chapter 1 was developed jointly with the FASB and issued in 2010 (see paragraph BC0.3). Consequently, this Basis for Conclusions includes some references to the FASB's literature.

Revision in 2018

BC1.2 When the Board restarted its work on the Conceptual Framework project in 2012, it did not reconsider Chapter 1 fundamentally (see paragraph BC0.11). Although some respondents to the 2013 Discussion Paper agreed with this approach, many stated that the Board should reconsider one or more aspects of Chapter 1. In the light of these comments, the Board considered whether to make changes in the following areas:

(a) primary users (see paragraphs BC1.18–BC1.20); and

(b) stewardship (see paragraphs BC1.32–BC1.41).

BC1.3 The FASB has not made any changes to its Concepts Statement No. 8 *Conceptual Framework for Financial Reporting—Chapter 1*, The Objective of General Purpose Financial Reporting corresponding to the limited changes made by the Board in 2018. The Board concluded that the clarity achieved by its improvements to Chapter 1 outweighs the disadvantages of divergence in those respects from the FASB's version.

General purpose financial reporting (2010)

BC1.4 Consistently with the Board's responsibilities, the *Conceptual Framework* establishes an objective of financial reporting and not just of financial statements. Financial statements are a central part of financial reporting, and most of the issues that the Board addresses involve financial statements. Although the scope of FASB Concepts Statement No. 1 *Objectives of Financial Reporting by Business Enterprises* was financial reporting, the other FASB concepts statements focused on financial statements. The scope of the Board's *Framework for the Preparation and Presentation of Financial Statements*, which was published by the Board's predecessor body in 1989 (1989 *Framework*), dealt with financial statements only. Therefore, for both boards the scope of the 2010 *Conceptual Framework* is broader than the scopes of their previous frameworks.[1]

BC1.5 Some stakeholders suggested that advances in technology may make general purpose financial reporting obsolete. New technologies, for example the use of eXtensible Business Reporting Language (XBRL), may make it practicable in the future for reporting entities

---

[1] With the exception of Chapters 1 and 2, the 2018 *Conceptual Framework* focuses on (general purpose) financial statements rather than on (general purpose) financial reports (see paragraph 3.1).

either to prepare or to make available the information necessary for different users to assemble different financial reports to meet their individual information needs.

BC1.6 To provide different reports for different users, or to make available all of the information that users would need to assemble their own custom-designed reports, would be expensive. Requiring users of financial information to assemble their own reports might also be unreasonable, because many users would need to have a greater understanding of accounting than they have now. Therefore, the Board concluded that for now a general purpose financial report is still the most efficient and effective way to meet the information needs of a variety of users.

BC1.7 In the 2006 Discussion Paper, the Board used the term 'general purpose external financial reporting'. External was intended to convey that internal users such as management were not the intended beneficiaries for general purpose financial reporting as established by the Board. During redeliberations, the Board concluded that this term was redundant. Therefore, Chapter 1 uses 'general purpose financial reporting'.

Financial reporting of the reporting entity (2010)

BC1.8 Some respondents to the 2008 Exposure Draft said that the reporting entity is not separate from its equity investors or a subset of those equity investors. This view has its roots in the days when most businesses were sole proprietorships and partnerships that were managed by their owners who had unlimited liability for the debts incurred in the course of the business. Over time, the separation between businesses and their owners has grown. The vast majority of today's businesses have legal substance separate from their owners by virtue of their legal form of organisation, numerous investors with limited legal liability and professional managers separate from the owners. Consequently, the Board concluded that financial reports should reflect that separation by accounting for the entity (and its economic resources and claims) rather than its primary users and their interests in the reporting entity.[1]

Primary users (paragraphs 1.5, 1.8–1.10)

Primary users (2010)

BC1.9 The objective of financial reporting in paragraph 1.2 refers to existing and potential investors, lenders and other creditors. The description of the primary users in paragraph 1.5 refers to existing and potential investors, lenders and other creditors who cannot require reporting entities to provide information directly to them. Paragraph 1.10 states that 'regulators and members of the public other than investors, lenders and other creditors' may find information in general purpose financial reports useful but states that those are not the parties to whom general purpose financial reports are primarily directed.

BC1.10 Paragraph 9 of the 1989 *Framework* stated that users included 'present and potential investors, employees, lenders, suppliers and other trade creditors' (and later added advisers in the discussion of investors' needs), all of which are intended to be encompassed by the phrase in paragraph 1.2. Paragraph 9 of the 1989 *Framework* also included a list of other potential users such as customers, governments and their agencies, and the public, which is

---

1 See also paragraph 3.8 of the 2018 *Conceptual Framework* and paragraphs BC3.9–BC3.10.

BC1.11 Paragraph 10 of the 1989 *Framework* stated that 'as investors are providers of risk capital to the entity, the provision of financial statements that meet their needs will also meet most of the needs of other users that financial statements can satisfy', which might have been read to narrow the focus to investors only. However, paragraph 12 explicitly stated that the objective of financial statements is to provide information 'that is useful to a wide range of users in making economic decisions.' Thus, the 1989 *Framework* focused on investors' needs as representative of the needs of a wide range of users but did not explicitly identify a group of primary users.

BC1.12 FASB Concepts Statement 1 referred to 'present and potential investors and creditors and other users in making rational investment, credit, and similar decisions' (paragraph 34). It also stated that 'major groups of investors are equity securityholders and debt securityholders' and 'major groups of creditors are suppliers of goods and services who extend credit, customers and employees with claims, lending institutions, individual lenders, and debt securityholders' (paragraph 35). One difference in emphasis from the 1989 *Framework*, which emphasised providers of risk capital, is that Concepts Statement 1 referred to 'both those who desire safety of investment and those who are willing to accept risk to obtain high rates of return' (paragraph 35). However, like the 1989 *Framework*, Concepts Statement 1 stated that the terms investors and creditors 'also may comprehend security analysts and advisors, brokers, lawyers, regulatory agencies, and others who advise or represent the interests of investors and creditors or who otherwise are interested in how investors and creditors are faring' (paragraph 35).

BC1.13 Paragraphs 1.3, 1.5 and 1.10 differ from the 1989 *Framework* and Concepts Statement 1 for two reasons—to eliminate differences between the 1989 *Framework* and Concepts Statement 1 and to be more direct by focusing on users making decisions relating to providing resources (but not to exclude advisers). The reasons are discussed in paragraphs BC1.15–BC1.17 and BC1.21–BC1.26.

Should there be a primary user group? (2010)

BC1.14 The 2006 Discussion Paper and the 2008 Exposure Draft proposed identifying a group of primary users of financial reports. Some respondents to the 2008 Exposure Draft said that other users who have not provided, and are not considering providing, resources to the entity, use financial reports for a variety of reasons. The Board sympathised with their information needs but concluded that without a defined group of primary users, the *Conceptual Framework* would risk becoming unduly abstract or vague.

Why are existing and potential investors, lenders and other creditors considered the primary users? (2010)

BC1.15 Some respondents to the 2006 Discussion Paper and the 2008 Exposure Draft suggested that the primary user group should be limited to existing shareholders or the controlling entity's majority shareholders. Others said that the primary users should be existing shareholders and creditors, and that financial reports should focus on their needs.

BC1.16 The reasons why the Board concluded that the primary user group should be the existing and potential investors, lenders and other creditors of a reporting entity are:

(a) Existing and potential investors, lenders and other creditors have the most critical and immediate need for the information in financial reports and many cannot require the entity to provide the information to them directly.

(b) The Board's and the FASB's responsibilities require them to focus on the needs of participants in capital markets, which include not only existing investors but also potential investors and existing and potential lenders and other creditors.

(c) Information that meets the needs of the specified primary users is likely to meet the needs of users both in jurisdictions with a corporate governance model defined in the context of shareholders and those with a corporate governance model defined in the context of all types of stakeholders.

BC1.17 Some respondents expressed the view that the specified primary user group was too broad and that it would result in too much information in the financial reports. However, too much is a subjective judgement. In developing financial reporting requirements that meet the objective of financial reporting, the boards will rely on the qualitative characteristics of, and the cost constraint on, useful financial information to provide discipline to avoid providing too much information.

Primary user group (2018)

BC1.18 Views expressed by respondents to the 2013 Discussion Paper and to the 2015 Exposure Draft about the description of the primary user group were similar to those expressed by stakeholders and considered by the Board when it originally developed Chapter 1:

(a) some respondents commented that the primary user group is defined too narrowly. They argued that it should be expanded to include, for example, employees, customers, suppliers, regulators and others.

(b) in contrast, others said that the primary user group is defined too broadly. These respondents stated that the Board should describe primary users as holders of equity claims against the entity (or perhaps as the holders of the most residual equity claims against the entity). The respondents argued that holders of equity claims have different (and perhaps more extensive) information needs than other capital providers because they are exposed to more extensive risks.

BC1.19 In the light of views expressed by respondents, the Board reconsidered the description of the primary user group. Nevertheless, it concluded that its reasons for describing the primary user group as the existing and potential investors, lenders and other creditors of a reporting entity were still valid (see paragraph BC1.16). In addition, as explained in paragraph 1.8 of the 2018 *Conceptual Framework*, focusing on the common information needs of the primary users does not prevent a reporting entity from including additional information that is most useful to a particular subset of primary users. Consequently, the Board concluded that no changes to the description of the primary user group were needed.

BC1.20 In addition, the Board decided that there was no need for the 2018 *Conceptual Framework* to identify long-term investors as a particular subset of primary users with specific information needs (see paragraphs BC0.40–BC0.41).

Should there be a hierarchy of users? (2010)

BC1.21 Some respondents to the 2008 Exposure Draft who supported the composition of the primary user group also recommended that the Board should establish a hierarchy of primary users because investors, lenders and other creditors have different information needs. However, the Board observed that individual users may have information needs and desires that are different from, and possibly conflict with, those of other users with the same type of interest in the reporting entity. General purpose financial reports are intended to provide common information to users and cannot accommodate every request for information. The Board will seek the information set that is intended to meet the needs of the maximum number of users in cost-beneficial ways.

Information needs of other users who are not within the primary user group (2010)

Management's information needs (2010)

BC1.22 Some stakeholders questioned the interaction between general purpose financial reporting and management's needs. The Board stated that some of the information directed to the primary users is likely to meet some of management's needs but not all of them. However, management has the ability to access additional financial information, and consequently, general purpose financial reporting need not be explicitly directed to management.

Regulators' information needs (2010)

BC1.23 Some stakeholders said that maintaining financial stability in capital markets (the stability of a country's or region's economy or financial systems) should be an objective of financial reporting. They stated that financial reporting should focus on the needs of regulators and fiscal policy decision-makers who are responsible for maintaining financial stability.

BC1.24 Other stakeholders opposed establishing an objective to maintain financial stability. They said that financial statements should present the economic reality of the reporting entity with as little bias as possible, but that such a presentation is not necessarily inconsistent with a financial stability objective. By presenting economic reality, financial statements could lead to more informed decision-making and thereby support financial stability even if that is not the primary aim.[1]

BC1.25 However, advocates of a financial stability objective had a different outcome in mind. They did not encourage the Board to require reporting entities to provide information for use by regulators and fiscal policy decision-makers. Instead, they recommended that the Board consider the consequences of new Standards for the stability of the world's economies and financial systems and, at least at times, assign greater weight to that objective than to the information needs of investors, lenders and other creditors.

BC1.26 The Board acknowledged that the interests of investors, lenders and other creditors often overlap with those of regulators. However, expanding the objective of financial reporting to include maintaining financial stability could at times create conflicts between the objectives that the Board is not well-equipped to resolve. For example, some may take the view that the best way to maintain financial stability is to require entities not to report, or to delay reporting, some changes in asset or liability values. That requirement would almost certainly result in depriving investors, lenders and other creditors of information that they need. The only way to avoid conflicts would be to eliminate or de-emphasise the existing

---

1 One group expressing that view was the Financial Crisis Advisory Group (FCAG). The FCAG comprised approximately 20 senior leaders with broad experience in international financial markets and an interest in the transparency of financial reporting information. The FCAG was formed in 2009 to advise the Board and the FASB about the standard-setting implications of the financial crisis and of potential changes in the global regulatory environment.

objective of providing information to investors, lenders and other creditors. The Board concluded that eliminating that objective would be inconsistent with its basic mission, which is to serve the information needs of participants in capital markets. The Board also noted that providing financial information that is relevant and faithfully represents what it purports to represent can improve users' confidence in the information, and thus contribute to promoting financial stability.[1]

Usefulness for making decisions (paragraphs 1.2–1.4)

Usefulness for making decisions (2010)

BC1.27 Both the Board's and the FASB's previous frameworks focused on providing information that is useful in making economic decisions as the fundamental objective of financial reporting. Those frameworks also stated that financial information that is useful in making economic decisions would also be helpful in assessing how management has fulfilled its stewardship responsibility.

BC1.28 The 2006 Discussion Paper that led to Chapter 1 stated that the objective of financial reporting should focus on resource allocation decisions. Although most respondents to the 2006 Discussion Paper agreed that providing useful information for decision-making was the appropriate objective, they said that investors, lenders and other creditors make other decisions that are aided by financial reporting information in addition to resource allocation decisions. For example, shareholders who vote on whether to retain directors or replace them, and on how members of management should be remunerated for their services, need information on which to base their decisions. Shareholders' decision-making process may include evaluating how management of the entity performed against management in competing entities in similar circumstances.

BC1.29 The Board agreed with these respondents and noted that, in most cases, information designed for resource allocation decisions would also be useful for assessing management's performance. Therefore, in the 2008 Exposure Draft leading to Chapter 1, the Board proposed that the objective of financial reporting is to provide financial information about the reporting entity that is useful to present and potential investors, lenders and other creditors in making decisions in their capacity as capital providers. The 2008 Exposure Draft also described the role financial statements can have in supporting decisions related to the stewardship of an entity's resources.

BC1.30 The 2008 Exposure Draft discussed the *Objective of Financial Reporting and Decision-usefulness* in separate sections. The Board combined those two sections in Chapter 1 because usefulness in making decisions is the objective of financial reporting. Consequently, both sections addressed the same points and provided more detail than was necessary. Combining those two sections resulted in eliminating the separate subsections on usefulness in assessing cash flow prospects and usefulness in assessing stewardship. The Board did not intend to imply that assessing prospects for future cash flow or assessing the quality of management's stewardship is more important than the other. Both are important for making decisions about providing resources to an entity, and information about

---

[1] See also paragraphs BC0.34–BC0.43 for the Board's 2018 discussion on the role of Standards in promoting long-term investment and paragraph SP1.5 of the 2018 *Conceptual Framework* for an explanation of the *Conceptual Framework*'s contribution to the mission of the IFRS Foundation and of the Board, which is to develop Standards that bring transparency, accountability and efficiency to financial markets.

stewardship is also important for resource providers who have the ability to vote on, or otherwise influence, management's actions.

BC1.31 The Board decided not to use the term 'stewardship' in the 2010 *Conceptual Framework* because there would be difficulties in translating it into other languages. Instead, the Board described what stewardship encapsulates. Accordingly, the objective of financial reporting in the 2010 *Conceptual Framework* acknowledged that users make resource allocation decisions as well as decisions as to whether management has made efficient and effective use of the resources provided.

Stewardship (2018)

BC1.32 After Chapter 1 was issued in 2010, some stakeholders interpreted the chapter, and in particular the removal from it of the term 'stewardship', as neglecting the fact that users of financial statements need information to help them to assess management's stewardship. As mentioned in paragraph BC1.30, the Board had not intended to neglect that need. Nevertheless, the Board concluded subsequently that the wording in the 2010 *Conceptual Framework* was not clear enough.

BC1.33 Thus, in the 2018 *Conceptual Framework* the Board improved the wording to clarify its original intention. The Board reintroduced the term 'stewardship' and, in describing the objective of general purpose financial reporting, gave more prominence to the importance of providing information needed to assess management's stewardship of the entity's economic resources. That extra prominence contributes to highlighting management's accountability to users for economic resources entrusted to their care.

BC1.34 To provide that greater prominence, the 2018 *Conceptual Framework* identifies information needed to assess management's stewardship as possibly partly separate from the information needed to help users to assess the prospects for future net cash inflows to the entity. Both types of information are needed to meet the overall objective of financial reporting—that is to provide information that is useful for making decisions relating to providing resources to the entity (resource allocation decisions).

BC1.35 The Board also considered other approaches suggested by some stakeholders. Those approaches would have identified the provision of information to help to assess management's stewardship as part of the objective of financial reporting or as an additional and equally prominent objective. The Board rejected those approaches because:

(a) assessing management's stewardship is not an end in itself; it is an input needed in making resource allocation decisions. For example, a conclusion that management's stewardship is unsatisfactory may lead to a decision to replace management with the aim of increasing future returns.

(b) introducing an additional objective of financial reporting could be confusing.

BC1.36 Further, in the 2018 *Conceptual Framework* the Board clarified how the assessment of management's stewardship contributed to resource allocation decisions. The Board did this by expanding the explanation of resource allocation decisions. The feedback on the 2015 Exposure Draft indicated that some respondents interpreted resource allocation decisions as referring solely to buying, selling or holding decisions. Thus, in their view, resource allocation decisions excluded decisions made while holding an investment, for example, decisions to reappoint or replace management, to assess the adequacy of management's remuneration or to approve a business strategy proposed by management.

BC1.37 The Board did not intend resource allocation decisions to be interpreted narrowly as referring solely to buying, selling or holding decisions. Consequently, the 2018 *Conceptual Framework* states explicitly that resource allocation decisions involve decisions about:

(a) buying, selling or holding equity and debt instruments;

(b) providing or settling loans and other forms of credit; or

(c) exercising rights to vote on, or otherwise influence, management's[1] actions that affect the use of the entity's economic resources.

Users of financial statements need to assess both the amount, timing and uncertainty of future net cash inflows and management's stewardship of the entity's economic resources to make any of these decisions.

BC1.38 Paragraph BC1.37(c) refers to management's actions that affect the use of the entity's economic resources. One example of a decision about such actions is a decision in voting on the membership of the Board of directors. That vote will ultimately influence the Board of directors' subsequent actions affecting the use of the entity's economic resources. However, financial reporting is not designed to provide information that will help the primary users of that information to exercise their rights to vote on other actions by management, such as developing a statement on an issue of a public policy that does not directly affect the use of the entity's economic resources.

BC1.39 Some respondents to the 2015 Exposure Draft suggested that in some cases the information needed to assess management's stewardship differs from the information needed to assess prospects for future net cash inflows to the entity. In particular, these respondents focused on the selection of a measurement basis:

(a) some respondents suggested that, in some cases, historical cost measures are more useful than current value measures for assessing stewardship because, in their opinion, historical cost measures are more verifiable and provide a more direct link to the transactions actually undertaken by management; and

(b) in contrast, other respondents argued that, in some cases, current value measures may be more useful for assessing stewardship because, in their opinion, such measures can provide information about how well management has performed in comparison with other courses of action currently available.

BC1.40 In giving more prominence to stewardship within the description of the objective of financial reporting in the 2018 *Conceptual Framework*, the Board did not intend to imply a preference for any particular measurement basis. Factors to be considered in the selection of a measurement basis are discussed in Chapter 6—*Measurement* of the 2018 *Conceptual Framework*.

The term 'stewardship' (2018)

BC1.41 The revised Chapter 1 reintroduces the term 'stewardship' and explains that the assessment of management's stewardship involves assessing how efficiently and effectively the entity's management and governing board have discharged their responsibilities to use the entity's economic resources (see paragraphs 1.4 and 1.22–1.23). That assessment enables users of financial statements to hold management to account for its actions. The Board's use of the term 'stewardship' is consistent with the general understanding of that term: the careful and responsible management of something entrusted to one's care.[2] These improvements to Chapter 1 provide increased clarity and the Board concluded that this outweighs the translation difficulties identified in 2010.

---

1 The term 'management' refers to management and the governing board of an entity (see paragraph 1.4(b) of the 2018 *Conceptual Framework*).

2 This definition of stewardship is provided in the Merriam-Webster online dictionary (https://www.merriam-webster.com/dictionary/stewardship).

The objective of financial reporting for different types of entities (2010)

BC1.42 The Board considered whether the objective of general purpose financial reporting should differ for different types of entities. Possibilities include:

(a) smaller entities versus larger entities;

(b) entities with listed (publicly traded) debt or equity financial instruments versus those without such instruments; and

(c) closely held entities versus those with widely dispersed ownership.

BC1.43 External users of financial reporting have similar objectives, irrespective of the type of entities in which they invest. Therefore, the Board concluded that the objective of general purpose financial reports is the same for all entities. However, cost constraints and differences in activities among entities may sometimes lead the Board to permit or require differences in reporting for different types of entities.

Information about a reporting entity's economic resources, claims against the entity and changes in resources and claims (paragraphs 1.12–1.21)

The significance of information about financial performance (2010)

BC1.44 A long-standing assertion by many stakeholders is that a reporting entity's financial performance as represented by comprehensive income and its components is the most important information.[1] Concepts Statement 1 (paragraph 43) stated:

> The primary focus of financial reporting is information about an enterprise's performance provided by measures of comprehensive income and its components. Investors, creditors, and others who are concerned with assessing the prospects for enterprise net cash inflows are especially interested in that information.

In contrast, the 1989 *Framework* considered information on the reporting entity's financial position and financial performance of equal importance.

BC1.45 To be useful for decision-making, financial reports must provide information about a reporting entity's economic resources and claims, and the change during a period in economic resources and claims. A reporting entity cannot provide reasonably complete information about its financial performance (as represented by comprehensive income, profit or loss or other similar terms) without identifying and measuring its economic resources and the claims. Consequently, the Board concluded that to designate one type of information as the primary focus of financial reporting would be inappropriate.

BC1.46 In discussing the financial position of an entity, the 2008 Exposure Draft referred to 'economic resources and claims on them'. The chapter uses the phrase 'the entity's

---

[1] Concepts Statement 1 referred to 'earnings and its components'. However, FASB Concepts Statement No. 6 *Elements of Financial Statements* substituted the term 'comprehensive income' for the term 'earnings'. The latter term is reserved for a component of comprehensive income.

economic resources and the claims against the reporting entity' (see paragraph 1.12). The reason for the change is that in many cases, claims against an entity are not claims on specific resources. In addition, many claims will be satisfied using resources that will result from future net cash inflows. Thus, while all claims are claims against the entity, not all are claims against the entity's existing resources.

Financial position and solvency (2010)

BC1.47 Some stakeholders have suggested that the main purpose of the statement of financial position should be to provide information that helps assess the reporting entity's solvency. The question is not whether information provided in the financial reports should be helpful in assessing solvency; clearly, it should. Assessing solvency is of interest to investors, lenders and other creditors, and the objective of general purpose financial reporting is to provide information that is useful to them for making decisions.

BC1.48 However, some have suggested that the statement of financial position should be directed towards the information needs of lenders, other creditors and regulators, possibly to the detriment of investors and other users. To do so would be inconsistent with the objective of serving the common information needs of the primary user group. Therefore, the Board rejected the notion of directing the statement of financial position (or any other particular financial statement) towards the needs of a particular subset of users.

from paragraph

CHAPTER 2—QUALITATIVE CHARACTERISTICS OF USEFUL FINANCIAL INFORMATION

INTRODUCTION	**BC2.1**
Revision in 2018	BC2.2
THE OBJECTIVE OF FINANCIAL REPORTING AND THE QUALITATIVE CHARACTERISTICS OF USEFUL FINANCIAL INFORMATION (2010)	**BC2.5**
FUNDAMENTAL AND ENHANCING QUALITATIVE CHARACTERISTICS (2010)	**BC2.9**
FUNDAMENTAL QUALITATIVE CHARACTERISTICS	**BC2.12**
Relevance	BC2.12
Predictive and confirmatory value (2010)	BC2.15
The difference between predictive value and related statistical terms (2010)	BC2.17
Materiality (2010)	BC2.18
Materiality (2018)	BC2.20
Faithful representation	**BC2.21**
Replacement of the term 'reliability' (2010)	BC2.22
Retention of the term 'faithful representation' (2018)	BC2.28
Substance over form (2010)	BC2.32
Substance over form (2018)	BC2.33
Prudence and neutrality (2010)	BC2.34
Prudence (2018)	BC2.37
Measurement uncertainty (2018)	BC2.46
Can faithful representation be empirically measured? (2010)	BC2.50
Applying the fundamental qualitative characteristics (2018)	**BC2.52**
ENHANCING QUALITATIVE CHARACTERISTICS	**BC2.58**
Comparability (2010)	BC2.58
Verifiability (2010)	BC2.60
Timeliness (2010)	BC2.63
Understandability (2010)	BC2.66
QUALITATIVE CHARACTERISTICS NOT INCLUDED (2010)	**BC2.70**
THE COST CONSTRAINT ON USEFUL FINANCIAL REPORTING (2010)	**BC2.73**

CONCEPTUAL FRAMEWORK FOR FINANCIAL REPORTING

> *In 2018, the Board made limited changes to Chapter 2 of the* Conceptual Framework. *A description of the Board's considerations in developing those changes was added to the original Basis for Conclusions on this chapter. The Board added a date to the heading of each section of the Basis for Conclusions to indicate when that section was developed. Sections of the Basis for Conclusions that reflect the Board's considerations at the time of developing the chapter in 2010 were not updated in 2018 except to add and update cross-references and to make minor necessary editorial changes.*

Introduction

BC2.1 The first version of this chapter was developed jointly with the FASB and issued in 2010 as Chapter 3 of the 2010 *Conceptual Framework* (see paragraph BC0.3). Consequently, this Basis for Conclusions includes some references to the FASB's literature.

Revision in 2018

BC2.2 When the Board restarted its work on the *Conceptual Framework* project in 2012, it did not reconsider fundamentally the chapter on the qualitative characteristics of useful financial information (see paragraph BC0.11). Although some respondents to the 2013 Discussion Paper agreed with this approach, many stated that the Board should reconsider one or more aspects of this chapter. In the light of these comments, the Board considered whether to make changes in the following areas:

(a) materiality (see paragraph BC2.20);

(b) reliability and measurement uncertainty (see paragraphs BC2.28–BC2.31 and BC2.46–BC2.49);

(c) substance over form (see paragraph BC2.33);

(d) prudence (see paragraphs BC2.37–BC2.45); and

(e) applying the fundamental qualitative characteristics (see paragraphs BC2.52–BC2.57).

BC2.3 In addition, the Board renumbered the chapter on qualitative characteristics of useful financial information as Chapter 2. The Board also made some editorial changes to Chapter 2, mainly to use the term 'faithful representation' more precisely by discussing whether financial information faithfully represents what it purports to represent (for example, an economic phenomenon), rather than by discussing whether financial information itself is faithfully represented.

BC2.4 The FASB has not made any changes to its Concepts Statement No. 8 *Conceptual Framework for Financial Reporting—Chapter 3*, Qualitative Characteristics of Useful Financial Information corresponding to the limited changes made by the Board in 2018. The Board concluded that the clarity achieved by its improvements to Chapter 2 outweigh the disadvantages of divergence in those respects from the FASB's version.

The objective of financial reporting and the qualitative characteristics of useful financial information (2010)

BC2.5 Alternatives are available for all aspects of financial reporting, including recognition, derecognition, measurement, classification, presentation and disclosure. When developing Standards, the Board will choose the alternative that goes furthest towards achieving the objective of financial reporting. Preparers of financial information will also have to choose among the alternatives in a way that achieves the objective of financial reporting if no Standards apply or if application of a particular Standard requires judgements or provides options.

BC2.6 Chapter 1 specifies that the objective of general purpose financial reporting is to provide financial information about the reporting entity that is useful to existing and potential investors, lenders and other creditors in making decisions about providing resources to the entity. The decision-makers on which this *Conceptual Framework* focuses are existing and potential investors, lenders and other creditors.

BC2.7 That objective by itself leaves a great deal to judgement and provides little guidance on how to exercise that judgement. Chapter 2 describes the first step in making the judgements needed to apply that objective. It identifies and describes the qualitative characteristics that financial information should have if it is to meet the objective of financial reporting. It also discusses cost, which is a pervasive constraint on financial reporting.

BC2.8 Subsequent chapters use the qualitative characteristics to help guide choices about recognition, measurement and the other aspects of financial reporting.

Fundamental and enhancing qualitative characteristics (2010) (paragraph 2.4)

BC2.9 Chapter 2 distinguishes between the fundamental qualitative characteristics that are the most critical and the enhancing qualitative characteristics that are less critical but still highly desirable. The 2006 Discussion Paper did not explicitly distinguish between those qualitative characteristics. The Board made the distinction later because of confusion among respondents to the 2006 Discussion Paper about how the qualitative characteristics relate to each other.

BC2.10 Some respondents to the 2008 Exposure Draft stated that all of the qualitative characteristics should be considered equal, and that the distinction between fundamental and enhancing qualitative characteristics was arbitrary. Others said that the most important qualitative characteristic differs depending on the circumstances; therefore, differentiating qualitative characteristics was not appropriate.

BC2.11 The Board does not agree that the distinction is arbitrary. Financial information without the two fundamental qualitative characteristics of relevance and faithful representation is not useful, and it cannot be made useful by being more comparable, verifiable, timely or understandable. However, financial information that is relevant and faithfully represents what it purports to represent may still be useful even if it does not have any of the enhancing qualitative characteristics.

CONCEPTUAL FRAMEWORK FOR FINANCIAL REPORTING

Fundamental qualitative characteristics (paragraphs 2.5–2.22)

Relevance (paragraphs 2.6–2.11)

BC2.12 It is self-evident that financial information is useful for making a decision only if it is capable of making a difference in that decision. 'Relevance' is the term used in the *Conceptual Framework* to describe that capability. It is a fundamental qualitative characteristic of useful financial information.

BC2.13 The definition of relevance in the *Conceptual Framework* is consistent with the definition in FASB Concepts Statement No. 2 *Qualitative Characteristics of Accounting Information*. The 1989 *Framework* definition of relevance was that information is relevant only if it actually makes a difference in users' decisions. However, users consider a variety of information from many sources, and the extent to which a decision is affected by information about a particular economic phenomenon is difficult, if not impossible, to determine, even after the fact.

BC2.14 In contrast, whether information is capable of making a difference in a decision (relevance as defined in the 2010 *Conceptual Framework*) can be determined. One of the primary purposes of publishing exposure drafts and other due process documents is to seek the views of users on whether information that would be required by proposed Standards is capable of making a difference in their decisions. The Board also assesses relevance by meeting users to discuss proposed Standards, potential agenda decisions, effects on reported information of applying recently implemented Standards and other matters.

Predictive and confirmatory value (2010) (paragraphs 2.7–2.10)

BC2.15 Many decisions by investors, lenders and other creditors are based on implicit or explicit predictions about the amount and timing of the return on an equity investment, loan or other debt instrument. Consequently, information is capable of making a difference in one of those decisions only if it will help users to make new predictions, confirm or correct prior predictions or both (which is the definition of predictive or confirmatory value).

BC2.16 The 1989 *Framework* identified predictive value and confirmatory value as components of relevance, and Concepts Statement 2 referred to predictive value and feedback value. The Board concluded that confirmatory value and feedback value were intended to have the same meaning. The Board and the FASB agreed that both boards would use the same term (confirmatory value) to avoid giving the impression that the two frameworks were intended to be different.

The difference between predictive value and related statistical terms (2010)

BC2.17 Predictive value, as used in the *Conceptual Framework*, is not the same as predictability and persistence as used in statistics. Information has predictive value if it can be used in making predictions about the eventual outcomes of past or current events. In contrast, statisticians use predictability to refer to the accuracy with which it is possible to foretell the next number in a series and persistence to refer to the tendency of a series of numbers to continue to change as it has changed in the past.

Materiality (2010) (paragraph 2.11)

BC2.18 Concepts Statement 2 and the 1989 *Framework* discussed materiality and defined it similarly. Concepts Statement 2 described materiality as a constraint on financial reporting that can be considered only together with the qualitative characteristics, especially relevance and faithful representation. The 1989 *Framework*, on the other hand, discussed materiality as an aspect of relevance and did not indicate that materiality has a role in relation to the other qualitative characteristics.

BC2.19 The 2006 Discussion Paper and the 2008 Exposure Draft proposed that materiality is a pervasive constraint in financial reporting because it is pertinent to all of the qualitative characteristics. However, some respondents to the 2008 Exposure Draft agreed that although materiality is pervasive, it is not a constraint on a reporting entity's ability to report information. Rather, materiality is an aspect of relevance, because immaterial information does not affect a user's decision. Furthermore, a standard-setter does not consider materiality when developing standards because it is an entity-specific consideration. The boards agreed with those views and concluded that materiality is an aspect of relevance that applies at the individual entity level.

Materiality (2018)

BC2.20 In revising the *Conceptual Framework* in 2018, the Board concluded that the concept of materiality is described clearly in the 2010 *Conceptual Framework*. Hence, the Board did not amend that description of materiality, except to clarify that the users mentioned in the description are the primary users of general purpose financial reports, as described in paragraph 1.5 of the *Conceptual Framework*. This clarification emphasises that decisions about materiality are intended to reflect the needs of the primary users, not the needs of any other group.

Faithful representation (paragraphs 2.12–2.19)

BC2.21 The discussion of faithful representation in Chapter 3 of the 2010 *Conceptual Framework* differed from that in the previous frameworks in two significant ways. First, it used the term 'faithful representation' instead of the term 'reliability'. Second, substance over form, prudence (conservatism) and verifiability, which had been aspects of reliability in Concepts Statement 2 and the 1989 *Framework*, were not considered aspects of faithful representation in the 2010 *Conceptual Framework*. References to substance over form and prudence were removed in 2010 for the reasons described in paragraphs BC2.32 and BC2.34, but they were reinstated, with clarifications, in the 2018 *Conceptual Framework*. Since 2010, verifiability has been described as an enhancing qualitative characteristic rather than as part of this fundamental qualitative characteristic (see paragraphs 2.30–2.32).

Replacement of the term 'reliability' (2010)

BC2.22 Concepts Statement 2 and the 1989 *Framework* used the term 'reliability' to describe what is now called faithful representation.

BC2.23 Concepts Statement 2 listed representational faithfulness, verifiability and neutrality as aspects of reliability and discussed completeness as part of representational faithfulness.

BC2.24 The 1989 *Framework* said:

> Information has the quality of reliability when it is free from material error and bias and can be depended upon by users to represent faithfully that which it either purports to represent or could reasonably be expected to represent.
>
> The 1989 *Framework* also discussed substance over form, neutrality, prudence and completeness as aspects of faithful representation.

BC2.25 Unfortunately, neither framework clearly conveyed the meaning of reliability. The comments of respondents to numerous proposed standards indicated a lack of a common understanding of the term 'reliability'. Some focused on verifiability or free from material error to the virtual exclusion of faithful representation. Others focused more on faithful representation, perhaps combined with neutrality. Some apparently think that reliability refers primarily to precision.

BC2.26 Because attempts to explain what reliability was intended to mean in this context have proved unsuccessful, the Board sought a different term that would more clearly convey the intended meaning. The term 'faithful representation', the faithful depiction in financial reports of economic phenomena, was the result of that search. That term encompasses the main characteristics that the previous frameworks included as aspects of reliability.

BC2.27 Many respondents to the 2006 Discussion Paper and the 2008 Exposure Draft opposed the Board's preliminary decision to replace 'reliability' with 'faithful representation'. Some said that the Board could have better explained what reliable means rather than replacing the term. However, many respondents who made those comments assigned a different meaning to reliability from what the Board meant. In particular, many respondents' descriptions of reliability more closely resembled the Board's notion of verifiability than its notion of reliability. Those comments led the Board to affirm its decision to replace the term 'reliability' with 'faithful representation'.

Retention of the term 'faithful representation' (2018)

BC2.28 In developing the 2018 *Conceptual Framework*, the Board considered whether to reinstate the term 'reliability' as a label for the qualitative characteristic now called 'faithful representation'. Arguments given for such a reinstatement by some stakeholders included:

(a) the term 'reliability' is clearer and better understood than the term 'faithful representation'.

(b) the 2010 *Conceptual Framework* implies that anything can be faithfully represented if sufficient explanatory information is given. This interpretation of faithful representation would allow the recognition of items that cannot be measured reliably. Consequently, the qualitative characteristic of faithful representation does not act as an effective filter when identifying the types of information to be included in financial statements.

(c) the 1989 *Framework* acknowledged a trade-off between the qualitative characteristics of relevance and reliability. More relevant information may lack reliability and more reliable information may lack relevance. Some respondents expressed the view that this trade-off was missing in the 2010 *Conceptual Framework* (see paragraphs BC2.52–BC2.57).

(d) the idea that financial statements should be credible, that is, that users need assurance that they can depend on financial statements to faithfully represent what they purport to represent, is a key concept that should be acknowledged in the *Conceptual Framework*. Treating that concept solely as an enhancing qualitative characteristic (verifiability, see paragraphs BC2.60–BC2.62) gives it too little weight.

BC2.29 The Board noted that the notion of reliability was used in two different ways in Standards:

(a) to mean that the level of measurement uncertainty is tolerable. This use of the word reflects the recognition criteria included in the 1989 *Framework* (and not reviewed in amending the 1989 *Framework* in 2010)—an item that meets the definition of an element is recognised only if it is probable there will be a flow of economic benefits and it has a cost or value that can be measured with reliability.

(b) to refer to a qualitative characteristic of useful financial information—the characteristic previously called 'reliability' and now called 'faithful representation'. This use of reliability is much less frequent in Standards.

BC2.30 The decision to change from the term 'reliability' to the term 'faithful representation' was made to avoid confusion between the two uses of the word 'reliability' described in paragraph BC2.29. The responses both to the 2013 Discussion Paper and the 2015 Exposure Draft seemed to confirm that many respondents continue to equate the word 'reliability' with a tolerable level of measurement uncertainty, not with the qualitative characteristic described in the 1989 *Framework*. Hence, the Board retained the term 'faithful representation' as the label for the qualitative characteristic previously called 'reliability'. However, to address concerns that the 2010 *Conceptual Framework* did not adequately discuss the role of measurement uncertainty in financial reporting, the Board included in the 2018 *Conceptual Framework* a discussion of how measurement uncertainty affects the usefulness of financial information (see paragraphs 2.19, 2.22 and BC2.46–BC2.49). Furthermore, the 2018 *Conceptual Framework* discusses the role of measurement uncertainty in decisions about recognition and measurement (see paragraphs 5.19–5.23 and 6.60).

BC2.31 Following the 2018 amendments to the discussion of prudence and substance over form (see paragraphs BC2.37–BC2.45 and BC2.33), the description of the qualitative characteristic of reliability in the 1989 *Framework* and the description of the qualitative characteristic of faithful representation in the 2018 *Conceptual Framework* are substantially aligned. Table 2.1 compares those descriptions.

Table 2.1—Reliability in the 1989 *Framework* and faithful representation in the 2018 *Conceptual Framework*

1989 *Framework* **Reliability**	2018 *Conceptual Framework* **Faithful representation**
Can be depended on by users to faithfully represent what it purports to represent	Faithfully represents the phenomena that it purports to represent (see paragraph 2.12)
Complete	Complete (see paragraph 2.14)
Neutral	Neutral (see paragraph 2.15)
Free from material error or bias	Free from error and neutral (see paragraphs 2.18 and 2.15)
Substance over form	Substance over form (see paragraph 2.12)

1989 *Framework* Reliability	2018 *Conceptual Framework* Faithful representation
Prudence	Prudence (see paragraphs 2.16–2.17)

Substance over form (2010) (paragraph 2.12)

BC2.32 In the 2010 *Conceptual Framework*, substance over form was not considered a separate component of faithful representation because the Board concluded that it would be redundant. Faithful representation means that financial information represents the substance of an economic phenomenon rather than merely representing its legal form. Representing a legal form that differs from the economic substance of the underlying economic phenomenon could not result in a faithful representation.

Substance over form (2018)

BC2.33 In developing the 2018 *Conceptual Framework*, the Board noted that some stakeholders had inferred that the 2010 deletion of the reference to substance over form meant that the Board was no longer committed to depicting the substance of an economic phenomenon. The Board did not intend to imply such a change. Accordingly, to avoid any further misunderstandings and to highlight the Board's intention, the Board reinstated in paragraph 2.12 of the 2018 *Conceptual Framework* an explicit reference to the need to faithfully represent the substance of an economic phenomenon. The Board explained further how to provide a faithful representation of the substance of contractual rights and contractual obligations in paragraphs 4.59–4.62 of the 2018 *Conceptual Framework*.

Prudence and neutrality (2010) (paragraph 2.15)

BC2.34 Chapter 2 of the 2010 *Conceptual Framework* did not include prudence or conservatism as an aspect of faithful representation because the Board concluded then that including either would be inconsistent with neutrality. Some respondents to the 2006 Discussion Paper and the 2008 Exposure Draft disagreed with that view. They said that the framework should include conservatism, prudence or both. They said that bias should not always be assumed to be undesirable, especially in circumstances when bias, in their view, produces information that is more relevant to some users.

BC2.35 Deliberately reflecting conservative estimates of assets, liabilities, income or equity has sometimes been considered desirable to counteract the effects of some management estimates that have been perceived as excessively optimistic. However, even with the prohibitions against deliberate misstatement that appeared in the 1989 *Framework*, an admonition to be prudent is likely to lead to a bias. Understating assets or overstating liabilities in one period frequently leads to overstating financial performance in later periods—a result that cannot be described as prudent or neutral.

BC2.36 Other respondents to the 2008 Exposure Draft said that neutrality is impossible to achieve. In their view, relevant information must have purpose, and information with a purpose is not neutral. In other words, because financial reporting is a tool to influence decision-making, it cannot be neutral. Obviously, reported financial information is expected to influence the actions of users of that information, and the mere fact that many users take similar actions on the basis of reported information does not demonstrate a lack of neutrality. The Board does not attempt to encourage or predict specific actions of users. If financial information is biased in a way that encourages users to take or avoid predetermined actions, that information is not neutral.

Prudence (2018) (paragraphs 2.16–2.17)

BC2.37 In developing the 2018 *Conceptual Framework*, the Board noted that different stakeholders apply the term 'prudence' to mean different things. In particular:

(a) some use it to refer to being cautious when making judgements under conditions of uncertainty, but without employing more caution in judgements relating to income or assets than in those relating to expenses or liabilities ('cautious prudence'—see paragraphs BC2.39–BC2.40).

(b) others use it to refer to applying systematic asymmetry—expenses are recognised at an earlier stage than is income ('asymmetric prudence'—see paragraphs BC2.41–BC2.45). Stakeholders expressed a range of views on how to achieve such asymmetry and to what extent it should be achieved. For example, some advocate a concept of prudence that would:

(i) require more persuasive evidence to support the recognition of income or assets than the recognition of expenses or liabilities; or

(ii) require the selection of measurement bases that recognise losses at an earlier stage than gains.

BC2.38 An understanding of prudence is linked to an understanding of the term 'neutrality'. The Board has identified two aspects of neutrality:

(a) the neutral application of accounting policies—applying the selected accounting policies in a neutral (ie unbiased) manner (see paragraph BC2.39); and

(b) the selection of neutral accounting policies—selecting accounting policies in order to provide relevant information that faithfully represents the items that it purports to represent (see paragraph BC2.44). A faithful representation requires that the depiction is neutral.

Financial information is neutral if it is not slanted, weighted, emphasised, de-emphasised or otherwise manipulated to increase the probability that the information will be received favourably or unfavourably by users.[1]

BC2.39 The Board was persuaded by the arguments made by some stakeholders that applying prudence (defined as the exercise of caution when making judgements under conditions of uncertainty) can help to achieve neutrality in applying accounting policies. Thus, 'cautious prudence' (see paragraph BC2.37(a)) can help to achieve a faithful representation of assets, liabilities, equity, income and expenses. Setting out that message clearly is expected to:

(a) help preparers, auditors and regulators to counter a natural bias that management may have towards optimism; for example, the message underlines the need to exercise care in selecting the inputs used in estimating a measure that cannot be observed directly; and

(b) help the Board to develop rigorous Standards that would reduce the risk of management bias in applying the reporting entity's accounting policies.

BC2.40 The Board found that the removal of the term 'prudence' in the 2010 revisions had led to confusion and had perhaps exacerbated the diversity in use of this term. People continued

---

1 See paragraph 2.15 of the 2018 *Conceptual Framework*.

to use the term, but did not always say clearly what they meant by it. In addition, some stakeholders said that, because the term had been removed, financial information prepared using IFRS Standards was not neutral but was, in fact, imprudent. The Board concluded that it would reduce the confusion by reintroducing the term with a clear explanation that caution works both ways, so that assets and liabilities are neither overstated nor understated. Therefore, the Board reintroduced the term 'prudence', defined as the exercise of caution when making judgements under conditions of uncertainty, in the 2018 *Conceptual Framework*.

BC2.41 Some respondents to the 2015 Exposure Draft suggested that the Board should go further and identify 'asymmetric prudence' (see paragraph BC2.37(b)) as a necessary qualitative characteristic of useful financial information for these reasons:

(a) asymmetric prudence reflects the view that investors are more interested in downside risk than upside potential;

(b) asymmetric prudence is inherent in many Standards and the *Conceptual Framework* should acknowledge this fact so that asymmetric prudence could be applied consistently when developing Standards;

(c) by limiting distributions to shareholders, asymmetric prudence minimises the risk that today's shareholders would benefit at the expense of future shareholders; and

(d) by limiting management remuneration, asymmetric prudence would reduce management's opportunism and encourage long-term growth.

BC2.42 The Board did not include asymmetric prudence in the 2018 *Conceptual Framework* because a systematic requirement for asymmetry in the accounting treatment of assets and liabilities or of income and expenses could sometimes conflict with the need for financial information to be relevant and provide a faithful representation. The Board noted that, depending on its exact nature, the requirement to apply asymmetric prudence in all circumstances might:

(a) prohibit the recognition of all unrealised gains. In some circumstances, for example, in the measurement of many financial instruments, recognising unrealised gains is necessary to provide relevant information to users of financial reports.

(b) prohibit the recognition of all unrealised gains not supported by observable market prices. In some circumstances, measuring an asset or liability at a current value (which may require the recognition of unrealised gains) provides relevant information to users of financial reports even if the current value cannot be determined directly by observing prices in an active market.

(c) permit an entity to measure an asset at an amount lower than an unbiased estimate using the measurement basis selected for that asset or to measure a liability at an amount higher than such an estimate. Such an approach cannot result in relevant information and cannot provide a faithful representation.

BC2.43 Further, the Board noted that information in financial reports may be used as an input in determining distributions to shareholders and management remuneration, but such information is only one of the factors to be considered (see paragraph BC0.41(d)).

BC2.44 However, although the Board rejected a requirement for systematic asymmetry, the Board also concluded that not all asymmetry is inconsistent with neutrality. The selection of neutral accounting policies means selecting accounting policies in a manner that is not intended to increase the probability that financial information will be received favourably or unfavourably by users. The selection of neutral accounting policies:

(a) does not require an entity to recognise the value of the entity in the statement of financial position. Paragraph 1.7 of the 2018 *Conceptual Framework* states that general purpose financial reports are not designed to show the value of a reporting entity.

(b) does not require the recognition of all assets and liabilities. Chapter 5—*Recognition and derecognition* of the 2018 *Conceptual Framework* discusses recognition criteria for assets and liabilities.

(c) does not require the measurement of all assets and liabilities at a current value. Chapter 6—*Measurement* of the 2018 *Conceptual Framework* discusses factors to consider when selecting a measurement basis. Considering those factors would not lead to such a requirement.

(d) does not prohibit impairment tests on assets measured at historical cost. Measurement at historical cost, including an impairment test, is consistent with neutrality if that measurement basis is selected without bias. The absence of bias means that the measurement basis is selected without slanting, weighting, emphasising, de-emphasising or otherwise manipulating information to increase the probability that it will be received favourably or unfavourably by users.

BC2.45 Hence, the 2018 *Conceptual Framework* acknowledges that Standards may contain asymmetric requirements. This would be the consequence of the Board taking decisions that it believes require entities to produce the most relevant information that faithfully represents what it purports to represent, rather than a consequence of applying asymmetric prudence. Such decisions are reflected in several Standards developed before the 2018 *Conceptual Framework*. For example, IAS 37 *Provisions, Contingent Liabilities and Contingent Assets* requires one recognition threshold for contingent liabilities and a different recognition threshold for contingent assets.

Measurement uncertainty (2018) (paragraph 2.19)

BC2.46 As mentioned in paragraph BC2.28(b), some respondents to the 2013 Discussion Paper expressed concern that the qualitative characteristic of faithful representation did not act as an effective filter when identifying the types of information to be included in financial statements. These respondents said that the 2010 *Conceptual Framework* did not convey the idea that a high level of measurement uncertainty can make financial information less useful.

BC2.47 Paragraph QC16 of the 2010 *Conceptual Framework* already set out the idea that an estimate might not provide useful information if the level of uncertainty in the estimate is too large:

> A faithful representation, by itself, does not necessarily result in useful information. For example, a reporting entity may receive property, plant and equipment through a government grant. Obviously, reporting that an entity acquired an asset at no cost would faithfully represent its cost, but that information would probably not be very useful. A slightly more subtle example is an estimate of the amount by which an asset's carrying amount should be adjusted to reflect an impairment in the asset's value. That estimate can be a faithful representation if the reporting entity has properly applied an appropriate process, properly described the estimate and explained any uncertainties that significantly affect the estimate. However, if the level of uncertainty in such an estimate is sufficiently large, that estimate will not be particularly useful. In other words, the relevance of the asset being faithfully represented is questionable. If there is no alternative representation that is more faithful, that estimate may provide the best available information.

BC2.48 Nevertheless, it was apparent that the link between the level of uncertainty in an estimate and its usefulness was not very visible and many readers of the 2010 *Conceptual*

Framework seemed to overlook it. Consequently, the 2015 Exposure Draft discussed how measurement uncertainty could affect the relevance of financial information. Respondents to the 2015 Exposure Draft welcomed the discussion of measurement uncertainty. However, some argued that measurement uncertainty is an aspect of the fundamental qualitative characteristic of faithful representation rather than an aspect of relevance. The Board agreed with these arguments noting that:

(a) measurement uncertainty makes information less verifiable. As explained in paragraph 2.30 of the 2018 *Conceptual Framework*, verifiability helps to assure users of financial statements that information faithfully represents what it purports to represent. The higher the level of measurement uncertainty, the less assurance users have that a particular estimate provides a faithful representation of the phenomenon. Thus, measurement uncertainty affects whether economic phenomena can be faithfully represented.

(b) paragraphs 2.20–2.21 of the 2018 *Conceptual Framework* describe the most efficient and effective process of applying the fundamental qualitative characteristics. In line with that description, the qualitative characteristic of relevance is concerned with what particular piece of information is capable of being useful to users. On the other hand, the qualitative characteristic of faithful representation is concerned with whether that information can provide a faithful representation. Thus, measurement uncertainty associated with the estimation process does not affect relevance; it affects whether that measure can be provided in a way that produces a faithful representation.

(c) even if information is subject to a high level of measurement uncertainty, it can be relevant. For example, if the underlying phenomenon is subject to significant risks and uncertainties, a highly uncertain measure may provide the only relevant information about that phenomenon.

BC2.49 Hence, the 2018 *Conceptual Framework* describes measurement uncertainty as a factor that can affect whether it is possible to provide a faithful representation. In addition, the Board noted that addressing measurement uncertainty in the discussion of faithful representation is more consistent with a notion of a trade-off between the two fundamental qualitative characteristics—relevance and faithful representation (see paragraphs 2.22 and BC2.52–BC2.56).

Can faithful representation be empirically measured? (2010)

BC2.50 Empirical accounting researchers have accumulated considerable evidence, through correlation with changes in the market prices of entities' equity or debt instruments, supporting financial information that is relevant and provides a faithful representation. However, such studies have not provided techniques for empirically measuring faithful representation apart from relevance.

BC2.51 Both previous frameworks discussed the desirability of providing statistical information about how faithfully a financial measure is represented. That would not be unprecedented. Other statistical information is sometimes reflected in financial reports. For example, some entities disclose value at risk from derivative financial instruments and similar positions. The Board expects that the use of statistical concepts for financial reporting in some situations will continue to be important. Unfortunately, the Board and the FASB have not identified any way to quantify the faithfulness of the representations in a financial report.

Applying the fundamental qualitative characteristics (2018) (paragraphs 2.20–2.22)

BC2.52 In developing the 2018 *Conceptual Framework*, the Board discussed whether a trade-off may need to be made in applying the fundamental qualitative characteristics.

BC2.53 The notion of a trade-off between relevance and reliability—then both identified as qualitative characteristics of useful financial information—was present in the 1989 *Framework*. The 2010 *Conceptual Framework* did not mention such a trade-off but referred to the need for both characteristics—relevance and faithful representation—to be present for information to be useful. It further stated that neither a faithful representation of an irrelevant phenomenon nor an unfaithful representation of a relevant phenomenon helps users to make useful decisions. The discussion in paragraph QC16 of the 2010 *Conceptual Framework* of uncertainty in estimates[1] implied that a trade-off may need to be made between relevance and faithful representation (see paragraph BC2.47).

BC2.54 Some respondents to the 2013 Discussion Paper expressed concern about the lack of discussion of the notion of a trade-off between qualitative characteristics in the 2010 *Conceptual Framework*. Their main concern seemed to relate to the relationship between the relevance of information and the tolerable level of measurement uncertainty for that information.

BC2.55 As explained in paragraphs BC2.48–BC2.49, in the 2018 *Conceptual Framework* the Board described measurement uncertainty as a factor that can affect whether it is possible to provide a faithful representation. Further, the Board clarified in paragraph 2.22 that following the process described in paragraphs 2.20–2.21 a trade-off may need to be made between relevance and faithful representation. One case when such a trade-off may need to be made is when a high level of measurement uncertainty makes it questionable whether an estimate would provide a sufficiently faithful representation of an economic phenomenon. The material in paragraph 2.22 builds on the discussion of measurement uncertainty in paragraph QC16 of the 2010 *Conceptual Framework* (see paragraph BC2.47).

BC2.56 The Board concluded that an explicit acknowledgement of the trade-off between relevance and measurement uncertainty would help to explain why, in some cases, an estimate with a high level of measurement uncertainty might, nevertheless, provide useful information—for example, in cases when the only relevant information is a highly uncertain estimate.

BC2.57 In addition, the Board updated the terminology used in the description of the process of applying fundamental qualitative characteristics. To be consistent with the description of relevance in paragraph 2.6 of the 2018 *Conceptual Framework* and to avoid confusion with the use of the term 'potential' in the definition of an economic resource (see paragraphs BC4.8–BC4.9), the Board replaced the phrase 'has the potential to be' with 'is capable of being' in paragraph 2.21.

---

[1] In the context of paragraph QC16 of the 2010 *Conceptual Framework*, uncertainty of estimates refers to what the 2018 *Conceptual Framework* calls measurement uncertainty.

Enhancing qualitative characteristics

Comparability (2010) (paragraphs 2.24–2.29)

BC2.58 Comparability was an important concept in both the 1989 *Framework* and Concepts Statement 2, but the two previous frameworks disagreed on its importance. The 1989 *Framework* stated that comparability is as important as relevance and faithful representation.[1] Concepts Statement 2 described comparability as a quality of the relationship between two or more pieces of information that, although important, is secondary to relevance and faithful representation.

BC2.59 Relevant information that provides a faithful representation is most useful if it can be readily compared with similar information reported by other entities and by the same entity in other periods. One of the most important reasons that Standards are needed is to increase the comparability of reported financial information. However, even if it is not readily comparable, information that is relevant and faithfully represents what it purports to represent is still useful. Comparable information, however, is not useful if it is not relevant and may mislead if it does not faithfully represent what it purports to represent. Therefore, comparability is considered an enhancing qualitative characteristic instead of a fundamental qualitative characteristic.

Verifiability (2010) (paragraphs 2.30–2.32)

BC2.60 Verifiable information can be used with confidence. Lack of verifiability does not necessarily render information useless, but users are likely to be more cautious because there is a greater risk that the information does not faithfully represent what it purports to represent.

BC2.61 The 1989 *Framework* did not explicitly include verifiability as an aspect of reliability, but Concepts Statement 2 did. However, the two frameworks are not as different as it might appear because the definition of reliability in the 1989 *Framework* contained the phrase 'and can be depended upon by users', which implies that users need assurance on the information.

BC2.62 The 2006 Discussion Paper stated that reported financial information should be verifiable to assure users that it is free from material error and bias and can be depended on to represent what it purports to represent. Therefore, verifiability was considered an aspect of faithful representation. Some respondents pointed out that including verifiability as an aspect of faithful representation could result in excluding information that is not readily verifiable. Those respondents recognised that many forward-looking estimates that are very important in providing relevant financial information (for example, expected cash flows, useful lives and residual values) cannot be directly verified. However, excluding information about those estimates would make the financial reports much less useful. The Board agreed and repositioned verifiability as an enhancing qualitative characteristic, very desirable but not necessarily required.

Timeliness (2010) (paragraph 2.33)

BC2.63 The 1989 *Framework* discussed timeliness as a constraint that could rob information of relevance. Concepts Statement 2 described timeliness as an aspect of relevance. However,

---

[1] The term 'reliability' was used instead of 'faithful representation', but the meaning was intended to be similar.

the substance of timeliness as discussed in those two previous frameworks was essentially the same.

BC2.64 The 2006 Discussion Paper described timeliness as an aspect of relevance. However, some respondents pointed out that timeliness is not part of relevance in the same sense that predictive and confirmatory value are. The Board was persuaded that timeliness is different from the other components of relevance.

BC2.65 Timeliness is very desirable, but it is not as critical as relevance and faithful representation. Timely information is useful only if it is relevant and faithfully represents what it purports to represent. In contrast, relevant information that provides a faithful representation may still be useful (especially for confirmatory purposes) even if it is not reported in as timely a manner as would be desirable.

Understandability (2010) (paragraphs 2.34–2.36)

BC2.66 Both the 1989 *Framework* and Concepts Statement 2 included understandability, a qualitative characteristic that enables users to comprehend the information and therefore make it useful for making decisions. Both frameworks also similarly described that for financial information to be understandable, users should have a reasonable degree of financial knowledge and a willingness to study the information with reasonable diligence.

BC2.67 Despite those discussions of understandability and users' responsibilities for understanding financial reports, misunderstanding persists. For example, some have expressed the view that a new accounting method should not be implemented because some users might not understand it, even though the new accounting method would result in reporting financial information that is useful for decision-making. They imply that understandability is more important than relevance.

BC2.68 If understandability considerations were fundamental, it might be appropriate to avoid reporting information about very complicated things even if the information is relevant and provides a faithful representation. Classifying understandability as an enhancing qualitative characteristic is intended to indicate that information that is difficult to understand should be presented and explained as clearly as possible.

BC2.69 To clarify another frequently misunderstood point, since 2010 the *Conceptual Framework* has explained that users are responsible for actually studying reported financial information with reasonable diligence rather than only being willing to do so (which was the statement in the previous frameworks). In addition, since 2010 the *Conceptual Framework* has stated that users may need to seek the aid of advisers to understand economic phenomena that are particularly complex.

Qualitative characteristics not included (2010)

BC2.70 Transparency, high quality, internal consistency, true and fair view or fair presentation and credibility have been suggested as desirable qualitative characteristics of financial information. However, transparency, high quality, internal consistency, true and fair view or fair presentation are different words to describe information that has the qualitative characteristics of relevance and representational faithfulness enhanced by comparability, verifiability, timeliness and understandability. Credibility is similar but also implies trustworthiness of a reporting entity's management.

BC2.71 Interested parties sometimes suggested other criteria for standard-setting decisions, and the Board has at times cited some of those criteria as part of the rationale for some decisions.

Those criteria include simplicity, operationality, practicability or practicality, and acceptability.

BC2.72 Those criteria are not qualitative characteristics. Instead, they are part of the overall weighing of benefits and costs of providing useful financial information. For example, a simpler method may be less costly to apply than a more complex method. In some circumstances, a simpler method may result in information that is essentially the same as, but somewhat less precise than, information produced by a more complex method. In that situation, a standard-setter would include the decrease in faithful representation and the decrease in implementation cost in weighing benefits against costs.

The cost constraint on useful financial reporting (2010) (paragraphs 2.39–2.43)

BC2.73 Cost is a pervasive constraint that standard-setters, as well as providers and users of financial information, should keep in mind when considering the benefits of a possible new financial reporting requirement. Cost is not a qualitative characteristic of information. It is a characteristic of the process used to provide the information.

BC2.74 The Board has attempted and continues to attempt to develop more structured methods of obtaining information about the cost of gathering and processing the information that proposed Standards would require entities to provide. The primary method used is to request interested parties, sometimes formally (such as by field tests and questionnaires), to submit cost and benefit information for a specific proposal that is quantified to the extent feasible. Those requests have resulted in helpful information and have led directly to changes to proposed requirements to reduce the costs without significantly reducing the related benefits.

CHAPTER 3—FINANCIAL STATEMENTS AND THE REPORTING ENTITY

from paragraph

FOCUS ON FINANCIAL STATEMENTS	**BC3.1**
OBJECTIVE AND SCOPE OF FINANCIAL STATEMENTS	**BC3.3**
Information about risks	BC3.7
PERSPECTIVE ADOPTED IN FINANCIAL STATEMENTS	**BC3.9**
GOING CONCERN ASSUMPTION	**BC3.11**
THE REPORTING ENTITY	**BC3.12**
Description and boundary of the reporting entity	BC3.13
Combined financial statements	BC3.20
Consolidated and unconsolidated financial statements	BC3.22
Joint control and significant influence	BC3.26

Focus on financial statements (paragraph 3.1)

BC3.1 Chapter 1 sets the objective of general purpose financial reporting. Chapter 2 discusses the qualitative characteristics of financial information that is useful for achieving that objective. Those qualitative characteristics apply to both financial information provided in financial statements and financial information provided in other financial reports.

BC3.2 Financial statements are a central part of financial reporting and most issues that the Board addresses involve financial statements. Moreover, addressing issues related to other forms of financial reporting could have substantially delayed completion of the 2018 *Conceptual Framework*, thus delaying the improvements it brought. Consequently, Chapters 3–8 of the 2018 *Conceptual Framework* focus on information provided in financial statements and do not address other forms of financial reporting, for example, management commentary, interim financial reports, press releases and supplementary material provided for analysis.[1]

Objective and scope of financial statements (paragraphs 3.2–3.3)

BC3.3 The Board based the description of the objective of financial statements in the 2018 *Conceptual Framework* on the description of the objective of general purpose financial reporting (see paragraph 1.2 of the 2018 *Conceptual Framework*) and the description of the objective of financial statements in paragraph 9 of IAS 1 *Presentation of Financial Statements*, which states:

> Financial statements are a structured representation of the financial position and financial performance of an entity. The objective of financial statements is to provide information about the financial position, financial performance and cash flows of an entity that is useful to a wide range of users in making economic decisions. Financial statements also show the results of the management's stewardship of the resources entrusted to it. To meet this objective…

BC3.4 The description of the objective of financial statements in the 2018 *Conceptual Framework* differs from the description of their objective in IAS 1 in the following ways:

  (a) to provide a link to the elements of financial statements, the description of the objective in the 2018 *Conceptual Framework* refers to:

   (i) assets, liabilities and equity instead of financial position; and

   (ii) income and expenses instead of financial performance.

  (b) the description of the objective in the 2018 *Conceptual Framework* does not refer to providing information about cash flows. Although information about cash flows is important to users of financial statements, the 2018 *Conceptual Framework* does not identify cash inflows and cash outflows as elements of financial statements.

  (c) the description of the objective in the 2018 *Conceptual Framework* expands on what makes information useful to primary users of financial statements in making decisions relating to providing resources to the entity. Information needs to be useful in assessing the prospects for future net cash inflows to the reporting

---

1 In 2010, the Board issued IFRS Practice Statement 1 *Management Commentary*—a broad, non-binding framework for the presentation of management commentary to accompany financial statements prepared in accordance with the Standards.

BC3.5 The description of the information provided in financial statements refers to the statement of financial position and the statement(s) of financial performance. A few respondents to the 2015 Exposure Draft suggested that this description should also refer to the statement of cash flows and the statement of changes in equity. They argued that making explicit references only to the statement of financial position and the statement(s) of financial performance could be interpreted as implying that these two statements are more important than statements providing information about cash flows or about contributions from holders of equity claims and distributions to those holders.

BC3.6 Paragraph 3.3(c) of the 2018 *Conceptual Framework* refers to information about cash flows and about contributions from holders of equity claims and distributions to them. The Board does not view that information as less important than information provided in the statement of financial position and the statement(s) of financial performance. Nevertheless, the 2018 *Conceptual Framework* refers only to those statements because only those statements provide a summary of recognised elements—assets, liabilities, equity, income and expenses. In addition, it is necessary to identify those statements as the place where recognition occurs because otherwise it would not be possible to describe recognition clearly. In contrast, because cash inflows and cash outflows and contributions from holders of equity claims and distributions to them are not elements of financial statements, statements providing information about those items do not provide a summary of recognised elements.

Information about risks (paragraphs 3.3(c)(i)–3.3(c)(ii))

BC3.7 The 2018 *Conceptual Framework* states that financial statements provide information about the risks arising from recognised and unrecognised items that meet the definitions of an element of financial statements. Some respondents to the 2013 Discussion Paper expressed a concern that the term 'risk' was not explicitly defined. Hence, they argued that 'information about risks' could be understood to include almost any type of information, including information that would be best reported outside financial statements. Indeed, some argued that the information about how an entity manages risks belongs outside financial statements.

BC3.8 However, the Board noted that information about the risks associated with an entity's recognised and unrecognised assets and liabilities is likely to be useful in assessing the entity's ability to generate cash flows and in assessing management's stewardship of the entity's economic resources. Thus, this information contributes to meeting the objective of financial statements.

Perspective adopted in financial statements (paragraph 3.8)

BC3.9 The 2018 *Conceptual Framework* states that financial statements provide information from the perspective of the reporting entity as a whole (often referred to as 'the entity perspective'), not from the perspective of any particular group of the entity's existing or potential investors, lenders or other creditors. This reflects the Board's view that the reporting entity is separate from its investors, lenders and other creditors (see paragraph BC1.8).

BC3.10 The Board adopted the entity perspective because it is consistent with the objective of general purpose financial reporting set out in paragraph 1.2. This objective is to provide useful information to existing and potential investors, lenders and other creditors rather

Going concern assumption (paragraph 3.9)

BC3.11 The description of the going concern assumption is brought forward from the 2010 *Conceptual Framework* largely unchanged, except that the phrase 'cease trading' replaces the phrase 'curtail materially the scale of its operations'. This change aligned the description more closely with that used in IAS 1 *Presentation of Financial Statements* and IAS 10 *Events after the Reporting Period*.

The reporting entity (paragraphs 3.10–3.18)

BC3.12 The 2010 *Conceptual Framework* did not discuss what a reporting entity is; nor did it describe how to determine what a reporting entity comprises. In developing concepts on the reporting entity for the 2018 *Conceptual Framework*, the Board considered comments received on the 2010 Exposure Draft developed jointly with the FASB[1] and comments received on the 2015 Exposure Draft.

Description and boundary of the reporting entity (paragraphs 3.10 and 3.13–3.14)

BC3.13 The 2018 *Conceptual Framework* provides a general description of a reporting entity, rather than stating who must, should or could prepare general purpose financial statements. The Board has no authority to determine who must, should or could prepare such statements.

BC3.14 When developing the description of a reporting entity for the 2018 *Conceptual Framework*, the Board considered whether that description could be improved by including material that described some key features of a reporting entity from the 2010 Exposure Draft. In particular, in the 2010 Exposure Draft the Board:

(a) described a reporting entity as a circumscribed area of economic activities whose financial information has the potential to be useful to existing and potential equity investors, lenders and other creditors who cannot directly obtain the information they need in making decisions about providing resources to an entity and in assessing whether management and the governing board of that entity have made efficient and effective use of the resources provided; and

(b) set out three features that are necessary—but not always sufficient—for identifying a reporting entity:

(i) economic activities of an entity are being conducted, have been conducted or will be conducted;

---

[1] See the Exposure Draft *Conceptual Framework for Financial Reporting—The Reporting Entity* published in March 2010.

(ii) economic activities of the entity can be objectively distinguished from those of other entities and from the economic environment in which the entity exists; and

(iii) financial information about the economic activities of that entity has the potential to be useful in making decisions about providing resources to the entity and in assessing whether the management and the governing board have made efficient and effective use of the resources provided.

BC3.15 The Board concluded that the feature mentioned in paragraph BC3.14(b)(iii) plays a role in determining the boundary of the reporting entity (see paragraph BC3.18). However, the Board did not use other material from the 2010 Exposure Draft to expand the description of the reporting entity in the 2018 *Conceptual Framework* for the following reasons:

(a) the financial statements of an entity that has never conducted and will never conduct economic activities are unlikely to provide useful information to users of financial statements; and

(b) the terms 'circumscribed area' and 'objectively distinguished' are vague and unclear, so they would not provide clear guidance on what constitutes a reporting entity.

BC3.16 In the 2015 Exposure Draft the Board proposed that the boundary of a reporting entity would be set in such a way that its financial statements provide relevant information to existing and potential investors, lenders and other creditors and faithfully represent the economic activities of the entity. It further proposed that financial statements should describe the set of economic activities included within the reporting entity.

BC3.17 Some respondents to the 2015 Exposure Draft expressed concern that the proposal would not sufficiently restrict what can constitute a reporting entity and that, as a result, financial statements could be prepared for any arbitrary collection of assets and liabilities and thus provide incomplete and therefore misleading information. In particular, they were concerned that a reporting entity that is a portion of an entity could choose to report on an incomplete set of economic activities, for example, by excluding from its financial statements the reporting entity's share of overheads. In addition, there may be difficulties in identifying which claims should be included in financial statements if the reporting entity is a portion of an entity.

BC3.18 In the light of those concerns, the Board revised the discussion of the determination of the boundary of a reporting entity. The 2018 *Conceptual Framework* explains that, in determining the boundary of a reporting entity that is not a legal entity and does not comprise only legal entities all linked by a parent-subsidiary relationship, the focus is on users' information needs. As stated in paragraph 2.4, users need information that is relevant and faithfully represents what it purports to represent. The Board concluded that the completeness and neutrality aspects of the qualitative characteristic of faithful representation are particularly important in determining the boundary of a reporting entity. For example, if the boundary of a reporting entity were determined in such a way that the boundary contains an arbitrary or incomplete set of economic activities, financial information provided in that reporting entity's financial statements would be incomplete and may also lack neutrality. Thus, if the boundary were to be determined in such a way, the resulting information would not meet users' information needs. The Board also concluded that to help users to understand what is included in a set of financial statements, those financial statements need to describe how the boundary of the reporting entity was determined and what constitutes the reporting entity.

BC3.19 Determining the boundary of a reporting entity is normally straightforward if that entity is a legal entity or if that entity comprises only legal entities all linked by a parent-subsidiary relationship. In those cases, the boundary of the legal entity or legal entities determines the boundary of the reporting entity. Determining the boundary in this way meets users' information needs.

Combined financial statements (paragraph 3.12)

BC3.20 The 2010 Exposure Draft stated that combined financial statements might provide useful information about a reporting entity that comprises entities under common control. Many of those who commented welcomed a discussion of this issue, but disagreed with restricting the preparation of combined financial statements to entities under common control.

BC3.21 The Board concluded that combined financial statements can provide useful information to users of financial statements in some circumstances. Accordingly, paragraph 3.12 of the 2018 *Conceptual Framework* acknowledges the concept of combined financial statements. However, the 2018 *Conceptual Framework* does not discuss when or how entities could prepare combined financial statements. The Board concluded that such discussion would be best developed if the Board decides in the future to develop a Standard on this topic.

Consolidated and unconsolidated financial statements (paragraphs 3.11 and 3.15–3.18)

BC3.22 The 2018 *Conceptual Framework* discusses the usefulness of financial information provided in consolidated and unconsolidated financial statements. As stated in paragraph 3.2, the objective of financial statements is to provide useful financial information to primary users of those financial statements. In the case of consolidated financial statements, the information needs of primary users may differ depending on whether their focus is on the parent (see paragraphs BC3.23–BC3.24) or on the subsidiaries (see paragraph BC3.25).

BC3.23 In developing the 2018 *Conceptual Framework*, the Board concluded that information about the assets, liabilities, equity, income and expenses of the parent with its subsidiaries is useful to existing and potential investors, lenders and other creditors of the parent (see paragraph 3.15). Consolidated financial statements provide that information.

BC3.24 The Board also concluded that information about assets, liabilities, equity, income and expenses of the parent alone is another type of information that may be useful to existing and potential investors, lenders and other creditors of the parent (see paragraph 3.17). Hence, the 2018 *Conceptual Framework* states that a parent may be required, or choose, to:

(a) prepare unconsolidated financial statements in addition to consolidated financial statements it prepares; or

(b) provide information about the assets, liabilities, equity, income and expenses of the parent alone in consolidated financial statements, in the notes.

BC3.25 Financial statements are designed to meet the common information needs of the maximum number of primary users, so they do not necessarily include some information that is useful to only a particular subset of primary users, such as investors, lenders and other creditors of a subsidiary. For example, some information about a subsidiary's assets, liabilities, equity, income and expenses may be material to the financial statements of the subsidiary, but may not be material to the consolidated financial statements of the parent. The subsidiary's own financial statements are designed to provide the primary users of its financial statements with information about the subsidiary's assets, liabilities, equity, income and expenses.

Joint control and significant influence

BC3.26 In developing the 2018 *Conceptual Framework*, the Board considered whether the *Conceptual Framework* should explain the notions of joint control and significant influence. The 2010 Exposure Draft stated that joint control and significant influence do not give rise to control. The Board still agrees with that conclusion, but sees no need to embed the notions of joint control and significant influence in the *Conceptual Framework*. Hence, the 2018 *Conceptual Framework* does not refer to these notions. In developing the 2018 *Conceptual Framework*, the Board did not discuss whether these notions should continue to play a role in standard-setting.

CONCEPTUAL FRAMEWORK FOR FINANCIAL REPORTING

from paragraph

CHAPTER 4—THE ELEMENTS OF FINANCIAL STATEMENTS

INTRODUCTION	**BC4.1**
DEFINITIONS—ISSUES COMMON TO BOTH ASSETS AND LIABILITIES	**BC4.3**
Separate definition of an economic resource	BC4.6
Deletion of the notion of an expected flow	BC4.8
Past event	BC4.15
Testing of revised definitions	BC4.19
DEFINITION OF AN ASSET	**BC4.23**
Economic resource	BC4.24
Focus on rights	BC4.28
Goodwill	BC4.32
Identifiability and separability	BC4.34
Other sources of value	BC4.35
Goods or services that are immediately consumed	BC4.37
Economic benefits available to all other parties	BC4.38
Control	BC4.40
Risks and rewards of ownership	BC4.41
Rejected suggestions	BC4.43
DEFINITION OF A LIABILITY	**BC4.44**
Obligation	**BC4.47**
No practical ability to avoid	BC4.49
Interpreting 'no practical ability to avoid'	BC4.54
Terminology	BC4.56
An obligation for one party is a right for another party	BC4.59
Transfer of an economic resource	**BC4.62**
Present obligation as a result of past events	**BC4.64**
ASSETS AND LIABILITIES	**BC4.69**
Non-reciprocal transactions	**BC4.69**
Contingent liabilities and contingent assets	**BC4.71**
Unit of account	**BC4.74**
Executory contracts	**BC4.78**
Reporting the substance of contractual rights and obligations	**BC4.88**

DEFINITION OF EQUITY	**BC4.89**
DEFINITIONS OF INCOME AND EXPENSES	**BC4.93**
Income and expenses defined in terms of changes in assets and liabilities	BC4.93
Types of income and expenses	BC4.96
OTHER POSSIBLE DEFINITIONS	**BC4.97**

Introduction

BC4.1   The 2010 *Conceptual Framework*, and previously the 1989 *Framework*, defined the following elements of financial statements:

(a) an asset—as a resource controlled by the entity as a result of past events and from which future economic benefits are expected to flow to the entity;

(b) a liability—as a present obligation of the entity arising from past events, the settlement of which is expected to result in an outflow from the entity of resources embodying economic benefits;

(c) equity—as the residual interest in the assets of the entity after deducting all its liabilities;

(d) income—as increases in economic benefits during the accounting period in the form of inflows or enhancements of assets or decreases of liabilities that result in increases in equity, other than those relating to contributions from equity participants; and

(e) expenses—as decreases in economic benefits during the accounting period in the form of outflows or depletions of assets or incurrences of liabilities that result in decreases in equity, other than those relating to distributions to equity participants.

BC4.2   In the 2018 *Conceptual Framework* the Board amended these definitions.

Definitions—issues common to both assets and liabilities

BC4.3   The Board found the definitions of an asset and a liability in the 2010 *Conceptual Framework* to be useful for solving many issues in standard-setting. However, some aspects of those definitions caused confusion in practice because:

(a) the explicit reference in the definitions of an asset and a liability to the flows of economic benefits blurred the distinction between the economic resource or obligation and the resulting flows of economic benefits; and

(b) some readers interpreted the term 'expected' as a probability threshold. In addition, some readers were unclear about the relationship between the terms 'expected' in the definitions and 'probable' in the recognition criteria.

BC4.4   To address these issues, and for the reasons given in paragraphs BC4.6–BC4.18, the Board revised the definitions to read as follows:

(a) an asset is a present economic resource controlled by the entity as a result of past events;

(b) a liability is a present obligation of the entity to transfer an economic resource as a result of past events; and

(c) an economic resource is a right that has the potential to produce economic benefits.

BC4.5 Supporting guidance for the definition of an asset is discussed in paragraphs BC4.23–BC4.43 and for the definition of a liability in paragraphs BC4.44–BC4.68.

Separate definition of an economic resource (paragraph 4.4)

BC4.6 The main structural change from the 2010 *Conceptual Framework* definitions is the introduction of a separate definition of an economic resource. This moved the references to future flows of economic benefits so that they now appear in the supporting definition of an economic resource instead of in the definitions of an asset and a liability.

BC4.7 The Board concluded that this separation would help to remove the confusion mentioned in paragraph BC4.3(a). It emphasises more clearly that an asset (or liability) is an economic resource (or obligation) and that it is not the ultimate inflow (or outflow) of economic benefits that the economic resource (or obligation) may produce. This approach also streamlines the definitions and shows more clearly the parallels between assets and liabilities.

Deletion of the notion of an expected flow (paragraphs 4.14 and 4.37)

BC4.8 The 2018 *Conceptual Framework* replaces the notion used in the 2010 *Conceptual Framework* that an inflow or outflow of resources is 'expected' with the concept that an asset (or liability) 'has the potential to produce economic benefits' (or 'has the potential to require a transfer of an economic resource'). References to that concept appear in the definition of an economic resource and in the guidance supporting the definition of a liability.

BC4.9 The Board replaced the notion of an expected inflow or outflow of resources for the following reasons:

(a) removal of 'expected' appropriately focuses the definition on the economic resource or obligation. To retain a notion of expected or probable outflows or inflows could exclude many items that are clearly assets and liabilities, for example, out-of-the money purchased and written options, insurance contracts and obligations to transfer an economic resource if a specified uncertain future event occurs (see paragraph BC4.63).

(b) the notion of expected flows is unhelpful because interpretations of this term can vary widely and are often tied to a notion of a threshold level of probability.

BC4.10 The 2013 Discussion Paper used the term 'capable of' producing economic benefits rather than 'has the potential to'. However, 'capable of' is already used in the discussion of relevance in paragraphs 2.6–2.7 of the 2018 *Conceptual Framework*. It could be confusing to use the term 'capable' with one meaning describing what information is relevant and with a different meaning in defining an economic resource. To avoid such confusion, the Board introduced the phrase 'has the potential to' in the definition of an economic resource.

BC4.11 The phrase 'has the potential to produce economic benefits' (or similarly 'has the potential to require a transfer of an economic resource') captures the following points:

(a) it is not sufficient that the economic benefits may arise in the future. Those economic benefits must arise from some feature that already exists within the economic resource. For example, a purchased option has the potential to produce economic benefits for the holder, but only because the option already contains a right that will permit the holder to exercise the option.

(b) the definition is not intended to impose a minimum probability threshold. The important thing is that in at least one circumstance the economic resource will produce economic benefits.

BC4.12 Some stakeholders stated that the Board should retain the notion of an expected inflow or outflow of resources. They stated that users and preparers of financial statements do not regard an item as an asset if inflows of economic benefits are not expected or are not at least reasonably possible. Those respondents argued that the revised definitions would considerably widen the range of items identified as assets and liabilities, which might lead to:

(a) pressure to identify every possible asset and liability, imposing a significant operational burden for little benefit if ultimately the asset or liability is not recognised or is measured at nil;

(b) recognition as assets and liabilities of more items that are uncertain, improbable or hard to measure, unless the recognition criteria are made more robust;

(c) a presumption that, in principle, all assets and liabilities should be recognised even if inflows or outflows are not expected; and

(d) pressure to provide in the notes irrelevant information about unrecognised assets and liabilities for which inflows or outflows are unlikely.

BC4.13 The Board concluded that removing the notion of 'expected'—interpreted by some as a probability threshold—would not impose a significant operational burden. In practice, an entity considers the definitions of an asset and a liability and recognition criteria at the same time to identify those assets and liabilities that the entity might need to recognise, or about which it might need to provide information in the notes.

BC4.14 In addition, the Board concluded that stakeholders' concerns about recognising assets or liabilities when the probability of an inflow or outflow of economic benefits is low are best addressed in decisions about recognition, not in the definitions (see paragraphs 4.15, 4.38, 5.15–5.17 and BC5.15–BC5.20). This approach is consistent with how the Board had applied the 2010 *Conceptual Framework* definitions for several years.

Past event (paragraphs 4.26 and 4.42–4.47)

BC4.15 In the 2018 *Conceptual Framework*:

(a) the phrase 'as a result of past events' remains in the definitions of an asset and a liability; and

(b) the word 'present' remains in the definition of a liability and is inserted in the definition of an asset.

BC4.16 In developing the 2018 *Conceptual Framework* the Board considered whether references to both 'present' and 'as a result of past events' are needed in the definitions of an asset and a liability.

BC4.17 The Board did not identify any significant problems that had arisen from including the phrase 'as a result of past events' in the definitions of an asset and a liability. Moreover, by identifying the past event, an entity can determine how to report that event in its financial statements; for example, how to classify and present income, expenses or cash flows arising from that event. Paragraphs BC4.64–BC4.68 discuss why the phrase 'as a result of past events' is particularly important to the revised definition of a liability. Hence, the Board retained that phrase in the definitions.

BC4.18 If a past event created an asset or liability, that fact alone does not confirm that the asset or liability still exists: it is also necessary to consider whether the entity still controls a present economic resource or is still bound by a present obligation. Thus, the Board also retained the reference to 'present' in the definition of a liability and added it to the definition of an asset. That addition emphasises the parallels between the two definitions.

Testing of revised definitions

BC4.19 In 2016, the Board analysed the effects of changes to the definitions of an asset and a liability proposed in the 2015 Exposure Draft. This exercise had two objectives:

(a) to enable both the Board and stakeholders to assess implications of the proposals for future Standards; and

(b) to help to identify any problems with the proposed definitions and supporting guidance.

BC4.20 This exercise involved:

(a) analysing the outcome of applying the proposed definitions and supporting guidance to 23 illustrative examples;

(b) identifying ways in which the proposed definitions and supporting guidance could help the Board to reach decisions in some of its current projects; and

(c) discussing the illustrative examples with participants at the meeting of World Standard-setters in September 2016.

BC4.21 The examples were selected and developed to examine questions raised by respondents to the 2015 Exposure Draft. These examples included rights and obligations that meet the definitions of an asset or a liability but have a low probability of inflows or outflows of economic benefits or have highly uncertain outcomes. The analysis of those examples explained not only why an asset or liability exists, but also why, applying the recognition criteria in Chapter 5, that asset or liability would not necessarily be recognised in the financial statements. The examples also included transactions for which respondents to the

2015 Exposure Draft thought the implications of the proposed definitions and supporting guidance were unclear and were possibly inconsistent with requirements in Standards. The analysis of those examples illustrated how and why applying the proposed definitions and supporting guidance could, in many cases, lead to conclusions consistent with the requirements in the Standards.

BC4.22 Feedback from the participants at the World Standards-setters meeting in September 2016 highlighted a few areas in which the wording of the proposed guidance was not sufficiently clear. In developing the revised definitions and supporting guidance, the Board considered this feedback together with other feedback received on the proposals.

Definition of an asset

BC4.23 This section discusses the following aspects of the definition of an asset:

(a) economic resource (see paragraphs BC4.24–BC4.27);

(b) focus on rights (see paragraphs BC4.28–BC4.39); and

(c) control (see paragraphs BC4.40–BC4.43).

Economic resource (paragraphs 4.4 and 4.14–4.18)

BC4.24 Paragraphs BC4.6–BC4.7 explain the Board's decision to introduce a separate definition of an economic resource and paragraphs BC4.8–BC4.14 discuss the Board's decision to remove the notion of expected flows from the definition of an asset and not to include that notion in the definition of an economic resource.

BC4.25 The Board concluded that the definition of an asset should refer to the economic resource, not to the resulting economic benefits. Although an asset derives its value from its potential to produce future economic benefits, what the entity controls is the present right that contains that potential. The entity does not control the future economic benefits.

BC4.26 The Board considered whether to use the term 'resource' instead of 'economic resource'. Some respondents to the 2013 Discussion Paper suggested that the term 'economic resource' is too limiting and would cover only resources that have a market value. The Board intended that the term 'economic resource' cover all resources that have the potential to produce economic benefits rather than be limited to resources for which a market currently exists. The Board chose the term 'economic resource' because it helps to emphasise that the resource in question is not, for example, a physical object, but rights over a physical object, as discussed in paragraphs 4.11–4.12 of the 2018 *Conceptual Framework*.

BC4.27 In some jurisdictions, the Board's *Conceptual Framework* is applied in the public sector and in other settings outside the financial markets, including the not-for-profit sector. Consequently, some stakeholders stated that the definition of an asset should include resources that produce benefits other than cash flows, for example, social or environmental services or benefits to the reporting entity, to other parties or to wider society. Similarly, the definition of a liability should, some stakeholders suggested, include obligations to transfer such benefits as well as obligations entered into for prudential or moral purposes, to meet expectations of a broader group of stakeholders or to maintain public support. However, the Board focuses currently on for-profit entities, and, therefore, concluded that the definition of an asset should continue to focus on resources that have the potential to produce economic benefits and that the definition of a liability should continue to focus on obligations to transfer an economic resource.

CONCEPTUAL FRAMEWORK FOR FINANCIAL REPORTING

Focus on rights (paragraphs 4.6–4.13)

BC4.28 Prior to the publication of the 2018 *Conceptual Framework*, the definition of an asset included the term 'resource'. The 2018 *Conceptual Framework* uses the term 'economic resource' and defines an economic resource and, hence, an asset as a right. To illustrate the effect of this change in emphasis, the 2018 *Conceptual Framework* states that, for a physical object, such as an item of property, plant and equipment, the economic resource is not the physical object but a set of rights over that object. Examples of such rights are listed in paragraph 4.11.

BC4.29 In developing the 2018 *Conceptual Framework*, the Board considered a suggestion made by some respondents to the 2013 Discussion Paper and a few respondents to the 2015 Exposure Draft that an asset should be defined as a right or resource, not merely as a right. These respondents argued that:

(a) some assets, for example, tangible assets, are best described as resources instead of rights. The concept of accounting for tangible assets as a set of rights is inconsistent with practice, they argued, especially when that concept is combined with the idea of 'unbundling' rights and recognising them as separate assets.

(b) unless the *Conceptual Framework* explains what factors drive the identification of the unit of account, it would be difficult to explain consistently for a single asset comprising several rights whether to recognise that single asset as a whole or to recognise some of those rights separately.

(c) a focus on rights within a larger set of rights would put more pressure on the recognition and derecognition criteria and the unit of account. Entities would need to ask themselves numerous questions in order to confirm whether new assets or liabilities exist, without providing any clear benefit to users of financial statements. These respondents argued that the rights approach has caused challenges in developing Standards and also in applying them, particularly in relation to derecognition decisions.

BC4.30 The Board noted that many assets are rights that are established by contract, legislation or similar means, for example, financial assets, a lessee's rights of use of a leased machine, and many intangible assets, such as patents. It is equally true that ownership of a physical object arises because of rights conferred by law. Furthermore, although they differ in extent, the rights conferred by full legal ownership of a physical object and by a contract to use an object for 99% (or 50% or even 1%) of its useful life are all rights of one kind or another. In addition, because of legal differences or changes, a particular set of rights may constitute full legal ownership in one jurisdiction but not in another jurisdiction, or at one date but not at another date.

BC4.31 Hence, the Board saw no advantage in defining two separate types of asset, one described in financial statements as a resource (for example, in cases of full legal ownership of a physical object) and the other described as a right (all other rights over all or part of a resource). Nevertheless, the 2018 *Conceptual Framework* notes in paragraph 4.12 that describing the set of rights as the physical object will often provide a faithful representation of those rights in the most concise and understandable way.

Goodwill

BC4.32 In developing the 2018 *Conceptual Framework*, the Board did not reconsider the conclusions in paragraphs BC313–BC323 of the Basis for Conclusions on IFRS 3 *Business*

BASIS FOR CONCLUSIONS ON THE CONCEPTUAL FRAMEWORK FOR FINANCIAL REPORTING

Combinations. Those paragraphs explain what constitutes 'core' goodwill and state that core goodwill meets the definition of an asset.

BC4.33 In finalising the 2018 *Conceptual Framework*, the Board concluded that including in the *Conceptual Framework* a reference to one particular asset—goodwill—was not appropriate. Accordingly, the 2018 *Conceptual Framework* does not mention goodwill.

Identifiability and separability

BC4.34 IAS 38 *Intangible Assets* requires an intangible asset to be identifiable, so as to distinguish it from goodwill. IAS 38 states that an asset is identifiable if it either is separable from the entity, or arises from contractual or other legal rights. Therefore, in developing the 2018 *Conceptual Framework*, the Board discussed whether the definition of an asset should require an asset to be identifiable and whether that definition should require an asset to be separable. The Board concluded that if an asset is separable or arises from contractual or other legal rights, it is likely to be easier to identify, measure and describe the asset. This may affect whether recognising the asset would provide relevant information and whether it is possible to represent it faithfully. However, the Board concluded that identifiability and separability should not form part of the definition of an asset.

Other sources of value

BC4.35 In developing the 2018 *Conceptual Framework*, the Board discussed items, such as know-how, that an entity obtains in ways other than by contract, legislation and similar means. The Board concluded that such items can be assets. It considered whether the term 'right' was broad enough to capture such items, or whether the Board should instead define an economic resource by reference to a 'right or other source of value'.

BC4.36 The Board concluded that the notion of 'other sources of value' was too vague to be useful in a formal definition. Instead, the 2018 *Conceptual Framework* explains that the term 'right' captures not merely rights obtained by contract, legislation and similar means, but also rights obtained in other ways, for example, by acquiring or creating know-how that is not in the public domain. Paragraph 4.22 further explains why the entity could control the right to use such know-how even if that know-how is not protected by a registered patent. This explanation of the concept is not new—it builds on material in paragraph 4.12 of the 2010 *Conceptual Framework*.

Goods or services that are immediately consumed (paragraph 4.8)

BC4.37 The 2018 *Conceptual Framework* clarifies that goods or services that are received and immediately consumed create a momentary right to obtain the economic benefits produced by those goods or services. That right exists momentarily until the goods or services are consumed, at which point the consumption is recognised as an expense. This is consistent with IFRS 2 *Share-based Payment*, which treats employees' services received as an asset that is immediately consumed.

Economic benefits available to all other parties (paragraph 4.9)

BC4.38 The 2018 *Conceptual Framework* explains that if rights are available to all other parties without significant cost, those rights are typically not assets for the entities that hold them. The Board included this explanation in the 2018 *Conceptual Framework* to clarify that defining an asset as a right would not compel entities to identify and recognise as assets their holdings of a possibly large array of rights.

BC4.39 There are various ways to explain why rights available to all other parties are typically not assets of a particular entity. One reason could be that such rights, for example, public rights of way over land, do not have a potential to produce for that entity economic benefits beyond those available to all other parties. An alternative or additional reason could be that such rights are not controlled by the entity—the entity cannot deny other parties access to any economic benefits that may flow from those rights.

Control (paragraphs 4.19–4.25)

BC4.40 The 2018 *Conceptual Framework* kept in the definition of an asset the requirement for the economic resource to be 'controlled by the entity'. It also introduced a definition of control. The Board built that definition on the definitions of control in IFRS 15 *Revenue from Contracts with Customers*, which defines control of an asset, and in IFRS 10 *Consolidated Financial Statements*, which defines control of an entity.[1] Although the definitions in these Standards differ, they are based on the same basic concepts—that the entity has the ability to direct the use of the asset (or of the entity) and to obtain economic benefits (or returns). The 2018 *Conceptual Framework* uses the concept of control both in the definition of an asset and in its description of a parent's control of its subsidiaries.

Risks and rewards of ownership

BC4.41 The Board considered whether the definition of an asset should incorporate the notion of exposure to risks and rewards of ownership. Some Standards identify that exposure (or the related notion of exposure to variable returns) as either an aspect of control or an indicator of control:

(a) IFRS 10 states that 'an investor controls an investee when it is exposed, or has rights, to variable returns from its involvement with the investee and has the ability to affect those returns through its power over the investee'.

(b) IFRS 15 states that one of the indicators that control of an asset has been transferred to a customer is that 'the customer has the significant risks and rewards of ownership of the asset'. The Basis for Conclusions on IFRS 15 explains that exposure to the risks and rewards of ownership of an asset may indicate control.

BC4.42 The 2018 *Conceptual Framework* explains in general terms the relationship between control and exposure to the risks and rewards of ownership. However, instead of using the phrase 'risks and rewards of ownership', the 2018 *Conceptual Framework* refers to 'exposure to significant variations in the amount of economic benefits' (see paragraph 4.24).

Rejected suggestions

BC4.43 In developing the 2018 *Conceptual Framework*, the Board considered and rejected other suggested changes to the definition and treatment of control:

(a) a suggestion to exclude a reference to control from the definition of an asset because it is implicit in the definition of an economic resource as a right that the

---

1 See paragraph 33 of IFRS 15 and paragraphs 5–7 of IFRS 10.

entity controls the resource. The Board agreed that this is implicit in the definition of an economic resource but decided that explicitly referring to control is a helpful way of structuring the definition and supporting guidance.

(b) a suggestion that the requirement for control to exist should be a recognition criterion, instead of part of the definition of an asset. A few stakeholders argued that this approach would separate two questions that are independent of each other (namely: does an asset exist? and to whom does the asset belong?). The Board did not move the reference to control into the asset recognition criteria because such a move would be unlikely to change which assets would be recognised and because the Board has identified no problems in practice that would be addressed by such a move.

(c) a suggestion that the Board should amend the definition of control to refer to 'substantially all' economic benefits. The Board noted that the reference to 'substantially all' economic benefits would be redundant, and possibly confusing, if an entity recognises only the rights it controls. For example, if an entity controls the right to obtain 20% of the economic benefits from a building, its asset is the right to obtain 20% of the economic benefits from the building. The entity would not need the right to obtain all, or even substantially all, the economic benefits from the building because its asset is not a right over the whole building. The question of whether to include a threshold such as 'substantially all' may arise when developing Standards, for example, if a Standard requires an entity to account for a group of rights as a single asset (a single unit of account).

Definition of a liability (paragraphs 4.26–4.47)

BC4.44 The 2018 *Conceptual Framework* defines a liability as a present obligation of the entity to transfer an economic resource as a result of past events. The main changes from the previous definition are as follows:

(a) deletion of the reference to an expected outflow of economic benefits. For reasons discussed in paragraphs BC4.8–BC4.14, that reference was replaced by supporting guidance explaining that an obligation to transfer an economic resource must have the potential to require the entity to transfer an economic resource to another party (see paragraph 4.37).

(b) replacement of the phrase 'resources embodying economic benefits' with the new defined term 'economic resource' (see paragraphs BC4.6–BC4.7).

BC4.45 As mentioned in paragraph BC0.15, the 2018 *Conceptual Framework* does not address classification of financial instruments with characteristics of both liabilities and equity. The Board is exploring how to distinguish liabilities from equity in its research project on Financial Instruments with Characteristics of Equity. If necessary, the *Conceptual Framework* will be updated as one possible outcome of that project. In finalising the 2018 *Conceptual Framework*, the Board sought not to add new concepts and new guidance that it may need to revisit after that research project.

BC4.46 In developing the 2018 *Conceptual Framework*, the Board concluded that for a liability to exist, three criteria must all be satisfied:

(a) the entity has an obligation (see paragraphs BC4.47–BC4.61);

(b) the obligation is to transfer an economic resource (see paragraphs BC4.62–BC4.63); and

(c) the obligation is a present obligation that exists as a result of past events (see paragraphs BC4.64–BC4.68).

Obligation (paragraphs 4.28–4.35)

BC4.47 In applying the previous definition of a liability, it was generally accepted that an entity has a present obligation to transfer an economic resource when that obligation is unconditional and legally enforceable—in such situations, the entity clearly has no ability to avoid the transfer. However, in some other situations an entity has some limited ability to avoid a future transfer. Both in developing Standards and in applying them, problems had arisen because it was unclear how limited that ability must be for an entity to have a 'present obligation'.

BC4.48 The 2018 *Conceptual Framework* defines an obligation as a duty or responsibility, as did the 2010 *Conceptual Framework*. However, to clarify the meaning of the term 'obligation', the 2018 *Conceptual Framework* states that an entity has an obligation if it has a duty or responsibility that it has no practical ability to avoid.

No practical ability to avoid (paragraphs 4.29–4.34)

BC4.49 The Board developed the 'no practical ability to avoid' criterion by considering the problems arising when:

(a) an entity does not have a legally enforceable obligation to transfer an economic resource, but its ability to avoid the transfer is limited by its customary practices, published policies or specific statements (such obligations are sometimes referred to as 'constructive obligations'); or

(b) a requirement already exists for an entity to transfer an economic resource, but the outcome of that requirement is conditional on the action that the entity itself may take.

BC4.50 Although the 2013 Discussion Paper considered those two situations separately, some respondents noted that the underlying issues are similar in both situations—the entity's ability to avoid a transfer is limited. In the 2018 *Conceptual Framework*, the 'no practical ability to avoid' criterion applies in both situations. However, the factors used to assess whether an entity has the practical ability to avoid a particular transfer would depend on the nature of the entity's duty or responsibility and would be considered when developing Standards.

BC4.51 Different Standards required different approaches to situations in which an entity can avoid a transfer of economic resources through its future action. The Board identified three views applied at that time in Standards to determine when a present obligation to transfer an economic resource has arisen:

(a) View 1—an entity must have no ability to avoid the future transfer. For example, IAS 37 *Provisions, Contingent Liabilities and Contingent Assets*, as it had been interpreted in IFRIC 21 *Levies*, required that for a present obligation to exist, the entity must have no ability, even in theory, to avoid the future transfer.

(b) View 2—an entity must have no practical ability to avoid the future transfer. For example, IAS 34 *Interim Financial Reporting* specified that, if a lease provides for variable lease payments based on the entity achieving a specified level of annual sales, an obligation can arise before that level has been achieved if that level is expected to be achieved and the entity therefore has no realistic alternative but to make the future lease payments.

(c) View 3—there need be no limits on an entity's ability to avoid the future transfer. It is sufficient that, as a consequence of a past event, the entity may have to transfer an economic resource if further conditions are met. For example, IAS 19 *Employee Benefits* required a liability to be recognised for benefits that are conditional on future employment (unvested benefits) if those benefits are given in exchange for service already provided by employees. IAS 19 did not require an entity to assess whether it has the practical ability to avoid paying those benefits.

BC4.52 In the 2018 *Conceptual Framework* the Board adopted View 2 for the following reasons:

(a) the Board rejected View 1 because when an entity has the theoretical ability to avoid transferring an economic resource but no practical ability to avoid that transfer, omitting from a list of the entity's obligations the requirement to make that transfer would exclude information that many users of financial statements would find useful. That omission would place too much emphasis on legal form and not enough weight on faithfully representing the substance of obligations that are, in practice, as binding as obligations that are legally enforceable. Moreover, if an entity has a theoretical right to take action that would avoid an obligation, but has no practical ability to exercise that right, that obligation binds the entity as effectively as if it did not have that theoretical right.

(b) the Board rejected View 3 because the term 'obligation' implies some limit on the entity's ability to avoid the transfer of an economic resource.

BC4.53 The Board rejected a suggestion made by several stakeholders to apply a threshold based on the probability of future outflows. Those respondents suggested that an entity should be regarded as having an obligation if it were probable or, perhaps, reasonably certain that the entity would transfer an economic resource. They argued that such a threshold would provide the most relevant measure of the expenses in the period. Nevertheless, in the 2018 *Conceptual Framework* the definition of a liability focuses on the existence of an obligation for the reasons set out in paragraphs BC4.9(a), BC4.52(b) and BC4.94(d). The supporting guidance focuses on what an entity is obliged to do—not on the likelihood of the possible outcomes.

Interpreting 'no practical ability to avoid'

BC4.54 The Board concluded that the factors used to assess whether an entity has the practical ability to avoid a particular transfer should depend on the nature of the entity's duty or responsibility. Applying the criterion of 'no practical ability to avoid' will require judgement. Some stakeholders were concerned that allowing preparers of financial statements to apply this criterion would lead to diverse practice and that in some circumstances entities would recognise a liability when, in the view of some of those stakeholders, the entity does not have a genuine obligation. However, the Board noted that preparers of financial statements will rarely be required to apply that criterion without further requirements and guidance. The Board will, if necessary, develop guidance on applying that criterion to particular cases as it develops Standards.

BC4.55 Paragraph 4.34 of the 2018 *Conceptual Framework* refers to actions that would have economic consequences significantly more adverse than a transfer of economic resources as an example of when an entity may have no practical ability to avoid a transfer. This is intended to mean not just that it would be economically advantageous to make the transfer. Rather, the adverse economic consequences of not making the transfer are so severe that the entity has no practical ability to avoid the transfer. Although the entity has the theoretical right to avoid the transfer, it has no practical ability to exercise that right.

Terminology

BC4.56 The Board considered whether phrases such as the following could be easier to interpret than 'no practical ability to avoid':

(a) 'no realistic alternative'; or

(b) 'little or no discretion (in practice) to avoid'.

BC4.57 These two phrases have a meaning similar to 'no practical ability to avoid'. The Board chose the phrase 'no practical ability to avoid' because it most effectively conveys the need to identify what an entity is obliged to do, instead of focusing on the probable outcome. Furthermore, it mirrors the term 'practical ability', which is applied in some Standards in assessing whether an entity controls an asset, and the term 'present ability' used for a similar purpose in paragraphs 4.20 and 4.22 of the 2018 *Conceptual Framework*.

BC4.58 Some Standards developed before the 2018 *Conceptual Framework* use the term 'constructive obligation' to refer to some circumstances that give rise to an obligation or the term 'economic compulsion' to refer to some circumstances that give rise to no obligation. The 2018 *Conceptual Framework* does not use those terms to distinguish circumstances when an obligation exists from circumstances when an obligation does not exist because the Board concluded that those terms have not proved helpful for that purpose and are not necessary.

An obligation for one party is a right for another party

BC4.59 Paragraph 4.30 of the 2018 *Conceptual Framework* states that if one party has an obligation to transfer an economic resource, it follows that another party (or parties) has a right to receive that economic resource. The Board decided that this statement would help entities to apply the definition of a liability because it may sometimes be easier to identify whether that other party (or parties) has a right than to identify whether the first party has an obligation.

BC4.60 The Board considered whether another party has any asset that it controls if the reporting entity's obligation is not legally enforceable but arises from the reporting entity's customary practices, published policies or specific statements, or is conditional on the entity's own future actions. The Board concluded that the counterparty does control an asset in such cases. According to paragraph 4.23, if an entity is the party that will obtain economic benefits produced by an economic resource, that entity controls the economic resource.

BC4.61 In developing the 2018 *Conceptual Framework*, the Board discussed whether environmental obligations are an exception to the general principle that for every obligation, a corresponding right to receive the economic resource exists. It concluded that in the case of such obligations a corresponding right is controlled by society at large—the people living in the area. They have the right to receive the services required to restore their environment. Therefore, the 2018 *Conceptual Framework* identifies no exception to the general principle.

Transfer of an economic resource (paragraphs 4.36–4.41)

BC4.62 The 2018 *Conceptual Framework* states that the second criterion for a liability is that the obligation must have the potential to require the entity to transfer an economic resource.

Paragraphs BC4.8–BC4.14 explain why the Board replaced the notion that an outflow of resources is expected with the concept that a liability has the potential to require a transfer of an economic resource.

BC4.63 An obligation to transfer an economic resource if a specified uncertain future event occurs has the potential to require a transfer of an economic resource and hence can give rise to a liability. That would be the case if the obligation is a present obligation that has arisen as a result of the past events discussed in paragraphs BC4.64–BC4.68. Such obligations are sometimes referred to as 'stand-ready obligations'. The 2018 *Conceptual Framework* does not use that term because the Board considered it unnecessary.

Present obligation as a result of past events (paragraphs 4.42–4.47)

BC4.64 The definition of a liability in the 2010 *Conceptual Framework* required a present obligation to be the result of past events but did not specify how to identify which event results in creation of a present obligation (sometimes referred to as the 'obligating event'). The 2018 *Conceptual Framework*, however, explains how to interpret the phrase 'as a result of past events'.

BC4.65 Some obligations arise from a single obligating event, for example, receiving goods. Other obligations build up over time through a continuous obligating event, for example, conducting a continuous activity.

BC4.66 In some cases, a chain of events creates an obligation. For example, an obligation may arise if a minimum threshold is reached in a period (such as a minimum amount of revenue, a minimum number of employees or a minimum amount of assets) and if the reporting entity is still operating on a specified later date. In such cases, identifying which of those events (reaching the threshold or operating on the specified date) is the obligating event can be particularly difficult. If the definition of obligations encompassed only unconditional obligations (View 1 discussed in paragraph BC4.51(a)), the explicit reference to a past event would, arguably, have been redundant. That is because under View 1 the obligating event would be the event that makes the obligation unconditional. In the example given in this paragraph that event is operating on the specified later date.

BC4.67 However, the Board adopted a broader 'no practical ability to avoid' approach (View 2 discussed in paragraph BC4.51(b)). Applying this concept, an entity may have an obligation if only some of the events in the chain have occurred: an entity could have an obligation if it has no practical ability to avoid the events that have not yet occurred. Therefore, it is important to explain which of the events in the chain must have occurred for an entity to have a present obligation 'as a result of past events'.

BC4.68 The Board concluded that the concept 'as a result of past events' means that:

(a) an entity has obtained economic benefits or taken an action.

(b) as a consequence, the entity will or may have to transfer an economic resource that it would not otherwise have had to transfer. The activity increases the magnitude of the economic resources that the entity will or may have to transfer.

Assets and liabilities

Non-reciprocal transactions

BC4.69 The Board considered whether the 2018 *Conceptual Framework* should explicitly discuss assets and liabilities that arise in non-reciprocal transactions, for example, donations, income taxes and other taxes and levies. It noted that the guidance in the 2018 *Conceptual Framework* had been developed without assuming that all transactions are reciprocal exchanges. Indeed, some guidance—in particular, the guidance supporting the liability definition—was developed with significant thought given to non-reciprocal transactions.

BC4.70 The Board concluded that its guidance supporting the definitions of an asset and a liability is equally suitable for reciprocal exchange transactions and non-reciprocal transactions. In both cases, the starting point is to identify the rights and obligations arising from the transaction. Therefore, the 2018 *Conceptual Framework* does not contain guidance that specifically addresses non-reciprocal transactions.

Contingent liabilities and contingent assets

BC4.71 The 2018 *Conceptual Framework* does not use the terms 'contingent liability' and 'contingent asset'. In IAS 37 *Provisions, Contingent Liabilities and Contingent Assets*, developed before the 2018 *Conceptual Framework*, the term 'contingent liability' is used as a collective label encompassing three categories of items that fail to meet that Standard's recognition criteria:

 (a) the first category is possible obligations whose existence is uncertain and will be confirmed only by the occurrence or non-occurrence of uncertain future events not wholly within the control of the entity. Paragraphs 4.35 and 5.14 of the 2018 *Conceptual Framework* analyse such items as cases of existence uncertainty—it is uncertain whether a liability exists.

 (b) the second category is present obligations that arise from past events but are not recognised because it is not probable that an outflow of economic resources will be required to settle them. Paragraphs 4.37–4.38 and 5.15–5.17 of the 2018 *Conceptual Framework* analyse these items as cases of liabilities with a low probability of an outflow of economic benefits.

 (c) the last category is present obligations that arise from past events but are not recognised because their amount cannot be measured with sufficient reliability. Paragraphs 2.19, 2.22 and 5.19–5.23 of the 2018 *Conceptual Framework* analyse these items as cases of liabilities that are subject to a high level of measurement uncertainty.

BC4.72 The term 'contingent liability' is not used in the 2018 *Conceptual Framework* because:

 (a) the three categories of item encompassed by the IAS 37 definition do not form a single natural class. The items in category (a) may be liabilities but are subject to existence uncertainty. The items in categories (b) and (c) are liabilities but might or might not be recognised after applying the recognition criteria described in Chapter 5—*Recognition and derecognition*.

 (b) contingent liabilities are not a further element of financial statements, additional to liabilities and equity. Moreover, some 'contingent liabilities' are liabilities, but others are not.

(c) in common usage, the term 'contingent liability' is not used in the same way as in IAS 37. It often refers to an item that may give rise to an outflow of economic resources if some uncertain future event occurs. Depending on the circumstances, an obligating event might or might not have occurred. If an obligating event has occurred, the item might be a liability subject to existence uncertainty, outcome uncertainty, measurement uncertainty or any combination of those uncertainties. The liability might be recognised or unrecognised.

BC4.73 Similar considerations apply for 'contingent assets'.

Unit of account (paragraphs 4.48–4.55)

BC4.74 It would be impossible to set out recognition requirements or a measurement basis for a particular item without selecting a unit of account to which those requirements apply. Likewise, selecting a unit of account without considering how recognition or measurement requirements would apply may not result in useful information. Therefore, the 2018 *Conceptual Framework* explains that the unit of account and recognition and measurement requirements for a particular item are all considered at the same time.

BC4.75 In developing the 2018 *Conceptual Framework*, the Board considered whether the unit of account for recognition could differ from the unit of account for measurement. In the Board's view, it is possible for items to qualify for recognition on an individual basis and to be measured on a group basis. For example, a collection of items qualifying for recognition on an individual basis:

(a) could be measured as a single unit of account when estimating their recoverable amount; or

(b) may sometimes, as a practical expedient, be measured as a portfolio.

Hence, the Board concluded that sometimes it might be appropriate to select one unit of account for recognition and a different unit of account for measurement.

BC4.76 Decisions about the unit of account are linked to decisions about recognition and measurement that are made in developing Standards. Hence, the Board concluded that decisions about selecting a unit of account will need to be made in developing Standards, not in the *Conceptual Framework*.

BC4.77 The 2018 *Conceptual Framework* includes a discussion of the factors to consider when determining which unit of account to use. The Board did not rank the factors by priority because their relative importance depends on the specific features of the item for which the entity is accounting. In the Board's view, no single ranking could be used to determine the most useful unit of account consistently for a broad range of Standards.

Executory contracts (paragraphs 4.56–4.58)

BC4.78 The 2018 *Conceptual Framework* provides revised and more extensive supporting guidance on executory contracts. It clarifies that:

(a) an executory contract establishes a combined right and obligation to exchange economic resources;

(b) that combined right and obligation to exchange economic resources are interdependent and cannot be separated; and

(c) the combined right and obligation constitute a single asset or liability.

BC4.79   Although some stakeholders expressed a view that executory contracts give rise to a right (to receive one economic resource) and a separate obligation (to transfer a second economic resource), the Board noted that the right and obligation are highly interdependent: the right to receive the first resource is conditional on fulfilling the obligation to transfer the second resource and the obligation to transfer the second resource is conditional on receiving the first resource.

BC4.80   The Board further noted that even if the parties transfer economic resources at different times, a simultaneous exchange occurs at the time of the first transfer. For example, an entity might have a contract to sell goods to a customer and receive payment from the customer at a later date. When the entity transfers the goods to the customer, it simultaneously receives a right to receive payment from the customer. At that time, the customer receives the goods and incurs an obligation to pay for them. Each party's combined right and obligation to exchange economic resources is satisfied at the time of the first transfer and replaced at that time by a new right (in this example to receive payment) or obligation (in this example to make payment).

BC4.81   The Board therefore concluded that an executory contract contains a combined right and obligation to exchange economic resources, not a right to receive one economic resource and a separate obligation to transfer another economic resource.

BC4.82   The Board considered whether the combined right and obligation to exchange economic resources could give a reporting entity both a separate asset (a right to exchange resources, equivalent to a purchased option) and a separate liability (the obligation to exchange resources, equivalent to a written option).

BC4.83   A purchased option to exchange economic resources gives the holder the right either to make an exchange or to withdraw from the exchange without penalty. Conversely, the issuer of the written option undertakes the obligation to make the exchange, if the holder exercises its right. However, if an entity is both the holder of a purchased option and the issuer of an identical written option for the same underlying exchange of economic resources:

(a)   the entity's right under its purchased option to withdraw from the exchange is nullified by its obligation to exchange if the counterparty exercises its right under the entity's written option; and

(b)   the counterparty's right under the entity's written option to withdraw from the exchange is nullified by its obligation to exchange if the entity exercises its right under its purchased option.

BC4.84   Consequently, if an entity is both the holder of a purchased option and the issuer of a written option for the same underlying exchange on the same terms, neither party has the right to avoid exchanging economic resources. It follows that for an executory contract, the terms of the contract provide for only one outcome—the exchange will occur unless both parties agree to terminate the contract. Moreover, the entity's right and obligation to exchange economic resources are so interdependent that they cannot be separated. Hence, the contract cannot be separated into more than a single asset or liability. If the exchange is on terms that are currently favourable to the reporting entity, the contract is an asset; if it is on terms that are currently unfavourable, it is a liability.

BC4.85   Some respondents to the 2015 Exposure Draft asked how the Board's conclusion on executory contracts could affect the treatment of assets and liabilities arising in a lease contract or could affect trade date accounting for financial assets:

(a)   as explained in the Basis for Conclusions on IFRS 16 *Leases*, at the commencement date, a lessee has obtained the right to use an underlying asset for a period of time and the lessor has delivered that right by making the asset available for use by the lessee. Once the lessor has performed its obligation to deliver that right, the lease contract is no longer an executory contract. The lessee controls the right-of-use asset and has a liability for the lease payments.

(b) IFRS 9 *Financial Instruments* permits 'trade date accounting' for a 'regular way' purchase or sale of a financial asset. Trade date accounting treats the financial asset as having already been delivered at the commitment (trade) date, instead of accounting for the purchase or sale contract as a derivative until settlement. IFRS 9 permits trade date accounting as a simple and practical method of managing and recording transactions that have only a short duration. In other words, permitting this method results from considering the cost constraint—from considering the relative costs and benefits of trade date accounting and settlement date accounting (the other method permitted by IFRS 9).

BC4.86 The 2018 *Conceptual Framework* does not specifically discuss recognition of executory contract assets and liabilities because it does not set out specific recognition requirements for any other types of assets and liabilities. The Board will set recognition requirements for executory contracts in developing Standards in the same way it sets recognition requirements for other assets and liabilities.

BC4.87 In the light of stakeholders' concerns, the Board considered whether the revised concepts on executory contracts could result in more assets and liabilities arising from executory contracts being recognised. In many cases in current practice, an asset or liability is not recognised for an executory contract. The Board expects that this will continue to be so. The same measurement considerations that apply to all other assets and liabilities (see Chapter 6—*Measurement*) apply also to the single asset or liability that arises from an executory contract. When a historical cost measurement basis is applied to an executory contract, the contract is typically measured at zero (which has the same practical effect as not recognising the contract) unless it is onerous. For example, the historical cost of an executory contract for the purchase of inventories is zero (assuming no transaction costs) unless the contract is onerous.

Reporting the substance of contractual rights and obligations (paragraphs 4.59–4.62)

BC4.88 As explained in paragraph 2.12, the 2018 *Conceptual Framework* explicitly states that, to provide a faithful representation of an economic phenomenon, an entity should report the substance of that phenomenon. The 2018 *Conceptual Framework* includes concepts for reporting the substance of contractual rights and contractual obligations. Those concepts drew on concepts developed by the Board in standard-setting projects. The Board decided that including the underlying concepts in the 2018 *Conceptual Framework* would help to ensure that these concepts are applied more consistently in Standards.

Definition of equity (paragraphs 4.63–4.67)

BC4.89 The 2018 *Conceptual Framework* continues:

(a) to make a binary distinction between liabilities and equity;

(b) to define equity as the residual interest in the assets of the entity after deducting all its liabilities; and

CONCEPTUAL FRAMEWORK FOR FINANCIAL REPORTING

(c) not to discuss what forms of presentation and disclosure are appropriate if an entity's equity comprises different classes of equity claims and different components of equity (see paragraphs 7.12–7.13).

BC4.90 The Board considered whether continuing to make a binary distinction between liabilities and equity is sufficient to provide users of financial statements with useful information about claims against the entity. The inherent limitation of a binary distinction between liabilities and equity is that it attempts to make a single distinction between claims that have various characteristics in varying degrees. Eliminating that binary distinction and defining a single element for all claims would allow the accounting for each type of claim to be determined individually to depict its specific characteristics. However, unless all claims are measured directly, any approach would need to identify at least one residual class of claim that would be measured indirectly by reference to the carrying amounts of assets and liabilities. Moreover, it is not possible to measure all claims directly without valuing the entire entity, which goes beyond the stated objective of general purpose financial reports. Thus, dividing claims into at least two classes is unavoidable.

BC4.91 Some respondents to the 2013 Discussion Paper suggested that defining equity directly and introducing another element (a third class of claim) may better depict claims that have some characteristics of both liabilities and equity. However, the Board concluded that introducing another element would make the classification and resulting accounting more complex. In addition, it would be necessary to determine whether changes in this third class of claim should meet the definition of income or expenses. An outcome similar to introducing a new element could instead be achieved by separately presenting different classes within liabilities or within equity.

BC4.92 The Board will further explore how to distinguish liabilities from equity in its research project on Financial Instruments with Characteristics of Equity. That research project:

(a) will consider approaches to distinguishing liabilities from equity, including approaches that could require changes to the definitions of a liability or equity in the *Conceptual Framework*. The Board will use the output from that project when it decides, in due course, whether to add to its active agenda a project to amend the relevant Standards, the *Conceptual Framework*, or both. Any decision to start an active project would require the Board to go through its due process for adding a project to its agenda.

(b) is unlikely to result in changes to the supporting guidance in paragraphs 4.28–4.35 that focuses on identifying whether the reporting entity has an obligation to transfer an economic resource. That guidance was not designed to help to distinguish liabilities from equity (see paragraph BC4.45).

Definitions of income and expenses (paragraphs 4.68–4.72)

Income and expenses defined in terms of changes in assets and liabilities

BC4.93 The 2010 *Conceptual Framework* defined income and expenses in terms of changes in assets and liabilities. A few respondents to the 2013 Discussion Paper questioned this approach. They argued that it gives undue primacy to the statement of financial position over the statement(s) of financial performance and insufficiently acknowledges the importance of accounting for transactions in the statement(s) of financial performance or of matching income and expenses.

BC4.94 The Board disagreed with these arguments, concluding that:

(a) it is incorrect to assume that the Board focuses solely or primarily on the statement of financial position. Financial statements are intended to provide information about an entity's financial position and its financial performance (see paragraph 3.3). Hence, when making decisions about recognition, measurement and presentation and disclosure, the Board considers whether the resulting information provides useful information about both an entity's financial position and its financial performance. The Board has not designated one type of information—about financial position or about financial performance—as the primary focus of financial reporting.

(b) information about transactions is relevant to users of financial statements. Hence, much of financial reporting is currently based on transactions and will continue to be so.

(c) transactions that result in income and expenses also cause changes in assets and liabilities. Consequently, identifying income and expenses necessarily leads to identifying which assets and liabilities have changed. The Board and other standard-setters have found over many years that it is more effective, efficient and rigorous to define assets and liabilities first and to define income and expenses as changes in assets and liabilities, instead of trying to define income and expenses first and then describe assets and liabilities as by-products of the recognition of income and expenses.

(d) the definitions of an asset and a liability are not merely accounting technicalities. They refer to real economic phenomena (economic resources and obligations to transfer economic resources). A statement of financial position depicting assets, liabilities and equity provides users with more relevant and understandable information about an entity's financial position than does a mere summary of amounts that have arisen as by-products of a matching process. Those amounts do not necessarily depict economic phenomena.

(e) an approach based on matching income and expenses does not define the period to which the income and expenses relate. As explained in paragraph 5.5 of the 2018 *Conceptual Framework*, if income and expenses relate to each other, they will often be recognised simultaneously because of simultaneous changes in related assets and liabilities. However, an intention to match income and expenses does not justify the recognition in the statement of financial position of items that do not meet the definitions of an asset or a liability.

BC4.95 The Board noted that no major problems had been identified with the definitions of income and expenses. Hence, the only changes made in the 2018 *Conceptual Framework* were those necessary to make the definitions of income and expenses consistent with the revised definitions of an asset and a liability.

Types of income and expenses

BC4.96 Much of the discussion of income and expenses in the 2010 *Conceptual Framework* related to their presentation and disclosure. Presentation and disclosure are discussed in Chapter 7—*Presentation and disclosure* of the 2018 *Conceptual Framework*. The rest of the discussion in the 2010 *Conceptual Framework* referred to various types of income and expenses, for example, revenue, gains and losses. That material was not included in the 2018 *Conceptual Framework*. The material was originally included to emphasise that income includes revenue and gains and that expenses include losses. The Board decided that that emphasis is now unnecessary and the implication that the *Conceptual Framework* defines subclasses of income and expenses is unhelpful. The Board does not expect the removal of that material to cause any changes in practice.

Other possible definitions

BC4.97 In developing the 2018 *Conceptual Framework*, the Board considered whether to define as elements of financial statements contributions from holders of equity claims and distributions to holders of equity claims, and cash inflows and cash outflows. Because the Board concluded that the absence of such definitions had not caused major problems, it did not include such definitions in the 2018 *Conceptual Framework*.

from paragraph

CHAPTER 5—RECOGNITION AND DERECOGNITION

RECOGNITION **BC5.1**

Relevance **BC5.12**

    Existence uncertainty **BC5.13**

    Low probability of an inflow or outflow of economic benefits **BC5.15**

Faithful representation **BC5.21**

DERECOGNITION **BC5.23**

Recognition (paragraphs 5.6–5.25)

BC5.1 The recognition criteria in the 2010 *Conceptual Framework* stated that an entity recognises an item that meets the definition of an element if:

(a) it is probable that any future economic benefit associated with the item will flow to or from the entity; and

(b) the item has a cost or value that can be measured with reliability.

BC5.2 The recognition criteria created the following problems:

(a) some Standards developed before the 2018 *Conceptual Framework* applied a probability recognition criterion, but they did not use it consistently. They used different probability thresholds which included 'probable', 'more likely than not', 'virtually certain' and 'reasonably possible'.

(b) the application of the probability criterion to some recognition questions could lead to loss of relevant information or a misleading representation of the entity's financial position or financial performance. For example, applying the criterion could prevent the recognition of some derivative financial instruments. Moreover, it could result in a gain being recognised for a transaction when no economic gain has occurred. For example, suppose that, in exchange for receiving cash, an entity incurs a liability to pay a fixed amount if some unlikely event occurs in the future. If the liability is not recognised because an outflow of economic benefits is not considered probable when the entity receives the cash, the entity will recognise an immediate gain at that time. To avoid such problems, some Standards developed before the 2018 *Conceptual Framework*, for example, IFRS 9 *Financial Instruments*, applied no probability recognition criterion.

(c) the reference to reliability was unclear and could result in inappropriate outcomes. Although reliability was identified as a qualitative characteristic in the 1989 *Framework*, in the 2010 *Conceptual Framework*, the term 'reliability' was no longer used to refer to a qualitative characteristic and was not defined (see paragraphs BC2.21–BC2.31). In practice, a 'reliable' measure was usually interpreted as one with a tolerable level of measurement uncertainty and perhaps also as verifiable and free from error. Hence, a recognition criterion referring to reliable measurement could be interpreted as one prohibiting recognition of any item that has a high level of measurement uncertainty, even if recognising such an item would provide useful information.

BC5.3 The 2018 *Conceptual Framework* states that an asset or liability is recognised only if such recognition provides users of financial statements with useful information, namely:

(a) relevant information about the asset or liability and about any resulting income, expenses or changes in equity; and

(b) a faithful representation of the asset or liability and of any resulting income, expenses or changes in equity.

BC5.4 The approaches in the 2010 *Conceptual Framework* and the 2018 *Conceptual Framework* have similar objectives but sought to achieve them by different means:

(a) the 2010 *Conceptual Framework* set up practical, but subjective filters for cases where recognition is not likely to provide information with the qualitative characteristics of useful financial information. Those filters referred to probability and reliability.

(b) the 2018 *Conceptual Framework* refers directly to the qualitative characteristics and then provides guidance on how to apply them. That guidance explains when recognition might produce information that lacks those qualitative characteristics—including some (but not necessarily all) cases where applying the 2010 *Conceptual Framework* might have led to a conclusion that a flow of economic benefits is not probable or that reliable measurement is not possible.

BC5.5 The Board considered whether the 2018 *Conceptual Framework* should include a presumption (or overarching principle) that every item meeting the definition of an asset or a liability is recognised. This would have meant that if the Board had decided that recognition of a particular item would not provide useful information, it would have had to include an exception to this principle in particular Standards.

BC5.6 The Board rejected that approach because it expects that in some circumstances it will continue to conclude that recognising particular assets or particular liabilities will not provide useful information or that the costs of recognising them would exceed the benefits of doing so. To be useful to the Board, the *Conceptual Framework* needs to give guidance on how to approach decisions about setting recognition requirements in Standards. A presumption or overarching principle that every item meeting the definition of an asset or a liability should be recognised would be too restrictive and would not provide such guidance.

BC5.7 Some stakeholders expressed a concern that the approach now included in the 2018 *Conceptual Framework* would not provide enough direction because it is too abstract and subjective. These stakeholders suggested that the Board needs more concrete and robust recognition criteria to ensure that it develops Standards with consistent requirements that result in useful information.

BC5.8 In considering that concern, the Board noted that the 1989 *Framework* and the 2010 *Conceptual Framework* also set abstract and subjective criteria—probability and reliability. The revised approach in the 2018 *Conceptual Framework* is linked directly to the qualitative characteristics of useful financial information and provides clearer and more developed guidance than the previous approach. In the Board's view, setting more rigid recognition criteria in the *Conceptual Framework* would not help the Board to set recognition requirements in Standards that result in useful information to users of financial statements at a cost that does not exceed the benefits.

BC5.9 Some stakeholders disagreed with the revised approach to recognition because they were concerned that it could increase the range of recognised assets and liabilities.

BC5.10 In developing the revised recognition criteria, the Board aimed to develop tools that would help it to base decisions on a more coherent set of principles. It did not have an objective of either increasing or decreasing the range of assets and liabilities recognised. Paragraphs BC5.15–BC5.20 provide the Board's responses to specific concerns in relation to situations when probability of inflows or outflows of economic benefits is low and paragraphs BC5.21–BC5.22 provide the Board's responses to specific concerns in relation to measurement uncertainty.

BC5.11 Further, the Board noted that, as explained in paragraph SP1.2 of the 2018 *Conceptual Framework*, the *Conceptual Framework* does not override requirements in Standards, so the 2018 revision of recognition criteria will not affect how preparers of financial statements apply recognition criteria developed in Standards issued before the 2018 *Conceptual Framework*.

Relevance (paragraphs 5.12–5.17)

BC5.12 The guidance supporting the revised recognition criteria provides examples of factors that may indicate when recognising an asset or liability may fail to provide users of financial statements with relevant information. Two of those factors relate to cases in which:

(a) it is uncertain whether an asset or liability exists (see paragraphs BC5.13–BC5.14); or

(b) an asset or liability exists, but the probability of an inflow or outflow of economic benefits is low (see paragraphs BC5.15–BC5.20).

Existence uncertainty (paragraph 5.14)

BC5.13 It is sometimes uncertain whether an asset or liability exists (existence uncertainty). The Board concluded that it is helpful to consider existence uncertainty separately from outcome uncertainty and separately from measurement uncertainty. Although existence uncertainty may contribute to outcome uncertainty and measurement uncertainty, conceptually it is different and could affect recognition decisions differently. Distinguishing different types of uncertainty makes it easier to decide what information is most likely to be relevant to users of financial statements and how to provide that information in a way that provides a faithful representation.

BC5.14 The 2018 *Conceptual Framework* does not provide detailed guidance on how to consider existence uncertainty in making recognition decisions because the appropriate approach will depend on facts and circumstances.

Low probability of an inflow or outflow of economic benefits (paragraphs 5.15–5.17)

BC5.15 Many respondents both to the 2013 Discussion Paper and to the 2015 Exposure Draft argued that the recognition criteria should continue to refer to probability. They argued that:

(a) the probability criterion had proved to be a practical way of applying the qualitative characteristics. The proposed supporting guidance on items with a low probability of generating a flow of economic benefits was not clear enough and would lead to doubt and inconsistency.

(b) the removal of the probability criterion, in combination with the removal of the reference to 'expected' from the definitions of an asset and a liability, could lead to requirements for entities to recognise more assets and liabilities with a low probability of inflows or outflows of economic benefits. Recognising such assets and liabilities would not provide useful information. In addition, preparers of financial statements might have to search extensively for rights and obligations. (The deletion of the notion of an 'expected' flow is discussed in paragraphs BC4.8–BC4.14.)

(c) if assets and liabilities with a low probability of future inflows and outflows were recognised, they might have to be measured at amounts based on expected value. Such measurement is difficult and puts a burden on preparers of financial statements. Sometimes, providing information about the range and distribution of possible outcomes is more useful than providing a measure based on expected value. Such measures may provide an illusion of precision that does not exist.

BC5.16 Some respondents suggested applying a probability filter for some assets or liabilities (for example, for patents or research and development), but not for all (for example, not for derivative financial assets), or for some transactions but not for others (for example, not for the acquisition of an asset for cash). Those respondents suggested it is not reasonable to remove the probability requirement from the recognition criteria simply to permit the recognition of some financial instruments. Including an exception for particular financial instruments in a Standard would be sufficient to achieve that result.

BC5.17 The Board acknowledged that a probability threshold could be a practical way to filter out assets and liabilities whose recognition might not provide relevant information. However, this approach would lead to not recognising assets and liabilities in some cases when recognition could provide relevant information. It would also be difficult to set a probability threshold that could be applied across all Standards and in all recognition events.

BC5.18 The Board also noted that, whatever measurement basis is used for an asset or liability with a low probability of an inflow or outflow of economic benefits, that basis would be likely to reflect that low probability—it is unlikely that a required measurement basis would reflect only the maximum inflow or maximum outflow of economic benefits.

BC5.19 The 2018 *Conceptual Framework*, therefore, does not include a probability threshold. Instead, the low probability of an inflow or outflow of economic benefits is discussed as an indicator that, in some cases, recognition may not provide relevant information, for the reasons discussed in paragraphs 5.16–5.17.

BC5.20 Some stakeholders expressed a concern that the term 'low probability' is too subjective to be interpreted consistently. However, the Board's objective in discussing situations of low probability was to indicate that in some such situations, the Board might conclude that some information may not be relevant. The Board's objective was not to identify a threshold above which information would always be relevant and below which it would always be irrelevant.

Faithful representation (paragraphs 5.18–5.25)

BC5.21 As discussed in paragraphs BC5.2–BC5.4, the recognition criteria in the 2018 *Conceptual Framework* do not include a requirement to recognise an asset or liability only if it has a cost or value that can be measured with reliability. The Board concluded that a high level of measurement uncertainty would not necessarily preclude a measure from providing useful information about an asset or liability, so it would be difficult to set a single threshold based on measurement uncertainty that could be applied across all Standards and in all recognition events. Hence, the 2018 *Conceptual Framework* discusses measurement uncertainty as a factor that may affect whether faithful representation can be provided by recognition of an asset or liability, supported, if necessary, by explanatory information. This discussion is based on the discussion of measurement uncertainty in Chapter 2—*Qualitative characteristics of useful financial information* (see paragraphs 2.19, 2.22 and BC2.46–BC2.49).

BC5.22 Some respondents to the 2013 Discussion Paper and to the 2015 Exposure Draft suggested that a higher level of measurement uncertainty is tolerable when recognising liabilities or expenses than when recognising assets or income. They described this as an application of prudence (asymmetric prudence, applying the terminology used in paragraph BC2.37). The Board concluded that the level of measurement uncertainty beyond which a measure does not provide a faithful representation depends on facts and circumstances and so can be determined only when developing Standards (see paragraph 5.9). Paragraphs

Derecognition (paragraphs 5.26–5.33)

BC5.23 The 2010 *Conceptual Framework* did not define derecognition; nor did it describe when derecognition occurs.

BC5.24 Discussions about derecognition have typically contrasted two approaches to derecognition:

(a) a control approach—derecognition is the mirror image of recognition. Thus, an entity derecognises an asset or liability when it no longer meets the criteria for recognition (or no longer exists, or is no longer an asset or liability of the entity).

(b) a risks-and-rewards approach—an entity continues to recognise an asset or liability until the entity is no longer exposed to most of the risks and rewards generated by that asset or liability. This continued recognition would apply even if that asset or liability would not qualify for recognition at the date when the entity disposed of the transferred component, if at that date it acquired only the retained component and had not previously recognised the retained component.[1]

BC5.25 To address some apparent conflicts between the control approach and the risks-and-rewards approach, the Board explained in the 2018 *Conceptual Framework* that:

(a) if an entity has apparently transferred an asset but retains exposure to significant positive or negative variations in the amount of economic benefits that may be produced by the asset, this sometimes indicates that the entity might continue to control that asset; and

(b) if an entity has transferred an asset to another party that holds the asset as an agent for the entity, the transferor still controls the asset.

BC5.26 In developing the 2018 *Conceptual Framework*, the Board concluded that accounting requirements for derecognition should aim to faithfully represent both:

(a) any assets and liabilities retained after the transaction or other event that led to the derecognition (including any asset or liability acquired, incurred or created as part of the transaction or other event); and

(b) the change in the entity's assets and liabilities as a result of that transaction or other event.

BC5.27 In the Board's view, the control approach focuses more on the aim described in paragraph BC5.26(a) and the risks-and-rewards approach focuses more on the aim described in paragraph BC5.26(b). If an entity transfers an entire asset or an entire liability and retains no exposure to that asset or liability, the control approach and the risks-and-rewards approach both lead to the same outcome. Moreover, in such cases, achieving both aims described in paragraph BC5.26 is straightforward.

BC5.28 In contrast, the Board has encountered difficulties in standard-setting when an entity transfers only part of an asset or liability or retains some exposure to variations. In those cases, the control approach does not always lead to the same outcome as the risks-and-rewards approach and the two aims described in paragraph BC5.26 sometimes conflict. The Board views both aims as valid. Accordingly, in the 2018 *Conceptual*

---

[1] Paragraph 5.28 of the 2018 *Conceptual Framework* explains what is included in the transferred component and the retained component.

Framework the Board did not specify the use of the control approach or the risks-and-rewards approach.

BC5.29 Instead, the Board adopted an approach that involves:

(a) derecognising the transferred component.

(b) continuing to recognise the retained component, if any.

(c) applying one or more of the following procedures if necessary to achieve one or both of the aims described in paragraph BC5.26:

  (i) present any retained component separately in the statement of financial position;

  (ii) present separately in the statement(s) of financial performance any income and expenses recognised as a result of derecognition of the transferred component; and

  (iii) provide explanatory information.

(d) as a last resort, if derecognition of the transferred component is not sufficient to achieve both aims described in paragraph BC5.26 even when supported by separate presentation or by explanatory information, considering whether continuing to recognise the transferred component would achieve those aims. That continued recognition would need to be supported by separate presentation or explanatory information because financial statements would include as assets and liabilities, and as related income and expenses, items that do not meet the definition of an element of financial statements.

BC5.30 The Board considered whether the description of aims of accounting requirements for derecognition should explicitly refer to the qualitative characteristic of relevance in addition to the qualitative characteristic of faithful representation. The Board noted that the aims described in paragraph BC5.26 identify what economic phenomena need to be represented faithfully when derecognition is being considered. In the Board's view, information about those economic phenomena is what would be relevant to users of financial statements. Therefore, the Board concluded that adding an explicit reference to relevance would not change how it would seek to achieve the two aims.

from paragraph

CHAPTER 6—MEASUREMENT

INTRODUCTION	BC6.1
MIXED MEASUREMENT	BC6.5
MEASUREMENT BASES AND THE INFORMATION THEY PROVIDE	BC6.12
Historical cost	BC6.19
Current value	BC6.23
Transaction costs	BC6.30
FACTORS TO CONSIDER WHEN SELECTING A MEASUREMENT BASIS	BC6.34
Effect on both the statement of financial position and the statement(s) of financial performance	BC6.36
Relevance	BC6.37
Faithful representation	BC6.43
Enhancing qualitative characteristics	BC6.46
Factors specific to initial measurement	BC6.49
More than one measurement basis	BC6.50
MEASUREMENT OF EQUITY	BC6.52

Introduction

BC6.1 In developing the 2018 *Conceptual Framework*, the Board did not provide detailed guidance on when a particular measurement basis would be suitable because the suitability of particular measurement bases will vary depending on facts and circumstances. Instead, the 2018 *Conceptual Framework*:

(a) describes measurement bases and the information they provide; and

(b) discusses the factors to consider when selecting a measurement basis.

BC6.2 Some respondents to the 2015 Exposure Draft questioned whether simply describing the measurement bases and discussing the factors to consider when selecting a measurement basis would provide the Board with sufficient guidance to develop measurement requirements in Standards. These respondents suggested that the Board should undertake further research on measurement and either:

(a) delay issuing a revised *Conceptual Framework* until that research is completed;

(b) issue a revised *Conceptual Framework* without a measurement section; or

(c) develop high-level interim guidance on measurement for use until more complete concepts and principles can be developed.

BC6.3 The Board rejected these suggestions. The 2010 *Conceptual Framework* provided little guidance on measurement. This lack of guidance was a significant gap in the 2010 *Conceptual Framework* that needed to be addressed. The Board concluded that the guidance in the 2018 *Conceptual Framework* will help it to develop measurement requirements in Standards.

BC6.4 Further, the Board considered whether the 2018 *Conceptual Framework* needs to identify a separate overall objective for measurement. The Board concluded that a separate measurement objective is unlikely to provide useful additional guidance to help it to develop measurement requirements. Instead, the 2018 *Conceptual Framework* describes how measurement contributes to the objective of general purpose financial statements—see paragraph 6.45.

Mixed measurement (paragraph 6.2)

BC6.5 In developing the 2018 *Conceptual Framework*, the Board considered whether the *Conceptual Framework* should advocate using a single measurement basis. The main advantages of using a single measurement basis would be:

(a) the amounts included in the financial statements could be more meaningfully added, subtracted and compared; and

(b) the financial statements would be less complex and, arguably, more understandable.

BC6.6 In addition, if the Board were to identify a concept of wealth or capital that would meet the information needs of users of financial statements, a single measurement basis would be required in order to produce a measure of that wealth or capital. However, as discussed in paragraphs BC8.1–BC8.4 the Board decided not to update the discussion of capital and capital maintenance and not to seek to identify a concept of wealth or capital that would meet the information needs of users of financial statements.

BC6.7 Both the 2013 Discussion Paper and the 2015 Exposure Draft suggested that a single measurement basis for all assets, liabilities, income and expenses might not always provide the most relevant information to users of financial statements. Nearly all respondents who commented on this issue supported the suggested approach.

BC6.8 However, a few respondents disagreed and proposed one of the following as a single measurement basis:

(a) historical cost;

(b) fair value;

(c) current entry value (for example, current cost, see paragraphs 6.21–6.22 of the 2018 *Conceptual Framework*); or

(d) deprival (relief) value (see paragraph BC6.29(a)).

BC6.9 Most of the respondents who suggested the use of a single measurement basis conceded that this could not be achieved in practice, at least in the short term. However, they said that the Board should describe a default measurement basis that it would use when developing Standards. The Board should then commit to explaining any decisions to use any other measurement basis.

BC6.10 The Board concluded that in different circumstances different measurement bases may provide information relevant to users of financial statements. In addition, in different circumstances, a particular measurement basis may be:

(a) easier to understand and implement than another;

(b) more verifiable, less prone to error or subject to a lower level of measurement uncertainty than another; or

(c) less costly to implement than another.

BC6.11 Hence, the 2018 *Conceptual Framework* states that consideration of the qualitative characteristics of useful financial information and of the cost constraint is likely to result in the selection of different measurement bases for different assets, liabilities, income and expenses.

Measurement bases and the information they provide (paragraphs 6.4–6.42)

BC6.12 The 2018 *Conceptual Framework* identifies two categories of measurement bases. Paragraphs BC6.19–BC6.22 discuss historical cost measurement bases and paragraphs BC6.23–BC6.29 discuss current value measurement bases.

BC6.13 The 2013 Discussion Paper identified cash-flow-based measurements as a separate category of measurement bases. The 2018 *Conceptual Framework* does not do so because the Board concluded that cash-flow-based measurements are not measurement bases in their own right. Instead, cash-flow-based measurement techniques can be used to estimate a measure in applying a specified measurement basis. Paragraphs 6.91–6.95 of the 2018 *Conceptual Framework* discuss how those techniques can be used in this way.

BC6.14 The Board considered and rejected the idea of categorising measurement bases according to whether they provide information about the cost of inputs to an entity's business activities—entry values such as historical cost and current cost—or information about the cost of outputs from an entity's business activities—exit values such as fair value, value in use and fulfilment value. The Board did not find such a distinction useful when describing

BC6.15 The 2018 *Conceptual Framework* describes the measurement bases the Board is likely to consider selecting when developing Standards. It acknowledges in paragraph 6.3 that a Standard may need to describe how to implement the measurement basis selected in that Standard.

or selecting a measurement basis for use in a particular Standard because the difference between entry and exit values in the same market is often small, except for transaction costs (see paragraphs BC6.30–BC6.33).

BC6.16 In addition, the 2018 *Conceptual Framework* discusses the information provided by particular measurement bases. Identifying that information will help to identify whether a particular measurement basis is likely to provide useful information to the users of financial statements in particular circumstances.

BC6.17 A few respondents to the 2015 Exposure Draft said the discussion of measurement bases is biased: some suggested that the discussion is biased against historical cost; conversely, others perceived a bias against current values. In developing the 2018 *Conceptual Framework*, the Board sought to provide a balanced description of the measurement bases and the information that they provide. The Board did not intend to favour one measurement basis over the others.

BC6.18 In the measurement chapter, the term 'value' is used to refer in general terms to an economic value of an asset or liability, rather than its carrying amount (see paragraph 5.1) and rather than a specific current value such as fair value. That term is used, for example, when that economic value may differ from the amount of a future cash payment or future cash receipt, for example, because of factors such as the time value of money.

Historical cost (paragraphs 6.4–6.9 and 6.24–6.31)

BC6.19 The 2018 *Conceptual Framework* explains that the historical cost of an asset is initially the value of the costs incurred in acquiring or creating the asset, comprising the consideration paid to acquire or create the asset plus transaction costs. The historical cost of a liability when it is incurred or taken on is initially the value of the consideration received to incur or take on the liability minus transaction costs. When developing Standards, the Board will decide whether to specify how those initial values are determined.

BC6.20 Consumption of all or part of an asset leads to derecognition of the part of the asset that is consumed. If the asset is measured at historical cost, this derecognition is reflected through depreciation or amortisation of the asset. Similarly, fulfilment of all or part of a liability leads to derecognition of the part of the liability that is fulfilled.

BC6.21 If an asset has become impaired or a liability has become onerous, the cost determined at initial recognition is unlikely to provide relevant information if it is not updated. Consequently, the 2018 *Conceptual Framework* describes the historical cost of an asset as being updated to reflect the fact that part of the historical cost is no longer recoverable, that is, the carrying amount of the asset is updated to reflect impairment. Similarly, the historical cost of a liability is updated to reflect changes that result in the liability becoming onerous, that is, the consideration received to incur or take on the liability is no longer sufficient to depict the obligation to fulfil the liability. However, historical cost does not reflect changes in value of an asset that is not impaired or of a liability that is not onerous.

BC6.22 The amortised cost of a financial asset or financial liability reflects estimates of future cash flows discounted at a rate that is not updated after initial recognition, unless the asset or liability bears interest at a variable rate. For loans given or received, if interest is receivable or payable regularly, the amortised cost of the loan typically approximates the amount originally paid or received. In addition, the carrying amount of a loan given is reduced if it is impaired. Therefore, the 2018 *Conceptual Framework* categorises amortised cost of financial assets and financial liabilities as a form of historical cost.

Current value (paragraphs 6.10–6.22 and 6.32–6.42)

BC6.23 The 2018 *Conceptual Framework* identifies current value measures as providing monetary information about assets, liabilities and related income and expenses using information updated to reflect conditions at the measurement date. It states that current measurement bases include fair value, value in use (for assets), fulfilment value (for liabilities) and current cost.

BC6.24 The description of fair value in the 2018 *Conceptual Framework* is consistent with its description in IFRS 13 *Fair Value Measurement*. The descriptions of value in use and fulfilment value are derived from the definition of value in use in IAS 36 *Impairment of Assets*, which is the most explicit of the various definitions of entity-specific value in Standards developed before the 2018 *Conceptual Framework*. The description of current cost is derived from descriptions of current cost in various academic sources.

BC6.25 Some Standards developed before the 2018 *Conceptual Framework* use value in use, but not as a separate measurement basis. In those Standards, value in use is used in determining the recoverable amount of an asset that is measured at historical cost and may be impaired. Within that context, if value in use is used to determine the recoverable amount of an impaired asset, immediately after the impairment loss has been recognised, the carrying amount of the asset equals its value in use. Nevertheless, the 2018 *Conceptual Framework* identifies value in use as a separate measurement basis because:

(a) it differs conceptually from historical cost, even though value in use is used in determining recoverable historical cost; and

(b) the Board might decide that in some circumstances an entity should measure an asset using an entity-specific current value (ie value in use) instead of fair value.

BC6.26 The 2018 *Conceptual Framework* explains that value in use and fulfilment value reflect the same factors as fair value, but using entity-specific assumptions, not assumptions by market participants.

BC6.27 Value in use and fulfilment value, therefore, reflect the price for bearing the uncertainty inherent in the cash flows—a risk premium. Including such a risk premium produces information that can be relevant because it reflects the economic difference between items subject to different levels of uncertainty. The inclusion of a risk premium is implicit in how value in use is described in IAS 36.[1]

BC6.28 Although current cost is not widely used in IFRS Standards, there is a significant body of academic literature that advocates the use of current cost in financial reporting. Consequently, the 2018 *Conceptual Framework* describes current cost.

BC6.29 The 2018 *Conceptual Framework* does not describe the following current value measurement bases:

(a) deprival value for assets or relief value for liabilities. The deprival value of an asset is the loss that an entity would suffer if it were deprived of the asset being measured. Similarly, the relief value of a liability is the benefit that an entity would enjoy if it were relieved of the liability being measured. The Board did not include a discussion of deprival value or relief value because they are more complex than other measurement bases and have been used in few jurisdictions.

---

1 See paragraphs 55–56, A1 and A15–A21 of IAS 36 *Impairment of Assets*.

Hence, the Board concluded that it is unlikely to use deprival value or relief value when developing Standards.

(b) net realisable value. Net realisable value depicts the estimated consideration from the sale of the asset reduced by the estimated costs of sale. The Board concluded that it is unnecessary to describe net realisable value separately, because it is derived from another current measure.

(c) cost of release. Cost of release depicts the estimated cost (including transaction costs) of obtaining release from a liability by negotiation with the counterparty. Because it is relatively unusual for entities to obtain release from liabilities, instead of fulfilling them, the Board concluded that it is unnecessary to describe this measurement basis in the 2018 *Conceptual Framework*.

Transaction costs

BC6.30 Transaction costs can arise both when:

(a) an asset is acquired or a liability is incurred or taken on; and

(b) an asset is sold or disposed of or a liability is settled or transferred.

BC6.31 Defining which costs are transaction costs is beyond the scope of the *Conceptual Framework*. They have normally been defined in particular Standards as incremental costs, other than the transaction price, that would not have been incurred if the particular asset (or liability) being measured had not been acquired (incurred) or sold or disposed of (transferred or settled).

BC6.32 Transaction costs incurred in acquiring an asset or incurring a liability are a feature of the transaction in which the asset was acquired or the liability was incurred. Hence:

(a) the historical cost and current cost of an asset or liability reflect those transaction costs. Although the transaction costs are not part of the transaction price, the entity could not have acquired the asset or incurred the liability without incurring those transaction costs.

(b) if the measure is intended to depict the fair value, fulfilment value or value in use of an asset or liability, the measure does not reflect those transaction costs. Those costs do not affect the current value of that asset or liability.

BC6.33 Transaction costs that would be incurred in selling or disposing of an asset or in settling or transferring a liability are a feature of a possible future transaction. Hence:

(a) value in use and fulfilment value reflect those transaction costs if the entity expects to incur them;

(b) fair value does not reflect those transaction costs; and

(c) historical cost and current cost do not reflect transaction costs that would be incurred in selling or disposing of an asset or in settling or transferring a liability because these measurement bases are entry values—they reflect the costs of acquiring the asset or incurring the liability.

CONCEPTUAL FRAMEWORK FOR FINANCIAL REPORTING

Factors to consider when selecting a measurement basis (paragraphs 6.43–6.86)

BC6.34 To meet the objective of financial statements, information provided by a particular measurement basis must be useful to users of financial statements. A measurement basis achieves this if it provides information that is relevant and faithfully represents what it purports to represent. The 2018 *Conceptual Framework* discusses how relevance and faithful representation affect the selection of a measurement basis.

BC6.35 The Board considered whether to prescribe the order in which factors should be considered in selecting a measurement basis (for example, using a hierarchy or decision tree). However, the Board concluded that this would not be possible or desirable. The relative importance of the factors will depend on facts and circumstances. Indeed, in many cases it will be important to consider several factors when selecting a measurement basis.

Effect on both the statement of financial position and the statement(s) of financial performance (paragraph 6.43)

BC6.36 The 2018 *Conceptual Framework* states that when selecting a measurement basis it is necessary to consider the nature of the information that the measurement basis will produce in both the statement of financial position and the statement(s) of financial performance. Some respondents to the 2015 Exposure Draft stated that the *Conceptual Framework* should give more weight to the effect that a particular measure would have on the statement(s) of financial performance. In their view, the statement(s) of financial performance is more useful than the statement of financial position to users of financial statements. However, the Board concluded that the relative importance of the information produced in those statements will depend on how users will use the resulting information in their analysis, which will, in turn, depend on facts and circumstances.

Relevance (paragraphs 6.49–6.57)

BC6.37 The 2018 *Conceptual Framework* discusses the following factors that can affect the relevance of the information provided by a measurement basis:

(a) characteristics of the asset or liability; and

(b) contribution to future cash flows (see paragraphs BC6.38–BC6.42).

BC6.38 Paragraph 1.14 notes that some economic resources produce cash flows directly, whereas other economic resources are used in combination to produce cash flows. Building on this idea, the 2018 *Conceptual Framework* identifies as one factor in the selection of a measurement basis the way in which an asset or liability contributes to future cash flows.

BC6.39 The 2018 *Conceptual Framework* states that the way in which an asset or liability contributes to future cash flows depends, in part, on the nature of the business activities conducted by the entity. For example, depending on the nature of an entity's business activities, the same asset could be sold as inventory, leased to another entity or used in the entity's business. The Board acknowledged that measuring in the same way assets or liabilities that contribute to cash flows differently could reduce comparability by making different things appear the same.[1]

---

[1] Paragraph 2.27 of the 2018 *Conceptual Framework* states: 'Comparability is not uniformity. For information to be comparable, like things must look alike and different things must look different.'

BC6.40 Although some respondents to the 2015 Exposure Draft expressed a concern that subjectivity could result if the nature of an entity's business activities were to be considered when selecting a measurement basis, many supported this approach. In addition, the Board noted that, in many cases, the nature of an entity's business activities is a matter of fact, not an opinion or management intent. When this is not the case, the Board will need to consider how to address any subjectivity.

BC6.41 The 2018 *Conceptual Framework* does not refer explicitly to any particular business activity, for example, long-term investment, for the reasons set out in paragraph BC0.39.

BC6.42 To help in the selection of a measurement basis, the 2018 *Conceptual Framework* also provides guidance on when historical cost or current value measurement bases might provide relevant information about financial assets and financial liabilities. That guidance builds on concepts identified by the Board in developing IFRS 9 *Financial Instruments*. The Basis for Conclusions on IFRS 9 explains why the Board decided to use those concepts.

Faithful representation (paragraphs 6.58–6.62)

BC6.43 The 2018 *Conceptual Framework* identifies the following as factors that can affect whether the information provided by a particular measurement basis provides a faithful representation of the economic phenomena that are being depicted:

(a) whether the assets and liabilities are related in some way; and

(b) measurement uncertainty (see paragraphs BC6.44–BC6.45).

BC6.44 Some respondents to the 2013 Discussion Paper suggested that one factor to be considered in selecting a measurement basis is the level of measurement uncertainty associated with that measurement basis. Some respondents used the term 'reliability' to describe that factor. As discussed in paragraphs BC2.28–BC2.31, the Board did not reintroduce the term 'reliability'. Paragraph 2.22 of the 2018 *Conceptual Framework* explains that if a high level of measurement uncertainty is involved in making an estimate, that may indicate that different information about the economic phenomenon might be more useful (see paragraphs BC2.55–BC2.56). In addition, Chapter 6—*Measurement* discusses how measurement uncertainty can affect the selection of a measurement basis.

BC6.45 Some respondents to the 2015 Exposure Draft stated that applying prudence as they understand the term would imply that the tolerable level of measurement uncertainty would always be higher for liabilities than for assets (see paragraphs BC2.37(b), BC2.41–BC2.45 and BC2.55–BC2.56). The Board disagreed with this view, concluding that the tolerable level of measurement uncertainty depends on facts and circumstances and can be decided only when developing Standards.

Enhancing qualitative characteristics (paragraphs 6.63–6.76)

BC6.46 The 2018 *Conceptual Framework* identifies four 'enhancing qualitative characteristics' that make financial information more useful—comparability, verifiability, timeliness and understandability. In developing the 2018 *Conceptual Framework*, the Board identified no specific implications of timeliness for selection of a measurement basis beyond those discussed in Chapter 2—*Qualitative characteristics of useful financial information*. The 2018 *Conceptual Framework* discusses the general implications that comparability, verifiability and understandability have for the selection of a measurement basis.

BC6.47 In developing the 2018 *Conceptual Framework*, the Board considered these suggestions made by respondents:

(a) verifiability should play a more significant role in selecting a measurement basis; and

(b) comparability could be enhanced if the Board, when developing Standards, prevented preparers of financial statements from choosing between measurement bases.

BC6.48 The Board concluded that the discussion of verifiability appropriately reflects the role of verifiability as a factor to consider when selecting a measurement basis. Further, the Board concluded that additional discussion of the disadvantages of developing Standards that allow preparers to choose between alternative measurement bases is unnecessary because paragraph 2.29 acknowledges that permitting alternative accounting methods for the same economic phenomenon diminishes comparability.

Factors specific to initial measurement (paragraphs 6.77–6.82)

BC6.49 The 2015 Exposure Draft discussed both exchanges of items of similar value and exchanges of items of different value. Respondents to the 2015 Exposure Draft commented that the meaning of the terms 'similar value' and 'different value' was unclear. To respond to such concerns, the 2018 *Conceptual Framework* refers instead to whether the terms of a transaction are market terms.

More than one measurement basis (paragraphs 6.83–6.86)

BC6.50 The 2018 *Conceptual Framework* discusses situations in which more than one measurement basis is needed for an asset or liability and for related income and expenses to provide users of financial statements with useful information.

BC6.51 One way in which such information could be provided is to use a current measurement basis for an asset or liability in the statement of financial position and to use a different measurement basis for the related income or expenses in the statement of profit or loss. In such cases, the difference between the income or expenses included in the statement of profit or loss and the change in current value of the asset or liability is included in other comprehensive income. As discussed in paragraph 7.17, the Board would decide to require information to be provided in this way only in exceptional circumstances—and only if doing so would result in the statement of profit or loss providing more relevant information or providing a more faithful representation of the entity's financial performance for the period.

Measurement of equity (paragraphs 6.87–6.90)

BC6.52 Although total equity is not measured directly, it may be appropriate to measure directly individual classes of equity or components of equity to provide useful information. The 2018 *Conceptual Framework* discusses this idea.

BC6.53 A few respondents to the 2015 Exposure Draft disagreed with the proposal that some individual classes or components of equity could be measured directly. The respondents said they disagreed because:

(a) measuring a class of equity or a component of equity directly would be inappropriate because equity is defined as a residual interest; and

(b) it would be inconsistent with the reporting entity perspective because dividing total equity between classes and into components would result in the reporting of items that do not have a financial effect on the reporting entity as a whole.

BC6.54 Although the total carrying amount of equity (total equity) is measured as a residual, the Board noted that equity is defined as a type of claim—a residual interest in the assets of the entity after deducting all its liabilities. Measuring some classes of equity, or some components of equity, directly does not contradict that definition and differs from measuring total equity directly. Even if some individual classes or components of equity are measured directly, total equity will continue to equal the total of the carrying amounts of all recognised assets minus the total of the carrying amounts of all recognised liabilities. Consequently, if an entity has more than one class of equity or more than one component of equity, at least one of them is measured as a residual.

BC6.55 The Board also concluded that the direct measurement of some individual classes of equity or components of equity would not contradict the entity perspective adopted in financial statements. Those direct measures might provide users of financial statements with information useful in making decisions relating to providing resources to the entity. This information would be provided from the perspective of the entity and reflect the equity claims held against the entity. Such information would not be provided from the perspective of a particular claimholder.

CHAPTER 7—PRESENTATION AND DISCLOSURE

	from paragraph
INTRODUCTION	**BC7.1**
CLASSIFICATION OF EQUITY	**BC7.4**
CLASSIFICATION OF INCOME AND EXPENSES	**BC7.6**
Terminology	BC7.6
Approach to guidance on presentation and disclosure of income and expenses	BC7.9
Describing profit or loss	BC7.15
Profit or loss and other comprehensive income	BC7.21
Reclassifying items into the statement of profit or loss	BC7.26

Introduction

BC7.1 The topic of presentation and disclosure was not addressed in the 2010 *Conceptual Framework*. Respondents to the Board's public consultation on its agenda in 2011 identified this topic as a priority. A particular issue identified was providing information about an entity's financial performance, including the use of other comprehensive income.

BC7.2 In response to that feedback, the 2018 *Conceptual Framework* introduces for the first time:

(a) concepts that describe how information should be presented and disclosed in financial statements. Those concepts will guide the Board in setting presentation and disclosure requirements in Standards and may guide entities in providing information in financial statements.

(b) guidance on classifying income and expenses for the Board to use when it decides whether they are included in the statement of profit or loss or are included outside the statement of profit or loss, in other comprehensive income (see paragraphs 7.15–7.18).

(c) guidance for the Board on whether and when income and expenses included in other comprehensive income should subsequently be reclassified into the statement of profit or loss (paragraph 7.19).

BC7.3 When it issued the 2018 *Conceptual Framework*, the Board was undertaking:

(a) a Disclosure Initiative, a collection of implementation and research projects aimed at improving disclosure in financial statements by providing additional guidance that builds on the presentation and disclosure concepts set out in the *Conceptual Framework*.

(b) a research project on primary financial statements. That project was examining potential targeted improvements to the structure and content of the statement(s) of financial performance and the statement of cash flows and perhaps also the statement of financial position and the statement of changes in equity.

Classification of equity (paragraphs 7.12–7.13)

BC7.4 The 2018 *Conceptual Framework* provides only high-level guidance on when it may be appropriate to present separately different classes of equity claims, and different components of equity. This guidance is based on the concepts for classification in paragraphs 7.7–7.8.

BC7.5 The Board may explore enhancements to the statement of changes in equity or other enhancements to presentation or disclosure requirements as part of its research project on Financial Instruments with Characteristics of Equity. Such enhancements might include some approaches the Board explored in the 2013 Discussion Paper.

Classification of income and expenses (paragraphs 7.14–7.19)

Terminology

BC7.6 The 2018 *Conceptual Framework* introduced the term 'statement(s) of financial performance' to refer to the statement or section of profit or loss together with the statement or section showing other comprehensive income.

BC7.7 The 2018 *Conceptual Framework* uses that term because it is consistent with the term 'statement of financial position' used in Standards and is clearer than the term 'statement of comprehensive income' sometimes used by the Board.

BC7.8 In 2007, the Board introduced a requirement to present all income and expenses recognised outside profit or loss in a statement of comprehensive income. The Board also introduced the term 'other comprehensive income' at that point. That term refers to income and expenses not included in the statement of profit of loss. Some respondents suggested that the term 'other comprehensive income' is neither particularly descriptive nor well understood by users of financial statements. Nonetheless, the Board concluded that avoiding the use of that term or using a different term could be confusing. Hence, the 2018 *Conceptual Framework* uses that term.

Approach to guidance on presentation and disclosure of income and expenses

BC7.9 Over the years, the Board has decided that several items of income and expenses may or must be recognised outside profit or loss. Those decisions were made for particular reasons in particular projects, not for a single consistently applied conceptual reason.

BC7.10 The 1989 *Framework* and the 2010 *Conceptual Framework* contained no reference to income or expenses presented outside the statement of profit or loss and no reference to other comprehensive income.

BC7.11 The Board decided it was important for the *Conceptual Framework* to include some discussion of this topic. However, the Board decided that the *Conceptual Framework* should not discuss whether income and expenses should be presented in a single statement of financial performance or in two statements, viewing this as a decision to be made when developing Standards. Since 2007, that decision has been set out in IAS 1 *Presentation of Financial Statements*.

BC7.12 In developing the 2018 *Conceptual Framework*, the Board considered the following questions:

(a) how to define or describe profit or loss (see paragraphs BC7.15–BC7.20);

(b) how to decide which income and expenses are included in the statement of profit or loss and which income and expenses are included in other comprehensive income (see paragraphs BC7.21–BC7.25); and

(c) whether and when the amounts included in other comprehensive income should be reclassified into the statement of profit or loss (see paragraphs BC7.26–BC7.33).

BC7.13 Many respondents to the 2013 Discussion Paper and to the 2015 Exposure Draft expressed a view that the proposed guidance on presentation of income and expenses was insufficient and would not provide the Board with a clear basis for standard-setting. Many respondents asked the Board to do further work on reporting financial performance.

BC7.14 However, the Board decided that the lack of guidance on the presentation of income and expenses was a significant gap in the 2010 *Conceptual Framework*. The Board concluded that it had made significant progress in developing high-level guidance on presentation of income and expenses and that this guidance would help the Board to develop presentation requirements in Standards. Hence, the Board decided to include such guidance in the 2018 *Conceptual Framework*, rather than to explore the use of the statement of profit or loss and other comprehensive income in a separate project. That decision will not preclude further work on reporting financial performance.

Describing profit or loss (paragraph 7.16)

BC7.15 The 2018 *Conceptual Framework* describes:

(a) the statement of profit or loss as the primary source of information about an entity's financial performance for the reporting period; and

(b) the total or subtotal for profit or loss as a highly summarised depiction of the entity's financial performance for the period.

BC7.16 Those descriptions are consistent with the fact that many users of financial statements incorporate the total or subtotal for profit or loss in their analysis, either as a starting point or as the main indicator of an entity's financial performance.

BC7.17 Merely describing the statement of profit or loss in the manner set out in paragraph 7.16 will be unlikely to satisfy those who asked for a definition of 'profit or loss' or for a more precise description. However, on the basis of its previous work the Board concluded that no single characteristic, or small number of characteristics, is shared by all items included in the statement of profit or loss but not shared by items that are most appropriately included in other comprehensive income. Consequently, the Board concluded that it is not possible to produce a robust conceptual definition of profit or loss or of other comprehensive income.

BC7.18 The Board also concluded that it could not create a prescriptive list of all categories of items that are most appropriately included in the statement of profit or loss. Such a list could never be complete and would inevitably lead to reporting in other comprehensive income some, perhaps many, items that would generally be regarded as being more appropriately included in the statement of profit or loss.

BC7.19 A number of stakeholders repeatedly asked the Board to define profit or loss. A few of them provided suggestions for how to develop such a definition or for distinguishing income and expenses to be included in the statement of profit or loss from income and expenses to be included in other comprehensive income. However, no consensus on a viable approach emerged.

BC7.20 As discussed in paragraphs BC7.17–BC7.19 of this Basis for Conclusions, the Board concluded that it was not possible to develop a robust conceptual definition of profit or loss or of other comprehensive income or a prescriptive list of all categories of items that are most appropriately included in the statement of profit or loss. Nevertheless, the 2018 *Conceptual Framework* introduces for the first time guidance on when it might be appropriate for the Board to include income or expenses in other comprehensive income. The Board concluded that introducing guidance on this topic was a significant improvement.

Profit or loss and other comprehensive income (paragraph 7.17)

BC7.21 As mentioned in paragraph BC7.17, the Board did not identify a single characteristic or a single set of characteristics shared by all items that are most appropriately included in the statement of profit or loss.

BC7.22 Further, the Board explored whether it might be possible to define a small number of categories of items that would or might be included in other comprehensive income. The Board described one approach to doing that in the 2013 Discussion Paper, but that approach did not attract significant support from respondents.

BC7.23 For the 2018 *Conceptual Framework*, the Board developed an approach to classifying income and expenses that is based on the description of the statement of profit or loss. As mentioned in paragraph BC7.15, that description states that the statement of profit or loss is the primary source of information about an entity's financial performance for the reporting period. If that statement is the primary source of that information, excluding income and expenses from that statement without compelling reasons could make that statement less useful.

BC7.24 Accordingly, the 2018 *Conceptual Framework* sets out a principle that all income and expenses are included in the statement of profit or loss. The Board's intention in establishing this principle was to emphasise that the statement of profit or loss is the default location for income and expenses. Thus, decisions to exclude any income and expenses from the statement of profit or loss and to include them in other comprehensive income can be made only in exceptional circumstances. Those exceptional circumstances would be when the Board concludes that requiring or permitting the exclusion of particular items of income or expenses from the statement of profit or loss would result in the statement of profit or loss providing more relevant information or providing a more faithful representation of an entity's financial performance for that period.

BC7.25 The 2018 *Conceptual Framework* does not include specific guidance on how the Board might reach that conclusion. The Board expects to take that decision when developing Standards and to explain its reasons in the bases for conclusions on those Standards. Entities cannot take that decision (see paragraph 88 of IAS 1).

Reclassifying items into the statement of profit or loss (paragraph 7.19)

BC7.26 The Board considered whether items of income and expenses included in other comprehensive income should be subsequently reclassified into the statement of profit or loss. Such reclassification is sometimes referred to as 'recycling'.

BC7.27 Some of the Standards developed before the 2018 *Conceptual Framework* require such reclassification; other Standards prohibit reclassification. The differences between these requirements arose because the Board had taken different approaches to the issue at different times. Sometimes, the Board's approach was to view the statement(s) of financial performance as a single performance statement so that each item of income or expenses should appear only once in that statement. To be consistent with that approach, the Board generally prohibited reclassification in Standards it developed at those times. At other times, the Board's approach was that all income and expenses should be included in the statement of profit or loss at some point. To achieve that objective, reclassification would be necessary.

BC7.28 It would have been undesirable for the Board's decisions on reclassification to continue to fluctuate over time in line with changes in the composition of the Board and in the Board's approach. Accordingly, the 2018 *Conceptual Framework* sets out the principle that the Board will apply in making decisions about reclassification.

BC7.29 The Board concluded that if the statement of profit or loss is the primary source of information about an entity's financial performance for the period, the cumulative amounts included in that statement over time need to be as complete as possible. Hence, income and expenses can be permanently excluded from the statement of profit or loss only if there is a compelling reason in that particular case.

BC7.30 Accordingly, the 2018 *Conceptual Framework* includes a principle that income and expenses included in other comprehensive income are subsequently reclassified into the statement of profit or loss. The reporting period in which reclassification takes place is the period when doing so results in the statement of profit or loss providing more relevant information or providing a more faithful representation of the entity's financial performance for that period.

BC7.31 Paragraphs 6.83–6.86 describe an approach that uses one measurement basis in the statement of financial position and a different measurement basis in the statement of profit or loss. When this approach is used, reclassification is the only way to ensure that, over the holding period of the asset or liability, the cumulative amount of income or expenses included in the statement of profit or loss for that asset or liability is the amount determined using the measurement basis selected for that statement.

BC7.32 In some cases, it might not be possible to identify any period when reclassifying income and expenses into the statement of profit or loss would have the result described in paragraph BC7.30. In such cases, without an appropriate, non-arbitrary basis for reclassification, reclassification would not provide useful information.

BC7.33 The 2018 *Conceptual Framework* does not include specific guidance on when reclassification would not provide useful information. The Board expects to take that decision when developing Standards and to explain its reasons in the bases for conclusions on those Standards. Entities cannot take that decision.

CHAPTER 8—CONCEPTS OF CAPITAL AND CAPITAL MAINTENANCE

BC8.1   The Board decided that updating the discussion of capital and capital maintenance was not feasible when it developed the 2018 *Conceptual Framework* and could have delayed the completion of the 2018 *Conceptual Framework* significantly.

BC8.2   The Board decided that it would be inappropriate for the 2018 *Conceptual Framework* to exclude a discussion of capital and capital maintenance altogether. Those concepts are important to financial reporting and influence the definitions of income and expenses, the selection of measurement bases, and presentation and disclosure decisions.

BC8.3   Therefore, the material in Chapter 8—*Concepts of capital and capital maintenance* of the 2018 *Conceptual Framework* has been carried forward unchanged from the 2010 *Conceptual Framework*. That material originally appeared in the 1989 *Framework*.

BC8.4   The Board may decide to revisit the concepts of capital and capital maintenance in the future if it considers such a revision necessary.